Judicial Review and the National Political Process

JESSE H. CHOPER is professor in the School of
Law, University of California, Berkeley. He is
the author of numerous publications including *Constitutional Law: Cases, Comments,
and Questions; The American Constitution:
Cases and Materials; Constitutional Rights
and Liberties: Cases and Materials;* and *Cases
and Materials on Corporations.*

Jesse H. Choper

Judicial Review and
the National Political Process

*A Functional Reconsideration of the
Role of the Supreme Court*

The University of Chicago Press
Chicago and London

The University of Chicago Press, Chicago 60637
The University of Chicago Press, Ltd., London

© 1980 by The University of Chicago
All rights reserved. Published 1980
Printed in the United States of America

85 84 83 82 81 80   6 5 4 3 2 1

Library of Congress Cataloging in Publication Data

Choper, Jesse H
  Judicial review and the national political
process.

  Includes bibliographical references and index.
    1. United States. Supreme Court. 2. Political
questions and judicial power—United States.
I. Title
KF8748.C39   347′.73′262   79-21135
ISBN 0-226-10443-5

Jesse H. Choper is professor of law at the
University of California Law School at Berkeley.
He is the author of numerous publications including
*Constitutional Law: Cases, Comments, and
Questions; The American Constitution: Cases
and Materials; Constitutional Rights and Liber-
ties: Cases and Materials;* and *Cases and Materials on
Corporations.*

For Sonya—with love
May fortune smile

Contents

Detailed Contents,
Chapters 1–6

Preface

This book has been with me much longer than I desire to recall and certainly for more years than I am willing to admit in print. It would be impossible, therefore, to acknowledge properly all of those who have graciously given me their time and thoughts over this period. But I wish to offer special thanks to a number of regular and visiting colleagues at Berkeley who have very helpfully commented on drafts of various chapters. They are, in alphabetical order, Vincent A. Blasi, William A. Fletcher, Sanford H. Kadish, Nelson W. Polsby, Stephen J. Schulhofer, Martin Shapiro, Jan Vetter, and Mark G. Yudof. Above all, I owe an enormous debt to two colleagues, Paul J. Mishkin and Michael E. Smith, who at one point or another reviewed virtually the entire manuscript. Although they must be absolved of any responsibility for errors of fact or analysis that persist—indeed, I hope only that I may have persuaded them somewhat as to some of the ideas advanced—they have been unstintingly generous and patient and unfailingly helpful and encouraging during the entire process. To them both, I am extremely grateful.

At various points throughout the book, I have made reference to statements by the framers of the Constitution. Recognizing that "a selective interpretation of history can provide much satisfaction to the interpreter,"[1] I have not used these materials to suggest that the major propositions advocated in the book were originally ordained. Rather, attempting to avoid resort to "law-office" history—"the selection of data favorable to the position being advanced without regard to or concern for contradictory data"[2]—I mean only to show that my proposals are not at war with original intent. To support my arguments I have, instead, placed stronger emphasis on many empirical examples. Although these are obviously neither all-encompassing nor conclusive, I have sought to present them in sufficient number and with adequate texture so as not to be merely selective or anecdotal.

Much of this book was the basis for the Thomas M. Cooley Lectures delivered at the University of Michigan Law School in March 1977. I wish again to express my deep appreciation to all there for their kindness and hospitality. Chapter 1 is an updated version of an article that appeared in volume 122 of the *University of Pennsylvania Law Review*. A small part of chapter 2 was included in the Ralph E. Kharas Visiting Scholar's Lecture delivered at the Syracuse University College of Law in March 1979 and printed in volume 30 of the *Syracuse Law Review*. Chapter 4 is a relatively substantial revision of a paper published in volume 86 of the *Yale Law Journal*.

Several former students at Boalt Hall—Leonard J. Martiniak, Stephen B. Sadowsky, and Robert H. Whalen, Jr.—provided excellent research assistance in connection with sections of chapter 2 that seek to document the effects of various Supreme Court decisions. Brian E. Gray of the class of 1979 carefully and thoughtfully edited the final manuscript and Carol L. Matchett of the class of 1981 cheerfully and tirelessly checked all citations. I should like especially to thank my secretary, Dorothy M. Snodgrass, for her continued efforts on the manuscript at all stages along the way.

Finally, but most important, I wish to express love to my wife, Sonya, and to my sons, Marc and Teddy—with understanding and appreciation of the toll imposed on them.

J.C.

Berkeley, California
July 1979

Introduction

This book concerns the proper role of the United States Supreme Court in our representative democracy when the Court engages in constitutional adjudication and thereby exercises the power of judicial review. In the main, analysis of the Court's role has addressed two broad areas. The first involves *substance*—that is, *how* the Court should interpret various provisions of the Constitution. The enormously complicated and profound issues that surround this question are generally beyond the scope of this book. Rather, in searching for the Court's proper function, I wish to explore the other major area—the *jurisdictional* or *procedural* role of the Supreme Court and judicial review. In particular, the book focuses on the question of justiciability—that is, whether the Court should adjudicate certain constitutional issues at all.

Most major provisions of the Constitution may be separated into three general categories. One involves our system of federalism, allocating power between the national government and the states. The second concerns the separation of powers at the national level, distributing the authority granted to the federal government among the legislative, executive, and judicial branches. The third category consists of personal liberties, which, either by explicit statement or judicial interpretation,

1

limit *all* government power—that of the three federal branches and of the states—vis-à-vis the individual.*

The purpose of this book is to examine these three broad categories of constitutional provisions and to advance a principled, functional, and desirable role for judicial review in our democratic political system. The major theme is that although judicial review is incompatible with a fundamental precept of American democracy—majority rule—the Court must exercise this power in order to protect individual rights, which are not adequately represented in the political processes. When judicial review is unnecessary for the effective preservation of our constitutional scheme, however, the Court should decline to exercise its authority. By so abstaining, the Justices both reduce the discord between judicial review and majoritarian democracy and enhance their ability to render enforceable constitutional decisions when their participation is critically needed.

Chapter 1 contends that neither in theory nor in practice is the Supreme Court as democratic as the political branches (Congress and the President) and that judicial review is the most anti-majoritarian of all exercises of national governmental power.

Chapter 2 submits that the essential role of judicial review in our system is to prevent violations of that category of constitutional provisions that secure individual liberties.

Chapter 3 discloses that the Court, in employing the power of judicial review and thus thwarting popular will by rejecting judgments of electorally responsible political institutions, expends its limited capital and diminishes its ability to gain compliance with the decisions it renders and those it may seek to render in the future.

Chapter 4 argues that since federalism issues involve considerations of practicality rather than principle and since state interests are forcefully represented in the national political process—which is peculiarly capable of fairly reconciling the competing interests—the Court should not decide constitutional

---

* Most other constitutional clauses concern "housekeeping" matters. These deal with details of the federal departments (for example, the minimum ages for elected national officials) or with relations among the states (for example, the extradition clause).

questions respecting the power of the national government vis-
a-vis the states.

Chapter 5 advocates that the Court should not decide constitutional questions concerning the respective powers of Congress and the President because the line separating legislative
from executive authority is ambiguous and shifting and these
issues can be trustworthily resolved without judicial involvement.

Chapter 6 urges that since the federal judiciary is not well
represented in the national political process, the Court should
continue to use its power of judicial review to reject attempts by
Congress and the President that improperly restrict or expand
federal judicial authority.

One

The Supreme Court and the Political Branches

Democratic Theory and Practice

I. THE CONFLICT BETWEEN MAJORITARIAN DEMOCRACY AND JUDICIAL REVIEW

Reconciling judicial review with American representative democracy has been the subject of powerful debate since the early days of the Republic. Much of the controversy has been due to the large number of varied and often vague theories of "democracy" and to the absence of any clear consensus on its definition and that of such other highly abstract concepts as a "democratic society" and a "democratic political system." But certain critical elements are beyond reasonable doubt. Whether one looks to such classical theorists as Aristotle, Locke, and Rousseau, to such mainstays of American political thinking as Madison, Jefferson, and Lincoln, or to this nation's constitutional development from its origin to the present time, majority rule has been considered the keystone of a democratic political system in both theory and practice.[1] Effective majoritarianism in turn depends on the preservation of two fundamental rights of the individual, the right to vote and the right freely to express and exchange ideas. Although the nature of operating government permits neither right to be absolute and although complex questions exist as to their precise scope—such as the particular qualifications of those to whom the franchise is to be granted and the permissible restrictions on the freedoms of speech, press, and association—the right of persons generally to vote rests at the heart of popular democracy and the intelligent exercise of the ballot demands robust free expression. In theory, the majoritarian ideal would be most faithfully fulfilled by having all governmental regulations enacted by plebiscite or, better yet, at national "town meetings" in which all electors could participate by framing the issues as well as by casting their ballots. But, because of the cumbersome and impractical quality of these devices, they have been largely rejected in favor of lawmaking by representative assemblies. Thus, although the history of modern democratic theory and the development of American democratic government may call for some amplifications and qualifications, a "democratic political system" may basically be defined as one in which "public policies are made, on a majority basis, by representatives subject to effective popular control at periodic elections which are conducted on the principle of political equality and under [general] conditions of political freedom."[2]

If it is not simply undemocratic when measured by this standard, the federal judiciary, presided over by the United States Supreme Court, is the least democratic of the three branches of American national government. It is true that various provisions of our Constitution—such as the age and citizenship requirements for elected officers contained in Articles I and II, and the two-term maximum for Presidents found in the twenty-second amendment—limit the majority's unfettered choice of representatives, senators, and chief executives. But to preclude the people from electing *A* is fundamentally different than to assign the office to *B*. Federal judges not only are appointed rather than elected but they are removable only by an exceedingly intricate and extra-majoritarian process of impeachment and protected absolutely against any diminution of compensation. Although, as recognized in *The Federalist*, such an institution may fit within the broad boundaries of a democratic government,* the lower federal judges and Supreme Court Justices

* In his "Definition of a Republic," Madison made clear that "it is *sufficient* for such a government that the persons administering it be appointed, either directly

appear to be wholly without political responsibility. This seeming conflict with the principle of majority rule is tempered by the fact that when the federal courts engage in nonconstitutional adjudication their rulings are subject to change by the political branches. But when they exercise the power of judicial review to declare unconstitutional legislative, executive, or administrative action—federal, state, or local—they reject the product of the popular will by denying policies formulated by the majority's elected representatives or their appointees. Apart from the rarely used and difficult political recourse of constitutional amendment, which itself requires substantially more than a simple majority, the Supreme Court's constitutional pronouncements are held to be final—the law of the land. Not merely antimajoritarian, judicial review appears to cut directly against the grain of traditional democratic philosophy.

The conclusion that judicial review is antithetical to democracy is by no means an inescapable one, however. The general definition of a "democratic political system," used above to evaluate the judicial branch and the institution of judicial review, may legitimately be found to be incomplete—inadequate even though not inaccurate. Despite the tendency of many classical and modern democratic political theorists to equate democracy with pure majoritarianism,[3] "the attempt to identify democracy with the unlimited power of majorities has usually gone hand in hand with an attempt to include in the definition some concept of restraints on majorities."[4] Madison, in particular, "wished to erect a political system that would guarantee the liberties of certain minorities whose advantages of status, power, and wealth would, he thought, probably not be tolerated indefinitely by a constitutionally untrammeled majority."[5] Thus, only representatives "were made directly elective by the people, for brief

---

or indirectly, by the people; and that they hold their appointments . . . either [tor a limited period, or during good behavior] . . .; otherwise every government in the United States as well as every other popular government that has been or can be well organized or well executed, would be degraded from the republican character . . . . [A]ccording to . . . the most respectable and received opinions on the subject, the members of the judiciary department are to retain their offices by the firm tenure of good behavior." The Federalist, No. 39, at 163 (C. Beard ed. 1959).

terms and under minor property restrictions .... Not only would the President be chosen for a longer term, but his electors would not necessarily be chosen by the people—certainly would not be nominated by them—and would meet in secrecy in the different states to cast their ballots. Senators would be chosen for still longer terms by state legislatures whose upper houses were normally based on a restricted electorate. The judges, who would serve for life, would be selected by the combined action of the President and Senate. Thus the influence of numbers, acting especially through the House of Representatives, was to be balanced by non-democratic influences."[6]

Furthermore, most contemporary defenders of judicial review explicitly reject the notion that democracy is synonymous with pure majoritarianism. They persuasively contend that the essential values of a democratic society, of a libertarian democracy, assume the existence of certain inalienable minimums of personal freedom (beyond the political rights of the ballot and free expression) that guard the dignity and integrity of the individual. They argue that "rational limitation on power is ... not a contradiction to democracy, but is of the very essence of democracy as such";[7] that "freedom is the informing ideal of the American system of government";[8] that "the object of the men who established the American Constitution, like the object of democratic theorists in all countries, and at all times, was not omnicompetent popular government, but the freedom of man as an individual being within a free society whose policies are based ultimately upon his consenting will."[9]

The postulate that a truly democratic society stops short of entrusting popular government with unlimited power over all individual action is appealing both philosophically and empirically. But critical questions remain unanswered: what are the specific personal liberties that transcend the authority of the state, and who determines when they have been abridged?

Three alternatives come quickly to mind. The first—one which may readily be found to be unacceptable—is that the individual himself prescribes his inalienable rights. But if "liberty is the right to defy the majority,"[10] and if, in a democracy, each person has the unqualified right to define liberty for himself, we have entered a quagmire that rapidly swallows democracy's central feature of majority rule. Indeed, the theory seemingly conflicts with all governmental rule as that term is ordinarily understood.

A second possible source for designating the appropriate restraints on majoritarianism—the one most compatible with orthodox democratic precepts and implicit in the views of classical democratic theorists[11]—is the legislative process itself. The sacrosanct liberties of the individual may either be enumerated in some constitutional document or perceived by the people's elected representatives in the course of the operation of the lawmaking process. Under this view, the assumption (and hope) is that the decisions of the representative bodies will be rational and just and that the social conscience of the majority of the populace—as molded and articulated by its leaders—will prevent invasion of the rights of the minority. In general, this is the scheme in England and in many other western democracies with written constitutions. Early confidence for this assumption in American society is found in the fact that the Constitution and the Bill of Rights—which contain definite and substantial limitations on both the national and state governments, many of which favor minorities—were promulgated by majorities through the political process. Furthermore, without denying that some serious abridgments of important personal liberties have periodically occurred, American history has shown, certainly at the national level and generally at the state and local levels as well, that with relatively few exceptions—usually regarding peculiarly identifiable, despised, and defenseless groups—the political process has not tyrannized minorities. Whether this experience may in part be attributed to the fact that the ever present threat of judicial review has deterred additional political excess is unknown and probably unknowable.[12] But it may be effectively explained by the analysis suggested by Carl Auerbach in describing national politics:

"The multiplicity and variety of interest groups in the United States, and the countervailing power they possess, keep any one interest, or combination of interests, from dominating our society. Furthermore, the power of pressure groups, the 'mobilizers of minorities,' is curbed by the exercise of political power which, in turn, is diffused by our political parties, the 'mobilizers of majorities' . . . . And the power of the parties is further checked by that of the pressure groups.

"To mobilize a majority of the votes in an election, each political party must appeal to a variety of 'interests' and a wide spectrum of opinion. As a consequence of their catholicity, the major parties are unthinkable as instruments of tyranny because 'it is impossible for the party in power to oppress any element of the opposition party without oppressing a corresponding element within its own ranks.' In addition, the party in power knows that any effort to 'tyrannize' a particular minority may also antagonize other groups in the majority coalition, as well as the 'independents' pursued by both major parties, and, therefore, may cost it the next election.

"In short, the 'monolithic' majority . . . does not exist; the majority is but a coalition of minorities which must act in a moderate, broadly representative fashion to preserve itself. Political conciliation and accommodation characterize the legislative and administrative processes, as well as the competition for votes. This aspect of our political system is accentuated because we do not have disciplined, programmatic political parties and the individual legislative representative is left with a great deal of discretion."[13]

A third method for defining and securing personal freedoms against the popular will—the one favored by champions of judicial review—is to assign this task to some government institution that functions at least somewhat outside the mainstream of the political process. Although a number of possible candidates may be suggested, in the United States the mantle has fallen upon the Supreme Court. In brief, the theory is that the Supreme Court constitutes "a working part of the democratic political life of the nation"[14] because the power of judicial review has been historically exercised to restrain the majority from impinging on the constitutionally designated liberties of the individual, thus to assure those ultimate values that are integral to a democracy.

The difficulty with this position is that it commingles substance with procedure. The Supreme Court does advance democratic values by rejecting political action that threatens individual liberty. Its rulings requiring popular policies to adhere to constitutional precepts do enhance the democratic nature of our society. But irrespective of the *content* of its decisions, the *process* of judicial review is not democratic because the Court is not a politically responsible institution.[15] "The Court is not saved from being oligarchic because it professes to act in the service of humane ends."[16] Although the Supreme Court may play a vital role in the preservation of the American democratic system, the procedure of judicial review is in conflict with the fundamental principle of democracy—majority rule under conditions of political freedom.

Heroic efforts have been made to demonstrate that judicial review is compatible with democratic theory, that in exercising this power the Supreme Court is neither a "bevy of Platonic guardians,"[17] an "aristocracy of the robe,"[18] nor an "autocratic member of a democratic process."[19] Few have launched a frontal attack on the principle that political responsibility is the crucial ingredient for the making of public policy in a democratic state. Rather, the most sophisticated approach has been to establish that Congress and the executive, the so-called political branches of our government, are by no means as democratic as standard belief would hold and that the Court is much more subject to the popular will than conventional wisdom would grant. According to this view, analysis based on observations such as Tocqueville's—that the legislature "represents the majority and implicitly obeys it" and that the executive "is appointed by the majority, and serves as a passive tool in its hands"[20]—is found to be greatly oversimplified—"the most starry-eyed political naivete."[21] Such reasoning is described as having "abandoned most of the fictions which previously protected the power and dignity of the Court, [yet insisting] on returning to the cliches of the high school civics books when describing the political process."[22]

In support of this challenge, it must be acknowledged that *all* of our notable governmental and quasi-governmental agencies, especially at different times, contain undemocratic as well as democratic features.[23] Democracy in action is not simply a mirror reflection of popular will. Rather—as we shall soon note in greater detail—American working democracy is the grand product of the efforts and interactions of all legal and political structures in the nation, influenced at different points with varying intensities by the multitude of economic and social organizations that function outside the formal system of government.[24] For reasons such as these, knowledgeable and perceptive students of the American political system such as Martin Shapiro have decried the utility of "issuing blanket condemnations of judicial action on the basis of an abstract model of democratic policy-making that does not reflect the realities of American government." In his judgment, "so long as the Supreme Court functions within a governmental matrix of mixed democratic and nondemocratic elements, whether or not to assign certain tasks to the Justices is no more and no less a question of democracy than whether or not to assign those tasks to any other government agency .... Certainly nothing can be solved by calling down a plague on both their houses because neither is selected by annual elections. It seems preferable to determine in each separate policy area whether judicial policy-making contributes to well rounded representation of interests or to popular control more or less than policy-making by some rival agency."[25]

This argument—an especially powerful one owing not only to its substantial empirical premises but also to its signal theoretical force in making judicial review a legitimate element of a democratic society—merits careful consideration. There has surely been no paucity of surveys and descriptions by various commentators and journalists of the argument's empirical foundation—the general electoral responsibility of the three branches of our national government. And several scholars who have explored the consonance of the role of the Supreme Court and judicial review with our theory of government have made observations and references to the matter. But because the pursuit has usually been fragmentary and the conclusions often intuitive, doubts have persisted and the debate has continued. A more intensive examination of the practical operation of the American political process from the perspective of democratic theory—with particular emphasis on the specific way in which the institution of judicial review functions—is therefore both appropriate and desirable.

This chapter first supports the proposition that the legislative branch—traditionally perceived to be the most broadly representative of all government institutions—in fact operates undemocratically. This premise is then reappraised: the negative quality of the antimajoritarianism of the lawmaking process and its consequences for judicial review are explored; the institutions of Congress are reviewed in a more balanced fashion; and the role of the executive is examined. Finally, the political accountability of the Supreme Court is assessed and weighed against that of the elected branches.

II. THE DEFECTIVE CHARACTER OF CONGRESS'S MAJORITARIAN RESPONSIBILITY

A. The Process of Election and Interelection Representation

If there is any single axiom that describes the Congress, it is that neither the method for selection of its members nor its actual modes of behavior result in the automatic translation of the majority will into detailed legislation. As with all representative legislative bodies, "neither elections nor interelection activity provides much insurance that decisions will accord with the preferences of a majority of adults or voters."[26] The result is the possibility, indeed not infrequently the actuality, of minority control over the making of government policy.

To begin at bedrock, since members of both houses of Congress are elected from geographical districts rather than at large, it is at least theoretically possible (assuming a particular distribution of voter interests among the states and districts) that, even at the very moment the successful candidates assume office, they represent the views of but a small fraction of the electorate.[27] The venerable art of gerrymandering in the creation of legislative districts—which has been performed nationally and locally throughout our history and has yet to be constitutionally condemned (at least not by a holding of the Supreme Court in any specific instance, even a racial one)—has been nurtured with this knowledge.

Wholly apart from academic theories respecting voter allocation, even when we assume a normal dispersal of constituent
interests, the election of lawmaking representatives produces no
more than a very crude approximation of majority rule. Elections
occur only intermittently, thus permitting the once coincident
views of representative and constituent to drift radically apart.
Nonetheless, periodic rather than constant recurring elections
are obviously required for reasons of efficiency and practicality.
This pattern is necessary to achieve effective and stable government and to afford legislators some opportunity for
independence—to permit them to use their ability and experience to educate and lead popular opinion and to empower them
at least partially to perform the role of "Burkean Trustee" rather
than "Instructed Delegate" (a topic to be addressed in more detail shortly). But none of this denies the resulting imperfection in
respect to the theory of pure majoritarianism.

That the people go to the polls only occasionally is, however,
but a minor cause of the failure of elections to assure majority
rule. More important, in contrast to the direct or participatory
democracy of the town meeting, it is inherent in the system of
representative government that the electorate must buy its
political representation in bulk form. The voter is invariably offered only a few candidates (rarely more than two who have any
realistic chance of being elected) to reflect his will on the myriad
issues, large and small, that must be resolved in the operation of
day-to-day government. Hardly ever will a candidate share all
the preferences of an individual elector. Given the alternatives,
agreement with a candidate on most matters will be a sufficient
reason to vote for him; differences regarding a few issues,
perhaps even some of real concern to the voter, ordinarily will
not cause him to withhold his support for a nominee. Thus, the
hypothetical meticulous elector will, either overtly or implicitly,
list the issues he considers to be germane, assign them varying
weights depending on his intensity of feeling, and cast his ballot
for that entrant whose projected score comes closest to his own.[28]
The more casual voter—and, unfortunately, in all likelihood the
more typical one—will rest his judgment on some less refined
basis, broadly ranging from the candidate's party affiliation to his

personal acquaintance with the voter. But whichever nominee is finally settled upon, the voter's choice is necessarily a highly qualified one.

Further, the larger the constituency and the broader its political base, the more accentuated this factor becomes. Thus, the major political parties in the United States submit their basic policy positions to the electorate at wholesale. In the absence of a truly extraordinary situation, they solicit support not for a full complement of specific, detailed issues but rather for candidates who run on the basis of either an integrated proposed platform or total past performance. They seek to build or maintain an electoral majority composed of people who have similar views on many questions, but they recognize that these same people will have conflicting views on other questions. "To make the same point in another way, every aggregate of American citizens large enough to constitute a majority of voters is necessarily a rather heterogeneous collection of individuals and groups who may agree on some matters but are sure to disagree on others. No group of like-minded citizens can ever win a national election merely by mobilizing themselves and others who think exactly the way they do. To win national elections, even to win influence over national policies, every group must participate somehow in the politics of coalition building. To be sure, it can pursue its own goals; and it must engage in conflict; but it must also conciliate, compromise, negotiate, bargain—and in the process often forego its lesser goals for its greater objectives. In this sense, no single group can win national elections—only a heterogeneous combination of groups can."[29] As a consequence of this kind of averaging and compromising in selecting a delegate, as well as the fact that disagreements on particular issues frequently occur within a single party, there is simply no guarantee in representative government that a legislative vote on any single matter will produce the same result as would a popular referendum, even assuming equal knowledge and interest of all participants in both instances.

The electorate itself contributes another important element to the flawed reflection of majoritarianism in the legislative branch. Empirical studies confirm the widely held intuitive judgment

that many citizens know little and care less about particular candidates and issues and that no majority preferences are discernible on the overwhelming number of issues decided by legislators.[30] In respect to what professional and concerned observers
of government would consider to be both major questions of
public policy and minor matters of detail, a distressingly large
percentage of voters is almost totally uninformed. As a result,
they lack awareness of many, if not most, of their representatives'
viewpoints on policy issues.* This state of affairs has been
exacerbated by the complexity of sundry congressional procedures, especially the opportunity for anonymous voting, which
permit legislators to obfuscate and conceal the positions they
hold and the actions they have taken on many issues.

American voters often cast their ballots for congressional candidates not on the basis of ideology, the issues, or the candidates'
voting records, nor even on the ground of major party affiliation,
but rather because of their perception of how diligently the candidate has attended or will attend to his duties—with particular
emphasis on whether and how well the legislator has obtained
particular benefits for his district, and has serviced the various
requests of the voter himself or of other constituents for aid in
dealing with the bureaucracy of government.[31] These conditions
go far in explaining how the majority of a particular district may
vote for a President, senator, and representative—not to mention
varied state and local officers—none of whom agree with one
another regarding most prominent issues of public policy.

Furthermore, once a representative takes office, there are severe limits on the extent to which he may be depended on to
reflect accurately the majoritarian preferences of his constituency. The threat of reelection challenge may not be a
significant force, for the reelection process cannot be expected to
be any more discriminating than that of original election, and the
incumbent may comfortably rely on the great advantage for reelection that statistics show incumbency produces.[32] Apart from

---

* A Gallup poll several years ago indicated "that 57% of Americans cannot name
their congressman, and only 19% can cite a single thing he has done." Time, Jan.
15, 1973, at 17. For an earlier similar poll, see R. Dahl, Democracy in the United
States: Promise and Performance 169 n.9 (2d ed. 1972).

this, the legislator's information respecting the desires of his general constituency—at least as to some matters—is highly imperfect. One careful study of this question, "which compared the views and voting records of one hundred sixteen Congressmen in 1958 with the views of their constituents, revealed a surprisingly low relationship between the majority attitude in each district on social welfare and foreign policy and what the Congressman from the district *thought* was the majority view among his constituents."[33] As a result of all these phenomena, legislative enactments frequently deal with subjects of indifferent or indecisive electorate concern.

B. THE LAWMAKING MACHINERY IN OPERATION

1. The Congressional Structure

The most serious antimajoritarian forces in the congressional system, however, are found not in the scheme of elections and interelection devices to assure accurate representation but in the structure and inner workings of the legislative process itself. At the apex, the bicameral construction of Congress (and of all state legislatures save one) arms minorities with peculiar influence in impeding popular will—a capability that is augmented by the authority of the executive veto over legislation which may nullify the vote of substantial majorities in both houses. More important, the structure of the Senate insures that certain groups representing a minority of the national population may constitute a majority.

The Senate is composed of two legislators from each state who have equal voting power irrespective of their state's population. Mathematically, this permits senators who represent about 15 percent of the national citizenry—and who were elected by just more than half of that number—to constitute a voting majority, able to overrule the preferences of senators representing 85 percent of the population. This arrangement, constitutionally ordained and unchangeable without the consent of the states themselves, has caused the Senate to be labeled "perhaps the worst 'rotten borough' system in the democratic world "[34] Further-more, the constitutional scheme of staggered elections for members of the Senate compounds the effort required of those persons who wish to obtain a reversal of its policies. The members of the House of Representatives are elected from districts whose populations closely approach the one person–one vote status mandated by the Supreme Court's interdiction of malapportionment.[35] Nonetheless, its constitutional organization guarantees each state at least one legislator despite the fact that several states—those most overrepresented in the Senate—have a significantly smaller population than the average congressional district. In addition to these structural asymmetries, each chamber contains a raft of devices and practices that undermine fulfillment of true majority rule.

2. Filibuster

The obstructional advantage for a minority in the filibuster and the supermajority vote required for cloture is obvious. The filibuster is a device no longer used solely by southern obstructionists to halt civil rights advances; it has been employed more recently by conservatives to block consumer protection and public campaign financing and by liberals to thwart extension of the military draft, prohibition of busing for school desegregation, and construction of the supersonic transport and the antiballistic missile.[36] In addition, the technique's potential for thwarting majority will is compounded when the minority that supports the filibuster is already overrepresented by its votes in the Senate.

3. Congressional Committees

The critical role played by congressional committees and subcommittees in modern times derives from the practical impossibility of each legislator's giving intensive consideration to the myriad consequential measures brought before him. The ostensible purpose of the committee system is to enable selected members to devote the time and energy required for mature and detailed review of proposed legislation, and to afford different congressmen the opportunity to develop expertise in designated areas. The committees were conceived to investigate and determine the need for legislation, study the alternatives, shape proposals for presentation to the whole body, and make recommendations. Over the years, this design has been grandly executed. And because of the extreme complexity of the great number of issues confronting Congress, as well as the incredible demands that are made on late-twentieth-century congressmen (especially in regard to reelection campaigning and "servicing" constituents),[37] the strength of many committees (especially in the House) in determining crucial questions respecting the detail and timing of legislation has become enormous.

Two specific illustrations should suffice:

i) The House Committee on Ways and Means "originates all laws raising revenues, including tax laws; laws regulating foreign trade (because of their tariff aspect); and laws pertaining to the social-security system (including medicare). Because of the complexity of the bills this committee writes and because of the temptation that exists for congressmen to add special exemptions and provisions to tax bills, legislation originating in the Ways and Means Committee normally comes before the House under rules of debate that limit amendments."[38] In 1962, a group of Democratic representatives defeated the bid of one of their distinguished southern colleagues for a seat on Ways and Means because they "believed that the fate of President Kennedy's trade program, of his tax program, and of the Medicare bill might be at stake in that single assignment."[39]

ii) The House Committee on Appropriations "is regarded as something of a law unto itself, even within the House."[40] Its dozen subcommittees scrutinize budget requests for the financing of all government programs and are largely joined in the common effort of guarding the fisc. In the period 1958–65, they reduced over one quarter of all desired expenditures by more than 20 percent and over half by more than 5 percent, despite the near-unanimous view of executive officials interviewed that a 5 percent decrease must be considered "serious" and "harmful to the operation of [one's] bureau (or department)."[41] These subcommittees "may effectively nullify the will of Congress expressed through ordinary legislation by refusing to appropriate money authorized by law" and their decisions "are rarely challenged in full committee." The whole committee "has privileged access to the floor" and "when the committee has been united, it has almost always gotten its way."[42]

There is no blinking the reality that few, if any, congressional committees are either microcosms of the entire Congress or reflective of the views of the electorate as a whole. Quite to the contrary, a highly significant consideration for deciding who is assigned to what committee—if not the most powerful factor—is the special (often parochial) interest of the aspiring congressman in the subject area of the committee's work.[43] The frailty of the representative character of the committees is accentuated by the influence from within held by less than a majority of their members. Even a medium-sized minority can prevent a bill it opposes from emerging—"the number and variety of objections [it] can raise is quite staggering."[44]

4. Committee Chairmen

The chairmen of the various committees have traditionally occupied the real seats of power within the committee system. Through their control of agenda, they have been able to determine when and whether bills should be considered by the full committee. In their committee executive role, they have been able to decide when and whether to call meetings at all. By their authority to select the committee's professional staff, conservative chairmen have been able to blunt the thrust of a committee composed mainly of liberals. The same result has been accomplished by skillful appointment of members of subcommittees, to which the chairmen have had the power to refer various bills. The chairmen have been empowered to decide whether particular investigations should be launched, whether and when hearings should be held, and who the witnesses should be. When bills are reported from committees, the chairmen have managed their consideration on the floor. In the House, where debate is limited, the chairmen have had the prerogative to open and close debate, allot the speaking time, and move the previous question whenever they think it appropriate. When bills that have been carried in each house go to conference, it has been the respective chairmen in each chamber who have been the bills' principal managers in the Conference Committee.

Again, just a few examples of the long-standing authority of these "lord-proprietors"[45]—reported by Douglass Cater in the mid-1960s—are necessary to suggest the limits to which this power may extend:

i) Representative Otto Passman, chairman of the House Appropriations Subcommittee on Foreign Operations, "is a professed enemy of the foreign aid program which he oversees. . . . Regularly he and his little subcommittee cut deeply into the sums already authorized by Congress. Just as regularly, the full Appropriations Committee, whose chairman shares Passman's hostility toward foreign aid, leaves the cuts untouched. The full House has made restorations only twice, both in the military-assistance categories. During the annual ritual, the President turns desperately to the Senate for more substantial help only to watch the effects be whittled away again by Passman's influence on the Senate-House Conference."[46]

ii) Representative Harold Cooley, chairman of the House Agricultural Committee, "rules the nation's sugar economy. . . . [He] works out the schedule of quotas . . . . Because the Sugar Act contains an excise tax, Cooley asserts the Constitutional prerogative of the House of Representatives to initiate all revenue measures. Because the legislation is highly technical, he claims that only his committee is able to cope with it. Within the committee itself, whose thirty-five members compete in their concerns for cotton, tobacco, wheat and the other commodities, a skillful Chairman dominates by playing off one interest against another. It permits him remarkable discretion. In reviewing the sugar quotas, Chairman Cooley has had the habit of receiving the interested parties one by one to make their presentations, then summoning each afterward to announce his verdict."[47]

Despite their nationwide lawmaking impact, committee chairmen have ruled far removed from the reins of national political responsibility. Traditionally selected on the basis of seniority—a custom, it is ironic to recall, that became virtually inviolable[48] as an antidote to the antimajoritarian tactics of a repressive leadership—these congressional hierarchs have thus invariably come from a limited number of safe districts (preponderantly in the South when the Democrats have controlled Congress). Whatever their accountability to their local constituencies, their immense influence is in disharmony with the democratic precept of majority rule.

5. Party Leaders

The party leadership in both houses has also occupied a key position in the congressional power structure. The long-institutionalized social dynamics of Congress have led American legislators—with just a few maverick exceptions—to set a high value on "getting along" internally. This means keeping their vote in tune with the expressed wishes of the leaders of their party as often as they deem possible. Even the committee chairmen realize that they cannot ordinarily overcome the active opposition of the leadership and that they almost always need at least its passive support to get laws enacted.

But neither does the crucial function of the party leadership guarantee majority rule. Much like committee chairmen, the leaders' immediate base of political responsibility is not nationwide but confined to a single state or congressional district.[49] Although their ascension is not strictly linked to seniority, it usually requires the longevity afforded by a safe constituency. And once they have attained their position, apart from extraordinary circumstances, it is not popular opinion but only age or intense peer dissatisfaction that can dislodge them.[50]

6. Conference Committee

No description of the antimajoritarian force of the committee system and party leadership in both houses of Congress would be complete without an examination of the Conference Committee—that unique device to effect reconciliation between the different versions of legislation on the same subject enacted by the House and the Senate. Appointments to this committee are formally made by the presiding officer in each house, but the wishes of the chairmen of the respective committees that originally considered the legislation have traditionally been respected. This not infrequently has resulted in conference members who are personally opposed to key provisions in their own chamber's version of the bill, notwithstanding the fact that their function is nominally to advance that version. Since the conference compromise report that is returned to each house may not be amended and must be either accepted or rejected in toto, the conferees potentially possess vast power to eliminate critical provisions; and both they and other congressmen are presented with a peculiar opportunity to play tricks with months of prior legislative effort. Several examples demonstrate the significance of the technique:

i) "Sophisticated liberal members of the House, realizing that the House of Representatives tends to be more conservative than the Senate, often make no attempt to insert liberal provisions into House measures initially but may arrange for them to be put into the Senate version of the bill. In this way they avoid the strong possibility that the House of Representatives will explicitly reject provisions they are interested in. Once there is such an explicit rejection in the House, it is very difficult to pass any conference report that includes the offending language, because conservative House members will make much of the fact that the House has already rejected the provisions of the bill. Thus the technique is to see that the liberal provisions are introduced on the Senate side and then make every effort to assure that the combined bill that comes out of the conference has predominantly Senate provisions in it."[51]

ii) In 1970, "on the controversial bill to continue federal funding for the supersonic transport plane, the House had voted to authorize $290 million, while the Senate refused to authorize any financial assistance. Yet the conferees 'compromised' at $210 million after a brief conference. Of the seven Senate conferees, four had voted to provide federal funding for the aircraft, and one, Senator Warren G. Magnuson (D-Wash.), a staunch SST-supporter, openly declared before the conference agreement was reported that he was still seeking the full $290 million."[52]

iii) In 1962, "after winning overwhelming approval in both Houses, aid to higher education was killed" because of the conflicting views of the Conference Committee, despite the fact that either the House or Senate version was acceptable to the President.[53]

These illustrations may be especially poignant ones. But they are in no way wholly atypical of what has transpired. As described by a once active Senate reformist, Albert Gore of Tennessee, "the archaic ways and the often dictatorial-like powers of conference committees"[54] have contradicted majority will in the halls of Congress.

7. Interest Groups

In exploring the assortment of undemocratic forces at work in the legislative process, some recognition must also be given to the influence held by what are popularly known as "interest" or "pressure groups." There is a sizable literature describing and appraising the complicated and potent role that the various types of factions falling under this label have assumed in government.[55] More shall be said shortly about some of these kinds of groups. At this point, it is enough to note the well-identified existence of one set—the organized lobbies. Although our knowledge of the nature, frequency, and success of the various methods they employ is far from complete,[56] it is generally agreed that by transmitting pertinent information to key lawmakers, by skillfully and selectively applying pressure at critical points in the system, and by expending massive sums of money—not infrequently in an abusive, and occasionally criminal, manner—they are able to exercise power well beyond the force of the numbers of people they represent.

These lobbies ply their trades not only within the offices of particular legislators and relevant congressional committees. They also effectively pierce the bureaucratic maze of the executive branch and the independent regulatory agencies which, because of their extensive rulemaking authority, and especially because of their status as the source of many of the programs considered by Congress, play an important part in the national legislative process. Conventional belief, supported by at least some hard and often disconcerting empirical evidence, holds that specific lobbies have been particularly successful on the latter front—e.g., the Farm Bureau in the Department of Agriculture, the "military-industrial complex" in the Department of Defense, the National Association of Manufacturers in the Department of Commerce, the railroads and truckers in the Interstate Commerce Commission, the oil and gas industry in the Federal Power Commission, and even certain foreign governments in parts of the Department of State. Indeed, the charge is often heard that some government agencies were either originally sponsored and engineered by, or have subsequently fallen captive to, the very private interests that are supposed to be the subjects of their regulation.[57]

To cap all this, the interaction among the lobbies, the executive and administrative bureaus, and the pertinent legislative committees is seen as producing enormous political clout. Described by one observer as "government by whirlpools,"[58] it has led another to conclude that "since the bureau generally drafts initial legislation and the committee has paramount powers over the bill once it reaches Congress, these alliances are of tremendous importance. They tend to protect subordinate, and frequently group dominated, segments of government from whatever democratic and broadly popular control one might expect from Congress as a whole and from the President."[59]

C. A Summary and Qualification

The preceding picture of the national lawmaking process reveals anything but a system that simply articulates some readily identifiable popular will. Rather, the business of legislating solutions to the exceedingly difficult and intricate problems confronting American society is seen as a complicated interplay among nonmajoritarian based organs of power within the government and various organized vested interest groups

without, which are continually engaged in activities of consultation, negotiation, and conciliation. At best, the voice of the
people is recognized as only one of a multitude of interacting
forces—and a relatively minor one at that.

If this were a complete and accurate portrayal, unburdened by
serious ambiguities, the task of legitimately fitting the Supreme
Court and judicial review into the working machinery of American democratic society would not be a very uncomfortable one.
But the foregoing description of the antimajoritarian nature of the
federal legislative scheme has been one-sided and, thus, dis-
torted. True enough, "there can be no automatic and blanket
equation of Congress or the Executive branch with the voice of
the people,"[60] and "democracy conceived populistically simply
does not comport with political reality."[61] Nevertheless, as will
soon be shown, the lawmaking process is greatly more responsive
to constituent will and much more aligned with traditional
democratic precepts than the prior recitation would have us
believe.

III. THE "NEGATIVE" QUALITY OF THE ANTIMAJORITARIANISM OF THE LAWMAKING PROCESS AND ITS CONSEQUENCES FOR JUDICIAL REVIEW

In comparing the undemocratic features of our national legislative system with those of the power of judicial
review—a contrast undertaken for the purpose of examining the
latter's validity in the American plan of democracy—one central
factor bears emphasis at the outset. In the main, the effect of
judicial review in ruling legislation unconstitutional is to nullify
the finished product of the lawmaking process. It is the very rare
Supreme Court decision on constitutionality that affirmatively
mandates the undertaking of government action. And even when
it does—as when the judiciary fashions a reapportionment
scheme or institutes a school desegregation plan—it substitutes
its own program for a popularly sponsored one that it finds constitutionally deficient. To make the point in another way, when
the Supreme Court finds legislative acts unconstitutional it holds

invalid only those enactments that have survived the many hurdles fixed between incipient proposals and standing law.

The significance of this evident fact for our purposes is that most of the antimajoritarian elements that have been found in the American legislative process—both quantitatively and qualitatively—are negative ones, i.e., they work to *prevent* the translation of popular wishes into governing rules rather than to *produce* laws that are contrary to majority sentiment. Conceding the validity of the broad contention that the national lawmaking machinery contains a host of multifaceted undemocratic features, it is critical to recognize the primary consequence—and the most frequently voiced major objection—that follows: It is not that far-reaching laws promulgated by the legislative system are opposed by a predominant segment of the populace, but rather that Congress too often refuses to ordain solutions supported by national majorities.[62]

The phenomenon of negativism operates in the lawmaking process at several levels. The effect of the bicameral legislature is to require the mustering of two separate majorities to carry a bill while permitting either body to frustrate its passage. Thus it is true, as noted earlier, that senators representing only 15 percent of the population may hold sway in the upper house; but their real impact (as is obviously the case with the filibuster as well) is to halt ultimate action rather than facilitate it. For the enactment of law also requires the concurrence of the lower chamber—and the House of Representatives in recent years has become well known as a frequently uncompromising "naysaying" body to measures passed by the Senate. Furthermore, within each legislative chamber, the ability of the committees and their chairmen and minority members—and frequently of the lobbies and other interest groups as well—to circumvent the majority will of the assembly is most saliently manifested in obstructing rather than making laws. It must be conceded that on occasion a skillful, highly informed lobbyist may outwit the staff of a congressional committee and cause a "special-interest slant" to "slip through without critical analysis."[63] But the more typical force of pressure groups is exemplified by the ability of the automobile industry to block government support of mass transit

and of the National Rifle Association to thwart gun control legislation despite sharp public sentiment to the contrary.[64] The more
formidable task usually is not to stall or defeat a proposal but to
organize the requisite support among the dispersed powers so as
to form a coalition for its passage. This is all the more true when
the issue at hand is one of real public visibility and concern,
causing a legislator to be especially wary of bargaining away or
compromising his vote. Above all, the force of the executive veto
in rendering congressional majorities ineffectual also operates to
deny rather than decree legislation. Thus, although exceptions
exist, "a distinguishing feature of our system, perhaps impelled
by heritage of sectional division and heterogeneity, is that our
governmental structure, institutional habits, and political parties
with their internal factional divisions, have combined to produce
a system in which major programs and major new directions cannot be undertaken unless supported by a fairly broad popular
consensus. This normally has been far broader than 51 percent,
and often bipartisan as well."[65] Indeed, it has been persuasively
argued that even after a material reform has been legislatively
promulgated by an overwhelming margin, its implementation
requires continuing deep-rooted popular pressure to overcome a
disciplined resistance to unwanted regulatory initiatives.[66]

To have underscored this point does not end the subject, however. By no means are all the undemocratic aspects of the federal
legislative process negative in character. For example, the same
inertia in the lawmaking system that operates to block the passage of new statutes supported by the people may also work to
hinder the repeal of existing laws despite their loss of majoritarian backing. And further inquiry on the subject remains to be
undertaken. But two basic matters should be acknowledged at
this point. First, the crucial issue is not simply whether the national legislative process is, in all, more electorally responsible
than the federal judiciary, but rather whether the institution of
judicial review is compatible with American democratic theory
and practice. Second, there is substance to the message that
when the Supreme Court, itself without conventional political
responsibility, says "thou shalt not" to acts of Congress, it usually
cuts sharply against the grain of majority rule. The relatively few

laws that finally overcome the congressional obstacle course generally illustrate the national political branches operating at their majoritarian best while the process of judicial review depicts that element of the Court's work, and that exertion of federal authority, with the most brittle democratic roots.

(No detailed examination of the legislative systems in the states and their subdivisions has been ventured here. But a parallel conclusion—that laws finally enacted by state and municipalities most likely have staunch popular backing within their political units—appears to have substantially similar merit in respect to the Court's overturning such regulations. Nonetheless, it may be that, at least on some occasions, when the Court invalidates such laws (the usual ground being that they abridge individual rights—a subject that is the principal concern of chapter 2), it acts in consonance with the sentiment of a nationwide majority which, because of the inertia of the national political process, cannot obtain a congressional reversal of the local rules. This would appear to be the exceptional situation. But to this limited extent, this phenomenon may relieve the tension between judicial review and majoritarianism when the Court passes on the constitutionality of action by governments below the national level. Further, in some few instances, special doctrines that the Court employs to overturn legislation less clearly reject majority will. Thus, when a statute that allocates government largesse is held violative of equal protection on the ground that it is underinclusive, denying benefits to groups who are constitutionally indistinguishable from recipients, it may be that the excluded class had majority sympathy but simply could not muster adequate force to move the lawmakers to include it. But even if this is so, the Court's invalidation of the statute often results in withholding benefits to the law's beneficiaries whom popular consensus plainly believed should have them.)

The case that judicial review operates against government action with especially strong majoritarian foundations is not as persuasive when it is the conduct of judges or, even more often, of lower echelon administrative officials (municipal, state, or federal) that the Court finds constitutionally objectionable—for example, a rule of court respecting the admission of illegally seized evidence, a local police practice regarding lineups, a state welfare board procedure governing the termination of benefits, a Civil Rights Commission regulation concerning confrontation of adverse witnesses, a Navy Department program dealing with security clearance for employees on bases. And it must be admitted that, at least in recent experience, measures such as these composed the major segment of the Court's constitutional adjudications. But it must also be recognized that all these policies are promulgated by public officers who, though not commonly subject to direct recall at periodic elections, obtain and hold their positions under the authority of other government officials who are immediately responsible to the people. Further, it is fair to observe that the bulk of these administrative practices, especially those of law enforcement agencies, command broad popular support. If the people or their elected representatives disapprove of their continuance, these policies may be altered by ordinary legislation or directive. And although the forces of inertia that we have noticed as operative in the lawmaking process render change no automatic endeavor, it is still much less difficult for a majority to reverse an existing administrative policy through commonplace legislative methods than it is to reinstate it after a judicial declaration of invalidity.

IV. THE MAJORITARIAN RESPONSIBILITY OF CONGRESS REEXAMINED

When viewed from a less adversary perspective, it becomes clear that the antimajoritarian ingredients of Congress are not as forceful in operation—even in obstructing legislation—as they were earlier made out to be.

A. THE PROCESS OF ELECTION AND INTERELECTION REPRESENTATION

American history has shown the mathematical possibility of true minority control of legislatures through districting without gerrymandering to exist in theory only. Moreover, even assuming its continuance without further specific judicial intervention, gerrymandering itself, although not just a theoretical construct, is "an increasingly risky enterprise" for state legislatures to undertake because of "the great mobility of the American people, the accelerating pace of socioeconomic change and the increasing uncertainties in the futures of both major parties."[67]

The criticisms of the limited choices offered the electorate by individual candidates and political parties, of voter ignorance and apathy regarding nominees and issues, and of elected representatives' not reflecting the majority will are, however, very serious ones. First, as to the major political parties and their nominees, it may be "that the removal of a government carries no necessary assurance that its successor will proceed in a markedly different direction."[68] But this does not prove that the American party system defeats the democratic ideal. Nor is such a claim substantiated by the fact that "all too often the major political parties are agreed on a specific measure or policy."[69] For the chances are far greater than not that the policy at issue is one on which most of the electorate, as well as the parties, are in accord. The available empirical evidence—tentative as it may be— indicates that when the average American voter casts his ballot along party lines, he is fairly knowledgeable about which party better reflects the positions he holds.[70]

Thus, as Robert Dahl, one of the most eminent scholars of American politics, concludes, "What happens if a party responds more to its leaders than to the voters? The answer seems obvious: It will probably be defeated in elections—if the other party is closer to the views of the electorate."[71] Even presidential elections have not infrequently turned on a single great question, or a closely bracketed set of critical issues, over which the parties or their nominees have been divided—as would have been attested, for example, by President John Adams in 1800, President John Quincy Adams in 1828, William Jennings Bryan in 1896, President Taft in 1912, Governor Landon in 1936, Senator Goldwater in 1964, and Senator McGovern in 1972. Perhaps the citizenry cannot always "secure the reversal of a particular measure" but they usually can "readily overturn [or reject] fundamental policies,"[72] if they feel strongly about them—as President

Johnson manifestly perceived in 1968, and President Nixon even more clearly came to realize six years later.

That many citizens are ill-informed about the complex policies and detailed issues confronted by their representatives, thus affording the legislators a spacious discretion and independence in lawmaking, need not be as incompatible with majority rule as it is made to sound. The specific details of most solutions ultimately passed on by the legislature cannot, in the nature of things, be in the minds of the voters at the time of the elections. Further, a great many of the legislative issues that do not concern large numbers of voters probably should not. Therefore, it is not inconsistent with majority rule to permit these categories of decisions to rest within the judgment of the legislator himself, even if his verdict is influenced significantly by pressure groups. On such issues, the latter may well be the most efficient representatives of those truly interested. Even if not, to characterize this as minority rule closely parallels finding pervasive minority rule in the fact that a substantial portion of the eligible population—indeed, often exceeding half—choose not to vote at all on election day.

More important, some empirical surveys tend to confirm the intuitive notion that voters elect candidates, and representatives act on the assumption that they have been selected, for dual purposes: citizens choose legislators who they believe will, when possessed with the requisite knowledge concerning alternative courses, vote the citizens' general preferences—thus to operate as "Instructed Delegates"; but the electorate also supports those candidates in whose values and judgments they have confidence, implicitly authorizing these representatives to vote their own perception of the public good—thus to act as "Burkean Trustees."[73] Whether in a given situation the elector intends his representative to perform as Instructed Delegate or Burkean Trustee depends mainly on the specific issue involved and the intensity of the elector's opinion regarding it. But the hard evidence that exists tends to show that voters recognize both their unfamiliarity and incompetence regarding many policy matters and that, in consequence, they "choose *to be* governed *by* the officials elected *as well as* to govern *through* them."[74]

It is less evident whether this usually inexplicit popular intention actually extends—as conceived by Hamilton—to charging "those to whom they intrust the management of their affairs" with the "duty" to disregard certain of their preferences ("every sudden breeze of passion" or "every transient impulse") on those occasions "in which the interests of the people are at variance with their inclinations ... in order to give them time and opportunity for more cool and sedate reflection."[75] But, as we have seen and will see, it is clear that if the people's elected guardians ignore the popular will too often, they will soon be retired. Nonetheless, the citizenry does expect their officials to lead as well as follow and to engage in an informed dialogue with them. The essential difference between this educational experience conducted by legislators and, as put by Eugene Rostow, Supreme Court Justices as "teachers in a vital national seminar"[76] through constitutional decisionmaking is that the legislators, but not the Justices, may readily be deposed if the received learning is found to be too distasteful.

The foregoing discussion indicates that, at least at a general level, the national process for choosing legislators conforms much more closely to Madison's original conception of truly representative houses of Congress[77] than our earlier, one-sided version depicted, and that constituency policy preference is in fact a signally important component in delegate selection. Thus, for example, in 1958, Representative Brooks Hays, after lengthy service in the House, was defeated for reelection by Dale Alford, a write-in candidate. In the sample of voters in the Arkansas district surveyed, not one was unaware of either candidate. "What is more, these interviews show[ed] that Hayes was regarded both by his supporters and his opponents as more moderate than Alford on civil rights and that this perception brought his defeat."[78] As another illustration: "Former Senator Paul Douglas (D., Ill.) tells of how he tried to persuade Senator Frank Graham (D., N.C.) to tailor his issue positions in order to survive a 1950 primary. Graham, a liberal appointee to the office, refused to listen. He was a 'saint,' says Douglas. He lost his primary."[79] In a study of the relationship between congressmen's roll call records and their election percentages, it was estimated that "an unusually liberal Republican Representative gets at least 6 per cent more of the two-party vote ... than his extreme conservative counterpart would in the same district."[80] A more recent detailed analysis of a 1974 election upset in Oregon, in which 73 percent of the respondents felt that they knew enough about the incumbent to rate his performance, found that "a congressman's reputation among his constituents has a strong bearing on his electoral fortunes."[81] Many additional illustrations could readily be found in the series of House and Senate—indeed, presidential—elections in the 1960s and early 1970s that constituted little more than popular referendums on the Vietnam war issue, or on Watergate,[82] or on school busing.[83] And although the expanding influence in the late 1970s, especially in off-year elections, of what has come to be known as "single issue voting"—on issues such as abortion and budget balance—has yet to be systematically documented, its threatening force is generally conceded.

The ultimate significance of this lies, of course, in its effect on legislative policymaking. A number of empirical studies reveal that, although the matter depends very heavily on the legislative issue involved, almost all congressmen—whether from "marginal" or "safe" districts—hold the firm belief that their election turns largely, if not exclusively, on how their constituents view their voting records.[84] "Outraged public opinion," one inquiry concludes, "is the single most effective pressure on Congress."[85] Moreover, the studies corroborate the probable inference that the more prominent the issue and the more intense the voters' feelings, the more substantial the impact on the legislator. As put by one southern congressman in explaining his vote to unseat Representative Adam Clayton Powell, "It was either his seat or mine."[86] Thus, "when two North Carolina nonsigners of the 1956 Southern Manifesto immediately lost their primaries, the message was clear to southern members that there could be no straying from a hard line on the school desegregation issue." And "any breath of life left in the cause of school bussing was squeezed out by House returns from the Detroit area in 1972."[87]

Similarly, in 1937, the first minimum wage bill "was tied up in the House Rules Committee, and there was an effort to get it to the floor through use of a discharge petition. Then two primary elections broke the jam. Claude Pepper (D., Fla.) and Lister Hill (D., Ala.) won nominations to fill vacant Senate seats. 'Both campaigned on behalf of the Wages and Hours bill, and both won smashing victories.... Immediately after the results of the Florida and Alabama primaries became known, there was a stampede to sign the petition, and the necessary 218 signatures were quickly obtained.' The bill later passed."[88]

Finally, in 1955, a number of southern congressmen, traditionally strong supporters of free trade, opposed the leadership of Speaker Rayburn and voted against reciprocal trade—"chiefly the result of the communications they received from their districts, largely from textile interests .... If industry and the workers in their district [were] convinced that reciprocal trade [would] hurt them, they [were] willing to go along."[89] The proposition, it might be useful to underline, is not that legislators bow to constituent will on each and every issue before them, or even on all issues about which a large group of the electorate holds a discernible view. Rather, the conclusion is that distinct voter preferences on major issues do customarily prevail.

This reality is closely bound, and thus similarly responds, to a factor earlier mentioned as one of the antimajoritarian features of Congress: the flawed system of communication between voters and legislators. Whatever the deficiencies in information transmission, if the issue is big enough and the electorate feels strongly enough, as was true regarding American participation in the League of Nations,[90] the message reaches Washington loudly and clearly. And it is important to observe that the clarity of the response from the Capitol has been heightened by several recently inaugurated disclosure devices. For example, both the House and the Senate have adopted rules stipulating that virtually all committee meetings (apart from those dealing with designated confidential subjects) must emerge from behind closed doors unless a majority of committee members publicly votes otherwise; as a result, the long-standing prohibition against open

mark-up sessions has been abandoned and only a tiny fraction of committee deliberations are now held in camera.[91]
In addition, both chambers determined to open Senate-House
conferences—"traditionally the most secretive meetings in
Congress"[92]—except when either group's conferees vote otherwise publicly, the House of Representatives subsequently going
even further by providing that its vote to close conference sessions must be cast by the full body.[93] Further, the House of
Representatives decreed that all teller votes be recorded and
published, thus deterring members from anonymously opposing
measures that they would otherwise feel compelled to support.*
Finally, even more "sunshine" reforms—in addition to televis-
ing congressional floor proceedings—appear to be in the works.

The gap in communications that exists between constituents
and congressmen also has a broader significance in our examination of whether legislators attend to voters' desires—and one that
interacts to a degree with the matter of pressure group influence.
As just noted, the empirical surveys divulge that congressmen
feel that their voting records will contribute significantly to their
election and thus they are strongly influenced by their *perception* of their constituents' preferences. But this does not assure
undeviating fulfillment of majority sentiment. One widely cited
study concludes that congressmen tend "to overestimate their
visibility to the local public, a tendency that reflects the difficulties of the Representative in forming a correct judgment of
constituent opinion"; and, while congressmen do frequently assume the role of Instructed Delegates, their instructions are
often "heavily biased" because "the communication most Congressmen have with their districts inevitably puts them in touch

---

* "The impact an alteration in the rules of procedure can have on the decisionmaking processes in Congress and on the legislative output was vividly illustrated early in the first session of the 92nd Congress, when the House, in casting
its first recorded vote on the question of federal assistance for development of a
supersonic transport plane, reversed its position of seven years and voted to end
the controversial subsidy. There were a number of factors behind the turnabout,
but the foremost among them was the newly created recorded teller vote, which
forced House members to take a position in the public eye." Hopkins, Congressional Reform: Toward a Modern Congress, 47 Notre Dame Law, 442, 450
(1972).

with organized groups and with individuals who are relatively well-informed about politics."[94]

This should not, however, be viewed as an unhealthy development in a democracy. It should rather be seen as furthering majoritarian representation. Regardless of the actual imperfections in legislative reflection of majority will on some issues (and their presence has been openly acknowledged throughout), they are ameliorated—at least in terms of democratic theory—by the fact that congressmen probably *believe* that they represent the preponderant views of the voters in their districts more often than they do so in practice; the important fact is that congressmen do feel obliged to respect constituents' interests. Nor is it at all unlikely that the vocal elements in the community normally reflect whatever broader citizen sentiment exists, especially on those issues on which the electors' preference has not been expressed. As we have seen and shall see, the lines of communication between Main Street and Capitol Hill are continually improving. And, in any case, however clogged they may be, they are both more direct and more informative than those running to the chambers of the Justices of the Supreme Court. Even the highly publicized Nader-sponsored indictment of the national legislative department concluded: "For all its flaws, Congress is still the most responsive and open branch of the government."[95] Indeed, a recent study contends that, both theoretically and empirically, overall congressional responsiveness to electoral wishes is probably even greater when measured by the actions of all congressmen collectively than by the relationship between a particular legislator's vote and the wishes of his immediate constituency.[96]

That the people's voice is quite distinctly understood when raised vigorously about prominent issues on which many voters hold opinions is further supported by the highly respected empirical analysis of Warren Miller and Donald Stokes. In their study, a very high correlation between what congressmen *thought* was the dominant opinion of all their constituents and what these views really were was found on the question of civil rights,[97] which was likely the most vital issue of the time. Further, on the matter of government social welfare policy—a salient topic on which the long-conflicting and plainly articulated views of the major parties and their candidates greatly facilitated communication between voter and representative—the survey results as to the correlation between the attitudes of the representative's electoral majority and his voting record were especially revealing: "Whereas the correlation between the constituency majority and congressional roll call votes [was] nearly +0.4 on social welfare policy, the correlation of the district majority with the non-incumbent candidate [was] −0.4. This difference, amounting to almost 0.8, between these two coefficients is an indicator of what the dominant electoral element of the constituency gets on the average by choosing the Congressman it has and excluding his opponent from office."[98]

On the other hand, on foreign policy issues, the correlation was markedly lower. This may plausibly be explained by pragmatic indifference, for, at the time of the study (which was before Vietnam became a political byword), the evidence was that many representatives based their foreign policy votes neither on constituent preferences nor on their own instincts, but rather tended to follow the lead of the executive branch. And there is probably some justification in democratic theory for this disposition; perhaps on these far-reaching questions of distinctly national scope, the legislators felt obliged to take a special sort of Burkean stand, either responding to a perceived nationwide attitude rather than to the soundings in their districts or deferring to presidential responsibility and expertise. Indeed, the national citizenry itself has often manifested a similar tendency—for example, voicing general support for President Johnson in 1966 far more substantial than its concurrence with his specific actions in Indochina.[99] But, as many hawkish (as well as some dovish) incumbents came to know, the dialogue between Burkean Trustee and the voters is subject to cloture—and the electorate, if it so wishes, may exercise the right of last rebuttal.

The Burkean model seems also to account in part for the fact that the safer the district, the stronger the legislator's display of independence of popular will on specific issues.[100] And it is surely reasonable for a continually reelected lawmaker to infer that his constituents have authorized him to exercise personal judgment with greater than normal freedom. But, once again, it is obvious without citation that some have learned—as often in primaries as in general elections—that this liberty has its limits.

To conclude the point, no claim is made here that the votes of congressmen perfectly mirror the desires of their constituents. The conduct of legislators is complicated by a host of interactive elements. The empirical evidence is relatively sparse and undoubtedly more remains to be discovered than ever will be. But, in admittedly varying degrees, all senators and representatives are, as Dahl noted, certainly "right in thinking that they would place themselves in serious jeopardy at the polls if they were to vote counter to the views of a majority of their constituents on any matter that is salient and important to a sizeable share of the voters at home."[101]

B. The Lawmaking Machinery in Operation

1. Bicameralism and Filibuster

The particularly negative character of bicameralism and filibuster so far as majoritarianism is concerned, has already been noted. Beyond this, it is pertinent to recognize that bicameralism actually serves democratic ends by forcing fuller and more open congressional consideration of great issues and by improving the flow of information to the electorate. The same is at least arguably, if somewhat perversely, true of the filibuster, which may "generate awareness of an issue and so potentially can bring the public into deliberations through letter writing and mass organizing."[102]

2. Congressional Committees and Chairmen

The committees, however, constitute more than a negative force. These power cliques, and especially their chairmen, elected but not nationally responsible, have, at least on occasion, seen their prejudices become law. But the committee system is changing.

Traditionally, the bane of promajoritarian critics has been the

Rules Committee of the House of Representatives. For many years, this assemblage was perhaps the most effective bill stopper in the Congress. The ingenuity in modern times of its several conservative chairmen—backed by a conservative coalition of their colleagues—in delaying legislation until they struck a bargain satisfactory to themselves, but often distasteful to a majority of the House, became legendary. But this committee has been caught in the net of reform, mainly by a change in its composition through enlargement and attrition so that it presently approximates more closely the political leanings of the leadership of the majority party.[103] It is no longer the signal object of scorn among those who indict the Congress as being unrepresentative. Indeed, the decline of this despotic group's influence suggests that no matter how ingrained an antimajoritarian stain in the lawmaking process may be, it is not ineradicable. Even the longstanding rule in the House of Representatives forbidding floor amendments to measures proposed by the Ways and Means Committee—which, it should be emphasized, is itself meant to shield against the machinations of avaricious special interests[104]—has been recently altered. At the request of fifty of its members, the Democratic party caucus may now demand a vote on a specific provision by the full House.[105]

Furthermore, there are other operative forces which limit the grip of a committee and its chairman. Even the general naysaying ability of committees is by no means unqualified. If a majority of either house truly desires action, it may resort to a discharge procedure to wrest a pending measure from the clutches of any of its committees. Although infrequently utilized, the threat of this method, as well as respect for the will of the body as a whole, usually prohibits committee chairmen from blocking consideration of issues that a majority deems fundamental and limits their impact to matters of timing and subordinate policy.[106]

Although we have seen instances, such as the sugar quota affair, in which a dominant chairman legislates for the nation, these are exceptional. Without in any way denying the autocratic nature of such conduct or devaluing its undemocratic force, the fact is that actions such as this virtually always concern matters of specific detail and hardly ever questions of central concern. The judgment of Nelson Polsby, a leading congressional scholar, that it would be "futile" for a chairman "to promote legislation that cannot command widespread support, at least from the leadership of his own party or from a vast majority of his colleagues on the floor,"[107] may be buttressed by countless illustrations that cover the full spectrum of congressional activities. In reference to taxation, for example, Douglass Cater reports that Representative Wilbur Mills, then chairman of the Ways and Means Committee and perhaps the most commanding figure in both houses at the time, "argue[d] that his primary concern must be to coalesce majority support for a bill in Committee and in the full House. The Ways and Means Chairman, he believe[d] firmly, must guard a reputation for invincibility if his handicraft is not to be torn apart by the competing pressures."[108] And in respect to the location and amount of defense spending, Cater describes in detail the lengthy and painstaking process of negotiation that takes place in the quest for broad-based support.[109]

Furthermore, the dictatorial authority of chairmen within their committees has recently been significantly diluted, to counter antimajoritarian tendencies. As a result of important reforms, clarifications, and codifications in the Legislative Reorganization Act of 1970,[110] chairmen may not obstinately refuse to convene the committee, for a majority of the members may call a meeting. Standing committees have regular meeting days with an alternative presiding officer if the chairman is absent. Committee hearings must generally be scheduled in advance through public announcement. Minority members are entitled to call some witnesses (and have also been provided with their own staff).[111] All witnesses must ordinarily file a written statement prior to their proposed testimony so as to alert interested legislators of the precise subject of the hearings. Finally, if the chairman delays in filing committee reports, a majority of his committee associates may require that it be done.

Modifications of the procedures in both chambers for choosing chairmen and other committee members have also been substantial. Challenges to length of tenure as the exclusive criterion for chairmanship have been facilitated in the House by the caucuses of both parties, which now require that all their committee leaders be elected by automatic secret ballot through majority vote of each party's full membership. On the Senate side, both the Democrats and the Republicans recently provided that nominees for committee chairman and top-ranking member must be individually approved by the senators of the respective parties—the Democrats provided for secret election when requested by one-fifth of the caucus. In 1977 the Senate, for the first time ever, approved all chairmen by secret ballot. Probably most important of all, recently adopted regulations bar any congressman from occupying the chair of more than one subcommittee. In addition, the rules of both House caucuses now affirmatively state that seniority is not required as a basis for committee assignment. In enacting a "Subcommittee Bill of Rights" to enforce subcommittee autonomy against many previously autocratic chairmen, House Democrats have redesigned their system for all committee positions so as to assure a more equitable distribution to junior members and to prevent chairmen from "stacking" key subcommittees with handpicked disciples. The Senate has taken similar, though less detailed, action.[112]

These reforms were most dramatically fulfilled in practice in 1975 when the House of Representatives toppled three committee potentates who had previously achieved their status through electoral longevity, and followed this by unseating two Appropriations subcommittee leaders (one in 1975 and another in 1977) and seriously compromising another.[113] As a consequence, "oligarchical chairmen" may no longer "forestall consideration of important legislation within their committee's jurisdiction. As Phil Burton, caucus chairman during the 94th Congress, stated, committee chairmen 'now know that they cannot act independently of the will of a majority of the Democrats in the House, and bottle up key legislation.'"[114] Finally, the fact that the seniority system is no longer sacrosanct has immeasurable symbolic importance for future progress. Although history indicates that confident predictions are risky, it appears that overall the congressional committee system may be due for yet additional reforms which, like those extensive ones that have already occurred, more closely approach the democratic model.

3. Party Leaders

One of the principal restraints on the affirmative power of committee chairmen that we have observed is the fact that they usually need the backing of the party leadership to enact legislation. But earlier the majoritarian political responsibility of that very leadership was itself made the subject of criticism. Thus, a dilemma of sorts arises. On the one hand, if the party chieftains heed the views of their respective constituencies, then these congessional districts exert an enormously disproportionate influence on fundamental policies of nationwide import. On the other hand, if the party leaders do not abide by their electorates' preferences—and empirical data suggest this to be the case*—then these leaders appear to be responsible only to themselves.

These conditions are plausibly (albeit intuitively) reconcilable with the projection of a democratic image for Congress, however. To begin with—and to accept the validity of the empirical data—legislators who have reached the peaks in Congress, and who are thus peculiarly entrusted with solemn responsibility for addressing the profound problems that confront the nation and the world, are very likely to be regarded by their constituents, and to view themselves, as Burkean representatives. The authorized boundaries of their independent judgments are very apt to be unusually wide, investing them with much greater than average margin in which to follow their own best instincts.

Indeed, their perceived constituency is probably the nation as a whole, and this political responsibility is traditionally reflected at several levels. First, in developing positions and supporting

---

* A Kraft poll some years ago found that "the voting records of ten House leaders have not reflected their constituents' views on such key issues as Vietnam, the draft and the supersonic transport" and "that very few voters in the ten congressional districts know how their representatives had voted" on these issues. S. F. Chronicle, Aug. 25, 1971, at 10, col. 1.

programs, they incorporate their understanding of national elections,[115] a phenomenon confirmed by the observation that when
a national political party suffers a bad year at the polls, its leadership is more likely to be replaced.[116] Second, if we view the party
leaders' congressional colleagues—who, after all, elected them
to their leadership positions—as their true constituents, then by
formulating policies in response to the predilections of their
peers, the party leaders reflect, albeit derivatively, the preferences of that segment of the national electorate that supported
their party.[117] Nonetheless, third, in seeking to persuade their
congressional colleagues to advance leadership policies, they
ultimately respect the members' obligations to their own constituencies.* As David Mayhew has noted, "leaders in both
houses have a habit of counseling members to 'vote their constituencies.'"[118]

4. Conference Committee

The antimajoritarian role of the Conference Committee, the last part of the congressional committee structure
examined earlier, also requires qualification. Its lack of affirmative capacity to insert provisions enacted by neither chamber has
recently been clarified and codified.[119] Wide as its powers may
be, if its reports propose laws unsupported by the majority, they
may be rejected outright or, in the Senate, filibustered. In the
House, the conference report may be returned to the committee
with specific instructions, thus discouraging both House and
Senate conferees from venturing too far from the House bill because this may result in the House's mandating its own particular

---

* Party leaders "rely mainly on persuasion, party loyalty, expectations of reciprocal treatment, and, occasionally, special inducements such as patronage or
public works. But none of these is likely to be adequate if a member is persuaded
that a vote to support his party will cost him votes among his constituents. For he
is concerned about his own re-election. Fortunately, for him, the mores of Congress, accepted by the leaders themselves, are perfectly clear on this point: His
own election comes first." R. Dahl, Pluralist Democracy in the United States:
Conflict and Consent 131 (1967). See generally Dexter, The Representative and
His District, in New Perspectives on the House of Representatives 3 (R. Peabody
& N. Polsby, eds. 2d ed. 1969); Polsby, Two Strategies of Influence: Choosing a
Majority Leader, 1962, in New Perspectives on the House of Representatives
325

version. Members of the lower chamber may also seek to insure against restoration of a provision defeated in the House but passed in the Senate by exacting a pledge to this effect from the House conferees in exchange for the unanimous consent necessary in the House to send a bill to conference. Finally, the ability of conferees, who themselves deprecate their body's version of the legislation, to sabotage that effort has been curtailed by a recent House of Representatives rule directing that conferees be members who supported the major provisions of the bill.[120] Thus, a nearer view reveals closer conformity to democratic precepts.

5. Interest Groups

Of all the components that contribute to lawmaking in the United States, the significance for majority rule of the various interest and pressure groups and organized lobbies is probably the most complex and difficult to assess. It is indisputable that the election and actions of legislators are strongly affected by applications of pressure at a large variety of critical points in the system—whether by professional, paid lobbyists for specific economic, social, or political interests; by amateurs coordinating letter and telephone campaigns; by the increasing number of "citizens' lobbies" and "public interest" organizations headed by such persons as John Gardner and Ralph Nader;[121] or by some other organized or disorganized groups of people. And it appears to be nearly as certain that the contention that the dominance of special interests makes American government systematically undemocratic is no more factually supportable or inherently persuasive than the argument that the total impact of pressure groups with conflicting biases magically produces a perfect majoritarian equilibrium.

At the operational level, the ability of moneyed interests to influence the legislative process has been diminished by various laws that require disclosure of donors to national political campaigns and set limits on the amounts that may be funneled to lawmakers through either contribution or compensation.[122] Further, although we have seen how adept lobbyists may work their way in congressional committees to produce laws favorable to themselves, this opportunity has also been reduced by new procedures that open mark-up sessions to public scrutiny.

From a broader perspective, as an empirical matter, the several studies undertaken suggest that the various interest groups tend to fill existing gaps—or serve as effective links—between voters and representatives, especially between elections; that legislators tend to respond initially by seeking to determine whether the urgings of pressure groups reflect a generally held constituent view, are opposed by a majority of their electorates, or involve a matter that is of no special concern to most of the voters in their districts; and that the lawmakers then exercise that degree of judgment with which they feel empowered—but almost always with the next election in mind.[123] If this is an accurate description, it may fairly be said to comport with democracy, albeit somewhat murkily and imprecisely.

As an intuitive matter, it is difficult to dispute Alexander Bickel's comment that "no one has claimed that [pressure groups] have been able to capture the governmental process except by combining in some fashion, and thus capturing or constituting...a majority. They often tend themselves to be majoritarian in composition and to be subject to broader majoritarian influences. And the price of what they sell or buy in the legislature is determined in the biennial or quadrennial electoral marketplace."[124] Bickel relies on Dahl's thesis that if, because of pressure group coalitions, "the majority rarely rules on matters of specific policy, nevertheless the specific policies selected by a process of 'minorities rule' probably lie most of the time within the bounds of consensus set by the important values of the politically active members of the society, of whom the voters are a key group."[125] Bickel then offers the persuasive conclusion that if "we have 'minorities rule' rather than majority rule, it remains true nevertheless that only those minorities rule which can command the votes of a majority of individuals in the legislature who can command the votes of a majority of individuals in the electorate. In one fashion or another, both in the legislative process and at elections, the minorities must coalesce into a majority."[126]

V. THE ROLE OF THE EXECUTIVE BRANCH

No appraisal of the democratic quality of the federal legislative system would be adequate without focusing more on the executive branch than so far has been done.

The veto power, the inherently negative nature of which has already been mentioned, and the fact that the administration is the principal source of legislation acted on by Congress alone suggest the consequential role played by the executive in the lawmaking process. But its influence is considerably greater in both striking and subtle ways. The President may reach into a well-stocked arsenal of weapons to impose pressure on an individual congressman—by employing such carrots as granting patronage, awarding contracts in his district, supporting legislation that the congressman favors; and by wielding such sticks as withholding these, or inflicting the ultimate penalty of opposing the congressman for renomination or reelection. Further devices may be left to the imagination. Even without reliance on the disputed ability to impound appropriated funds, it is fair to say that, in late-twentieth-century America, few important national policies may be enacted or effectuated without executive acquiescence.

Given the immense legislative power of the executive branch, the degree of its political responsibility bears critically on the principal questions before us. The contention that the appointed federal civil service is more democratically representative than the elected Congress because it better mirrors the voters in origin, income level, attitudes, needs and desires, and associations[127] may be noted and passed. For it is the President himself, the single federal official with a nationwide constituency— politically accountable by election, in seeking his own reelection or that of his successor, in courting popular support for a Congress sympathetic to his views, and (as we shall see in detail in chapter 5) thus highly sensitive to the voice of national popular opinion—who greatly enhances the democratic image of the political branches.

This is not to say that the presidential will is equivalent to the enactment of legislation. Nor, even more clearly, is it to contend that the President's preference is synonymous with majority rule, for the systems of both nomination and election contain pitfalls. The metaphoric "smoke-filled-room" process for choosing presidential nominees has a particular antidemocratic scent—a malodor by no means completely erased by some of the recent experimental reforms in convention delegate selection.[128] Nonetheless, both the increasing use of the presidential primary (which, although no majoritarian panacea, has in the last three decades almost exclusively dictated the major parties' choices) and the fact that the traditional convention process, despite the metaphor, has been substantially similar to "minorities rule" through pressure, negotiation, and conciliation (producing nominees who have almost always been the choice of the parties' rank and file)[129] go far to meet this objection to the executive's majoritarian legitimacy.

The electoral college poses a major theoretical hurdle in the path of presidential quest for majoritarian political legitimacy. Originally conceived to insulate the chief executive from the immediate heat of politics, early electors were usually chosen by state legislators rather than by the people. But this practice fell into disuse before the middle of the nineteenth century. Still, the electoral college's winner-take-all method is less than pristinely democratic because of the possibility that the people's choice will be other than that of the electors and because of its tendency to exaggerate the power of key groups of voters in swing states.[130] Nonetheless, although more than a dozen presidential elections—including two of the last five—have produced plurality winners with less than a majority of the popular vote, only once in our history has the winner of the popular vote been denied election, and that was a century ago.

In sum, all these qualifications notwithstanding, it is fair to say that the American presidency does represent a majority of the people and comes closer to the majoritarian ideal than practically any other national office in the modern western democracies.

VI. THE POLITICAL ACCOUNTABILITY OF THE SUPREME COURT

As an interim conclusion it is clear that the national legislative process conducted by the political branches is not impeccable democracy in action. Infirmities appear at many important points on both its vertical and horizontal flow charts. Despite all the surface blemishes, however, closer examination reveals an underlying and unshrinking core of popular responsibility—not pure majority rule, but rule by government broadly accountable to the majority. (And, although state and local lawmaking bodies have been only sparingly mentioned, their majoritarian roots have been markedly enlarged through the elimination of malapportionment.) The burden of our inquiry, however, has not been simply to pass judgment on the democratic quality of the political branches. Rather, it has been the less onerous one of measuring this quality against that of the Supreme Court and judicial review. It must be acknowledged that the Court—especially under the aegis of Earl Warren—has often played a pivotal role in improving the democratic face of the political branches at all levels of government. But in comparison to the political branches, the Court, at least as conventionally perceived, must be found to be the loser in terms of political responsibility.

The undemocratic appearance of the Court, however, requires more intense scrutiny before this conclusion may be held with real conviction. As has been noted, valiant efforts have been made to prove this image inaccurate. The most encompassing argument to "democratize" the Court's power as ultimate constitutional arbiter has been that judicial review, "from the beginning," has been tolerated by the people and their elected representatives. Or, even more strongly, because the citizenry wants certain of its leaders to preserve immutable and fundamental values against the hasty and ill-considered decisions that the voters and their other leaders will inevitably make, judicial review has been institutionally adopted by continuing consensus of American society as an integral rule of the system. Thus, judicial review operates by majority will, with the consent of the governed.[131]

Proper evaluation of this broadly sweeping contention necessitates detailed review of the efficacy and legitimacy of both the general force of public opinion and the particular controls available to elected and appointed officials in responding to the

Court's constitutional pronouncements. But some generalizations are safe at the outset. Almost two hundred years of
judicial review show many periods of serious popular and political disagreement with the Court's work.[132] Effective implementation of its decisions has greatly varied in degree from
time to time and from case to case—and, not infrequently, the
dynamics of the matter have been such that those rulings that
have been least fulfilled were not those most strenuously opposed. Both literal and informal alterations of its decisions have
occurred, but often only after considerable time has passed and
their impact has already been meaningfully felt. And the most
honored methods for political reversal of its judgments require
extraordinary time and effort, i.e., more than simple majority
will.

A. CONSTITUTIONAL AMENDMENT

The amendment process, that technique of constitutional change with the most solid and dignified credentials,
has been employed but four times in our history to overcome the
Court's view.[133] Such meager utilization evidences the difficulty
involved. More important, there is no more plainly designated
antimajoritarian force in our governmental system—or, now that
malapportionment is gone, no more clearly operative one—than
the constitutionally prescribed amendment procedures.

B. POLITICAL CONTROL OVER BUDGET AND TERMS

Less direct—and less reputable—political weapons for
doing battle with the Court are available. Of minor significance,
because it has been used more in pique than with seriousness of
purpose, is congressional control over the Court's budget and
over increases (but not reductions) in the Justices' compensation.
In addition, through its capacity to regulate the times when the
Court sits, Congress may abolish certain of the Court's terms.
Employed but once in our history, this technique is only of
slightly more meaningful thrust because it is capable only
of postponing, but not finally avoiding, the Justices' pro-

nouncements—although delay at a critical point or even for a brief period of time may sometimes accomplish much of what is desired.

C. POLITICAL CONTROL OVER COMPOSITION

Of greater import is the ability of the political branches to determine the Court's composition. The authority to impeach sitting Justices, the gravest aspect of this power, may be readily discredited as a factor that enhances the Court's democratic image. The use of this power simply because Congress disapproves of a Justice's votes or opinions cannot be seriously defended—though legislators have sought to employ impeachment for this reason. Because of its severe consequences, prodigious energy is needed to put the impeachment machinery in motion. And the critical fact for our purposes is that the two-thirds Senate vote required for conviction strips it of any majoritarian pretenses.

The authority to appoint new Justices, vested in the President and—as several recent occurrences confirm, despite semantic quibbles—the Senate (which has rejected nearly one of every five executive nominees),[134] may be seen as a powerful political tool to manipulate constitutional decisionmaking. But this ability alone—although its use to elevate persons of particular constitutional leanings is (or should be) unquestioned—depends on natural fortuities that are beyond even the reach of the most indomitable President; and only infrequently does the Court's composition engage the attention of the chief executive.[135] It may well take several successive like-minded presidential terms—and, it merits reemphasis, cooperative Senates—to change the judicial philosophy of a majority of the bench. Moreover, it requires a keen executive prediction of appointees' present and future views on known and unknown issues, a clairvoyance that our history, even the most recent, has proved to be far short of wholly reliable. Even nominees who have been public figures in their own right with announced policy positions, once elevated to the Court,[136] have disappointed presidential expectations. Manipulation through use of the appointment power further assumes that the new appointees will disregard precedent. Although the willingness and ability to do this, even when denying that it is being done, is surely well supported by its own precedent, it nonetheless demands a readiness to depart from the strong tradition of stare decisis—a quantity that no President can buy with real assurance. In sum, the sustained effort needed to reverse (or even halt) a course of constitutional interpretation through the appointing process is much greater than that required for vitually any legislative program—certainly for any that has the backing of a majority of the electorate.

The power of the political branches over the Court's composition includes the right to alter the number of Justices—to reduce the size of the Court and not fill vacancies, or to enlarge it by creating new seats. As a practical matter, the former course requires only executive action—or, more precisely, inaction. But even then the difficulties of awaiting normal attrition and depending on disregard of precedent remain, although perhaps in slightly ameliorated form. Probably because of these uncertainties, because executive nonuse of the appointment power for this end would be highly questionable in light of our constitutional traditions, and because it would constitute a de facto reduction of the Court's membership by the President alone without the consent of Congress, this method appears never to have been attempted.

While history provides several illustrations of efforts by Congress to diminish the number of positions, usually it did so for the specific purpose of curtailing the influence of a President it opposed (Jefferson in 1801 and Andrew Johnson in 1866). To reverse particular constitutional paths the Court had taken—for our purposes, the more significant goal—the political departments more often have used the power of increasing the number of Justices, coupled with the making of new appointments. After Chief Justice Marshall's departure in the Jackson administration, Justices were added, supposedly to counter his remaining influence. During the Civil War, the Court's membership was briefly enlarged to ten, seemingly to afford a greater margin of security in response to the Court's closely split decision upholding the blockade of the confederacy.[137] The most dramatic example concerned the *Legal Tender Cases*. President Grant, on the day that *Hepburn v. Griswold*[138] was decided, nominated two new Justices following a resignation and an increase in the Court's membership from eight to nine. Although the reasons for selecting and confirming the particular nominees ranged far beyond the legal tender issue,[139] in just a little more than a year the *Hepburn* decision was overruled[140] because of the determination and votes of the new appointees.[141]

This last occasion, over a century ago, appears, however, to be the only clear victory achieved by the political branches in exercising the authority to enlarge. Indeed, the technique is distinguished not by success but rather by failure. Its most celebrated day occurred when President Franklin Roosevelt, just elected by an overwhelming popular majority and possessed of a legendary influence over Congress, nonetheless saw his Court-packing plan defeated—and this despite the extremely disreputable position of the Court for having thwarted both executive *and* legislative efforts to combat a great national crisis. Because of the Court's subsequent modification of its course (the true motivation for which remains incalculable),[142] the President, although losing the formal battle, may well have won the larger campaign—but at very high cost, owing to the widely acknowledged fact that his legislative mastery suffered greatly from this effort.[143] And the yet firmer facts are that, even under this extraordinary combination of auspicious circumstances, the Court's traditional independence of the political will survived and that, during subsequent periods of momentous judicial impact and unpopularity, the political departments' power over the Court's composition, far from being seriously considered a consequential weapon, has been effectively discredited.

D. POLITICAL CURTAILMENT OF APPELLATE JURISDICTION

In the past forty years, the device most frequently threatened by the political branches for use against the Court has been Congress's power, specified in Article III, to make "Exceptions" to and "Regulations" of the Court's appellate jurisdiction. The starkness of the authorizing constitutional language appears to leave little room for disputing that Congress may divest the Court of its commission to review certain types or classes of cases, thus enabling the legislature to silence at least some of the Court's future constitutional pronouncements. The opinion of the Court itself, in the only executed congressional attempt in history to keep cases from it, gives credence to the existence of this broad legislative power.[144] Thus viewed, this politically responsible authority goes far in sustaining the contention that the Court acts only with the acquiescence, albeit often passive, of the popular will and that there remains a forceful and formal democratic check on judicial review.

For a variety of reasons, however, the apparent cogency of the proposition suffers serious weakness. First, the theoretical underpinnings for a wide legislative power to curtail the appellate jurisdiction, only most scantily explored by the Court and usually in casual dicta,[145] are hardly as firm as the literal phrasing of Article III and the quite sweeping judicial language would suggest. A number of persuasive (and quite different) interpretations of the delegated authority have been offered by prominent constitutional scholars, none of which results in any consequential political check on judicial review. Proceeding from such bases as the language itself and the intent and history of the Constitution as a whole, it has been plausibly argued that any case "excepted" from the Supreme Court's appellate function must concomitantly be included within its original jurisdiction;[146] that the pertinent clause of Article III was meant only to permit restriction of the Court's review of questions of fact, not of substantive constitutional matters;[147] that no matter how literally broad the general scope of legislative authority under Article III, its exercise (like that of all delegated powers) is limited by the other constitutional provisions, such as those in Art. I, §9 or in the Bill of Rights, which may themselves condemn certain denials of Court review to particular classes of cases or persons;[148] that, whatever the range of the power, it does not extend to the destruction of the essence of the Court's appellate function which contemplated ultimate resolution by the Justices of important federal questions;[149] and that, if a *case* is "excepted" from the Court's appellate purview, then jurisdiction over it must be vested in a lower federal court and some path must remain to permit its constitutional *questions* to reach the Supreme Court on appeal.[150] There is no need here to evaluate these theories. It is enough to conclude that the scope of congressional power to express discontent with the Court's work by legislation divesting it of certain jurisdiction is largely unresolved and totally unclear.

But even if this legislative ability to retaliate against the judiciary rested on a firm theoretical foundation, its pragmatic potential as a majoritarian restraint on judicial review would be severely limited. As Herbert Wechsler has lucidly revealed, since the political branches realize that the use of federal courts is essential to administer federal law—for purposes of both imposing government coercion and enforcing private remedies— Congress cannot, as a practical matter, withdraw all federal jurisdiction, even if it were authorized to do so constitutionally. If Congress instead were to choose only to curtail the Supreme Court's appellate jurisdiction, it could attempt to rest final resolution of all constitutional questions with the eleven federal courts of appeals. Although this may be preferable to leaving it to the highest courts of the fifty states—the result of abolishing *all* federal jurisdiction or of restricting the adjudication of some or all constitutional questions to the state courts (a course that I believe to be of most doubtful validity)—the potential for national inconsistency in constitutional interpretation would still be unbearable. Furthermore, the tradition of stare decisis could lead these other courts to follow the very Supreme Court decisions that sparked the congressional counteraction. "The jurisdictional withdrawal thus might work to freeze the very doctrines that had prompted its enactment, placing an intolerable moral burden on the lower courts . . . . The federal system needs federal courts and the judicial institution needs an organ of supreme authority."[151]

This convincing line of argument helps explain why on only one occasion in American history—the effect of which is of questionable significance and the scope of which ultimately has been determined to be incomplete[152]—has hostility prompted the political branches (Congress overriding a presidential veto) to use Article III to diminish the Court's jurisdiction, though many such efforts have been made. Without discounting the possibility that certain resolute legislative threats (such as the Jenner Bill in the 1950s) may have had some immeasurable impact on the Court's judgments,[153] strong reliance cannot be placed on the political authority of Article III if judicial review is to be democratized.

E. Summary

Having surveyed the various constitutional sources of indirect congressional and presidential authority that may serve as political brakes on the power of judicial review, we may fairly conclude that their highly infrequent and largely ineffective use gravely undermines the view that the people have continuously approved of the Court's function simply because, in the main, they have let the Court be. In general, the constitutional legitimacy of the use of these devices against the Court's rule is greatly suspect; most, if not unconstitutional in law, may be seen as anticonstitutional in tradition. Their exercise calls for one or the other of the elected branches to act affirmatively, and usually the concurrence of both departments is required. Moreover, all the dominant forces of inertia—of maintenance of the status quo, of inaction due to the frequent absence of cohesive majorities and to the fragmentation of power—that are present in the national political process work to safeguard the Court, and indeed are magnified in the case of an attack on the Court's historic independence. Thus, the majoritarian threat posed is more theoretical than real. Even if the necessary battalions could be enlisted, any habitual use of the "unwieldy and overly blunt weapons . . . would have disastrous results on the judicial process; yet infrequent use of them is not enough to satisfy our democratic standards."[154]

VII. CONCLUSION

The Supreme Court is involved in the political process in the sense that it participates in making public policy; it is not an organ of the political process in the sense that it is electorally responsible. The plan of the Constitution is that the federal judges are appointed with life tenure for the precise purpose of shielding them from the popular will. The Justices stand in sharp contrast to the many highly placed and greatly influential executive and administrative officials who are also appointed, for the persons in the latter group *are* politically responsible: all their terms of office are shorter; most are subject to removal at any time by the political branches, if not in law then in fact; and Congress designates their authority with its desired specificity and may reverse their policies by ordinary legislation.

The most trenchant popular barriers to the rule of the Court are both more discrete and less formalized than those mentioned. Although detailed exploration of the subject remains mainly for chapter 3, some brief indication of the dynamics involved is appropriate here. If either of the political branches opposes a judicial doctrine that requires support for its effectuation—and many do, in varying degrees—the legislative or executive opportunity is clear. The presidential response may range from Abraham Lincoln's outright refusal to obey Chief Justice Taney's order in *Ex parte Merryman,* to Franklin Roosevelt's plan to openly defy the full bench if it ruled adversely in the *Gold Clause Cases* or *Ex parte Quirin,* to Andrew Jackson's alleged edict that he would leave John Marshall to enforce his own decision in the *Cherokee Indian Cases,*[155] to Dwight Eisenhower's seeming ambivalence immediately following the *School Desegregation Cases.* The congressional power of the purse may be employed to enfeeble the Court's will—as is illustrated by the recent repeated efforts to deny funds for school busing to achieve racial desegregation. (At the opposite pole, the spending power may be used as a sharp-edged sword to obtain conformity to judicial rulings—as is exemplified by the enormous progress in southern school desegregation that immediately [and only] followed Congress's threat to withhold federal funds from noncomplying districts.) Furthermore, lesser officials (including the judges) at all levels of government, and, ultimately, the people themselves, may move grudgingly and hesitatingly in adhering to the Court's mandate, or they may simply refuse to obey, with varying degrees of blatancy.

Whether these types of conduct abide by the social compact of American society and whether they are constitutionally justifiable—they seem, at least in many instances, open to serious question—is beyond the scope of discussion here. Perhaps because of their availability there is truth in the observations that "the Supreme Court has seldom, if ever, flatly and for very long resisted a really unmistakable wave of public sentiment"[156] and that "when either [Congress or the President] has chosen to fight back the Court has generally failed, *in the long run*, to stop the two branches permanently."[157] But, for our purposes, the carefully injected qualifications within these statements are more significant than the generalizations themselves—and note the latter commentator's further view that "the Court does make many of its major constitutional decisions stick."[158] Similarly, perhaps there is validity in the conclusion that the visibly ascending threat of the more formal—but constitutionally even more debatable—political sanctions discussed above, when supported by a hostile national temper, will ultimately persuade the Court to bend from a course of decisions.[159] Instances of such tactical recessions during Reconstruction and by the Marshall, Hughes, and Warren Courts have been proclaimed by many observers.[160]

Neither this reasoning nor its supporting data, however, lead to making judicial review compatible with majoritarian democracy as it is traditionally conceived or practiced. Many eventful and controversial constitutional decisions—especially those involving use of the judicial system itself (as in the field of criminal procedure)—although subject to being undercut by resentful administrative officials and lower courts, do not depend on the cooperation of other public agencies or of the people in general for their complete effectiveness. Further, it must be conceded that it is only those Supreme Court mandates perceived as exceedingly flagrant that are capable of generating the intensity of opposition necessary to prevent enforcement. Nor is popular resistance universal in impact, either geographically or temporally; even if certain rulings eventually fall into disuse because they are opposed by the requisite majority will, their force will be felt by a segment of the people for some time and often by many of the people for a long time. And impelling the Court to bend or draw up in developing doctrine falls far short of causing the Court to break or retreat.

At the surface, the antimajoritarian features of all three federal departments bear a certain similarity. The leeway afforded the political branches by the people and the tenacity of popular feeling needed for radical change through election revolt are not absolutely different from the independence granted the judiciary by the Constitution and the assiduous efforts required to affect the Court and its decisions through the restraints ultimately retained by the citizenry and their elected representatives. But, in both democratic theory and practice, the distinction between control of the legislature and executive on one side and control of the judiciary on the other, if not one of kind, is one of substantial degree. That a majority of the people may ultimately prevail vis-à-vis the Court by outright resistance or through methods of dubious legitimacy under a rule of law, even if a reality, is not the same as their ordained ability to change the composition of the political branches at regularly scheduled periodic elections. Even if the Court can accomplish little beyond delaying strong popular passions—and the hard evidence for this is sparse and spotty at very best—so that its declarations of unconstitutionality do no more than afford the people a "sober second thought,"[161] because of the extraordinary time and energy required for finally successful political inebriation, the Court's role far exceeds Burke's most aggrandized view of a political trusteeship.

The case may be an uneasy one, but given a realistic and balanced view of the operation of the political branches, and especially considering the predominantly negative quality of their antimajoritarianism, the Supreme Court is not as democratic as the Congress and President, and the institution of judicial review is not as majoritarian as the lawmaking process. The sundry controls of the people and their elected representatives may succeed in some instances and pose perilous threats in others. But these political checks do not democratize the Court or its power of judicial review. To the contrary, as we shall see in chapter 2, the essential role of judicial review in our society is to guard against certain constitutional transgressions which popular majorities specifically seek to impose.

Furthermore, the effect of these antijudicial weapons (blunt as they are) is not to guarantee that only rulings with popular support are effectuated, or even to assure that only those decisions that draw intense popular opposition are denied—although that would be democracy in action, no matter how antithetical to the core of our constitutional plan. Rather, when used or threatened, these political instruments operate overbroadly and haphazardly, often undermining large areas of the Court's fundamental obligation in indiscriminate fashion, thus plurally frustrating the Court's vital functions. The great task, then, for the Court—and a major concern of this book—is how best to reject majority will when it must, without endangering not only that critical role but its other urgent duties as well.

Two

The Individual
versus Government
The Essential Function of
Judicial Review

To affirm that the federal judiciary is the least democratic branch of American government and that the Supreme Court generally acts contrary to the popular will in exercising the power of judicial review is neither to deny that the Court's role as final constitutional arbiter justifiably serves central and beneficial values in our society nor, indeed, to dispute the fact that it promotes the precepts of democracy. It is merely to state certain basic premises.

Deeper understanding of the function of the Supreme Court and judicial review can be achieved only by exploring several cardinal features of the genesis of our political system. The critical facts are that our written Constitution is a postulate against orthodox democracy in that no provision is alterable by simple majority will; the principal purpose for its adoption was to establish an essentially democratic government, yet one with limited powers; the preservation of certain individual liberties, mainly through its Bill of Rights, was one of its primary goals; and, in Madison's words, "in our Government the real power lies in the majority of the Community, and the invasion of private rights is chiefly to be apprehended, not from acts of Government contrary to the sense of its constituents, but from acts in which the Government is the mere instrument of the major number of the Constituents."[1]

I. CATEGORIES OF CONSTITUTIONAL PROVISIONS

Item-by-item examination of this antimajoritarian Constitution discloses that, apart from many clauses concerning what may be described as "housekeeping" details (in respect either to administration of the federal departments or to relations among the states), most significant provisions may be intelligibly separated into three broad categories. One deals with the separation of powers at the national level, distributing all the authority within the domain of the federal government among the legislative, executive, and judicial branches and setting the boundaries of each department's power vis-à-vis that of the others. Another involves our system of federalism, allocating power between the nation and the states by delegating certain governmental authority to the former and reserving the balance to the latter. The third category designates personal liberties which, either by explicit statement or judicial interpretation, limit all government power—that of the three federal branches and of the states—vis-à-vis the individual.

II. WHO DETERMINES CONSTITUTIONALITY AND BY WHAT STANDARD?

Many crucial constitutional ordinances fit handily into one or another of the stipulated categories; and, although some important provisions appear ambiguous in this respect, this need not detain us. The large question at this juncture, having recognized that the Constitution consists of a mass of antimajoritarian imperatives (perhaps including even some "unwritten higher law principles"),[2] is who determines when it has been violated—what institution in our society decides when the people's majority has transgressed its borders? An equally vital companion question is by what standard should the matter be judged—what is the measuring rod for resolving whether the constitutional lines of demarcation have been crossed? Much of this book will address these issues in terms of each of the three categories of constitutional provisions established above— categories that I hope will help to assess the appropriate role for the Supreme Court in our constitutional democracy in a meaningful, principled, and functional manner.

The first question—who shall decide matters of constitutionality?—was addressed early in our history. In 1803, in the seminal case of *Marbury v. Madison*,[3] Chief Justice Marshall ruled that the Supreme Court possessed the power to declare at least certain acts of its coordinate branches in the national government ultra vires and, several years later, the Court extended this authority to the actions of the states as well.[4] Thus was established the power of judicial review—although, especially for our purposes, it is essential to note that, beginning with Marshall's unveiled signal in the dicta of *Marbury*[5] and explicitly confirmed by his successor, Chief Justice Taney,[6] the Court has consistently acknowledged that the determination of *some* constitutional questions rests exclusively with the other federal departments.

Whether the framers originally intended to vest the Supreme Court with such an extensive authority has been the subject of powerful and painstaking scholarship.[7] The statements of various of the founding fathers—particularly those of Madison, the prime architect, and of Charles Pinckney—have been discovered to be in conflict.[8] Following ratification of the Constitution there is persuasive evidence—especially in the debates of the First Congress[9] and in the Judiciary Act of 1789[10]—that Congress intended courts (state and federal) to have the competence to pass on the constitutionality of both state and federal governmental actions. On the other hand, the prodigious power of judicial review was, at the time, not at all an accepted judicial tradition, either in America or abroad. In any case, probably because few of those historic figures who participated in the adoption and ratification process had matured views on the matter, the reported evidence appears—at least to a nonhistorian who has not carefully culled it for himself—to be inconclusive. Further, despite a number of careful efforts to find the judicial anointment in the language of the document, there appears to be no disputing Alexander Bickel's compelling demonstration that the constitutional text provides neither explicit nor firm support for the Court's assumption of authority—at least in respect to invalidating acts of Congress or the President.[11] Finally, whatever indications may be gleaned from intention or text on the issue of whether the Court should possess the power of judicial review, these sources afford virtually no assistance whatever on the related question of the form and scope of judicial review (assuming its legitimacy)[12]—of the standard to be employed; of whether the Court should find unconstitutionality only when nearly all informed persons would do so, or whether it should rely more on its own insights respecting the charter's commands; of whether—in now familiar terms—the Court should assume a stance of activism or restraint.

But enough has been said about original intent. That is no longer the real issue. As Eugene Rostow put it, the power of judicial review "has been exercised by the Court from the beginning.... And it stands now, whatever the Founding Fathers may in fact have meant, as an integral feature of the living constitution, long since established as a working part of the democratic political life of the nation."[13] Further, although careful parsing of judicial language would reveal that only of late has the Court explicitly claimed it is imbued not only with the authority to pass on most issues of constitutionality in the course of adjudicating cases before it but also with the supreme and final arbitral voice on these matters,[14] the principle has become generally accepted—though not without notable dispute (a topic to be later discussed)—that these judicial pronouncements bind the other branches of national and state government. Rather, the continuing controversy that has enveloped the Court has concerned the more refined problems of the quality and scope of judicial review and, nonetheless, as an adjunct, of which constitutional questions are to be committed for final resolution to the political branches.

III. PARAMOUNT JUSTIFICATION FOR JUDICIAL REVIEW

Whatever the standard of judicial review regarding issues of federalism or separation of powers, a pragmatic appraisal—historic or contemporary—of our antimajoritarian Constitution, of the undemocratic structure of the Court, of the dynamics of the American political process, and of the great scheme of our society ineluctably leads to the conclusion that the overriding virtue of and justification for vesting the Court with this awesome power is to guard against governmental infringement of individual liberties secured by the Constitution. In a moment we shall turn to the demanding and delicate problems involved in fixing the definition and content of these personal rights held against popular will, but the essential rationale for their judicial protection is relatively uncomplicated.

The political theory ordained by the Constitution forbids popular majorities to abridge certain rights of individuals even when the latter may be part of the majority and even though their interests may be forcefully represented and carefully considered in the political process. Thus, the fourth amendment's prohibition against unreasonable searches and seizures has been applied to electronic eavesdropping[15] despite heated political opposition to the practice at different times by influential business and labor groups, as well as important legislators.[16] But even a cursory examination of those liberties most unmistakably assigned by the Constitution to protect all persons manifests a primary, undisguised purpose to safeguard interests of minorities—mainly aberrant political and religious groups and persons accused of crime, but also individuals in certain economic positions (racial groups being added by later events). At base, the dominant concern was not that political majorities—or coalitions of influential minorities—would impose undue restrictions on their own vital interests but rather that they would either seek to advance their own ends at the expense of those politically less powerful or simply act malevolently to penalize those whose views, conduct, or appearance they feared or despised. Individual rights were mainly designated in the Constitution for those who could not be expected to prevail through orthodox democratic procedures, whose destinies were likely to be disregarded under a regime of simple majority rule, or who plausibly would be disadvantaged when the interests who prevailed by "minorities rule" were sufficiently "homogeneous and hostile"[17] to override the normal barriers to political action.

All that has been said being accepted, it would be neither unreasonable nor unparalleled, as we observed in chapter 1, to rely on the humane sensibilities of the people and the integrity of their elected representatives to assure the personal liberties afforded in the Constitution. John Adams was likely guilty of overstatement in insisting that "there is . . . no possible way of defending the minority . . . from the tyranny of the majority, but by giving the former a negative on the latter."[18] But, notwithstanding the distinctive libertarian traditions on which the nation was conceived (if not their vigilant fulfillment in practice) and the unusually diversified composition of its citizens, the experience of history strongly suggests that vesting the majority with the ultimate power of judgment, although far from being calamitous, would not sufficiently protect minority rights. Indeed, this may well be due to the very heterogeneity of our population. Unlike Great Britain, for example, the United States "is a sprawling country divided by regional and other animosities, with an unhappy tradition of corrupt and partisan officials, especially on the local level."[19] And more so than Americans, the British appear to "have a tradition of accepting the direction of their leaders, a respect for and acceptance of authority, which makes it possible for the more libertarian Member of Parliament to play a role somewhat similar to that of our principled Supreme Court justices."[20] In short, in America a "high degree of mutual empathy does not exist."[21] Thus, given the existence of any authority in our counter-majoritarian judiciary to review the constitutionality of political action, it should apply to claimed violations of individual rights.

A. DIFFICULTY OF EMPIRICAL VERIFICATION

In advancing this conclusion, it must be admitted that the data have not been scientifically tested in that the American experience has not been compared to what would have occurred in the absence of judicial review. In the nature of things, there is no way to conduct such a controlled inquiry. Thus, on the one hand, it is impossible convincingly to refute the propositions that lawmaking would be more sensitive to individual liberties if it were conducted with the knowledge that its resolutions were final, and that the ever present potential of judicial disapproval actually encourages popular irresponsibility and stultifies the poeple's sense of moral and constitutional obligation. On the other hand, it is equally impracticable to reject the contention that, without the threat of judicial invalidation in the background, majoritarian excesses in respect to minority rights would be all the less restrained. Although the issue will concern us again in chapter 4 (where supportive arguments are made), because of the inherent intractability of the empirical dilemma, at this point we must disregard both possibilities.

B. HISTORICAL AND CONTEMPORARY OPINIONS

Although there has been less than universal agreement that the security of individual liberty is *the* central function of judicial review, the argument that it constitutes a paramount justification has been made frequently and consistently throughout America's history by its foremost constitutional leaders. In introducing the Bill of Rights, the major source of personal constitutional liberties, to the First Congress, Madison declared that "independent tribunals of justice will consider themselves in a peculiar manner the guardians of those rights; they will be an impenetrable bulwark against every assumption of power in the legislative or executive."[22] Even prior to the formulation of the Bill of Rights, in the renowned 78th Federalist Paper, the historic fountainhead of intended judicial review, Hamilton designated the courts as "the bulwarks of a limited Constitution against legislative encroachments," referring to "certain specific exceptions to the legislative authority; such, for instance, as that it shall pass no bills of attainder, no *ex-post-facto* laws, and the like." In *Marbury v. Madison,* the wellspring judicial opinion, Marshall uttered the flat dictum (taken, for our purposes, somewhat out of context) that "the province of the court is, solely, to decide on the rights of individuals."[23] Over one hundred years later, Holmes recounted Brandeis's view that "the best defense . . . 'for leaving fundamental responsibilities to this Court' was that constitutional restrictions enabled minorities to get an untroubled night's sleep."[24] And near the end of his superintendence of the Court during one of its most dramatic periods, Earl Warren voiced his belief that "the essential function of the Supreme Court in our democracy is to act as the final arbiter of minority rights."[25] Perhaps the clearest and most succinct judicial expression is that of Justice Jackson, writing for the Court in the *Flag Salute Cases:* "The very purpose of a Bill of Rights was to withdraw certain subjects from the vicissitudes of political controversy, to place them beyond the reach of majorities and officials and to establish them as legal principles to be applied by the courts."[26]

It is noteworthy to observe that austere critics of the judicial prerogative as well as its staunch defenders acknowledge this as a cardinal purpose. Thus, when launching a bitter attack on the early efforts of the Warren Court, the House of Delegates of the American Bar Association carefully prefaced its condemnatory resolution with these words: "Whereas, the Supreme Court of the United States and an independent judiciary created by the Constitution have been and are the ultimate guardians of the Bill of Rights and the protectors of our freedom."[27] At diverse but continual periods of American history, individuals and minority groups of all ideological shades have looked to the Court as the supreme guarantor of personal liberty against majority will—be they the Ku Klux Klan or the National Association for the Advancement of Colored People seeking to protect associational privileges, conservatives wishing to insure property interests and preferred status, or liberals desiring to secure political and civil rights.

C. FUNCTIONAL JUSTIFICATION

The Supreme Court has been and should be the ultimate guardian of individual liberty not because its members are possessed of deeper wisdom or broader vision, nor simply because they command greater constitutional expertise than other institutional bodies in our society. Since, almost by definition, the processes of democracy bode ill for the security of personal rights and, as experience shows, such liberties are not infrequently endangered by popular majorities, the task of custodianship has been and should be assigned to a governing body that is insulated from political responsibility and unbeholden to self-absorbed and excited majoritarianism. The Court's aloofness from the political system and the Justices' lack of dependence for maintenance in office on the popularity of a particular ruling promise an objectivity that elected representatives are not—and should not be—as capable of achieving. And the more deliberative, contemplative quality of the judicial process further lends itself to dispassionate decisionmaking.

The thesis being advanced—hereafter referred to as the Individual Rights Proposal—should not be understood as contending that the political branches are either inherently incapable of heeding personal liberties or that they always ignore their vitality in practice. The momentous legislative and executive efforts at all levels of government that have been undertaken and consummated specifically in behalf of civil rights evidence the contrary. Indeed, in response to some judicial rulings—involving such matters as wiretapping,[28] electronic interception of conversations with the consent of one of the conversants,[29] noncustodial interrogation by law enforcement officials,[30] multiple prosecutions by state and federal government,[31] police searches of newspaper offices,[32] and the privilege of members of the press to preserve the anonymity of their sources[33]—political bodies have been more sensitive to important personal liberties than has the Court. But the predominant pattern is otherwise. As illustrated by such issues as slavery,[34] public financial assistance to church-related schools, the conflict of internal security and individual liberty, and the political and socioeconomic rights of racial minorities,[35] Congress has recognized that political expediency often renders it impotent to uphold the constitutional rights of vulnerable minorities and that it would not be displeased to have the Court set the record straight. Thus, when it seemed imminent that popular pressure would finally overcome the long-held congressional impression that aid to parochial schools violated religious freedom, the path of least resistance for many legislators lay in formally authorizing the Court to review the constitutionality of such appropriations.[36] And when Congress could not itself muster the strength to abolish poll taxes, its way out was to direct the Attorney General to request the judiciary to do so.

The smaller the allegedly aggrieved group and the more intense the felt need or the contempt of the majority, the greater the necessity of judicial review for the preservation of personal liberty. In part, this may explain the perceived irony of the Court's ostensible willingness, on the one hand, to afford relief to relatively insignificant nonconformist groups in society—such as Jehovah's Witnesses, illegitimates, and political extremists—and its seeming hesitancy, on the other, to hear causes supported by large and respected segments of the population—such as those who opposed the war in Indochina. Justice Frankfurter put it less charitably, but nonetheless in part accurately, in stating that "the safeguards of liberty have frequently been forged in controversies involving not very nice people."[37]

Wholly apart from constitutional matters, western judicial tradition has long proceeded on the plausible theory that individuals and politically isolated minorities are at a peculiar disadvantage in dealing with government, a position that is accentuated when such persons or groups challenge those government officials, representing the people as a whole, who administer the law. Therefore, "most sophisticated societies have been willing—and have thought it socially useful—to acknowledge the predicament of the individual who is making a claim for fair and equal treatment, not only against his fellows, but against government itself. They have set up, in the persons of judges, individuals specially trained and deputed to do justice even in the face of the society's very hostility, and to apply the policy which the society has preordained for the case."[38] And the Supreme Court is the most effective guarantor of the interests of the unpopular and unrepresented precisely because it is the most politically isolated judicial body. Even the judges of the inferior federal courts, although surrounded by the same constitutional perquisites as the Justices of the Supreme Court, cannot be relied on as confidently. Because of their long and strong personal and professional relationships with the local community and bar and their desire to sustain the prestige of their courts within their respective districts, the front-line federal judges are often more constrained to observe politically popular local rules and customs and more loath to invoke community disapproval and hostility.[39]

The need for enforcement by an independent judiciary is all the more cogent when constitutional liberties, rather than statutory rights, of individuals are at stake. Unlike those licenses granted merely by legislation, constitutional prerogatives are held to be so intrinsic that they are included in the fundamental charter itself, unalterable by normal legislative processes either directly or through the delegated discretion of administrators. The citizenry and its politically accountable representatives, legislative and administrative, are apt to be more hostile to the fulfillment of constitutionally ordained liberties than statutorily granted privileges because the former relate to matters more naturally subject to popular scorn and controversy, and the latter are more closely identified with the present attitude of the people. This is especially true when the individual claim is made against the clearly expressed will of the legislature rather than an administrative interpretation. The people having already unmistakably spoken, the absence of judicial review could well render the constitutional rights of politically weak minorities little more than grandly stated admonitions.

IV. SUBSTANTIVE SCOPE OF INDIVIDUAL
RIGHTS: AN OVERVIEW

As stated in the introduction, this book's principal task is to examine one part of what may be conveniently described as the jurisdictional or procedural aspect of the role played by the Supreme Court and judicial review in our democratic society—namely, *whether* the Court should adjudicate certain constitutional issues. The other major portion of the constitutional

work of the federal judiciary (which I believe to be most complicated of all to unravel and the most bedeviling in the search for
the Court's proper function) is substantive—that is, *how* the various provisions of the Constitution should be interpreted. A precise and exhaustive listing of the individual rights guaranteed by
the Constitution and a comprehensive discussion of the process
that should be employed by the Court in determining (or discovering) their nature and scope fall within the latter compart-
ment; neither will be undertaken here. But some brief inquiry
into the surface of the substantive problem may be helpful.

A. POLITICAL RIGHTS

It has been urged that the Court's critical yet fragile
faculty of assuring individual liberty should be reserved—to use
famous phrasing of the Court itself, though in a slightly different
context—for "legislation which restricts those political processes
which can ordinarily be expected to bring about repeal of undesirable legislation."[40] The underlying rationale is that careful
judicial protection of the "right to vote," the "dissemination of
information," and the rights of "political organization" and
"peaceable assembly"[41] promotes orthodox democratic precepts.
Although this view accords legitimacy to the antimajoritarian
principle of judicial review, it limits the Court's role to keeping
normal political channels unclogged and affording all participants in the democratic process a full and fair opportunity to
influence the promulgation and alteration of policies affecting
them. Beyond this, it leaves all other substantive decisions—
even those touching constitutionally designated liberties—to
majority rule.

From the perspective of traditional democratic theory, there is
much to be said for this approach. It does logically account for
the Court's enforcement of the first amendment's explicit protections of political and communicative freedom, the fourteenth
amendment's guarantee of citizenship, and the prohibition of
certain types of voting disqualifications specifically described in
the fifteenth, nineteenth, twenty-fourth, and twenty-sixth
amendments. But because the scheme of our political democracy

is qualified so as to preserve other libertarian values and the machinery of the political process is untrustworthy in sustaining them, the Court has rightfully gone beyond these bare minimums.

B. Specifically Designated Rights

Perhaps implicitly recognizing that, once it stepped beyond the area of political rights into the terrain of other substantive guarantees, the demarcation line between a limited judicial march and a fuller invasion of legislative prerogatives may be only most dimly perceived, the Court has not hesitated to bring within its protective ambit at least those other individual rights that are also specifically designated in the Constitution. The exact definition and scope of these particular provisions is by no means beyond controversy. But, at the core, the most apparent and least disputed of these personal liberties include, in addition to those already mentioned, the original Constitution's prohibitions of impairments of contractual obligations, ex post facto laws, and bills of attainder; the first amendment's security of religious freedom; the fifth amendment's requirement of just compensation for the taking of private property; the thirteenth amendment's ban on slavery; and, in historical context, the fourteenth amendment's proscription of discrimination against racial minorities.

C. Liberties Arising in the Judicial Process

Although this extension of judicial review unmistakably collides with orthodox majoritarian precepts, the Court's constitutional reappraisal of those popularly sponsored policies that arguably endanger one cluster of plainly articulated personal liberties, those that involve the administration of justice—such as Article III's strictures for criminal trials and treason convictions; the fourth amendment's restraint on unreasonable searches and seizures; and the further safeguards for those accused of or adjudged to be guilty of crimes found in the fifth, sixth, and eighth amendments—may be independently justified as being of intrinsic and intimate concern to the functioning of the judicial department itself.[42]

D. UNMENTIONED LIBERTIES

A major controversy in modern times—often conducted under the title of "applying the Bill of Rights to the states"—has been whether various constitutional provisions, which seemingly are directed to securing personal rights but explicitly limit only either the national government or the states, are sufficiently fundamental to be held to restrict all government power. This clash has now been largely (and, in my view, correctly) resolved.[43] The preeminent current debate is not whether a particular constitutional provision falls within the classification of rights that are judicially enforceable by the individual against all government. Rather the conflict centers upon two somewhat interrelated questions: first, whether and to what extent such personal rights exist—or may be found by the Court to exist—without specific textual support (the "fundamental rights" issue); and second, whether groups other than blacks (the clearly intended beneficiaries of the fourteenth amendment's equal protection clause) should enjoy a special judicial immunity from adverse political treatment (the "suspect classifications" issue).

1. "Fundamental" Rights

There are many persons parading under various banners who would confine the category of judicially enforceable individual liberties to rights that are firmly grounded in the historically bounded language of the Constitution. Some would make the literally modest but theoretically momentous addition of a general right to vote—or, as recently articulated by the Court, a "right to participate in elections on an equal basis with other citizens in the jurisdiction"[44]—which has no clear textual foundation. (Indeed some sections of the Constitution appear to vest voting rights largely with the states subject to designated limitations found in certain amendments.) But other observers would greatly amplify the Court's prerogatives in defining and protecting individual liberty from popular infringement.

Among the grantors of broad judicial discretion are such eminent constitutional scholars as Henry Hart, who found the Court to be "a voice of reason, charged with the creative function of discerning afresh and of articulating and developing impersonal and durable principles."[45] Archibald Cox, after observing that the due process clause "calls for some measure of judicial review of legislative enactments," maintained that "from that point forward all must be done by judicial construct with no real guidance from the document" but rather from "the strength of our natural law inheritance."[46] Robert Bork, a former Solicitor General of the United States, once urged that the Court become more "activist"—"working in the method familiar to lawyers trained in the common law, the judge can construct principles that explain existing constitutional rights and extrapolate from them to define new natural rights."[47] Harry Wellington suggested that "the Court's task is to ascertain . . . conventional morality and to convert the moral principle into a legal one by connecting it with the body of constitutional law."[48] Ronald Dworkin agreed that the Justices must face "the issue of what moral rights an individual has against the state" by identifying the nation's "constitutional morality," which he defined as "the political morality presupposed by the law and institutions of the community."[49] Rejecting a call for greater judicial restraint, Addison Mueller and Murray Schwartz have contended that "our constitutional guarantees of individual freedoms . . . are not static but are expressions of basic human values. They transcend day-to-day shifts in majority wishes and hence require re-definition from time to time to meet newly recognized—if not newly created—human needs."[50] Further illustrations of the most generous delegations of judicial authority may be found in the writings of such students of the American constitutional process as James Bryce, who thought of the Court as "the conscience of the poeple,"[51] and Charles Curtis, who believed that the Court should "articulate our creed for the era" "by becoming the Nation's philosopher."[52]

The judicial mandates set forth by these views are seemingly boundless. As admirably demonstrated by Terrance Sandalow[53] and John Ely,[54] by calling on the Justices to move beyond the core of individual rights that are established by the text and historical meaning of the Constitution and to define contemporary fundamental norms that are manifested by some evolving societal consensus, these prescriptions either strike at the very heart of majoritarianism or pose dilemmas for democracy that demand exceedingly wise resolution.

2. "Suspect" Classifications

Somewhat more finite theses have been advanced, however, addressed primarily to the "suspect classifications" approach, that urge the Court to articulate a span of personal immunities that is wider than the constitutional text would appear to support, yet narrow enough to account for our society's premises respecting popular will. Rather than calling on the Court to elevate particular interests of all individuals to a constitutionally protected status, these theories focus on groups in our society that are seen as lacking political strength. The most thoughtful developments of this approach find their source in Chief Justice Stone's famous footnote in the *Carolene Products* case in which he questioned "whether prejudice against discrete and insular minorities may be a special condition, which tends seriously to curtail the operation of those political processes ordinarily to be relied upon to protect minorities, and which may call for a correspondingly more searching judicial inquiry."[55] This has been reflectively expanded on more recently by Justice Goldberg, who recommended stricter judicial scrutiny of popular enactments "that adversely affect those who are not represented in the legislature."[56]

Majoritarians should have scant difficulty in reconciling traditional theory with the Court's assistance of persons who are not represented in the political process *at all*—best illustrated by aliens, nonresidents, perhaps minors or, as past experience unhappily reveals, minority racial groups who were illegally disenfranchised in certain parts of the nation. But the matter becomes painfully more complicated (both factually and theoretically) when the next step is taken—that is, when the judicially favored minority is one that, although fully enfranchised in accordance with its numbers, is nonetheless characterized as being "politically impotent," "not adequately represented," "discrete and insular," or the like.

The initial complexity arises because almost all, if not all, groups and interests in the American political process are "minorities." Thus, each time any group loses any political battle in which it has an interest—and some group always does—it may lay claim to the label of "political weakness" or "submerged and beaten minority." It is simply too facile to assert that "a claim of economic injustice can reasonably be referred to the political process for redress"[57] because "economic interests are typically represented in legislative bodies—or able to obtain a hearing from them."[58] The poor are with us in substantial numbers, yet, hearing or no, they may receive short shrift in political channels; the wealthy may often fare better, but at least some subgroups among them have been known to pay a heavy price at the hands of certain representative bodies. Nor does it solve the problem to say that every such group has the opportunity to join with others to form a "majority coalition of minorities." Rather than solve the problem, this response assumes it away from the outset.

It is true that some minorities, because of their sophistication and combined arithmetical and financial strength, are more influential than others on most political issues; and that some groups with modest numbers may win powerful surrogates who give them forceful representation.[59] Similarly, there are some minorities who are less effective than others on most legislative matters because of their geographic isolation, the general inexcitability or unpopularity of their ideas, their relative inarticulateness, their lack of numbers and resources, or because they are viewed with such resentment, distaste, or hatred that they can neither join working coalitions nor prevent hostile action.[60] But there are many disparate groups who may legitimately claim to meet some or all of these varied criteria for judicial solicitude. Thus, the Court may have to be as sympathetic to the pleas of apartment dwellers in Iowa, tobacco farmers in Massachusetts, debt adjustors in Kansas, oil well producers in New

York, and cedar tree owners in Virginia as it is to the complaints of Jehovah's Witnesses in Rhode Island, communists in New Hampshire, progressives in Ohio, Asian-Americans in California, and blacks in Mississippi—all these illustrations assuming a given temporal span, presumably also to be determined by the Court.

It may seem that the task would be significantly less intractable if the Court were to identify a "permanent minority" (the term is Justice Goldberg's)—one that never succeeds at all in the political process or even one that is never taken seriously on designated subjects. This notion has recently been elaborated upon superbly by Owen Fiss, who urges judicial scrutiny on behalf of "disadvantaged groups"—which he defines as social groups (1) that have distinct existence apart from that of their individual members and whose members' identity and well-being are determined by that of the group, (2) that have occupied or will occupy a position of subordination for an extended time, and (3) whose political power is severely limited.[61] But, as Fiss explicitly acknowledges, "the group-disadvantaging strategy" will cause the Court to become "heavily steeped in factual inquiries" and may "strain the resources, the imagination and even the patience of the judiciary."[62] For example, at any one time, even racial minorities, political and religious nonconformists, and the poor may be befriended by powerful factions either because of the latters' perceived self-interest or because of their more humane feelings of obligation. The problem is further confounded by the fact that, at least during particular periods, some groups that will invoke the judicial process because they are rarely forceful enough to obtain enactment of favorable legislation are, nonetheless, often strong enough to resist new laws that would adversely affect their central interests—for example, slaveholders prior to the Civil War, and those who desired greater racial equality after the Vietnam war.

E. ALTERNATIVE COURSES AVAILABLE

The principled delineation and interpretation of the judicially enforceable constitutional rights held by individuals against popular government is an awesomely perplexing responsibility for the Court. Yet determining its competence to do so vis-à-vis other institutions of state and national government probably represents the Court's most profound obligation. The Justices could reasonably restrict their authority to keeping the political passages unblocked and remitting all further matters to the trusteeship of democracy. But the clearly stated and commonly understood procedural and substantive guarantees of the Bill of Rights and analogous constitutional provisions appear to demand more. The Court could well draw the line at these, affording its protection for their historically intended beneficiaries—either actively including the interests of property (under the contracts, just compensation and due process clauses) in the fashion of the Court under Marshall, Fuller, White, Taft, and Hughes, or downgrading them more in the style of the Court under Stone, Vinson, Warren, and Burger.[63] Or the Court might enlarge the number of favored groups—for example from racial minorities to the illegitimate and underprivileged—by declaring that discriminations against them are "inherently suspect" under the equal protection clause; expand the list of "fundamental rights"—for example, from speech and religion to privacy, travel, procreation, and marriage (or even education)—by requiring that regulations affecting them be sustained by a "compelling" (or, perhaps, "substantial") interest under the due process and equal protection clauses, the ninth amendment, or the structure of the Constitution as a whole;[64] or to accomplish much the same via procedural due process by censuring classificatory laws (as most are) that create (as most do) a "permanent and irrebuttable presumption" that certain possessed characteristics produce certain undesired results, and by demanding instead that an individualized determination be made;[65] or extend procedural guarantees, traditionally reserved under the due process clause primarily for the imposition of criminal penalties, into the domains of disputes over private property or the distribution of government benefits. All of these alternative courses—which implicate such solemn considerations as how faithfully to adhere to the language or historic purposes of the Constitution,[66] how carefully to attempt to examine the adequacy of a group's influence in the political process, how to relate these factors, whether to grant greater deference to the political branches in respect to some liberties in contrast to others, whether to proceed broadly or narrowly—clearly require the least democratic branch to make critical public policy decisions.

Fortunately, as has been stated, full exploration and final clarification of these questions is beyond the scope of discussion. So, too, is a set of similar issues that also fall under the heading of the Court's *substantive* interpretation of personal liberties. These concern the standard to be used by the Court in reviewing alleged abridgments of individual rights and the factors that should influence the Court's formulation of that criterion—for example, whether the Justices should accord the action of other governmental agencies a general presumption of constitutionality, or an opposite presumption, or something in between; whether some personal liberties (such as the political rights of speech, press, association, and voting) should be held to occupy a "preferred position," while others do not; and whether and the extent to which the test should be guided by the amount of political influence possessed by the person or group claiming infringement, or by how broadly representative the decisionmaking political institution is and how deliberately it has considered the constitutional issue.[67] Although the Individual Rights Proposal plainly urges that judicial review should be exercised in behalf of personal constitutional liberties, this book in no way undertakes to say how this superintendence should be carried out. In short, it does not attempt to resolve what John Ely recently stated to be "the critical question facing constitutional scholarship": development of "a principled approach to judicial enforcement of the Constitution's open-ended provisions"[68] securing individual rights.

V. THE RECORD OF JUDICIAL REVIEW FOR INDIVIDUAL RIGHTS

A major justification for the Individual Rights Proposal is that experience, confirming the political theory elaborated in the Constitution, demonstrates the shortcomings of the political process in affording adequate security for fundamental personal liberties. Documentation of the people's frequent collective insensitivity (and that of their electorally responsible representatives) to constitutionally prescribed freedoms that were believed would be endangered by majoritarian institutions may be readily obtained from the pages of the *United States Reports*—at least from the last two hundred-odd volumes. This phenomenon, which is further illustrated in the specific instances to be described below, has not been seriously disputed from any quarter.

A. CRITICAL APPRAISALS

It has often been contended by distinguished observers, however—and not so long ago—that reliance on the Court for performance of the momentous task of safeguarding individual rights is misplaced. Whatever the deficiencies of the alternatives, Henry Steele Commager complained in 1950 that the judicial record in this area "as far as federal legislation is concerned . . . is practically barren."[69] Robert Dahl concluded in 1967 that "it is doubtful that the fundamental conditions of liberty in this country have been altered by more than a hair's breadth as a result of" the judiciary's invalidation of congressional action,[70] and reiterated this view with but the slightest qualification in 1972.[71] In 1954 John Frank observed that "for the most part, the civil rights limitations on the states have been a collection of magnificent trifles."[72] And as late as 1975 another commentator opined that overall "the traditional concept of the Court as the champion of minority rights . . . is *largely* incorrect."[73]

It may be unfair to read hastily too precise a meaning into these broadly phrased value judgments. Nonetheless, as we shall see, the evidence does not substantiate their basic thrust.

B. COMPLEXITIES IN DOCUMENTATION

Before proceeding to examine the data, several important qualifications must be noted. First, any attempt to measure the societal effects of judicial holdings is an enormously complicated task.[74] Perhaps the greatest difficulty is that "the decisions of the Supreme Court are part of a general milieu in which later events take place and part of a set of multiple causes of such events. If several factors are operating in the same direction, how does one 'separate out' the impact the Court's decision has by comparison with other elements of the situation?"[75] When libertarian reforms do take place in the aftermath of pronouncements by the Justices requiring them, how can it be confidently said that such advances would not have occurred in any event, if not as quickly then at least eventually? Perhaps the Court's rulings did no more than reflect, or perhaps anticipate, or at best reinforce, what would have ultimately happened anyway. "Even the most careful study cannot establish whether alleged changes were not merely coincidentally but actually consequentially related."[76]

Second, even if we assume a causal relationship, there is no automatic assurance that all constitutional pronouncements of the Supreme Court will be complied with in practice. Some rulings in favor of personal liberties are relatively self-enforcing. This is perhaps best illustrated by certain rights of the accused. For example, a person charged with a crime and faced with a prison sentence has every incentive to assert his constitutional right to counsel, and trial judges ordinarily have a comparable motivation to respect the claim, whether or not they are in sympathy with it, because they recognize that failure to do so may well result in reversal of the conviction. On the other hand, effectuation of some judicial rulings in behalf of individual rights against recalcitrant public officials may demand much greater commitment and fortitude on the part of their beneficiaries. This may be exemplified by the school prayer controversies. If a public school wishes to continue voluntary Bible-reading programs despite the Justices' proscription of the practice, vindication of the constitutional right requires objecting parents and students to initiate litigation and risk the social obloquy that is likely to result from their preventing the majority from engaging in a much desired activity from which it is already willing to permit dissenters to be excused.

Third, even if we assume literal compliance with the Court's mandates, the degree to which they are truly meaningful to the individuals affected varies considerably. For example, there is little doubt about the significance of the consequences for prisoners on death row of a judicial decision invalidating capital punishment. Be even if counsel is appointed at state expense for all indigent criminal defendants because of a ruling by the Justices, this does not insure that the quality of the representation afforded will be of any value to the accused or, even if only very talented lawyers are assigned, that their participation will make any real difference.

Finally, even if we assume that the Court's unconstitutionality holdings have effectively negated substantial political abridgments of personal liberty, history reveals that other decisions of the Justices that rejected claimed violations of individual rights have exacerbated the infringement of those rights. "For instance, after the Court reluctantly upheld the compulsory flag salute rule in *Minersville School District v. Gobitis*, the West Virginia legislature enacted a comparable statute for the state as a whole, and other states quickly joined the repressive band wagon."[77] Within one year of the Court's ruling in *Ginsberg v. New York*, that states have broad regulatory power over distribution of sexually related materials to minors, "at least twenty city councils across the country were found to have passed statutes like that validated."[78] And it has been observed that as a result of the Court's sanctioning of the separate-but-equal precept in *Plessy v. Ferguson*, "racial segregation came to dominate virtually all areas of Southern life,"[79] and the doctrine became "the linchpin of Jim Crow jurisprudence in America."[80] Can it be reliably concluded that, on balance, the state of freedom within the nation is better than it would have been without the Justices' involvement? On the other hand the existence of judicial review and the mere possibility that the Court will invalidate a governmental practice may have caused political officials to refrain from impinging on individual rights, perhaps to an even greater extent than the Justices would have demanded. Thus, "the Post Office often mooted cases involving restrictions on receipt of mail when an irate individual threatened to go to court, in order to avoid a court decision on its practices of holding mail."[81]

As observed above, when exploring the difficulty of scientifically verifying the related question of how the presence of judicial review has more generally affected the conduct of majoritarian government in respect to individual freedom,[82] that these imponderables are incapable of systematic resolution should not deter us from determining what is and can be known. The empirical studies that have been made on the impact of the Court's efforts in behalf of personal liberties are relatively few in number and methodologically uneven in thoroughness and quality. Some tend to be based more on opinion than on observation and hard data. But the available knowledge, as augmented by my own research (which draws almost exclusively on information gathered by others), is nonetheless revealing. I readily concede that the presentation that follows has been undertaken to make the point and therefore may, at least in part, be fairly characterized as being not only fragmented but adversarial as well. Further, to contend (as I do) that the Justices' rulings in favor of personal liberties have quite meaningfully affected the lives of many people is neither to approve all the substantive results reached (which I do not) nor to deny that advancing the interests of some persons may well retard the welfare of others. These disclaimers having been noted, I believe that the historical record discloses that the Court's accomplishments for individual rights have been substantial.

C. PRIOR TO 1935

As early as 1867, the Court's invalidation of post–Civil War federal and state loyalty oaths, which had prevented Confederate "sympathizers" from acting as lawyers or ministers,[83] meaningfully furthered the cause of individual liberty. Although national oaths for federal office, employment, and jury duty persisted, within months of the Justices' rulings, "ex-rebel attorneys could practice in all the courts of the nation."[84] "The boon presented by the Court to dispossessed lawyers in the *Garland* case, was of inestimable benefit to Southerners of the legal fraternity .... [I]t made possible the financial recuperation of great numbers of former Confederates."[85] Furthermore, several state courts (although not all) followed the *Garland* and *Cummings* mandate to abrogate similar impediments to voting and to teaching, thus freeing additional southerners from the oaths' political and economic shackles.[86]

The decisions of the nineteenth and early twentieth centuries, in which a majority of the Justices acted under several clauses of the Constitution to preserve economic interests, also spoke in behalf of personal rights. Although these rulings benefited persons of property and affluent minorities rather than unpopular individuals and downtrodden groups and, hence, may be disapproved under contemporary libertarian standards, the fact is that they served the ideal of limited democracy and secured interests that were originally regarded as fundamental. It is well known that one of Alexander Hamilton's primary concerns respecting judicial protection of personal liberties was that majority tyranny in state legislatures would subvert the vested rights of the creditor class.[87] And, as viewed by Henry Maine, the Court's very early interpretations of the contracts clause proved to be "the bulwark of American individualism against democratic impatience and Socialistic fantasy."[88] Because the state of empirical methodology was nascent during the first third of this century when the Court rejected governmental attempts to regulate various economic relationships on more than two hundred occasions,[89] "there is no way of estimating reliably the restraining effect of this cloud of negativisms on state legislators and congressmen who might otherwise have made haste more speedily along the road to the welfare state." And it may be "highly questionable" that this course of decisions was "a major factor in determining the drift of American economic policy during the period." Nonetheless, Robert McCloskey found "no doubt" that "the pace of social change was moderated"; that "a respectable number of 'excesses' were prevented"; that "a respectable amount of money was saved for the businessman"—and that "a good many laborers were left a little hungrier than they might have been if the Court had not been there to defend economic liberty."[90]

D. THE HUGHES, STONE, AND VINSON COURTS

Even in reference to the period before the era of the Warren Court, the positions stated above—either condemning or minimizing the Court's impact—unduly discounted the Court's vigorous protection of individual freedom. A host of decisions (under the first, fourteenth, and fifteenth amendments) overruled government action that prejudiced racial, religious, and political minorities and (under the fourth, fifth, sixth, and fourteenth amendments) rejected federal and state practices that disregarded critical rights of the accused. Again, rigorous empirical data measuring the effect of the Court's civil liberties rulings during the quarter-century stewardship of Chief Justices Hughes, Stone, and Vinson is unavailable. Some of the results— such as forbidding Congress to withhold salaries of named federal employees whom it found to be "subversive,"[91] prohibiting municipal officials from denying speaking permits in censorial fashion,[92] restricting judges from too easily holding judicial critics in contempt,[93] barring conviction of controversial public advocates on too sweeping charges,[94] and protecting activities of persons with sincerely held religious beliefs no matter how aberrant or unbelievable[95]—may have had no greater force than the vindication of the personal constitutional rights of the particular litigants involved. But this consequence in itself is by no means unimportant, wholly apart from the possible deterrence of other repressive state action that may have been caused. As to a number of other decisions, however, there is sundry evidence corroborating their broader effectiveness—some factual, some inferential—that may be gleaned from scattered sources:

i) In 1936, five years after the Wickersham Commission disclosed that police use of the "third degree"—"physical brutality, or other forms of cruelty, to obtain involuntary confessions or admissions"—was "widespread" in the United States,[96] the Court for the first time held that convictions based on such confessions violated due process.[97] No responsible person would contend that *Brown v. Mississippi* and its progeny have resulted in the complete eradication of all such crude conduct by law enforcement officers. And it may well be that the Justices' unanimous and consistent condemnation of beatings and threatened hangings to obtain confessions has simply produced a shift in police tactics to more subtle techniques than bodily violence or explicit intimidation. Nonetheless, as reported by the Civil Rights Commission in 1961, "it is noteworthy that, with two exceptions"—one concerning the use of a stomach pump[98] and the other actually occurring before the *Brown* denunciation of the practice had time to be absorbed at the grass roots[99]—"all Supreme Court confession cases since 1942 have involved psychological coercion alone."[100] And, in a recent survey of prosecutors, defense attorneys, police magistrates, and trial judges, "it was generally agreed that [the Court's] decisions were instrumental in directing critical public attention to the more extreme forms of 'third degree' methods of interrogation, long practiced but previously taken for granted in this country."[101]

ii) Prior to 1938, it was "common practice" in the federal district courts not to assign counsel to indigent criminal defendants who wished to plead guilty; and, even when the accused asserted his innocence and went to trial, "some district courts did not appoint counsel for a defendant who appeared without an attorney, unless the defendant affirmatively and expressly requested that a lawyer be designated to represent him."[102] Both of these conditions were remedied for all federal criminal prosecutions by *Johnson v. Zerbst*[103] and *Walker v. Johnston*,[104] in which the Court required counsel to be assigned to all indigent federal defendants who plead guilty or go to trial unless this sixth amendment right is intelligently and competently waived. In 1945, the Federal Rules of Criminal Procedure codified this mandate and further stipulated that defendants be specifically advised of their right to the assistance of a lawyer.

iii) In the last few years of the 1930s, a number of states and municipalities, responding to toughened antilabor sentiments, adopted a series of new laws against peaceful picketing and other forms of advertisement and communication in respect to labor controversies. The adverse impact of these laws on the labor movement was markedly reduced by the Court's holdings in *Thornhill v. Alabama*,[105] *Carlson v. California*,[106] and *AFL v.*

Swing,[107] which brought peaceful picketing under the protective umbrella of the first amendment and limited employers' ability to enjoin such activity. Whether these judicial pronouncements really constituted the "Magna Charta of Labor" (as they were often heralded at the time) or whether they were "of even greater value than the enactment by legislatures of state Norris-LaGuardia acts"[108] (as the counsel to the American Federation of Labor then believed) is highly speculative. We do know that the Court hastened to qualify the broadest reaches of the newly articulated doctrines[109] and that subsequent judicial development proceeded under the head of federal preemption rather than free speech.[110] But the fact remains that many state and lower federal courts followed the lead of the celebrated rulings to invalidate various prohibitions on peaceful picketing[111] and that labor's legal spokesmen were convinced that "complete familiarity with them [was] as important to labor as tools to the craftsman."[112]

iv) During the 1930s, the young religious sect known as the Jehovah's Witnesses generated widespread public hostility. The most formidable legal barriers to its practice of engaging in door-to-door canvassing on Sundays—which resulted in a wave of arrests—were local ordinances that forbade peddling without a permit (submission to which the Witnesses believed to be an insult to the Almighty) and barred leaflet distribution on the public streets.[113] These impediments to the Witnesses' exercise of their religion were greatly ameliorated by a series of Supreme Court rulings commencing in 1938.[114] Although it undoubtedly would be an oversimplification to attribute the subsequent decline in the group's conflicts with local police officials—and the increase in its American membership from about 29,000 in 1938 to over 72,000 in 1943[115]—exclusively to these decrees, it appears that, as stated by one of the sect's leading chroniclers, "the *Lovell* and *Schneider* decisions...put the anti-Witness forces once and for all on the defensive."[116]

The Jehovah's Witnesses' most serious clash with the established order was over the flag salute. By one count, as of 1940, Jehovah's Witness children who refused to salute the flag because of their religious beliefs were faced with actual or impending expulsion "in at least thirty-one states. According to

Witness sources, expulsions took place in all forty-eight states and totaled more than 2,000 by 1943."[117] Furthermore, in some states, "there were attempts to have the children declared delinquent or dependent and removed from their parents. Prosecutions were brought against parents for school law violation or for contributing to the delinquency of their offspring, or for 'obstructing' the ceremony."[118] This grave threat to the faith's survival was found to be unconstitutional by the Supreme Court in 1943.[119] Although "attempts to enforce the flag salute requirement did not die out altogether immediately after *Barnette*,"[120] on the whole—owing in no small measure to vigorous implementation by the Department of Justice[121] (as well as to a weakened public enmity toward the Witnesses)—"state and local compliance with the *Barnette* ruling was immediate and substantial . . . . The dearth of Witness complaints to the Justice Department about flag-salute expulsions, together with the almost total absence of new litigation, strongly suggests that Witness children were being readmitted to school in most localities without incident."[122] By 1955, Jehovah's Witness membership in the United States had grown to 187,000.[123]

v) As of 1932, the problem of disenfranchisement of black citizens was largely confined to twelve states—Alabama, Arkansas, Florida, Georgia, Louisiana, Mississippi, North Carolina, Oklahoma, South Carolina, Tennessee, Texas, and Virginia. In that year, fewer than 100,000 blacks voted in general elections in these states, and virtually no blacks were permitted to vote in the primaries.[124] Although literacy tests and poll taxes were significant contributing factors, the most formidable barrier was the "white primary" whose proscription by the Supreme Court in 1944,[125] according to V. O. Key, "precipitated a crisis in southern politics."[126] Despite manifold efforts of varying success to negate the decision's mandate in a number of states, those "around the rim of the Deep South accepted the new order more or less as a matter of course."[127] Within four years of *Smith v. Allwright*, it was reported that "remarkable changes have taken place both in the practical voting arrangements and in the viewpoints of many people within the South, and, as a result, large numbers of Negroes were admitted to the Democratic primaries of 1944 and 1946."[128] For example, in Texas, "since 1944, Negroes have been paying their poll taxes in greater numbers and have been admitted to Democratic primaries more or less freely in many counties";[129] in 1946, "for the first time, Negro delegates were selected to the county Democratic conventions in Dallas, Travis (Austin), and Harris (Houston) counties. Negro poll tax deputies were appointed by the county tax collector's office in Dallas, Tarrant (Fort Worth), Harris, and Travis counties. Dallas had no fewer than 28 Negroes deputized to collect poll taxes, Houston 18. Finally, some Negro Democratic precinct chairmen turned up in the colored precincts of the big cities—three in Dallas, five in Houston, two in Galveston, and one in Port Arthur."[130] In Arkansas, "registration of Negroes for 1946 was reported as heavy, although attempts were made, it is alleged, to dissuade many from voting."[131] Even in Georgia, where there was extensive opposition to implementation, "the state Democratic executive committee let down the bars for the primary of 1946, and nearly 125,000 Negroes were registered (100,000 are supposed to have voted)"; the black vote "helped elect a congresswoman from the fifth Congressional district whose opponent had declared for 'white supremacy.'"[132] There is no disputing that it was only aggressive congressional and executive enforcement, culminating in the Voting Rights Act of 1965, that finally fulfilled the fifteenth amendment's promise. But the fact is that, within three years of the outlawing of the white primary, the number of registered black voters in the twelve southern states had risen to 645,000, and by 1952 this figure exceeded one million.[133] "The most important change," observed the Civil Rights Commission, "was the virtual elimination of 'white primaries' in 1944."[134]

vi) Commencing with its decision in *Missouri ex rel. Gaines v. Canada*[135] in 1938 and ending with *Sweatt v. Painter*[136] and *McLaurin v. Oklahoma State Regents*[137] in 1950, the Supreme Court put teeth into the separate but equal doctrine in respect to public education by ordering black students to be admitted to state graduate and professional schools when no comparable segregated facilities existed. The response of the southern states was twofold. First, by the fall of 1950, in compliance with the

Court's mandates, eleven states with segregation laws "lowered the racial bar in professional and graduate schools. Thus the University of Oklahoma enrolled 60 Negroes; the University of Texas, 21; the University of Arkansas, 12; the University of Kentucky, 15; the University of Missouri, 9; the University of Virginia, 3. The University of Louisville admitted 18 Negroes." It was reported "that 1,000 or more Negroes were attending classes with white students in the 17 Jim Crow states . . . that 200 Negro students were engaged in graduate and professional studies at the University of Arkansas; the University of Kansas City had 54."[138] Other sources disclosed the attendance of blacks in state universities in Tennessee[139] and Louisiana.[140] Second, and more consequential, in order "to remedy a hundred years of neglect"—as Governor James F. Byrnes of South Carolina frankly confessed[141]—and concededly to ward off the threatened demise of the school segregation principle altogether lest the Court "take matters out of the state's hands,"[142] the states of the Deep South engaged in "frenzied spending campaigns and gigantic efforts . . . to equalize the educational opportunities of white and Negro pupils."[143] A modest illustration is found in the record of the *Sweatt* case itself: Texas opened its School of Law of the Texas State University for Negroes only after the trial court had held that the state must supply substantially equal facilities. More dramatic examples were South Carolina's $75 million school bond effort,[144] Virginia's $60 million "Battle Fund" (named coincidently after the incumbent governor),[145] Mississippi's $46 million school "overhaul" program,[146] and Georgia's $30 million "equalization" plan.[147] But probably the best evidence of the impact of these decisions on civil rights lies in the statistics compiled in the Biennial Survey of Education in the United States,[148] selections from which follow:

Alabama: In 1946, expenditures per pupil were $85 for whites and $38 for blacks; in 1954, the figures were $112 and $105. In 1946, average teachers' salaries were $1,451 for whites and $884 for blacks; in 1954, the figures were $2,834 and $2,681.

Arkansas: In 1946, expenditures per pupil were $74 for whites and $35 for blacks; in 1954, the figures were $99 and $72.

Florida: In 1946, pupil-teacher ratios were 26 for whites and 30 for blacks; in 1952 the figures were 27 and 27. In 1946, expenditures per pupil were $135 for whites and $62 for blacks; in 1954, the figures were $176 and $161. In 1946, average teachers' salaries were $1,862 for whites and $1,278 for blacks; in 1954, the figures were $3,836 and $3,613. In 1946, capital expenditures per pupil were $7 for whites and $2 for blacks; in 1952 the figures were $60 and $69.[149]

Georgia: In 1946, average teachers' salaries were $1,279 for whites and $651 for blacks; in 1952 the figures were $2,649 and $2,444.

Louisiana: In 1946, expenditures per pupil were $136 for whites and $44 for blacks; in 1954, the figures were $165 and $122. In 1946, average teachers' salaries were $1,797 for whites and $948 for blacks; in 1952, the figures were $3,248 and $2,864.

Mississippi: In 1946, expenditures per pupil were $75 for whites and $15 for blacks; in 1954, the figures were $98 and $43. In 1946, average teachers' salaries were $1,165 for whites and $427 for blacks; in 1954, the figures were $2,261 and $1,302.

Virginia: In 1946, pupil-teacher ratios were 31 for whites and 39 for blacks; in 1954, the figures were 27 and 29.

E. THE WARREN COURT

The Court's record since 1953 surely refutes the charge that judicial review has not significantly advanced the cause of individual freedom. This is not the place either to rehearse all of the numerous and important instances in which the Warren Court boldly moved to further civil liberties or to evaluate the doctrinal merits of the rulings. Elsewhere, I will seek to present a more comprehensive survey measuring the impact of the work of both the Warren and Burger Courts in behalf of personal liberties.[150] Here, a few examples should suffice.

1. Racial Equality

There is no denying that it fell to the Court to fulfill the promise of the equal protection clause by repudiating racial segregation in 1954 for, at least until then, the national and state political organs remained silent. As Justice Jackson remarked during oral argument in the Virginia and South Carolina suits, "I suppose that realistically the reason this case is here was that action couldn't be obtained from Congress."[151] Indeed, two years after the *Brown* decision, more than half the populace still disapproved of black children attending the same schools as whites.[152] Statistical evidence disclosed that, by the end of the decade following the Justices' decree, more than half the black pupils enrolled in the border jurisdictions—Delaware, Kentucky, Maryland, Missouri, Oklahoma, West Virginia, and the District of Columbia—attended integrated schools.[153] It is true that wide-scale implementation of *Brown*'s ban on legally imposed school segregation was accomplished only after the political branches afforded coercive support in the Civil Rights Act of 1964. But it was the Court's mandate that provided the indispensable impetus. Moreover, even if, in the long run, socioeconomic facts and politico-psychological attitudes render "the nationalizing, egalitarian, assimilationist conception of the public schools' mission"[154] to be either unattainable or unwanted, there is no demeaning the significance for individual liberty—both pragmatically and symbolically—of the elimination of enforced racial separation in schools and all other public facilities.

More important, however, it must be acknowledged that the overall consequences of the Court's historic ruling and its major contribution to the advancement of racial justice in the United States radiated far beyond the cold statistics in southern schoolhouses. Although a congeries of complex factors contributed to the civil rights upheaval in the 1960s,[155] in the words of Anthony Lewis, *Brown v. Board of Education* was the "catalyst" for "the revolution in American race relations," creating "a climate that encouraged the Negro to protest against segregation on buses, to demand coffee at a lunch counter, to stand in long, patient lines waiting to take a biased test for the right to vote . . . . It took the drama of school desegregation, and then of the protest movements, to make the possibility of freedom come alive."[156] (Indeed, Kenneth Karst has observed that the Justices' desegregation rulings not only "forever alter[ed] the substance and the tone of race relations in this country; they made us question the validity of all sorts of systems of dominance and dependency," thus "set[ting] in motion forces (moral and political) that fostered other 'liberation' movements.")[157]

That *Brown* sparked an erruption of emotion and energy in the "hearts and minds" of black Americans, young and old, "in a way unlikely ever to be undone"[158] has been attested by black leaders from all walks of life. Louis Lomax explained that "it would be impossible for a white person to understand what happened within black breasts on that Monday.... That was the day we won; the day we took the white man's laws and won our case before an all-white Supreme Court with a Negro lawyer.... And we were proud."[159]

In the opening paragraphs of "Soul on Ice," Eldridge Cleaver wrote from Folsom Prison:

"Nineteen fifty-four, when I was eighteen years old, is held to be a crucial turning point in the history of the Afro-American— for the U.S.A. as a whole—the year segregation was outlawed by the U.S. Supreme Court. It was also a crucial year for me because on June 18, 1954, I began serving a sentence in state prison for possession of marijuana.

"The Supreme Court decision was only one month old when I entered prison, and I do not believe that I had even the vaguest idea of its importance or historical significance. But later, the acrimonious controversy ignited by the end of the separate-but-equal doctrine was to have a profound effect on me. This controversy awakened me to my position in America and I began to form a concept of what it meant to be black in white America."[160]

Robert Carter found that, in *Brown,* "the psychological dimensions of America's race relations problems were completely recast.... As a result, the Negro was propelled into a stance of insistent militancy. Now he was demanding—fighting to secure and possess what was rightfully his. The appeal to morality and to conscience still was valid, of course, but in a nation that was wont to describe itself as a society ruled by law, blacks had now perhaps the country's most formidable claim to fulfillment of their age-old dream of equal status—fulfillment of their desire to become full and equal participants in the mainstream of American life."[161] And the fact that this judicial doctrine "fathered a social upheaval the extent and consequences of which cannot even now be measured with certainty"[162] underlines rather than negates its seismic thrust.

The particular effects for racial freedom resulting from one of *Brown*'s most famous progeny further illustrate the legacy of the Court's intervention. Fifteen years prior to the Justices' 1967 ruling in *Loving v. Virginia*,[163] that laws forbidding interracial marriage violate equal protection, twenty-nine states had such statutory provisions.[164] Between 1953 and 1967, thirteen of these states repealed their laws,[165] galvanized in part by a constitutional decision of the California Supreme Court[166] and in part by the revolutionary movement toward racial equality engendered by the *School Segregation Cases*.[167] Still, as late as 1967, the statutes of sixteen states continued to prohibit miscegenous marriages.[168]

The consequences of these laws were not inconsiderable. Ordinarily, the laws applied not only to marriages consummated within the prohibiting state but also to persons of different races who married outside such states and subsequently came to live in the state with an antimiscegenation law.[169] In some states where such unions were illegal, violation subjected the parties to prosecution for a felony.[170] Penalties ranged from 30 days (where the offense was only a misdemeanor) up to 5–10 years in other states.[171] In the 1940s, reported impositions of prison terms were not infrequent.[172] In 1959, the principals in the *Loving* case "were sentenced to one year in jail; however, the trial judge suspended the sentence for a period of 25 years on the condition that the Lovings leave the State and not return to Virginia together for 25 years."[173] Many of the statutes also made it a crime for any person to perform a marriage ceremony for an interracial couple or to issue a marriage license to them[174]—prohibitions whose effect was confirmed by a widely publicized incident in 1958 when longshoreman leader Harry Bridges was thrice rebuffed by county clerks in Nevada after he applied for permission to marry a Japanese-American woman.[175]

The antimiscegenation laws also produced serious noncriminal ramifications. Since the statutes made interracial marriages void, all offspring were considered illegitimate. Children and surviving spouses were denied the right to intestate inheritance, to take property under a will, to be granted letters of administration, and to receive workmen's compensation benefits.[176] In the late 1950s, black servicemen who had married white women while on European tours of duty were transferred from their military units on return to the United States when their divisions were stationed in jurisdictions that barred racially mixed unions.[177] Indeed, as recently as 1965—even after the Supreme Court had invalidated laws that imposed special penalties for interracial cohabitation[178]—the U.S. Comptroller General's office refused military death benefits to the Negro widow of a deceased white soldier because they had wed in a state forbidding miscegenous marriages.[179]

These varied disabilities of antimiscegenation laws—all with "the ultimate aim of preventing interracial couples from having any legal peace of mind"[180]—were removed by the *Loving* decision. The exact number of persons that *Loving* directly affected is incalculable. But a 1956 survey which indicated that in states where mixed marriages were lawful perhaps 5 percent of blacks had spouses of a different race[181] suggests the breadth of *Loving*'s impact on individual constitutional rights.

2. Rights of the Accused

It was also up to the Court to strike forcefully against unreasonable searches and seizures in 1961[182] because the legislative process had not—twelve years had passed since the Court informed the states that they were bound by the fourth amendment, yet still more than half continued to admit into evidence the fruits of illegal searches and seizures. This should not be particularly surprising. Students of police behavior have observed that the law enforcement profession is extremely sensitive and commonly resistant to regulation from without,[183] thus making legislative control, according to Anthony Amsterdam, a "politically suicidal undertaking."[184]

The extent to which the exclusionary rule has deterred official misconduct and thus secured the fourth amendment's promise of freedom is, of course, a matter of substantial debate. Some empirical surveys[185]—whose methodology, it should be noted, has been sharply criticized[186]—have simply concluded that *Mapp*'s stricture is ineffective, thus supporting the view that the Court's efforts in behalf of individual liberty have been largely inconsequential. The most celebrated study, by Dallin Oaks, returns an inconclusive verdict: "The data contains little support for the proposition that the exclusionary rule discourages illegal searches and seizures, but it falls short of establishing that it does not."[187] Again, however, the underlying evidence has been challenged as being "insufficient and largely inappropriate."[188] Perhaps the only position that may be taken with confidence is that *Mapp*'s "deterrent efficacy defies precise measurement."[189]

To concede that the exclusionary rule falls short of curing the disease and that it produces the undesired side effect of preventing otherwise justified criminal convictions, however, does not refute its prophylactic value—at least until a more effective antidote is discovered. For, although it is clear that the rule "does not produce police conformity with the requirements of law in all cases," it is equally plain that it "does have a significant impact upon police practice in some situations."[190] While "the evidence consists only of bits and pieces, . . . the fragments indicate it is a mistake to think that police behavior is never conditioned by the sanction of excluding evidence that might lead to conviction."[191] Thus, in the opinion of a substantial majority of prosecutors, defense lawyers, and judges surveyed in North Carolina, "exclusion of evidence is an effective way of reducing the number of illegal searches."[192] Similar views were expressed by police officials, public defenders, and judicial officers in small towns and rural areas of southern Illinois and western Massachusetts; "in general, the judges saw the police departments as making fewer illegal searches, as operating more carefully in their work, and as educating the men of the departments so that a situation won't arise where evidence will be suppressed."[193] And, in an intensive study of the administration of criminal justice in Oakland, Jerome Skolnick concluded that "the exclusionary principle puts pressure on the police to work within the rules in those cases where prosecution is contemplated."[194] Evidence gleaned from such cities as Baltimore, Boston, Buffalo, Detroit, New York, Philadelphia, San Francisco, and Washington indicates "that to a considerable extent the rule is producing the impact that was intended."[195] At least in some areas, "it is clear that the exclusionary rule has served as a stimulus to police training on the legal requirements of search and arrest."[196] Thus, the New York City police commissioner could "think of no decision in recent times in the field of law enforcement which had such a dramatic and traumatic effect as [Mapp].... Retraining sessions had to be held from the very top administrators down to each of the thousands of foot patrolmen and detectives engaged in the daily basic enforcement function. Hundreds of thousands of man-hours had to be devoted to retraining 27,000 men."[197] Reports from several cities found that police use of search warrants had increased enormously.[198] At the very least, Mapp "provides a counterweight within the criminal justice system that prevents the system from functioning as an unmitigated inducement to policemen to violate the fourth amendment on every occasion when there is criminal evidence to be gained by doing so."[199]

Several further examples, primarily involving the right to legal representation, may be drawn from the many other Warren Court rulings on behalf of persons accused of crime. When Gideon v. Wainwright[200] was decided in 1963, the number of states that provided counsel for all or virtually all indigent felony defendants who so requested had increased from thirty-five,[201] at the time of Betts v. Brady,[202] to forty-five. Thus, Gideon's greatest impact was felt by the destitute accused in only five states—Alabama, Florida, Mississippi, North Carolina, and South Carolina.[203] Indeed, even in those states, some cities and counties regularly assigned lawyers for the trial of poor persons who were charged with serious crimes.[204] But this is not to suggest that Gideon was of only minor significance for individual rights. In Florida alone, in the first months after the Justices' ruling, "1,000 prisoners were released because prosecutors could not or would not attempt to reprosecute. Of those 300 plus who were retried, most had their sentences reduced."[205] Further, "to facilitate compliance with Gideon (and other subsequent implementing cases), legislatures and courts in 23 states took specific actions within twenty-four months to expand or improve their assigned counsel or public defender systems in varying degrees"[206]—efforts that, as we shall see,[207] provided lawyers for many accused indigent misdemeanants as well as persons charged with more grievous offenses. In certain large cities where assigned counsel systems function, some degree of assembly-line justice undoubtedly results, thus producing less than the Supreme Court's sixth amendment rulings appear to promise.[208] Nonetheless, from the perspective of the security of personal liberty, surely even this form of legal representation is better than none at all.

Moreover, it may be that the greatest overall significance of the *Gideon* decision can be measured only when viewed in combination with the Court's rule—which was most emphatically established in 1962 in *Carnley v. Cochran*,[209] though it has earlier origins[210]—that "where the assistance of counsel is a constitutional requisite, the right to be furnished counsel does not depend on a request . . . . [Rather,] the record must show . . . that an accused was offered counsel but intelligently and understandingly rejected the offer."[211] As of the early 1960s, it appeared that in a majority of the forty-five states that mandated counsel for all indigent felony defendants the relevant statute or practice afforded this right only "on request" of the accused.[212] It is uncertain whether this meant, as it did in at least some states,[213] that the accused was always first advised of his right; or whether the accused obtained counsel only if he solicited assistance on his own initiative. If the latter were true, as was found to be so in at least eight states,[214] then, irrespective of how broad the sixth amendment right might be, it is reasonable to infer that a sizable percentage of those for whom the protection was intended would not receive it. This inference is confirmed by an empirical study of the operation of the *Miranda* rule which showed that, while almost two-thirds of arrestees who were informed of their right to counsel requested assistance, more than three-fourths of those who were not so advised failed to exercise the right.[215] The Court's stringent waiver rule in *Carnley* corrected this in respect to the right to counsel at trial.

As for the plight of poor persons in the criminal appellate process, prior to the Court's decisions in *Griffin v. Illinois*[216] and *Douglas v. California*,[217] the exact practice in each of the then forty-eight states respecting the rights of indigents to receive free transcripts or appointed counsel on appeal of their criminal convictions was uncertain. In a number of states no statute addressed the subject, and no empirical study systematically documented the law in action in every jurisdiction in the country— assuming that there was a consistent pattern in each state and, if there was, that some persons knew of it. But it was well established that a large percentage of persons convicted of crime were indigent (estimates often exceeding 50 percent)[218] and that a significant number of criminal convictions were reversed when appealed (statistics sometimes reaching as high as over 40 percent).[219]

In 1955, counsel for petitioner in *Griffin* reported that nineteen states refused to provide free trial transcripts to all indigents who sought to appeal their convictions of noncapital offenses.[220] Shortly thereafter, a more detailed and comprehensive survey indicated that twenty-two states fell into this category.[221] The more important finding of the later study, however, was that within three years of the *Griffin* ruling more than two-thirds of these states—including Colorado, Connecticut, Delaware, Illinois, Kansas, Maine, Maryland, Massachusetts, Minnesota, New Jersey, Texas, Washington, and West Virginia—appeared to have formally altered their procedures so as to remove this severe obstacle to effective appellate review of many convictions. And five years later, no evidence of any deviation from the *Griffin* principle was discovered.[222]

As for counsel on appeal, in 1959 no more than fourteen states followed the subsequently announced *Douglas* ruling. Among the remainder, some states appointed appellate counsel for indigents only in capital cases; others left the matter to the discretion of the reviewing court, the trial judge, or the trial lawyer (if there was one); in yet others the practice varied from county to county. Even in the fourteen states that did regularly assign counsel, some limited the practice to felony cases and at least five—Maryland, Massachusetts, Oregon, South Dakota, and

Virginia—had formulated their rules only in response to their prescient reading of the *Griffin* rationale.[223] In an extensive nationwide audit that was conducted just a few months after *Douglas*, however, it was found that "nearly all the sample counties had some system for providing counsel for appeals,"[224] thus affording what few lawyers or laymen would dispute to be a normally indispensable ingredient for successful appellate review.

Finally, apart from the direct effects of the Warren Court's rulings to secure constitutional justice for the accused, its equally significant legacy may be—as Jerold Israel has recently suggested—"the long-range consequences that flowed from its direction of public attention" to the general problem, leading to "various reforms in the criminal justice process that have benefited the accused." Thus, the populace "came to recognize that police training involves more than teaching people to shoot straight, that we must devote substantial resources to police training, and that we must recruit our police from all groups in the community." The bar came to perceive "criminal law as an area of intellectual and social challenge, and this, in turn, induced more able lawyers to enter that field, particularly in the offices of public defenders, and prosecuting attorneys." And the lawmakers, led by "various distinguished professional groups, such as the American Bar Association, American Law Institute, and the National Conference of Commissioners on Uniform State Laws," came to reexamine the role of legislation in the criminal procedure field. The proposed reforms "did not always indicate whole-hearted support of particular Warren Court decisions, but they certainly reflected a general concern for the rights of the accused and urged expansion of those rights in many areas, such as pretrial discovery."[225]

3. Freedom of Expression

The Warren Court's authority was also required to defend against sweeping governmental assaults on the communicative and associational rights of political dissidents[226] and racial minorities[227] because these groups had been reviled by various national, state, and local political institutions. (And only the Court could speak for religious noncomformists against devotional exercises in the public schools[228]—and against sundry disqualifications in other areas[229]—because legislators could not oppose God and retain their seats.)

Because these rulings usually concerned only trifling segments of the populace, and then only in respect to discrete interests, it may be true that the impact of each of these decisions, or even of their sum, has not radically changed the face of liberty in the country. It is fair, though, to speculate that their cumulative force has retarded further popular repression of advocacy critical of official policy. Thus, it has been recently urged that "tolerance for dissent over the war in Vietnam was in large measure a product of the Supreme Court's decisions in the area of freedom of speech."[230] But such large judgments are extremely difficult to substantiate. There is less doubt, on the other hand, that the Justices' approval, in over 90 percent of the cases during the period before the Civil Rights Act of 1964,[231] of the first amendment claims of demonstrators seeking integration of public accommodations contributed significantly to their ultimate legislative victory.[232]

In any event, it is certainly true that these rulings alone have not saved the nation from totalitarian rule. Perhaps this explains the critical evaluations of the effect of the Court's handiwork. But if it does, the reproval misconceives the Court's primary function respecting individual liberty which, in the main, is not to guard against wholesale destruction of the majority's constitutional rights but to shield the weak against popular excess.

4. Reapportionment

The judiciary's effort in the area of malapportionment is a vivid exception to the generally valid proposition that the Court comes to the aid only of insular minorities. Wholly apart from the strict doctrinal justification for the Court's rationale in this series of cases and from the propriety or wisdom of the one man–one vote principle, and no matter how different or subjectively desirable the operative results achieved by the newly constituted political bodies affected by the Court's rulings have been or will be (and the conclusions to date of political scientists who have systematically examined the effects of reapportionment on public policies have been sharply varied),[233] in these decisions the Court cogently repaired a crucial void in American democratic society. For, as Joseph Bishop succinctly put it, "legislative malapportionment had become a scandal and an affront to democracy."[234] By actively furthering—although by no means insuring or seeking fully to insure—the democratic ideal of majority rule (as well as that of equality), the Court successfully exercised its power on behalf of the majority of citizens and voters in the nation, mostly urban dwellers, whose political influence had been seriously diluted by entrenched minority interests. At least when dealing with the federal and state legislatures, only the Court seemed to be capable of improving the majoritarian quality of the political process. It is true that, in the past, legislators who had been the beneficiaries of existing arrangements for voting had moved on their own initiative to enfranchise additional groups of citizens (such as women). But the electoral effect of extending voting rights to such persons who were scattered throughout the population was much less certain than that of equalizing legislative districts. Because of the paralytic nature of malapportionment—whose cure would guarantee some lawmakers the loss of their seats and would imperil those of many others—there was no reason to believe that a nonjudicial remedy would ever be forthcoming.

Granting that the full complement of apportionment decisions shored the theoretical foundation of the political process at many levels of American government, they have by no means provided for the elimination of every influential antimajoritarian device. But the formal representative institutions with which the Court dealt, were perversely incompatible with the democratic ideal because they afforded no meaningful protection to individual constitutional rights—at least as commonly perceived—and were indeed able affirmatively to promulgate laws opposed by the majority of the constituency as a whole. As for those undemocratic elements untouched by the Court's rulings—a notable example being the legislative committee system—their affirmative influence (as we have seen in chapter 1) is quite limited. And although their negative power persists, it is realistically incapable of being used effectively on any regular basis to secure personal constitutional liberties. For this task, of the anti-majoritarian forces existing in government, the Court stands supreme.

F. THE BURGER COURT

It has become relatively commonplace to hear that judicial protection of personal liberties, which concededly blossomed under Earl Warren, withered rapidly in 1969 with the seating of his successor and died completely by 1972 when all four of President Nixon's appointees had been finally confirmed. Commenting on the Burger Court's 1972–73 product, Norman Dorsen, then general counsel of the American Civil Liberties Union and president of the Society of American Law Teachers, observed that "an entire generation of young Americans has come of age accustomed to looking to the Supreme Court to protect individual rights," but that "the first full year of the Burger Court reveals quite distinctly that this period has ended."[235] Similarly, in the preface to his influential treatise, published in 1978, Laurence Tribe declared "that the course of the Burger Court at least in its first years, will eventually be marked not as the end of an era of exaggerated activism on behalf of individuals and minorities, but as a sad period of often opposite activism, cloaked in the worn-out if well-meant disguise of judicial restraint."[236] More harshly, in 1974, Leonard Levy complained that a majority of the Justices "vote for the rights of the criminally accused about as often as snarks are sighted alighting on the roof of the Supreme Court building."[237] And, in 1978, Henry Steele Commager, echoing his criticism of nearly thirty years earlier, "condemned the current Supreme Court for what he called a 'tragic' lack of protection of individual rights."[238]

Although there is no denying that overall the Burger Court has been markedly less sympathetic than its predecessor to claims of infringement of constitutionally secured personal liberties, an objective appraisal of its record must be less pessimistic than the portrayals quoted above. (After all, *no* Supreme Court in our history has been as protective of individual freedoms as that of Earl Warren.) This is not the place for a thorough examination or evaluation of the matter. But, especially because of the frequently articulated view that the present Court is hostile to individual rights, a somewhat detailed overview is called for.

1. Retreats

It is true that in respect to some personal liberties there is substantial evidence for the deprecatory soundings that have been heard. The most obvious concerns the rights of the accused—particularly the *Miranda* rule,[239] the prohibition against unreasonable searches and seizures,[240] and the right to counsel (at least at lineups and for discretionary appeals).[241] But, as shall be specifically illustrated a bit more fully below, even though it may not be unfair to characterize the net product of the Burger Court's criminal procedure decisions as a retreat, a significant number of protective rulings clearly demonstrate that the Burger Court has pulled up far short of a total surrender.[242] Examples include such search and seizure holdings as *Mincey v. Arizona* (search at homicide scene),[243] *Michigan v. Tyler* (search at fire scene),[244] *Connally v. Georgia* (who may issue warrants),[245] *Gerstein v. Pugh* (requirement of hearing after arrest),[246] *United States v. Chadwick* (warrantless search of luggage),[247] and *United States v. District Court* (warrantless electronic surveillance for "domestic" security purposes);[248] and the hospitable application of *Miranda* in *Doyle v. Ohio* (prosecutor's use of accused's silence to impeach trial testimony);[249] and such extensions of the right to counsel as *Argersinger v. Hamlin* (any offense for which indigent is imprisoned),[250] *Morrissey v. Brewer* (parole revocation),[251] *Gagnon v. Scarpelli* (probation revocation),[252] *Faretta v. California* (right of self-representation),[253] *Holloway v. Arkansas* (appointment of separate counsel for co-defendant where there is potential of conflict of interest),[254] as well as several other favorable holdings for this "most pervasive right"[255] of an accused.[256]

Other areas of net retrenchment from the Warren era include

state action,[257] voting rights,[258] obscensity,[259] and the delineation of those personal property interests that cannot be denied by government without some form of notice and hearing.[260] Again, however, at least in regard to most of these issues, more than a few decisions reveal that the Burger Court's record has not been uniformly unresponsive to those who have suffered injury at the hands of the majority. For example, *White v. Weiser* (population equality for congressional apportionment),[261] *White v. Regester* (exclusion of minorities in state legislative apportionment),[262] and *O'Brien v. Skinner* (absentee ballots for accused persons being held for trial)[263] continued the Warren Court's quest to ensure fair and equal access to the political process;[264] *Kois v. Wisconsin* (poetry recounting sexual intercourse),[265] *Jenkins v. Georgia* (film, "Carnal Knowledge"),[266] *Erznoznik v. City of Jacksonville* (drive-in theater showing films containing nudity),[267] *Southeastern Promotions, Ltd. v. Conrad* (municipal theater's refusal to permit musical, "Hair"),[268] and *McKinney v. Alabama* (burden of proof in criminal prosecution)[269] protected sex-related expression; and *Goss v. Lopez* (suspension from public school)[270] and *Memphis Light, Gas & Water v. Craft* (municipal utility's termination of service)[271] extended the procedural protection of the due process clause.

The support of the incumbent Justices has also been diminished, relative to the Warren Court, by several lines of cases—concerning habeas corpus,[272] standing,[273] and enjoining state proceedings[274]—that have prevented individuals from obtaining hearings before federal courts in respect to alleged violations of their personal liberties. But once more, at least in respect to the latter two subjects, the Court's results have not been wholly regressive.[275]

2. Vacillations

In other areas of individual rights, the decisions of the Burger Court may be fairly described as mixed. For example, on the matter of racial equality, although the Court has made it clear that government action which results in a disproportionate disadvantage for racial minorities will not be subject to judicial scrutiny unless it is shown to be intentional rather than merely adventitious,[276] there was no well-grounded indication that the Warren Court would have held otherwise. On the other hand, the Burger Court explicitly abandoned the doctrine—which its predecessor periodically invoked[277]—that prohibited federal judges from inquiring into the motives behind such government action.[278] And while the present Court has shown an unmistakable aversion to judicially ordered wide-scale busing as a cure for deliberate school segregation,[279] especially if the transportation extends beyond the district lines of the offending school board,[280] it was a unanimous decision written by Chief Justice Burger that initially endorsed the use of this tool under proper conditions.[281] Additional cases have affirmed other expansive evidentiary rules[282] and remedial devices[283] for the problem, in the North as well as the South, and the Court has ordered an interdistrict remedy for segregation in housing.[284] Similarly, although the Burger Court has declined to invalidate all state laws or practices that operate to the disadvantage of the poor,[285] it has struck down statutory fees that prevented indigents from getting a divorce,[286] obtaining a position on a primary election ballot,[287] avoiding imprisonment because of inability to pay a fine,[288] and appealing a judgment of eviction from rented premises.[289]

The Burger Court's imprint in regard to first amendment freedoms has similarly been undulatory. It has indisputably reduced—but by no means eliminated—the availability of the vagueness and overbreadth doctrines[290] as weapons to challenge the application of broadly phrased laws to expressive activity.[291] But it has also vindicated the rights of a substantial number of political dissidents despite their public use of vulgar language,[292] their philosophy of violence and disruption,[293] and their openly communicated contempt (at least by majoritarian standards) for patriotic symbols.[294] Further, the Burger Court has forbidden the discharge of non–civil service public employees because they have fallen into political disfavor,[295] preserved the rights of individuals[296] and corporations[297] to expend funds in political campaigns, secured the liberty of clergymen to hold political office,[298] and safeguarded the beliefs of religious nonconformists in respect to education of their children.[299] As for freedom of the press, the Court has, on the one hand, refused to grant the media a special privilege to withhold information from investigative agencies[300] or to obtain information under government control.[301] On the other hand, the Justices have afforded the press a most spacious immunity—despite powerful countervailing public interests—from government restraints against publishing data revealing highly sensitive national policies,[302] describing critical evidence obtained by the police for subsequent introduction at a criminal trial,[303] and divulging what transpired at confidential proceedings of an administrative agency.[304] In addition, the Court has shielded the editorial judgments of newspapers by invalidating state right-of-reply laws.[305]

3. Advances

As we have observed, although the Burger Court has often upheld the claims of those alleging popular disregard of their constitutionally secured individual rights, its record suffers in comparison to the extraordinarily sensitive stance of the Warren Court. But it must also be recognized that in the process the Burger Court "has nullified more national laws on First Amendment and equal protection grounds than any predecessor,"[306] and, indeed, on several issues, has moved well beyond the lines established in 1969.

The most prominent advance concerns the "right of privacy." Although its seeds were planted under the stewardship of Chief Justice Stone[307] and sprouts appeared in 1965,[308] it reached full bloom only in such Burger Court rulings as *Roe v. Wade* and its several progeny (right to an abortion),[309] *Eisenstadt v. Baird* and *Carey v. Population Services, Int'l* (right of access to contraceptives by unmarried persons, including minors),[310] *Moore v. City of East Cleveland* (right of related persons to live together in same dwelling),[311] *Zablocki v. Redhail* (right to marry)[312]—and possibly also *O'Connor v. Donaldson* (right of persons involuntarily confined in mental institutions),[313] whose implications will be explored more fully below.

The Burger Court has also expanded the "suspect" classifications branch of equal protection doctrine to encompass almost all state discriminations against aliens,[314] and has closely approached this position for government disabilities imposed on the basis of sex[315] or illegitimate birth.[316] The Justices have rejected the more limited rule of their precursors[317] and have extended the first amendment's protective umbrella to include commercial advertising.[318] Finally, the present Court's delicate circumscription, if not total abolition, of the death penalty[319] has also entered territory beyond the Warren Court's march.

4. Effects

Ascertaining the extent to which each of the Burger Court's decisions favoring personal rights has had a meaningful impact on the lives and liberties of individuals is beyond the scope of this book;[320] but several illustrations are indicative:

i) In 1972, when the Court decided *Argersinger v. Hamlin*,[321] at least four or five states[322] completely refused to appoint counsel for indigent misdemeanor defendants. Beyond this, determining the exact practice throughout the nation is complicated by several factors. Statewide laws were applied differently in different areas of some states; there were conflicting rules within certain states; and in other states which wholly forbade assignment of counsel (such as Louisiana, Nebraska, and Virginia),[323] federal courts had ruled that lawyers must be provided for at least some indigent accused misdemeanants.[324] Despite these ambiguities, it is plain that only a minority of the fifty states afforded indigents counsel in all (or virtually all) nonfelony prosecutions where imprisonment might result.[325] States like Rhode Island assigned lawyers in but a few such instances; Maine, Montana, and South Carolina in some few more; Alabama and Maryland did so only for "serious" offenses or where "special circumstances" were found to exist. Other states appointed counsel only when incarceration exceeded six months (Arizona, Florida, Idaho, Nevada, New Mexico, North Carolina, Utah, and Wisconsin), or ninety days (Michigan), sixty days (Vermont), or thirty days (Iowa). Even in such states as Georgia, Indiana, and

Oklahoma, where statutes or judicial decisions required counsel in all cases, investigation has disclosed that the rule was administered unevenly.[326]

The number of indigent misdemeanor defendants who subsequently obtained the assistance of a lawyer because of the *Argersinger* edict cannot, of course, be computed precisely. But it was unquestionably substantial. For example, in the city of Cleveland alone it was shown that 4,000 misdemeanor cases annually would be affected.[327] Several broader estimates at the time, using different bases of calculation, found that between 1,000,000 and 1,250,000 persons annually charged with misdemeanors were without funds,[328] and one of the studies concluded that prior to *Argersinger* perhaps as many as 75 percent went unrepresented.[329] It is true that many of these poeple would not qualify under *Argersinger*'s limitation, confirmed by *Scott v. Illinois*,[330] that counsel must be appointed only when imprisonment is imposed. But it is equally beyond cavil that many of those indigents who *did* have lawyers provided at state expense at the time of *Argersinger* would not have had this benefit were it not for the Court's earlier right-to-counsel rulings. Thus, Alabama, which before *Gideon v. Wainwright*[331] had appointed counsel only in capital cases, implemented *Gideon* by assigning lawyers not only for felonies but for serious misdemeanor offenses as well.[332] The Supreme Court of Minnesota, in mandating the *Argersinger* approach as early as 1967, pointed to *Gideon* as the basis for its holding.[333] Indeed, whereas at the time of the *Gideon* decision only five states required appointment of counsel for any misdemeanor, by 1970 twelve states did so for at least some and nineteen more did so for most misdemeanors.[334] In addition, within eighteen months of the *Argersinger* decision, some states (Arizona, North Carolina, and South Dakota) moved to expand the announced right to encompass all or almost all misdemeanors even when only a fine could result.[335] And by 1979 nearly forty states appointed lawyers in connection with any offenses for which imprisonment is authorized, whether or not it is actually imposed.[336] Given the finding of one survey that "misdemeanants represented by attorneys are five times as likely to emerge from police court with all charges dismissed as are defendants who face similar charges without counsel,"[337] it may fairly be said that the *Argersinger* rule significantly affected the personal liberties of many Americans.

ii) The number of persons subject to revocation of probation or parole in the United States is huge. As of the mid-1960s, nearly 700,000 adults and juveniles who had been convicted of criminal offenses were on probation and over 100,000 felons who had been released from prison were on parole.[338] Although more recent figures as to probationers have not been found, by the mid-1970s, the number of parolees on active status had almost doubled.[339] Furthermore, a substantial portion—estimates run from about 25 percent to as high as 45 percent[340]—of all persons who are conditionally released have their probation or parole rescinded.

The precise extent to which the states had afforded procedural due process rights to persons whose probation or parole was sought to be revoked is difficult to ascertain. As for probation, a widely cited 1964 survey reported that the statutes of four jurisdictions (confirmed by judicial decisions in two) expressly authorized revocation without a hearing, and that in at least four additional states the courts had upheld revocation with no hearing whatever.[341] No detailed review of probation revocation procedure appears to have been subsequently undertaken, but the matter of parole has been somewhat more thoroughly examined. In 1970, an update of earlier studies concluded that nine states provided neither notice nor a hearing prior to a parolee's recommitment to prison.[342] Two years later, a Supreme Court review of statutes and judicial decisions observed that "very few States provide no hearing at all in parole revocations."[343] At the same time, a comprehensive national survey found "that by January 1972 *all* jurisdictions had chosen in fact to make use of *some* form of revocation hearing. Only four parole authorities (Iowa, Louisiana, Michigan, and Texas) did not grant parole-revocation hearings to *all* parolees facing return to incarceration."[344]

Assuming that the states followed a similarly progressive path in respect to affording hearings for persons charged with probation violations, the Court's rulings in *Morrissey v. Brewer*[345] and *Gagnon v. Scarpelli*[346] did not revolutionize the procedural rights of parolees and probationers. But the decisions did significantly expand the individual liberties of these groups by bringing about "major restructuring"[347] of state practices. Almost all states had prejudiced an alleged parole violator's opportunity to rebut the charges by granting hearings only at a time well after the parolee's arrest and at the prison in which he had previously been incarcerated, a site that often was a considerable distance from the place in which the purported violation had occurred.[348] In *Morrissey* and *Gagnon,* the Court sought to cure this defect by holding that due process requires that alleged probation and parole violators be granted hearings promptly after their detention at a place near the arrest and also before the final decision on revocation. In addition, *Morrissey* and *Gagnon* imposed a series of procedural safeguards that many states theretofore had not provided. A survey of every parole board in the country—fifty-four in all—completed on the eve of the *Morrissey* decision revealed that, contrary to the Court's mandate, nineteen did not grant the parolee notice of the specific charges, twenty-two did not permit the parolee to present witnesses, twenty-six denied the parolee the right to confront and cross-examine adverse witnesses, and fifty declined to afford the parolee a written statement of the evidence relied on and reasons for revoking parole.[349]

Within months of the Court's pronouncement, a study of parole boards in forty-five states concluded "that most of them are in formal compliance with most of the *Morrissey* requirements."[350] Eighty percent were conducting on-site initial hearings and allowing the parolee to present evidence and witnesses and to confront and cross-examine adverse witnesses. All these states also provided an impartial hearing officer and a final written statement of the reasons for decision. Two-thirds of these states were holding the initial hearing within ten days of notice or arrest, although some parole boards took up to thirty days. As for the revocation hearing, all reporting jurisdictions used impartial review panels. Forty-one of the forty-four states responding assured the parolee an opportunity to be heard and to present witnesses and evidence—nine of the states had instituted this practice in direct response to *Morrissey.* Thirty-eight of the forty states responding permitted confrontation and cross-examination—an immediate increase of ten states. Whereas just prior to *Morrissey* only four parole boards drafted a written statement justifying revocation, thirty-eight of forty-two states did so thereafter. One of the strongest points of compliance with the Court's edict was that all reporting states now provided parolees written notice of specific charges, a change in practice for at least eight boards.[351] Overall, of the forty-five states replying to the survey, seven "expressly pointed out that they were currently involved in efforts to determine what their responsibilities under *Morrissey* consisted of and how they would implement changes required under that decision."[352] In addition, the federal government promptly revised its established parole and probation revocation procedures to comply with the conditions laid down in both *Morrissey* and *Gagnon*.[353]

By 1976, a survey of parole boards of all fifty states, the national government, and the District of Columbia disclosed *unanimous* conformity with virtually all the Court's requirements (although six jurisdictions provided only verbal explanation of their revocation decision).[354]

Furthermore, as of 1972, nearly one-third of the parole boards refused to permit even retained counsel to be present at the revocation hearing, and only a handful appointed lawyers for indigents.[355] And these statistics undoubtedly would have been less generous to the parolees[356] were it not for the decision several years before, in *Mempa v. Rhay*,[357] that counsel is constitutionally required at sentencing even when sentencing is deferred to a probation revocation proceeding. The earlier and less comprehensive data for probation revocations were stronger but still indicated that only half the states provided a lawyer for an indigent alleged probation violator.[358] The extremely important role of counsel for alleged parole and probation violators in effectuating such rights as presentation of evidence and cross-examination of witnesses was confirmed by professional observers[359] of revocation hearings conducted between the time of the *Morrissey* decision (which did not reach the right to counsel issue) and the Court's ruling in *Gagnon* (which held that due process requires the assistance of counsel under certain circumstances). Although in *Gagnon* the Court declined to impose an automatic right to retained and appointed counsel in all revocation hearings, its requirement of legal assistance when needed to assure a fair hearing will surely improve the lot of many probationers and parolees; in fact *Gagnon* has led almost all jurisdictions to permit retained counsel as a matter of course and has caused a majority—including California, New York, and the federal government[360] to provide appointed counsel without any showing of special need.[361]

The Court's rulings have not eliminated all the injustices, present or perceived, in the parole and probation revocation process.[362] For example, it has been contended that, despite *Morrissey*'s establishment of the right to confront and cross-examine adverse witnesses, the New York parole board "never produces any witnesses, other than parole officers . . . . The parole officer's testimony usually contains substantial amounts of hearsay, and violation charges are not infrequently sustained, solely or in large part, on the basis of hearsay."[363] Nonetheless, the fact that the parole officer himself may be confronted at the hearing represents a significant advance over the revocation authorities' common previous practice of relying exclusively on written reports.[364] Further, at least in some instances, *Morrissey* and *Gagnon* have motivated reforms beyond the minimums stipulated— such as granting subpoena power to the parties in the revocation dispute,[365] permitting parolees some discovery rights prior to their revocation hearing,[366] providing them an opportunity to appeal an adverse revocation decision, and applying certain due process rights to parole release hearings as well as to revocation proceedings.[367] And parole officials' post-*Morrissey* statements that "fewer revocations are now proposed on the basis of technical violations,"[368] further evidences the favorable impact on personal liberty that the Court's efforts produced.

iii) In 1976, the Court announced that the death penalty did not, in all circumstances, violate the Constitution.[369] But other decisions in the 1970s, in which the Court held that various forms of capital punishment contravene the eighth amendment, were of literally life-saving importance to many people. The ruling in *Furman v. Georgia*,[370] invalidating the capital punishment laws of thirty-nine states and several federal statutory provisions, prohibited the execution of 633 prisoners on death row.[371] "All were entitled to new sentences of life imprisonment, to a term of years or, in a few cases, to new trials. The precise disposition was up to the state courts."[372] None was put to death.[373] The experience of the twenty-one Massachusetts persons affected by *Furman* is instructive: eighteen had their sentences reduced, two were retried and acquitted, and one committed suicide.[374] As a result of *Woodson v. North Carolina*,[375] in which the Court rejected mandatory capital punishment for specified offenses, 278 inmates had their death sentences rescinded.[376]

The consequences of the Justices' holding in *Lockett v. Ohio*,[377] which required that the sentencer consider all mitigating factors proffered by the defendant, are less precisely calculable. Since only nine of the thirty-four states that then had capital statutes conformed to this new standard,[378] serious doubt was cast over the laws of the other states, whose death rows contained approximately 135 prisoners.[379] What is clear, however, is that *Lockett*—and state court decisions from Pennsylvania and New York which anticipated its reasoning[380]—preserved the lives of ninety-nine inmates in Ohio and twelve in Pennsylvania (numbers from New York are unavailable),[381] apart from those others still to be tried before an acceptable death penalty statute is enacted.

Of probably greatest significance—at least for the future—is the Court's holding in *Coker v. Georgia*[382] that the death sentence may not be imposed for the crime of rape of an adult woman. *Coker*'s immediate effect was to save thirty-four persons then under such sentence from capital punishment.[383] The number whose lives will be spared in years that follow may, of course, only be conjectured. But the fact that 455 people were executed for rape between 1930 and 1968[384] foretells the substantial number of individuals involved.

It may be that even those rulings that upheld capital punishment have "opened up new possibilities that with imaginative and resourceful litigation may avoid or nullify many death sentences."[385] But there is no question that the Court's decisions upsetting death penalty laws have supremely influenced the personal liberties of thousands of people.

iv) As of the early 1970s, statutes in all states provided that persons might be civilly committed to public mental institutions against their will.[386] Although there were some indications that the annual number of involuntary admissions was declining,[387] and estimates of the exact number of such persons so confined at any time varied somewhat, there was no dispute that the figure was very large—ranging from about 500,000 to over 700,000.[388] Statutory criteria justifying involuntary commitment differed significantly, but as of 1974 less than one-third of the states limited such custody to persons who were either unable to care for their physical needs or were dangerous to themselves or others.[389] The great majority of jurisdictions authorized compulsory confinement under much more expansive standards, such as whether the individual was in need of care or treatment or was a fit subject for hospitalization.[390] Moreover, some states adopted criteria even looser for determining whether involuntarily confined persons could obtain their release than for justifying their initial commitment.[391]

For several reasons, it is not possible accurately to assess the precise effect of the Supreme Court's 1975 decision in *O'Connor v. Donaldson*,[392] which delineated a substantive "constitutional right to liberty"[393] for those held involuntarily in mental institutions. First, regardless of the scope of this personal right, the ruling's impact on individual liberty must be reduced somewhat by the relatively short time that the average person is confined. For example, in 1971 "86.9% of the total number of voluntary and involuntary patients who were admitted to state and county mental hospitals were discharged within 6 months of admission," and "the median length of stay in these hospitals was 41 days."[394] These naked statistics, however, should not mask *O'Connor*'s potential importance for the substantial number of mental patients whose much longer deprivation of freedom is submerged in the calculations. Thus, Donaldson himself was kept in custody against his will for nearly fifteen years;[395] 1973 data from West Virginia revealed that the average stay for involuntary admittees was over fifteen years and that more than half these inmates had been held for more than a decade;[396] National Institute of Mental Health figures for five states showed that in 1966 and 1968 the median period of confinement ranged between four and a half and eight and a half years; and in 1969 a majority of the patients in Saint Elizabeth's Hospital in Washington, D.C., had been there over five years.[397]

But the major obstacle in determining *O'Connor*'s direct consequences for individual rights is the extremely restricted scope of the Court's opinion. The record showed that Donaldson posed no danger to himself or others, had the capacity to earn his own living outside the institution in which he had been confined, had responsible people willing to provide him any help he might need on release, and had received nothing but custodial care while at the hospital.[398] On these facts, the Court held that "a State cannot constitutionally confine without more a nondangerous individual who is capable of surviving safely in freedom by himself or with the help of willing and responsible family members or friends."[399] But it specifically declined to decide "whether the State may compulsorily confine a nondangerous, mentally ill individual for the purpose of treatment"[400]—that is, "whether the provision of treatment, standing alone, can ever constitutionally justify involuntary confinement."[401]*

O'Connor was initially greeted by many observers as a near boundless declaration of freedom for mental patients—as a "renunciation of the past practice of warehousing human beings in conditions which were really comparable to Dante's Inferno."[402] Since it was believed that "the vast majority of mentally ill individuals will not engage in dangerous behavior if they are permitted to retain their freedom,"[403] on the day after the decision the *New York Times* speculated that the Court's edict "appeared likely to force the ultimate release from mental institutions of thousands of the estimated 250,000 patients regarded as untreated, harmless and not likely to become community charges."[404] A week later, *Time* magazine reported an American

---

* In a separate concurrence, however, Chief Justice Berger did advance the view that a state could not, consistently with due process, "confine an individual thought to need treatment and justify that deprivation of liberty solely by providing some treatment." 422 U.S. 563, 589 (1975).

Psychiatric Association estimate that 90 percent of compulsorily detained mental patients were not sufficiently damaging to themselves or others to require hospitalization.[405]

These early predictions, however, were not rapidly fulfilled. Surveys in the months immediately following the Court's pronouncement found that very few patients attained their freedom as a direct result of the decision.[406] Rather, mental institution officials explained the continued detention of almost all involuntary admittees by correctly pointing out that *O'Connor* "did not rule on the major form of treatment normally given state patients—drugs."[407]

These facts notwithstanding, the impact of judicial review—if not of the narrow holding in the *O'Connor* case itself—on the personal liberties of involuntarily confined mental patients has been very significant. Both shortly before and soon after the Supreme Court's decision in *O'Connor,* a number of lower federal courts ruled that due process forbids compulsory civil commitment of people unless they are either (1) likely to inflict physical harm on themselves or others, or (2) are not able to survive safely in freedom.[408] Under the rationale of these decisions, the mere fact that a person is considered to be mentally ill and in need of treatment cannot constitutionally support involuntary hospitalization. In at least five of the states in which the federal courts had held the involuntary commitment procedures to be invalid, the state legislatures responded by revising their statutes to conform to the judicially announced criteria.[409] Further, whereas a 1974 comprehensive survey of state civil commitment laws revealed that "fifteen jurisdictions authorize commitment only if the individual is mentally ill and dangerous to himself or others or is unable to care for his physical needs,"[410] within the next three years the lawmaking bodies of about fifteen additional states amended their more loosely drawn statutes to adopt this tighter definition.[411] The experience in Virginia—where the commissioner of mental health reported that the statute was reformed "in partial anticipation"[412] of *O'Connor*—is instructive: within a five-year period, the state's institutional population was reduced from seventeen thousand to ten thousand, of whom only seven hundred were involuntarily confined.[413]

Thus, the Burger Court's decision in *O'Connor*—along with its progeny and forebears in other federal courts—has, even in the short run, directly and indirectly advanced the cause of personal freedom. By preserving or restoring the liberty of many mentally ill persons, judicial review has greatly contributed to the prevention of the loss of various legal rights and the suffering of economic, social, and psychological injuries[414] which were "often barely distinguishable from the analogous burdens imposed on criminals"[415] and may have been even more severe.

v) Few decisions of the Supreme Court have invalidated as many state regulations as those dealing with the constitutional right to an abortion. As recently as 1967, just six years before the foundational ruling in *Roe v. Wade*,[416] no state in the nation permitted an abortion except to save the life of the mother.[417] By 1973, in response to positions espoused by several national professional groups (including both the American Medical Association and the American Bar Association) and to a rapidly growing public attitude favoring liberalized abortion,[418] four states— Alaska, Hawaii, New York, and Washington—enacted statutes that effectively legalized abortion on request and about fifteen other jurisdictions followed the Model Penal Code's proposal to authorize therapeutic abortions for the mental health as well as for the life or physical health of the pregnant woman.[419] Indeed, California might well be classed in the most lenient group—at least for those women who could afford a psychiatric opinion attesting to the emotional damage that childbirth would bring.[420]

On the other side of the spectrum, the laws of five states— Connecticut, Louisiana, Massachusetts, New Jersey, and Pennsylvania—blanketly prohibited abortions under all circumstances (although there were mitigating court rulings in each jurisdiction), and about half the states continued to follow the traditional pattern by allowing an abortion only to preserve the mother's life. Mississippi extended its exception to pregnancies caused by rape.[421] Even many of the permissive statutes limited abortions to a period of gestation which fell short of that prescribed by the Justices in *Roe*.[422] And a substantial majority of these more tolerant jurisdictions also imposed residency requirements and other sundry restrictions on abortions—such as demanding that they be performed in a hospital licensed by the state or approved by the Joint Commission on Accreditation of Hospitals, or concurred in by a second physician or hospital staff committee[423]—that were struck down by the Court in the companion case of *Doe v. Bolton*.[424] In the subsequent decision of *Planned Parenthood of Central Missouri v. Danforth*,[425] the Court invalidated additional barriers to abortion—which existed in about fifteen states[426]—such as the need for spousal consent and for parental consent in the case of an unmarried minor. The *Danforth* ruling also rejected the express or implied prohibition of five jurisdictions against use of the saline amniocentesis method of abortion.[427] Finally, in *Colautti v. Franklin*,[428] the Justices cast a considerable cloud on the validity of statutes in approximately one-third of the states that oblige doctors who perform abortions to take measures to preserve the life and health of the fetus if it appears to be viable.[429]

The consequences for individuals, while not precisely calculable, have, nonetheless, been momentous. As a statistical matter, the number of reported legal abortions in the United States has grown from about 50,000 in 1969 (before New York's reform) to just under 600,000 in 1972[430] (the final pre-*Roe* year) to nearly 1,000,000 in 1976.[431] This fact has several ramifications.

First, although estimates of criminal abortions prior to *Roe* and *Doe* vary drastically (ranging from 50,000 to 1,200,000 annually),[432] there is no doubt that their number has decreased sharply (perhaps as much as 70 percent since the late 1960s).[433] While liberalization has by no means eliminated all inept and malign abortion services,[434] the fact remains that the risk of death from an illegal abortion is twelve times greater than from a legal one[435] and that mortalities resulting from abortion have diminished markedly. Thus, in New York, whereas maternal death from criminal abortions comprised nearly half of all maternal mortalities in 1961, only one such death was recorded in the first six months under the liberalized regime.[436] In California, death from illegal abortions declined from twenty-seven in 1960 to none in 1976.[437] Nationally, although it has been asserted that 8,000 women were killed each year in criminal abortions,[438] more conservative estimates prior to the advent of reform in 1967 placed the figure at between 250 and 500.[439] In 1968 to 1970, an average of fifty-seven women died annually from illegal abortions;[440] the figures subsequent to *Roe* were nineteen in 1973, six in 1974, four in 1975, and three in 1976[441]—and in 1976 only ten maternal deaths were associated with legally induced abortions.[442]

Apart from mortalities, since legal abortions are indisputably safer than criminal ones, an untold number of women have also avoided being permanently maimed, becoming sterile, or suffering other serious illness as a result of the Court's mandate. Further, since it is generally agreed that the availability of lawful abortions will result in most being performed in the early stages of pregnancy, and since medical complications from abortion vary directly with the gestation period, all statistics imply a lower complication rate as the product of legalization.[443] For example, the number of women admitted to New York hospitals for abortion-related afflictions was cut in half between 1969 and 1973.[444]

Second, the Court's recognition of an individual's constitutional right to an abortion has meant that a great many women, either unwilling or afraid to violate the law, have been able to forgo unwanted pregnancy and childbirth. Whereas over 1,000,000 women who sought an abortion in 1973 could not obtain one, by 1977 this figure had been reduced by 50 percent.[445] This has resulted in substantial benefits for maternal life and physical health since it has been found anywhere from four to eight times more dangerous to complete a pregnancy than to have a legal abortion[446]—indeed, in 1976 there were nearly fifteen times more deaths per 100,000 births than per 100,000 legal abortions.[447] Thus, after New York removed its prohibition, maternal mortality associated with childbirth fell nearly 60 percent—"the most logical explanation for this dramatic improvement in public health is that a large number of abortions are being performed on women in high-risk age and health groups, thus significantly lowering childbirth fatality."[448] The extent to which undesired pregnancies and children impair the mental health and stability of mothers and their families is less ascertainable. But psychiatric studies attest to the general phenomenon,[449] and the existence of children with mutilated minds and bodies attributable to such causes as thalidomide and rubella (30,000 in 1964 alone)[450] strongly indicate that these problems, too, have been greatly relieved.

Finally, by making legal abortions obtainable throughout the country, the Court's rulings have significantly eased the burden, peril, and expense of obtaining one. In 1972, 44 percent of all women who received lawful abortions were forced to travel outside their state of residence to do so,[451] thus frequently delaying the procedure "to a later and riskier period of gestation. Distance also makes rapid diagnosis and treatment of any post-abortion complications difficult."[452] By 1976, only 10 percent of the pregnant women were so encumbered[453] (though about 25 percent did have to go to another county within their own state).[454] Similarly, in 1970, after California and New York had removed their barriers to abortion but before the Justices mandated this system for the nation, 81 percent of all legal abortions performed in the United States took place in those two states (where approximately one-fifth of all women between the ages of fifteen and forty-four lived);[455] by 1976, this number had fallen to 29 percent.[456]

It is impossible to know at this time the full extent to which the Court's 1977 decision in *Maher v. Roe*,[457] which permitted the government to withhold medicaid benefits from indigent women for elective abortions, will diminish the impact of *Roe v. Wade* and its earlier progeny. In 1976, nearly one-third of all legal abortions were financed by medicaid,[458] and within just over a year of *Maher*, only fifteen jurisdictions continued to pay for all or most abortions for poor women.[459] In some "states where medicaid dollars have been cut off, the impact on abortion services has been dramatic. In Arkansas, for example, the number of abortions paid for by these funds has dropped from 500 in 1976 to 5 during the period of August, 1977, to June, 1978; in South Carolina from 1,400 to 14; in Texas from 13,300 to 59."[460] Although there is no doubt that many indigent women resigned themselves to completing their pregnancies, many others managed to gain assistance without reverting "to dangerous back-alley or coat-hanger abortions."[461] Some county governments granted funds despite their elimination by the state.[462] While private physicians often declined to provide services without assurance of their fees,[463] a number have been willing to make special arrangements for payment.[464] Once again, a growing number of women pursued the riskier and burdensome route of crossing state lines to satisfy their needs—an estimated 2,000 from Maine alone in less than a year after *Maher*.[465] And many private clinics either reduced their fees or abandoned them altogether—"for example, the Cullen Women's Center in Houston, Tex., where more than half the women requesting abortion services cannot pay, has spent $15,500 for abortions that used to be covered by public-assistance funds."[466] Thus, in mid-1978, it was reported that *Maher*'s adverse consequences were still relatively limited in that "70 percent of all medicaid-supported abortions are performed in a few major states such as New York, California and Pennsylvania, and up until now these states have continued liberal funding."[467] Within less than a month, however, California removed itself from this category, thereby rendering the situation considerably less encouraging.

Because the liberalizing statutory trend began several years before the Burger Court's auspicious abortion rulings in 1973, not all the imposing developments that have since occurred may be fairly attributed to the Justices' intervention. But especially because of the many hostile state legislative reactions, it is equally fair to conclude that *Roe v. Wade* greatly hastened the drive toward abortion legalization and dramatically affected the lives and liberties of an enormous number of women. It is this impact of the Supreme Court's abortion decisions, rather than the question of whether as a matter of substantive constitutional doctrine the Court overstepped its proper bounds, that is the critical issue here. The longevity of the decisions' effect, as we have seen, is highly uncertain at present, particularly because the matter of public funding for the indigent is in such a state of flux. But even if the statistical increases are reversed and eventually return to near their original position, the powerful consequences for personal liberty that have already taken place cannot be undone.

VI. LIMITS AND REACH OF JUDICIAL INFLUENCE

All the foregoing notwithstanding, the judiciary's power is neither unlimited nor a panacea for all of society's anti-libertarian ills. Its constitutional role is limited to protecting those individual rights that are unambiguously expressed or that at least may in some persuasive way fairly be found within the broad philosophical confines of the basic charter. And, as eloquently stated by Justice Jackson, "perfect resistance to forces of hysteria which sometimes permeate the whole social fabric is not to be expected from any institution."[468] Thus, in one recent account of the judicial defense of the first amendment rights of political radicals, it was argued that the Court cannot be viewed "as a bastion of liberty, holding out against the forces of repression."[469] More specifically, the Justices' failure to rule for personal freedom in the series of post–World War I cases under the Espionage and Sedition Acts (and state counterparts that sought to silence anarchists and syndicalists) is found explicable because "intervention on behalf of those whose expression was being curbed would have been highly unpopular and perhaps impolitic";[470] the Court's affirmances of legislative authority in the early 1950s (when McCarthyism was at its zenith) were "reflective of the general desire in our society to sacrifice the rights of radicals in the name of national security";[471] only the demise of Senator McCarthy and the Court's perception of a moderated popular emotion emboldened it in the mid-1950s to reject repressive action; but even this judicial thrust for freedom was short-lived because "the Court misjudged the temper of the times" and "proceeded to step back in the next three years,"[472] ultimately returning to the libertarian path after 1961 only when the political climate had changed in fact.

Whether this psycho-historical appraisal—and others that sound a similar theme in respect to virtually all that the Court has done—accurately describes the Justices' constitutional decisionmaking process, or whether it represents no more than a post hoc rationalization of decisions that would have come out otherwise if different judges had sat, or whether the broadly protective formulations of dissenting opinions would have become the holdings of the Court if the minority's sentiment had captured a majority are matters neither known nor demonstrable. But both the portrayal and its uncertainty are beside the point. For within a dozen years of such restrictive post–World War I rulings as *Schenck, Abrams,* and *Gitlow,*[473] the Court sustained free speech claims in *Fiske v. Kansas*[474] (on the same day of its denial in *Whitney*),[475] *Stromberg v. California,*[476] and *Near v. Minnesota;*[477] and within another six years it reversed convictions in *DeJonge v. Oregon*[478] and *Herndon v. Lowry.*[479] McCarthyism notwithstanding, in the same opening years of the 1950s in which the Court rejected first amendment pleas in *Dennis, Garner,* and *Adler,*[480] it provided some succor to suspected subversives under other constitutional clauses in *Blau v. United States,*[481] *Stack v. Boyle,*[482] and *Wieman v. Updegraff*[483]—at the same time opening other strictures on free expression in *Joseph Burstyn, Inc. v. Wilson.*[484] In the several succeeding years, the Court's narrow statutory reading in *Yates*[485] caused the Department of Justice to drop all relevant pending prosecutions save one;[486] and—just as earlier judicial pronouncements had aborted a 1940 congressional effort to deport Harry Bridges by name and had ameliorated even harsher provisions than those legislated in the McCarran Act of 1950[487]—so, too, the "cumulative impact" of the series of nonconstitutional rulings in *Cole v. Young,*[488] *Service v. Dulles,*[489] *Vitarelli v. Seaton,*[490] and *Greene v. McElroy*[491] "undoubtedly diminished the scope and curbed several excesses"[492] of the national government's loyalty programs. And, despite the hostile political reaction between 1958 and 1961, when a narrowly divided Court upheld government security measures in *Barenblatt, Scales,* and *Konigsberg II,*[493] the decisions in *Speiser v. Randall*[494] and *Noto v. United States*[495] show that the Court was not wholly disdainful of the speech and association interests of leftist dissidents. Indeed, in addition to continuing the invalidation of overbroad censorship regimes in *Kingsley Int'l Pictures Corp. v. Regents,*[496] it was during these years that the Justices first undertook—in *NAACP v. Alabama,*[497] *Bates v. City of Little Rock,*[498] and *Shelton v. Tucker*[499]—to secure the first amendment rights of minority groups and their members in their fight against racial injustice.

This is by no means to suggest that the Court's record in regard to the first amendment rights of political radicals and others has been uniformly libertarian or that its pronouncements in respect to individual rights have been completely uninfluenced by the popular mood. Nor is it to contend that those decisions that affirmed majority will were substantively wrong. Whether and to what degree the Justices, individually or collectively, are guided by perceived public attitudes is at least as complex a psycho-empirical problem as whether their constitutional interpretations are "right" as a doctrinal matter. But there has been no effective refutation of the well-grounded intuition that no matter how repressive the political climate, the cause of personal liberty has been better served by the Court's participation than it would have been without it. Further, our focus has been almost exclusively on the product of the Supreme Court. But, as illustrated by the discussion of *O'Connor v. Donaldson,* the recent achievements for individual liberties of the lower federal courts, largely undirected by specific precedents from the Justices—in regard to the interests of such persons as prisoners[500] as well as mentally ill detainees—underlines the effectiveness of judicial review.

It may well be that "when public opinion reaches the proportions of a tidal wave, no merely intellectual appeal can stop it."[501] In the long run, it is only an informed and sensitive citizenry and an educated and enlightened political process that will fulfill the nation's loftiest and proudest visions. But, for practical purposes, political sentiments that reach heights short of tidal waves and time spans briefer than the long run may be more pertinent. For our experience shows that numerous actions of the majority will that have sorely damaged constitutional freedoms remain in force until the Court rules, but subside thereafter. Much of the time, the Justices' mandate simply triumphs; on most other occasions, it prevails for long periods of time—"for more than a decade and even more than a generation."[502] Indeed, as we shall see in chapter 3, even when there are immediate and substantial pockets of resistance to the Court's pronouncements—as, for example, with denominational prayers and racial segregation in the schools—the fact is that in many parts of the country the beneficiaries of the Justices' decisions promptly enjoy the fruits.

The dynamics of the matter are complex and often interwoven. In part this may be attributed to the fact that—as one empirical study has concluded—quite often "the Court can take far-reaching action . . . [in behalf of individual liberty] without ever making a dent in the public consciousness."[503] Beyond this, the people, although often discontentedly, usually heed judicial appeals to conscience and selflesssness; the Court's message may have a proselytizing and sobering effect, often converting an impetuous popular mind into one more receptive to reason.[504] Moreover, the Court's rulings on behalf of personal rights may displace antilibertarian policies which commanded adequate popular support for enactment but which cannot muster sufficient political backing for reinstatement after judicial invalidation; inertia is a powerful ally for the sustenance of the Court's views. These phenomena, in turn, may be the product of the educative and symbolic force that the Court's constitutional views have on both the general citizenry and its elected leaders,[505] or of the psychological encouragement and enhanced ability for attracting adherents and resources that the Justices' imprimatur affords to those minority groups who are working in the political process as well as the courts to preserve individual liberties.[506] Perhaps this helps explain the fact that the incredibly oppressive intolerances for political dissent that existed during World War I,[507] before the Court had given substantive thrust to the first amendment, were not so ignominiously duplicated during World War II and were markedly less discernible during the prolonged conflict in Indochina.

Further, even when the Court admittedly retrenches in the face of public dissatisfaction, it often leaves a distinctly wider area of constitutional liberty than would have existed were it not for the judiciary's original intervention. It may be acknowledged, for example, that the Court's regression in *Miller v. California*[508] permits government a substantially broader authority to regulate sexual materials than did *Roth v. United States*[509] and its progeny. But surely the impact of the earlier rulings on the freedoms to communicate and receive information and ideas has been far from totally dissipated.[510] Indeed, experience—both recent and historic[511]—shows that in more than a few states the complete sphere of liberty opened by the Court's initial generous interpretations of personal rights remains, and may even be expanded, by the influence of those decisions—at least in part, it is fair to infer—on state courts' constructions of their own constitutions.[512]

Finally, to concede that occasions may arise when the political forces are so fervent and immense as completely to overcome the Court's edict or cause it eventually to succumb fully is not at all to refute the Court's essential role. For, in the other instances as well as these, the judiciary is literally the court of last resort since, by definition, the political agencies have patently determined to reject the claims of personal liberty.

VII. CONCLUSION

Like all human, as well as governmental, institutions, the Supreme Court does not have an unblemished record. Indeed, the advantage of hindsight has proved that some of its decisions regarding the line between individual autonomy and collective need—both validating and disapproving the popular will—have been manifestly wrong. Some have been failures when judged either by their internal logic or their public acceptance or both. The Court has at times in the past—as it assuredly will in the future—ruled both too timidly and too vigorously. It "may mistake what is fundamental and enduring, as we now think it mistook the importance of 'liberty of contract,' but where it errs, its judgments will surely yield, as they yielded in that instance, to the slow pressures of unfolding history."[513]

Nonetheless, the Court has also accomplished much, both for the substance of liberty and—especially under the equal protection clause in the apportionment cases and others which removed shackles on the exercise of the franchise—for the furtherance of the goals of democracy. Even when the Court's decisions reject the claim of violation of constitutional liberty, the availability of judicial review on behalf of political minorities often works to reassure these persons and groups and frequently tends to encourage acquiescence in laws they strongly deplore. Justice Story perhaps overstated when he opined that "in other governments, these questions cannot be entertained or decided by courts of justice; and, therefore, whatever may be the theory of the constitution, the legislative authority is practically omnipotent, and there is no means of contesting the legality or justice of a law, but by an appeal to arms."[514] But, if judicial review were nonexistent for popularly frustrated minorities, the fight, already lost in the legislative halls, would have only one remaining battleground—the streets. Apart from some radical change in our political ethos that would render consideration by the Court unnecessary, the alternatives to judicial review for individual constitutional rights are either disobedience of the law or discontented acceptance. Both options—violence and decadence—are antithetical to basic democratic precepts. These truths would be even more manifest if judicial review were unavailable to question the legitimacy and legality of the people's elected representatives' ceasing to represent the majority of their constituents.

In fulfilling this key role in American government, the Court is confronted with an inescapable dilemma. As will be explored in detail in the following chapter, on the one hand, the securing of personal liberty in opposition to majority will inevitably generates some degree of public disfavor—popular disapproval not infrequently passed deliberately on to the Court by political agencies who, as we have seen, well appreciate what they are doing. On the other hand, effective judicial defense of constitutional rights demands at least some degree of public acceptance. The Court's great task and responsibility is to negotiate these narrow straits successfully.

Three

The Fragile Character
of Judicial Review

*The Problems of Popular
Noncompliance and Exhaustible
Institutional Capital*

I. THE NATURE OF THE PROBLEM

Over the course of its constitutional stewardship, from
the earliest years of the nineteenth century to the closing decades of the twentieth, the Supreme Court's use of the power of
judicial review has made it a continuing subject of national controversy, often rendering its position highly insecure and several
times pushing it close to the brink of defeat. As will be discussed
in chapter 4, many of its rulings, such as *McCulloch v. Maryland,*
that have legitimated the exercise of government authority by
holding that political action conforms to the fundamental charter
have generated bitter hostility and genuine threats to the Court's
continued existence. But the most menacing challenges have
been reserved for those occasions when the Court, itself with no
direct political responsibility and with only the most tenuous
links to the popular will, commands that the wishes of the
people, expressed by elected representatives or designees
within their control, must be disregarded. The Court's capacity
to beget public enmity by decisions that reject political judgments believed necessary for effective governance is easily

fulfilled, and its ability to obtain compliance with those mandates that thwart the popular will is greatly circumscribed.

A. Invalidations Not Contrary to Popular Will

There are a series of related and progressively interacting factors at play that often expose the Court to antagonism when it invalidates actions by political bodies. It is true that some of the actions the Court finds unconstitutional do not represent deliberately considered judgments of effectively responsible political agencies. Rather, the judicially condemned program may be one of low visibility, promulgated and administered by an inconspicuous bureaucrat, which may have continued to operate because of public ignorance or political indifference. Or the Court's rulings may reject only narrow applications of federal or state laws—or, yet more frequently, of municipal ordinances—thus only marginally affecting the popular will and leaving largely intact the basic policies that the legislation seeks to further. Indeed, as adverted to in chapter 1,[1] the specific practice disapproved may actually be contrary to the values or desires of a majority of the people and their elected representatives but, because of the complexity or delicacy of the problem to which the action is directed or to its relative unimportance, the coalition of interests necessary for its replacement or outright elimination cannot be (or has not yet been) suitably organized. In instances such as these, the Court's invalidation may either be generally overlooked or greeted with varying degrees of approval or enthusiasm.

B. Invalidations Contrary to Popular Will

Judicial invalidation of unpopular programs is atypical, however. The customary exercise of judicial review, in the words of President William Howard Taft, "tends to put the court constantly in opposition to the legislature and executive, and, indeed, to the popular supporters of unconstitutional laws."[2] This is most apparent—as we shall soon observe in detail—when the Court strikes against an act of Congress (or the executive). It cannot be inferred from this, however, that federal judicial negations of state and local actions—by far the most frequent objects of the Court's maledictions—usually disapprove of mere isolated schemes without broad popular support. For, in a great many of these cases, the practice is not confined to a single state or locality but instead is widespread throughout the nation. Thus, for example, five months after the Supreme Court found the death penalty as it was then administered to be unconstitutional, 64 percent of the public respondents with an opinion on the issue advocated capital punishment for murderers.[3] Moreover, more than five years after the Court's rulings to the contrary, almost 75 percent of the populace continued to favor prayers in public schools[4] and nearly 60 percent would prohibit abortions during the second trimester when only the mental health of the pregnant women was endangered.[5] Indeed, as will be documented shortly, some of the Court's gravest difficulties, not only with state officials but with the national political branches as well, have come in response to judicial review of state and local programs.

II. THE REASONS FOR PUBLIC HOSTILITY

A. PECULIAR QUALITY OF CONSTITUTIONAL DECISIONMAKING

Certain unique characteristics of the Supreme Court as a government institution and of judicial review as an operating force merit emphasis in this context. It requires no elaboration to acknowledge that the Supreme Court passes on a great many fundamental questions arising in society and thus functions in a most highly charged political milieu, more so than virtually any other judicial body in the world, state or foreign, past or present. What is sometimes less clearly recognized are certain vital features that distinguish the normal work of courts, either in fashioning common law or interpreting statutes and the like, from the federal judiciary's exercise of the power of judicial review—traits that focus public attention and political debate on the Supreme

Court in a manner unknown to other courts. Unlike judicial review, which normally operates against—literally, "reviews"— value judgments that have already been delicately balanced and finally resolved in the political process, judicial development of common law principles occurs only when no such political action has been taken. Rather than being perceived as the censurer of the consensus of the popular will, which is the task of the Court in judicial review, the common law judge's duty—as Cardozo explained—"to declare the law in accordance with reason and justice is seen to be a phase of his duty to declare it in accordance with custom," to act "as the interpreter for the community of its sense of law of order."[6] In even starker contrast to the rejection-of-the-people's-choice function of judicial review, the judicial process of statutory interpretation is exclusively designed to fulfill the matured policy decisions of the political branches. And, if judges articulating common law precepts or interpreting enacted rules misconceive announced community sentiment or miscalculate values presently held, the legislative remedies available through conventional democratic means diminish the need for popular disagreement to be expressed by condemnation and disdain.

B. PROTECTION OF POLITICALLY WEAK AND UNPOPULAR GROUPS

The hostility engendered by these elements of judicial review is compounded by others. Not only do most judicial invalidations cut against the grain of deliberate majority choice, but many—especially those, as we have seen, in defense of individual constitutional liberties—do so in favor of small minorities against whom there are large numbers of people and with whom few segments of the population identify. Thus, in a recent statewide survey in Michigan, nearly four-fifths of those polled believed "that the courts have gone too far in making rulings which protect people who get in trouble with the law."[7] Of perhaps greater importance is the fact that many of these minorities—especially racial and religious groups, political dissidents, and persons accused of crime, who have been the most recent beneficiaries of the Court's mandates—are not only politically insignificant in quantitative terms but often in qualitative terms as well, frequently being bereft of any specific political force or general public influence. Unlike such earlier recipients of the Court's protection as the business community and propertied interests, these later groups are incapable of affording the Court organized political support.[8]

Even when the Court's decisions overturning politically enacted ordinances redound to the advantage of large portions of the population—indeed, on occasion, to the benefit of a numerical majority—reaction to them is usually not unmixed. For example, the Court's "one person–one vote" rulings of the mid-1960s in respect to state legislative apportionment, which enunciated a deep-rooted value shared by most Americans and enhanced the voting power of a majority of citizens, were generally received with popular acclaim. A Gallup poll at the time indicated that more than 60 percent of the responding public supported the Court's edicts.[9] Nonetheless, shortly thereafter, on two separate occasions, over half the members of the United States Senate joined in Senator Everett Dirksen's harsh criticism of the decisions and supported his proposed constitutional amendment to modify their impact.

C. Intense Reactions of Losers

This illustration of recent vintage is in accord with a phenomenon whose recurrence may be observed at varying times during the history of the Court's existence. All judicial decisions produce losers, and many exercises of judicial review—for minorities as well as for majorities, invalidations as well as legitimations—find the losers incensed over a burning issue of national moment with scant hope of change through democratic processes. The Court, being the agency of final resort and having spoken the last word, presents a convenient focal point for unhappiness and invective, irrespective of the direction in which its mandate happens to have run.

It is true that some groups who have triumphed in the process of judicial review will often rise to the Court's defense—as did the commercial and financial communities during the heyday of substantive due process in the first third of this century, and the voices of civil liberties through the halcyon days of the Warren Court. Indeed, there may be periods when the Court's invalidations of legislative and executive action actually enhance its overall public standing. But both intuition and experience indicate that, at least as compared to losers, winners' memories are shorter-lived and their Court-related efforts less sustained. Recent research in the fields of social psychology and political science tends to confirm this intuitive sense that "negative opinions exercise disproportionate influence in political behavior. Studies utilizing a variety of experimental settings have consistently shown that the perceived negative aspects of a stimulus object are more determinative of the overall evaluation of the object than its positive aspects."[10] Thus, in a detailed study of electoral contests, it appeared that "first, failures of incumbents are more important than their achievements, and despite a long list of accomplishments, a conspicuous failure may threaten re-election. Second, the greater strength of negative evaluations suggests that voters upset with an incumbent's performance will be more activated to vote against the individual than are satisfied voters likely to support him."[11] Just as it has been found that "political parties are 'punished' by the voters for economic downturns but are not 'rewarded' accordingly for prosperity,"[12] so, too, the Justices seem more readily to be the objects of scorn than the recipients of praise.

In practice, it is not that present victors (who were earlier losers) before the Court now join forces with the currently vanquished to challenge it. The recent winners may well support the Justices or at least remain passive when their opponents mount the offensive. But defeat seems to be the greater energizer, even when the attackers have been previous beneficiaries of the Court's rulings. Now having lost, many political or geographic segments of the populace find little difficulty in launching broad-side assaults on the Court. Thus, hauntingly paralleling the desertion and excoriation of Hubert Humphrey in 1968 by long-time devotees because of his association with the Vietnam war, at that same time—which was near the zenith of the Warren Court's liberalism—one NAACP official, disappointed principally by the Court's failure to invalidate de facto school segregation and its approval of some restrictions on civil rights demonstrators, condemned it as "an institution which has not departed from the American tradition of treating Negroes as second-class citizens" and which "has struck down only the symbols of racism while condoning or overlooking the ingrained practices which have meant the survival of white supremacy in the United States, North and South."[13]

Moreover, it is immediate results rather than legal theories that appear to make the difference. Selecting a specific area of doctrinal dispute, Charles Warren wrote in the 1920s that "throughout American history, devotion to State-Rights and opposition to the jurisdiction of the Federal Government and the Federal Judiciary, whether in the South or in the North, has been based, not so much on dogmatic, political theories or beliefs, as upon the particular economic, political or social legislation which the decisions of the Court happened to sustain or overthrow. No State and no section of the Union has found any difficulty in adopting or opposing the State-Rights theory, whenever its interest lay that way."[14]

This whose-ox-is-gored course of conduct was dramatically confirmed from the 1930s to the 1960s in the reversal by political conservatives on the one hand and traditional liberals on the other on the judicial activism–judicial restraint range. It has been further underlined by the often harsh and apocalyptic criticism of the incumbent Justices (who, as we have seen in chapter 2, are by no means singlemindedly conservative and are seemingly a good deal more sensitive to individual rights than is the citizenry as a whole) by many libertarian admirers of the Warren Court. For example, Laurence Tribe has expressed the belief that "the Burger Court has been animated by a specific substantive vision of the proper relationship between individuals and government—a vision I regard as bordering on the authoritarian, unduly beholden to the status quo, and insufficiently sensitive to human rights and needs."[15] And, with heightened rhetoric, Leonard Levy recently concluded that "the lawyers who today constitute the majority of the Court in most criminal-justice cases are no damn good as judges. They are more like advocates for law enforcement's cause."[16]

A further variation of the Court's exposure is manifested by one type of discontent expressed about the "quality" or "style" of some of the Warren Court's opinions. For example, in the criminal procedural area, the Court's ad hoc search and seizure rulings and coerced confession decisions were criticized as being so confined to the particular facts of the cases as not to provide law enforcement officials or lower court judges with an adequate understanding of what conduct was prohibited. But when the Justices promulgated a series of specific and plainly understood rules in *Miranda,* many of these same critics reversed their course and condemned the Court for acting like a legislative body. In the apportionment field, *Baker v. Carr* was assaulted because it afforded no meaningful guidelines to lower courts and legislatures while *Reynolds v. Sims* was discredited because its boldly stated standard was found to be too rigid and inflexible. The point is not that the Court's work product should be or should have been immune from criticism, or even that no preferable middle ground existed in the illustrations set forth above. Rather, the fact is that, regardless of how careful its efforts, the Court remains exeedingly vulnerable to reproach by those who are motivated to discover its shortcomings.

D. BREADTH OF CONSTITUTIONAL LANGUAGE

An allied component that arms those who are inclined to respond belligerently to declarations of unconstitutionality is the spacious and ambiguous language of many clauses in the Constitution that require interpretation and application in the course of judicial review. To cite the most obvious example, in determining whether popular action comports with "due process of law," a phrase which itself gives but the slightest hint of its content, the Court readily opens itself to the charge—not infrequently fueled by the rhetoric of the Justices themselves—of being no more than an added layer of the political process or no different from a continuing constitutional convention. And since the phrase is "as vast as 'goodness, beauty and truth' to some lawyers, and mean[s] no more than 'traditional legal procedures' to others,"[17] it is exceedingly difficult for the Court or its defenders to refute the charge. Furthermore, when the Court itself splits sharply on the meaning of these broad phrases, it becomes extremely simple for critics legitimately to differ with the majority's announced wisdom and it is quite understandable that those who are defeated in a contest involving high principles and momentous issues may respond intemperately. It was this imprecise and value-laden nature of the clauses that deal with individual constitutional rights which led Learned Hand to conclude that "if an independent judiciary seeks to fulfill them from its own bosom, in the end it will cease to be independent. And its independence will be well lost, for that bosom is not ample enough for the hopes and fears of all sorts and conditions of men, nor will its answers be theirs; it must be content to stand aside from these fateful battles."[18]

It may well be that the expansive nature of the Constitution's provisions affords its true genius for guiding the nation's destiny. But acknowledgment of the Constitution's flexibility magnifies the paradox of the institution of judicial review in a democracy because of the apparent unseemliness of empowering the Court, itself without real political accountability, to reject the policies and programs of majority will in the name of these vague clauses. And it greatly complicates the task if the Court seeks to provide vigorous protection for the constitutional rights of minorities by moving beyond existing precedents. For it then becomes virtually impossible to justify the Court's actions on the ground that it is doing no more than "finding" the law of the Constitution and fulfilling the intentions of its framers.

III. THE DYNAMICS OF POPULAR REACTION

A. RELIANCE ON PUBLIC ACQUIESCENCE

To this point, we have explored the reasons underlying the fact that the Court's decisions overturning the efforts of the people's representatives make it peculiarly susceptible to public hostility. But that consequence itself, apart from the resulting discomfort for the Justices, is not of great significance. The critical matter for our purposes is that the Court, having no electoral base of its own and equipped with neither physical nor monetary instruments of coercion, is almost totally dependent on the cooperation of politically responsible public officials to perform its function successfully, and on the confidence, goodwill, and respect of the people as a whole for the ultimate source of its strength. This becomes even more pronounced when the Court's efforts to secure personal liberty reach beyond its traditional posture of simply enjoining or refusing to enforce laws it finds to be unconstitutional. Rather, when—as in the desegregation, prison reform, and reapportionment areas—the Justices, in rejecting the product of the popular will, actually impose "affirmative undertakings of an essentially legislative character"[19] on public officials, their ability to do so effectively becomes all the more tenuous.

B. Symbolic and Educative Influence

The host of interrelated variable factors that may persuade the disparate members of American democratic society to abide by the Court's extremely consequential yet anti-majoritarian rulings are complex and subtle, and have undoubtedly differed at various times in our history.[20] It is believed (and it has been modestly substantiated)[21] that the Court has won public deference—and has resisted many offensives from political agencies at all levels of government—because of the reverence and tradition that have surrounded it as an institution in its historic role in the American system, as well as the prominence and distinction of its individual members. (National opinion polls often find that Supreme Court Justices rank at the very top of prestige vocations).[22] It is widely assumed that the moral and intellectual force of the Court's opinions—its appeal to conscience as well as political ideals and its invocation of fundamental tenets—has led the people to transcend their immediate interests in favor of allegiance to traditional values and to reconsider the merit and virtue of previously formulated popular decisions. It may be that, despite the strong majoritarian underpinning of our society, many citizens (at least at certain times) welcome the judgment of an authoritative and elitist government organ in the belief that it will aid in the preservation of stability as well as liberty.

C. PHENOMENON OF EXHAUSTIBLE CAPITAL

But no matter how speculative and undefined the forces that motivate public acceptance of the Court's invalidations may be, there is one point of common agreement among observers of all stripes, be they constitutional historians or political analysts, from America or abroad: The people's reverence and tolerance is not infinite and the Court's public prestige and institutional capital is exhaustible. The fortress of judicial review stands or falls with public opinion and the Court's symbolic image is not forever indestructible. It is true, as we have noted, that many exercises of judicial review may go largely unnoticed by all relevant constituencies. In other instances, judicial disapproval of local regulations may actually conform to the beliefs of a national majority and thereby increase the Court's store of esteem and good will. Moreover, on some occasions, the Justices' explanation for their invalidation of laws that had broad popular support may be so persuasive as to draw on the latently held moral values of a large percentage of the citizenry and thus produce their immediate agreement and enhance the Court's prestige and capital. But, overall, as plainly manifested by public opinion surveys during the Warren years (whose details will be recounted shortly),[23] the federal judiciary's ability to persuade the populace and public leaders that it is right and they are wrong is determined by the number and frequency of its attempts to do so, the felt importance of the policies it disapproves, and the perceived substantive correctness of its decisions. At some point—the exact location of which is unknown, but the existence in fact virtually undisputed—the Court's continued antimajoritarian rulings will tip the balance of credit accumulation and expenditures and animate a public sentiment that it has but a gossamer claim to legitimacy in a democratic society, thus either inducing popular disregard of the Court's decisions or inspiring political forces to seek to bring it to heel, or both. This ultimately fragile nature of the judiciary's ability to effectuate its rulings was early noted by Hamilton—albeit in another context—when, in arguing against assigning the Justices a role in impeachment proceedings, he "doubted whether they would possess the degree of credit and authority, which might, on certain occasions, be indispensable towards reconciling the people to a decision that should happen to clash with an accusation brought by their immediate representatives."[24] The fragility of the Court's influence has recently been confirmed by the conclusion of a detailed study of congressional voting divisions on proposals affecting the judiciary "that partisan and ideological considerations play a far greater role in Congressional behavior toward the Court than protagonists of the 'reverence' theme have recognized."[25]

IV. THE RECORD OF NONCOMPLIANCE

This is not the place for a comprehensive catalog of the occasions throughout our history in which the citizenry and public officials have either attempted to subvert the impact of the Court's constitutional invalidations or have refused outright to obey its mandates. Accurate evaluation of the law in action is normally a matter of low visibility. Careful empirical documentation requires a complex and time-consuming effort—and this has only recently begun in a serious way. Nonetheless, although representing merely the tip of the iceberg, a recitation of the most prominent illustrations may be useful.

A. STATE OFFICIALS

To begin generally: Up to the time of the Civil War, "the courts of seven States denied the constitutional right of the United States Supreme Court to decide cases on writs of error to State courts—Virginia, Ohio, Georgia, Kentucky, South Carolina, California and Wisconsin. The Legislatures of all these States (except California), and also of Pennsylvania and Maryland, formally adopted resolutions or statutes against this power of the Supreme Court."[26]

More specifically: The Pennsylvania affair, arising in 1809 over the case of *United States v. Judge Peters*,[27] required the presence of two thousand federal marshals and a not thinly veiled threat by President Madison to enforce the judicial decree. The imbroglio with Virginia, occasioned by the 1816 decision in *Martin v. Hunter's Lessee*,[28] is a familiar tale unnecessary to be retold here except to note that only fancy judicial footwork averted a more direct confrontation. In the first contest with Georgia, its House of Representatives sought to make any attempt to execute the 1793 mandate of *Chisholm v. Georgia*[29] a felony punishable by death without benefit of clergy.[30] The particular crisis was averted because the judgment was never executed and the broad issue was mooted by the eleventh amendment's ratification. Another Georgia crisis, revolving about its dispute with the Cherokee Indians, resulted in the state's formally ordering its officials to ignore the Supreme Court's directives in the 1831 decision of *Cherokee Nation v. Georgia*[31] and the 1832 sequel of *Worcester v. Georgia*.[32] Only when President Jackson, to serve independent political ends, belatedly persuaded Georgia to succumb, was a peaceful settlement finally secured.

Ohio's first turn came after *McCulloch v. Maryland* in 1819 when state officials, in the face of a federal court order, forcibly impounded funds of the Bank of the United States, which were recovered only after federal marshals imprisoned the state treasurer for contempt. Another Ohio turn came when, in direct defiance of the Supreme Court's 1859 decision in *Ableman v. Booth*,[33] the state court issued writs of habeas corpus for federal prisoners convicted under an act of Congress that was earlier sustained by the Court. A direct clash was avoided only when the state court independently held the statute to be valid. The *Booth* case was also the occasion for Wisconsin's day against the Court. That state's judges refused for several years to comply with a series of judicial mandates from Washington; the matter was finally resolved quietly and anticlimactically after the outbreak of the Civil War.

Soon after the end of the armed conflict, the highest court of West Virginia explicitly refused to abide by the ruling in *Ex parte Garland*[34]—indeed, the state went so far as to impeach and remove one of its judges for admitting a lawyer to practice who had not taken the loyalty oath that had been proscribed by the Supreme Court. Only a loosening of the radicals' grip in the state legislature finally resulted in the oath law's repeal.[35]

A great many other instances of state court resistance to Supreme Court orders before the mid-twentieth century, and various efforts to secure compliance, are chronicled elsewhere and need not be further recited here.[36] Of contemporary significance is a recent survey that documents the "organizational contumacy" and frequent explicit resistance by state appellate judges during 1961–72 to several controversial criminal procedure rulings by the Justices,[37] and the finding of another study—substantiating the normal relationship between energetic judicial action in behalf of insular minorities and official resistance to the Justices' efforts—that the "number of 'evasive' state court actions during the last decade of the controversial Warren Court . . . appears to be at least twice as high . . . as in either the 1930's or the 1940's."[38]

B. NATIONAL POLITICAL BRANCHES

Whereas all the above instances concerned state defiance of the Court's invalidations of state power, Georgia's, which was abetted by Andrew Jackson's well-known animus in the early stages of the Cherokee predicament,[39] also discloses an instance of antijudicial conduct by the nation's chief executive. It was the Civil War that afforded President Lincoln the opportunity to flout the authority of Chief Justice Taney's writ of habeas corpus in *Ex parte Merryman;*[40] and that was the end of the matter. Nor was Lincoln's attitude itself without precedent. Fifty-five years earlier, a general of the United States Army ignored two such writs issued by lower federal courts arising out of the Aaron Burr affair; and President Jefferson stopped just short of going this full distance himself when the Supreme Court ordered that the prisoners be released.[41] And seventy years after the Civil War, Franklin Roosevelt appeared to be fully prepared to rely on Lincoln's position in order to scorn an unfavorable decision in the *Gold Clause Cases*[42]—a ruling that the Court in fact delivered, but whose thrust was fortunately mooted by doctrinal byplay.[43] Finally, a 1975 incident demonstrates that the legislative branch is similarly capable of resisting the judiciary: The Senate, relying on a rule of confidentiality, "by voice vote and with scarcely a pause for debate, directed the comptroller general to reject a subpoena from the Florida federal district court trying former Senator Edward J. Gurney on bribery and perjury charges."[44]

Conceding that outright disobedience of judicial decrees by the President, his executive subordinates, and Congress has only infrequently occurred, there is no disputing the highly visible fact that Supreme Court abrogations of majority-sponsored activities have been the primary source of retaliation, real and seriously threatened, by the national political branches (as well as the states) against the federal judiciary. There is neither special utility nor available space to rehearse the full story here,[45] but some data may be briefly set forth. As reported broadly by David Currie, "every important decision invalidating a state law has brought forth a rash of irresponsible proposals to limit the Court's jurisdiction, to alter its procedures or composition, or to subject its decisions to review by an unwieldy tribunal composed of judges from the courts of each of the fifty states.... Others sought to deprive the Court of its jurisdiction over state judgments, to require the concurrence of five of the then seven Justices to hold a state law invalid, [or to require unanimity,] or to give appellate jurisdiction to the Senate whenever the validity of a state law was questioned."[46]

More specifically, no less than five times has the Justices' number been altered for political reasons, including fruitful efforts under the aegis of Presidents Jefferson, Jackson, and Lincoln, perhaps the three most severe executive antagonists of judicial review. And if a fourth president must be brought beneath this umbrella it likely would be Franklin Roosevelt. Although his notorious Court-packing plan was itself narrowly beaten, it may nonetheless have achieved its immediate goals and provided no infallible warranty against successful repetition. In fact, its failure may well have been less an institutional victory for the Court than a political defeat for the President. Because Roosevelt kept his plans secret until the final moment, he insulted many legislators and interest groups whose assistance was critical for enactment. Because he disguised his proposal as a judicial efficiency measure rather than candidly submitting it as an effort to change the Justices' philosophy, "public opinion, fired by conservative newspapers and fanned by bar association pronouncements, was more incensed at the deviousness and crassness of Roosevelt's scheme than at the Court decisions."[47] In addition, his move was sorely damaged while the bill was pending by the Court's radical change of course and Justice Van Devanter's announced retirement. In the end, fear of executive domination rather than support for judicial review more likely sealed its fate.[48] As Senator Wheeler concluded: "We must teach that man in the White House a lesson. We must show him that the United States Senate has to be consulted and is going to have something to say about how the Government is run."[49]

Finally, the political menace of impeachment was used as early as 1804 for Justice Samuel Chase and threatened as recently as 165 years later for Justice William Douglas; both cases were unmistakably linked to the exercise of judicial review.

The awesome power of the judiciary has also thrust the Court into the midst of battle strategies in national presidential campaigns: for example, in 1860 the Republican platform inveighed against *Dred Scott;*[50] in 1896, stimulated by the Court's denial of congressional authority in *Pollock v. Farmers' Loan & Trust Co.*[51] and *United States v. E. C. Knight Co.,*[52] both Democrats and Populists inserted antijudiciary planks; from 1908 to 1928 the Socialists included a proposal to forbid judicial review of all acts of Congress, and in 1912 and 1924 the Progressives urged a constitutional amendment simply to permit the alteration of judicial invalidations—all of which were responses to the Court's interferences with progressive economic regulations; in 1936 even the Republican convention adopted a policy repudiating the Court's decision in *Morehead v. New York ex rel. Tipaldo,*[53] which had negated state efforts to impose minimum wages for women; in 1964 Barry Goldwater launched a frontal attack against the Court in which he was supported by 70 percent of the public interviewees who professed to be somewhat knowledgeable about the matter;[54] in 1968 and 1972 Richard Nixon, capitalizing on a more pronounced popular sentiment which showed 75 percent of the public opposed to the Court's solicitude for accused criminals[55] and promising the appointment of "judicial conservatives," made "law and order" and "peace forces versus criminal forces" attractive catch phrases for many of America's ills; in 1968 George Wallace's strident disapproval of the judiciary was a major part of his campaign oratory; and in 1976 opposition to the Court's abortion decisions was one presidential candidate's sole issue.

The congressional weapon that is probably most often raised against the federal judiciary is that of curtailing its jurisdiction. Countless efforts of this kind have been recorded; casual perusal of Charles Warren's Supreme Court history for the nineteenth century alone discloses their occurrence in 1808, 1821, 1822, 1824, 1825, 1826, 1830, 1831, 1832, 1833, 1846, 1858, 1867, 1868, 1871, 1872, and 1882.[56] Almost every occasion is clearly traceable to momentous constitutional rulings, most of them declarations of unconstitutionality.[57] Indeed, the single consummated attempt, immediately following the Civil War, was for the specifically articulated purpose of preventing the Court from reviewing Reconstruction enactments. More recently the point is affirmed by Senator Jenner's well-known bill responding to the Court's internal security rulings of the 1950s, Representative Tuck's attempt to modify the reapportionment decisions of the 1960s, and President Nixon's proposed solution to judicial enforcement of public school desegregation in the 1970s.

Finally, history abounds with those national political offensives that are most directly related to judicial invalidations that seek straightforwardly to overturn the Court's decisions by ordinary legislation. Ambiguities in the recent legislative attack on the use of judicially compelled busing to achieve school desegregation probably disqualify the Education Amendments Act of 1974[58] from being illustrative. But a vivid recent example may be found in the provisions of the Omnibus Crime Control and

Safe Streets Act of 1968[59] which purported to repeal the thrust of *Miranda* and *United States v. Wade*[60] (extending the right of counsel to police lineups). Although somewhat analogous congressional attempts in the past to reimpose rapidly what the Court has just forbidden have been rejected again by the Court itself,[61] at this writing the ultimate fate of this freshest gambit is unknown. Also worthy of brief mention is the formal recommendation of a committee of the House of Representatives in 1947 that no funds be appropriated in order to negate the Court's mandate in *United States v. Lovett*[62] (a conclusion rejected by a one-vote margin in the House), as well as the more recent memorandum of a federal agency following a losing decision, "stating (confidentially) that the agency would not follow the majority opinion, but would adhere to the dissent."[63]

C. Citizenry at Large: Empirical Studies

The findings of the growing number of empirical studies that have been recently undertaken, mainly by social scientists, to determine how Supreme Court invalidations of widespread local practices are received at the grass roots is of equal moment for our purposes. Again, to begin generally, the conclusion of a 1970 overall review of these studies was that "survey research has thoroughly documented the oft-observed fact that Supreme Court decisions may produce only scattered changes in actual local practices."[64] Another review of work that had been done on a limited topic similarly stated that "in many districts policies remained as they were and in many where policies changed practices changed less."[65]

More specifically, the matter of constitutionally prohibited religious practices in the public schools has served as the basis for a number of empirical inquiries. After the Court's decision in *McCollum v. Board of Education*[66]—barring released-time classes in religious instruction on public school premises—one study concluded that "in some instances reaction was felt the day after the Court ruled. In others, the ruling seemed simply to be ignored. If any single generalization can be made from this discussion, it is that the impact nationwide of a Supreme Court decision is by no means uniform. The various patterns of compliance adopted in the local situations where the decision was sought to be enforced indicate that there is a considerable latitude of modes of compliance with a decision of the highest court of the land."[67] Another survey found that "many communities continued to hold released time classes in public school buildings. The most conservative estimate places noncompliance at 15 per cent of the programs, and other estimates run up to 40 and 50 per cent in some states."[68] Indeed, this inquiry disclosed that even after the Court upheld the alternative of off-premises released time for religious training in *Zorach v. Clauson*,[69] the on-premise programs continued unabated—especially in those districts where school officials were plainly aware of their unconstitutionality.[70]

Following the Court's *School Prayer* and *Bible Reading* invalidations,[71] one researcher believed that his work "along with other studies of compliance with Supreme Court decisions in the church-state area, should serve to dispel the notion that society automatically responds to the will of the Supreme Court. Indeed, this study indicates that 60 per cent of the states report continuing violations of the Court's *Bible Reading* decision."[72] "Surveys by the State Superintendent of Education in Kentucky, and by the Indiana School Board Association, both showed low compliance; only 61 of 204 school districts in Kentucky had discontinued prayers and Bible reading, and 121 superintendents had unwritten policies permitting both, while in Indiana fewer than 6 percent of the boards had changed policies to come into compliance with the Court. In Texas, in a survey conducted by the Council of Churches, the change was negligible, and few responding said they agreed in principle with the decision."[73] An intensive study of an anonymous midwestern community estimated that "at least half of the classrooms in Midway engage in some explicitly proscribed religious activity."[74] The impact revealed in a study of Wisconsin was substantially more friendly to the Court's rulings, but "compliance with the school prayer decision . . . [was] considerably less than perfect in Ohio."[75]

Response to the Supreme Court's landmark ruling in *In re Gault*[76] has been another subject of substantial empirical research. As I plan to detail elsewhere,[77] the results showed mixed acceptance of the Justices' requirements. In an intensive study, conducted shortly after the decision, of juvenile cases in three metropolitan areas in which the offender was not represented by a lawyer, full compliance with the right-to-counsel guarantee was achieved in 56 percent of the cases in one city. In the other cities, the written notice that all parents received was incomplete. And in one-third of the cases in one of the latter cities and 85 percent of those in another, the right to counsel was not mentioned by the judges to those youths who appeared without counsel. In the authors' view, "in virtually all of the other instances, the advice given was insufficient in content to comply with constitutional requirements."[78] Another observational survey of suburban juvenile courts in the greater Washington area, undertaken in the year following *Gault*, found that many juvenile judges "express doubts or downright disapproval of what they have been told to do" and that "in effect, most of their day-to-day practices still differ considerably from the changes called for by the Supreme Court and Federal experts, and they appear to discourage juveniles from exercising their rights."[79]

The substantial number of specific instances in which lower courts (state as well as federal) and law enforcement officials have sought to subvert the Warren Court's decisions expanding the safeguards of accused law violators fall within yet another principal area of recent empirical investigation.[80] *Miranda v. Arizona*,[81] probably the most controversial of these rulings, has been the subject of a series of detailed impact analyses by lawyers in a number of cities throughout the country. To mention but two, in the District of Columbia nearly 30 percent of persons who were arrested and interrogated after *Miranda* was decided "claimed that they had not been given a single *Miranda* warning and were therefore interrogated by the police in clear violation of *Miranda* and the Police Department's General Order";[82] in New Haven the study suggested "that detectives cannot be trusted to give warnings consistently and conscientiously."[83]

A comprehensive examination of the implementation of several lower federal court decisions that mandated changes in correctional facilities also reveals instances of significant noncompliance. In a case involving a major prison in New Orleans, research completed two years after the final judicial decree disclosed that despite the judge's imposition of strict prisoner population limits, there were "over nine times as many inmates as the decree permitted"; that although the prison was required to be shut, it "functioned as it had before the lawsuit"; and while the court ordered the establishment of a department of detentions and corrections, "the city never created or attempted to create any such department."[84]

Three additional areas of observation merit reference. First, despite the Court's invalidation of official demands that the NAACP disclose its membership lists,[85] "the refusal of the state courts to comply with the ruling in Alabama meant that the NAACP was out of business there for over a half-dozen years, 'its state-wide organization . . . destroyed and its activities on behalf of the state's Negroes . . . completely disrupted.'"[86] Second, a systematic study of the response by New York City welfare officials to the Court's requirement in Goldberg v. Kelly[87] of procedural due process prior to termination of benefits disclosed substantial evasion. "Based on a random sample of appeals filed in October 1972, the New York evaluation found, among many other defects, the following conditions which are directly relevant to Goldberg's constitutional requirements: (1) 5 percent of the appellants had received no notice of a proposed adverse action; (2) 25 percent did not receive timely notice; (3) two-thirds of all notices failed to give an adequate statement of what action was proposed and what the factual and policy bases for the action were; (4) in 15 percent of the cases aid had not been continued as required pending appeal; (5) only 25 percent of the appellants who requested access to relevant agency files prior to appeal were given such access; and (6) in only 7 percent of the cases was an opportunity for cross-examination afforded by having opposing witnesses present. . . . New York may be a special case. But there is also evidence of a fairly serious breakdown in the hearing process in other states."[88] Finally, an examination of the quality of local observance of the Court's pre-1965 restrictions on motion picture censorship, concluded that "each city and each state using a systematic program of movie censorship here surveyed operates under a legal framework that is in some measure at least, violative of procedural due process and at the most, in conflict with *Burstyn v. Wilson* and its free speech corollaries."[89]

The available evidence of popular noncompliance with the Supreme Court's constitutional invalidations, like that reported here, is fragmentary and incomplete. Moreover, to avoid distortions by intervening variables, such social science studies are often undertaken very soon after the Court's decision. As will be illustrated by a subsequent look at the impact of the *Miranda, School Prayer,* and *Gault* rulings,[90] since the studies observe complex organizations in a transitional stage, they may well overstate the actual degree of nonconformity even in the short run. And, because the empirical observations span only a limited time period, at least some will undoubtedly fail to account for compliance that naturally occurs over the longer term—e.g., a teacher who has led prayers for twenty years will more likely continue than will a newly appointed, young instructor who has learned in college that the practice is unconstitutional.[91] Nonetheless, more than enough is known to conclude confidently that a material gap exists between what the Court orders to be done and what the people in fact do.

Further, it is surely true that not all nonobservance can be attributed to knowing disobedience. Ignorance and unintentional nonconformance (some certainly due to a failure, probably an inevitable one, of clear communication on the part of the Court itself) surely play a role.[92] For example, a questionnaire survey of juvenile judges in rural Kentucky two years after *Gault* disclosed that "a good many . . . were not even aware that the Supreme Court had made a decision affecting juvenile procedure."[93] Whatever empirical omissions or behavioral uncertainties there may be, however, there is no question that popular and political resistance is a meaningful force with which judicial review must reckon. The need for both President Eisenhower and President Kennedy to use armed militia (with related loss of lives) to enforce the Court's ban on racial segregation in state schools unfortunately recalls a picture sufficiently familiar to most adults living today to eliminate the utility of further elaboration.

V. THE ROLE OF ELECTED LEADERS AND COMMUNITY ELITES

There are several notable points that may be drawn from the foregoing description of the dual circumstances of popular nonconformance with and political retribution for Supreme Court holdings of unconstitutionality. The first is the crucial role played by elected public representatives and other recognized community leaders, which accentuates the fragility of the Court's ability to obtain compliance with its antimajoritarian rulings. In chapter 1 we observed that the identity of government officials and especially the policy positions they held were perceived with greatly varying degrees of attentiveness and clarity by members of the public at large. This is at least equally true of the public knowledge about the work of the federal judiciary—e.g., in the poll referred to above, showing 70 percent public support for Senator Goldwater's criticism of the Court in 1964, fully 60 percent of all interviewees confessed that they were at best only vaguely familiar with what the Court had done.[94] Only very few of even the most fundamental of the Court's decisions immediately reach the view or touch the nerve of the general populace—e.g., in 1964, less than 3 percent of the respondents in a cross-sectional survey of the adult population expressed a view about the Court's reapportionment efforts despite the extraordinary publicity the cases engendered; in 1966, the figure fell below 0.5 percent.[95] It does not follow, however, that only this handful of the Court's rulings expose it to the phenomena of popular noncompliance and political attack that we have just recounted. Nor is it true that judgments that clash directly with deep-seated values held by large majorities of the people will necessarily be disobeyed.

A. EFFECT ON POPULAR ATTITUDES

Although, as we shall see, the dynamics of the process are complex and interactive and the factual documentation fragmentary, the fact is that leaders—respected and influential either by virtue of public office or attainments of other sorts—often possess the ability to overcome popular resistance[96] either by reshaping public opinion itself or by simply executing the Court's mandate despite the people's discontent. The precise impact of President Eisenhower's indifference and implicit disapproval on the public acceptance of the school segregation rulings is a matter of some speculation, as is the extent to which President Nixon's announced disagreement with busing engendered popular antipathy to *Swann* and its progeny across the nation. But there seems to be little question that if the sustained reaction of southern political leaders to *Brown* had been different than what it was, so too would have been the response of their constituents. A key factor that frequently emerges from the detailed empirical studies is exemplified by a survey reporting that the school prayer decision was implemented in one community because the "central decisionmaker for the school system" agreed with it and carried through[97] despite the fact that "a sizeable majority in the community did not agree with the substance of the court's policy," "felt that it had exceeded its proper range of power," and believed that "the rulings expressed a disdain for the values which they held paramount."[98] So, too, " 'almost all the compliance [with the prayer and Bible-reading cases] occurred in those states whose attorneys general supported the Court's decisions with official opinions . . . .' On the other hand, where the attorneys general opposed the Court, little compliance with the school prayer rulings came about."[99] In Tennessee, "the State Commissioner of Education . . . 'was reported as saying that it was permissible to read the Bible in public schools despite *Schempp*.' . . . Of the 121 of the state's 152 districts for which policy was ascertained, 51 did change their policy somewhat, but *only one* eliminated devotional exercises; the others made student participation voluntary and left matters to the individual teacher as to whether the exercises should be held."[100]

The critical part that may be played by the federal political establishment is highlighted by the progressive statistics of southern school desegregation. Although exact figures vary depending on their source, in the first decade following the *Brown* decision nationally unassisted judicial efforts resulted in only about 2 percent of the black students in the eleven southern states attending schools in which they were not in the racial majority. Within less than five years of the passage of the Civil Rights Act of 1964, in which Congress provided several enforcement devices, including the withholding of federal financial aid to noncomplying school districts, the figure had increased more than tenfold; by 1972 it stood at 46 percent,[101] and in 1973 it was reported that 79 percent of black students in the South were enrolled in racially mixed classrooms.[102] The power of the national political purse as compared with that of the federal judicial order is further startlingly indicated by 1968 statistics disclosing that more than twice as much racial desegregation had occurred in school districts affected by the federal funding remedy as in those subject to court mandates.

Care should be exercised, however, not to overstate the messianic influence or enforcement ability of political leaders and private statesmen—at least in respect to those relatively few judicial rulings that do arouse intense and widespread public opposition. Even when they are motivated to secure compliance with controversial decisions, elected officials with significant public exposure cannot successfully (at least not often or for long) speak and act in the teeth of concerted popular sentiment,[103] or even against the determined wishes of powerful interest groups (sometimes labeled "issue publics"). But the intuition, if not the proven reality, is that frequently the natural inclination of many public officials who are on the firing line is to accede unprotestingly to public outcries against the Court (or actually to fan flames) rather than to attempt to fulfill their legal obligation of enforcement and thus shift the abuse from the Court to themselves.

The complicated and interrelated quality of the public's opinion of the Supreme Court is suggested by Martin Shapiro's judgment that "(1) the public responds to major changes in the environment rather than specific Court decisions (2) for many purposes there is a two-stage process of public opinion formation in which opinion leaders transmit facts and evaluations to an attentive public (3) the fragmented issue publics do not form consistent alliances and (4) the 'public opinion' that seems to actually affect politics is some as yet not understood mixture of general public mood, the activities of issue publics and the selective perceptions and attitudes of political actors which they themsevles label public opinion but have only a partial and confused relation to actual public opinion as revealed in the polls. As a result we will always experience a great deal of difficulty in assessing the impact of the Supreme Court on public opinions and attitudes because public opinion is itself so fragmented, amorphous and generally non-opinionated."[104] Nonetheless, the strong inference remains that the heights to which popular sentiments rise are strongly influenced by how the "political stratum" handles the issue;[105] that even in regard to such highly sensitive matters as school segregation, political enforcement and opinion leadership are important factors in shaping public attitudes and fostering compliance. Witness, for example, the finding in the first decade after *Brown* that "in those parts of the South where some measure of school integration has taken place official action has preceded public sentiment, and public sentiment has then attempted to accommodate itself to the new situation."[106]

B. Direct Enforcement of Decisions

Whatever the degree and complexity of judicial dependence on political actors and private opinion leaders for effectuation of the Court's most deep-rooted judgments, the Justices more clearly rely on segments of public officialdom for enforcement of that enormously greater number of decisions in which the public is unaffected directly and is thus generally indifferent. And the supreme anomaly is that not infrequently it is those very officials who are most adversely affected by the decision whose cooperation is most urgently required—at least in the first instance—for its fruition. Thus, just as it was President Lincoln who held the key to enforcement of *Ex parte Merryman*, so, too, implementation of many of the Court's rulings invalidating public school practices lies with the very officials who had originally established the illegal programs, and the realization of many of the Court's criminal procedure edicts rests in the hands of law enforcement agencies.

It is true that the Supreme Court itself may police those few instances that wend their way to its docket, and that the inferior federal (and state) courts frequently assist—though, as we have seen, resistance at these levels is not unknown. The invaluable backing of the national political branches may also be forthcoming, as illustrated by the enactment by Congress of the Civil Rights Act of 1964, which finally reinforced the Court's ruling in *Brown v. Board of Education* of 1954. Indeed, despite President Eisenhower's seeming antipathy to desegregation and his disinclination—as a former military commander—to employ troops for a domestic problem, when he felt that soldiers were needed to support the Justices in Little Rock, he sent them. The complex (or perhaps simple) reasons that prompted Eisenhower and other presidents to so respond, yet failed to move Andrew Jackson and other chief executives, are probably beyond our ken. But, as numerous occasions in our history reveal, neither Congress nor the President can invariably be counted upon to support the Court's rulings.

It goes too far to assert that, because the national lawmaking machinery has always possessed the authority itself to invalidate the now judicially condemned state or federal practice and has never done so, that same machinery will automatically be hostile to the Court's decisions; rather, its lack of action may well have been political inertia or indifference. But if these factors (rather than congressional approval) explain the political inaction before the judicial ruling, it is also likely that political inertia or indifference will allow affected parties to disregard the Court's judgment. Indeed—again demonstrating the Court's indebtedness to political leaders—if we eliminate those instances of national political indifference, the record suggests that Congress and the President will challenge the Court's ruling at least as often as they push the noncomplying government agencies into line, even when the national political branches did not previously sponsor the invalidated policy. And here, given an originally detached public attitude, the opinion-molding influence of political leaders is markedly powerful—as evidenced no later than *Marbury v. Madison* when, in Justice Jackson's words, there was "little doubt" that President Jefferson could have "defied the Court" and the birth of judicial review "and at that time the people would probably have sustained him."[107] The conclusion is inescapable that the Court, in some wise and principled fashion, must ration its power of invalidation.

VI. THE CUMULATIVE IMPACT OF PUBLIC HOSTILITY

The Court's capacity to obtain popular compliance with, or to invite political retaliation for, any particular negation of the majority will is as much or more a function of its general public image at the time as it is a result of the particular case at issue. Just as voters with different sets of grievances coalesce to defeat incumbents, and Congress asserts itself more vigorously against a President whose public support is eroding,[108] the Court's prestige and authority is of a broad institutional nature, and when the Court expends its store of capital it tends to do so in a cumulative fashion. Since public antagonism, resistance, and retribution appear to have a spill-over effect, if one or another of the Court's rulings sparks a markedly hostile reaction, then the likelihood that subsequent judgments will be rejected is greatly increased even though the later invalidations would, in themselves, be only mildly productive of popular resentment.

A. CIVIL WAR ERA

The *Dred Scott* disaster illustrates this phenomenon—wholly apart from its abject failure to calm the passions surrounding the slavery controversy, a task that was (as we have seen) deliberately passed to the Court by the federal political branches. Although the grievous wound that the decision inflicted on the Court was not fatal[109] and there has been recent disagreement with the conclusion that the post–*Dred Scott* period "marked the nadir of judicial power and influence,"[110] in Edward Corwin's traditional view it enfeebled the Court for some years to come. Because of this single ruling, "during neither the Civil War nor the period of Reconstruction did the Supreme Court play anything like its due role of supervision, with the result that during the one period the military powers of the President underwent undue expansion, and during the other the legislative powers of Congress. The Court itself was conscious of its weakness, yet notwithstanding its prudent disposition to remain in the background, at no time since Jefferson's first administration has its independence been in greater jeopardy than in the decade between 1860 and 1870; so slow and laborious was its task of recuperating its shattered reputation."[111] Furthermore, it was *Dred Scott* that gave rise to Abraham Lincoln's oft-cited and unrestricted view that the Court's rulings be accorded only a very narrow binding effect. Because of its renowned authorship, this doctrine—like nullification and interposition—whose encouragement to disobedience long outlived the conditions that generated its birth, has served to haunt the Court ever since. (It might be noted, as an aside, that Lincoln's hostility was forthcoming despite the fact that his earlier enthusiasm for judicial resolution of the matter permitted him to avoid taking a firm stand either way when he was on the hustings.)[112]

B. BLUNTNESS OF POLITICAL CONTROLS

On a similar note, although many of the antijudiciary devices available to the national political branches, particularly the authority to curb the Court's jurisdiction and the control over its membership, may be employed in response to specific judicial invalidations, the impact of such a change may not be limited simply to repairing the unpopular decisions. Rather, as illustrated by the *McCardle* statute and even more by the Roosevelt packing plan and the Nixon replacement policy, the potential impact of these political retaliations extends well beyond their issue of origin, sometimes affecting the entirety of the Court's work. Thus, the income tax decision not only resulted in "a loss of public confidence in the Court's impartiality and a decline in respect for the rule of law"[113] but also generated a broad "demand that the Court should be shorn of its alleged 'usurped' power to pass upon the validity of [all] Acts of Congress."[114]

C. Progressive Transference of Antagonism

To turn to events of more recent vintage, a number of the grass-roots empirical studies mentioned earlier have identified—and none has discounted—the existence of a direct correlation between a community's overall esteem for the Court and the readiness with which the public tolerates particular unpopular decisions.[115] As with other government organs, it appears that "the legitimacy of the originating institution (in this case, the Supreme Court), if great in a particular context, will reduce the capacity of local forces to modify a policy initiative."[116] Thus, in the careful study of one school district in which the Court's prayer proscription was effectively implemented, "it was demonstrated . . . that whether or not a duty of compliance with Court policy was acknowledged depended upon positive or negative evaluations of the Court's legitimacy and expertise."[117] That the converse is also true—i.e., "that noncompliance with a specific Supreme Court decision is related to the more general question of support for the Supreme Court as an institution and the legitimacy of its actions"[118]—has been manifested in a variety of contexts. A survey of the extent to which schools conformed with the prayer decisions disclosed that "law enforcement agencies" and "business property owners," as well as religious interests, parents, and teachers, were among those groups most strongly aligned against the rulings; "general dissatisfaction—probably groups concerned with Supreme Court actions in general [rather] than Bible reading per se" was suggested as a particular source of opposition; "indeed, if one were able to pinpoint the opposition to the Supreme Court's decisions on desegregation, reapportionment, criminal due process, and Bible reading, he might find a considerable overlapping of groups."[119] With respect to the Warren Court's liberal criminal procedural rulings in the 1960s, knowledgeable observers believe that "the police and those supporting their position may have been particularly upset by a specific decision, for example, *Miranda,* but it is not that decision *by itself* which produced reaction so much as *Miranda* in relation to other, earlier decisions reaching in the same direction. In that set of cases, each reinforced the other, as far as the reaction of many law enforcement officials was concerned, and helped create a certain 'climate' regarding 'law and order.'"[120] Similarly, Franklin Roosevelt's Court-packing plan was plainly attributable "to the large number of decisions striking down New Deal legislation rather than to a single decision."[121]

These dynamics of the transference of antagonism from one judicial decision to another and the coalition of groups with separate grievances against the Court into a single front of opposition may help explain why the southern states, already stung by the Court's racial ventures in the public schools, were the most resentful and resistant to its religious decisions.[122] Conversely, it has been suggested that Virginia's "massive resistance"—supported by its attorney general and education officers—to the 1948 *McCollum* released-time ruling predisposed it to react in comparable manner to school desegregation.[123] This phenomenon may also account, at least in part, for the findings that in the Warren era southern state courts much more frequently evaded Supreme Court decrees than their counterparts in other sections of the nation, and that southerners as a group were "generally more critical of the Supreme Court's ... first amendment and procedural rights decisions" as well as those dealing with racial issues.[124] There are, however, other variables (such as the generally more conservative views in the South) that may have contributed to, or even independently produced, these responses. But this "cumulative grievance-reaction" phenomenon is surely more than just a plausible explanation, even for such a complex matter as the causes for attitudes and actions of the public at large.

The "cumulative grievance-reaction" phenomenon is also quite plainly revealed in the national political system where the traditional process of negotiation and compromise greatly strengthens the forces of retribution against the Court as each significant judicial invalidation is successively rendered. Thus, the racial segregation rulings in the mid-1950s sounded the battle cry mainly for southern legislators and the internal security decisions several years later added the cold warrior anticommunist bloc to the ranks. It was this ideological alliance—reinforced by conservative business groups who were frightened by contemporaneous holdings on labor relations, and encouraged by the American Bar Association, the Conference of State Governors, and law enforcement officials who were similarly offended by the Justices' sensitivity to individual rights—that formed in the late 1950s and came dangerously close to bringing the Court to heel.[125] This episode was followed by the school prayer mandates in the early 1960s, which unearthed another group of combatants; and after the legislative apportionment judgments in the mid-1960s rang the alarm for yet others, all finally turned their accumulated resentment against the Court. This coalition posed one of the most severe national political threats to the Court since the New Deal and was averted only by a liberal filibuster in the Senate.[126] Indeed, given the psychological penchant of those charged with solving the exceedingly perplexing problems of American society to find scapegoats when their own well-intentioned solutions fail (and secularism, sensualism, and crime in the streets is on the rise), it is not unusual for legislators truly incensed by judicial invalidations of popularly enacted programs to find comrades who have not been generally disposed unfavorably toward the Court to begin with. And the task of enlistment is made all the easier if one determined committee chairman whose political nerves are rubbed raw by the Court's action produces a biased record by stacking the hearing room with witnesses of similar persuasion.[127]

D. Judicial Cognizance of the Problem

By both words and action, the Court itself has long recognized that heightened judicial activism contrary to popular sentiment may weaken its authority to continue. As Justice Powell recently stated, "repeated and essentially head-on confrontations between the life-tenured branch and the representative branches of government will not, in the long run, be beneficial to either. The public confidence essential to the former ... may well erode if we do not exercise self-restraint in the utilization of our power to negative the actions of the other branches .... The power recognized in *Marbury v. Madison* is a

potent one.... Were we to utilize this power...indiscrimi-
nately...we may witness efforts by the representative branches
drastically to curb its use."[128]

History confirms Justice Powell's fears. Walter Murphy reports
that "Marshall was ready to submit to congressional review of
Court decisions, and while such a concession was never forced,
his Court did pass up the opportunity to declare unconstitutional
the peremptory removal of circuit judges by the Jeffersonians.
Twenty years later, in the face of new attacks, the Court cut back
into Marshall's earlier opinions and eased its restrictions on state
authority. During Reconstruction, the judges at first courageously defended civil liberties against martial law and bills of
attainder. When confronted with Radical threats, however, the
Justices, as Gideon Welles said, 'caved in.' Jeremiah Black was
less kind in his comments: 'The Court stood still to be ravished
and did not even hallo while the thing was being done.'"[129] Alan
Westin concludes that since the beginning, the Court has consciously avoided rulings against the President when the Justices
felt that such decisions would tarnish their image.[130]

The Hughes Court's legendary "switch in time" was followed
less dramatically, but still quite perceptively, by the Warren
Court's modification in the internal security area in the late
1950s[131] and, according to several astute commentators, in the
criminal procedure field in the late 1960s.[132] And while the
Burger Court's forays have themselves been more modest than
those of its predecessor, its refusal to extend the reach of its
abortion rulings to cover government payment of medical costs
for indigents[133] also illustrates the Court's inevitable self-
rationing of the power of invalidation. As Westin has observed,
"as constitutional statesmen, the justices must arrive at some
ultimate accommodation with dominant opinion."[134]

VII. THE THEORY OF CONSTANT GROWTH OF
CAPITAL

Having developed at some length the position that the
Court's guardianship of constitutional principles against majority
error rests on tenuous foundations, a contrary approach should

also be recognized. The argument, which may be termed the theory of constant growth of capital, contends that each assertion of the Court's negative authority of judicial review ultimately augments that authority and the more regular the judiciary's invalidating command, the more likely and accustomed the public acceptance. Indeed, the theory runs, although the Supreme Court does enjoy only a finite quantity of institutional capital, this public prestige is dissipated rather than enhanced when it fails to speak forthrightly in the name of constitutional principles, especially when it refuses to act courageously for the security of individual liberties in the face of popular abridgment.

This theory is an appealing one, its resonance strengthened by the degree to which the Court does appear to retain the faculty both of educating a majority that has temporarily foresaken constitutional values and of calling for adherence to profound ideals. Since certain of the Court's rejections of the popular will are perceived by the people and their representatives as legitimate and worthy acts of authority by the nonpolitical branch of government, some exercises of judicial review do earn public respect for the judiciary. Indeed, given the function that the Justices historically have assumed in our system, it may well be that if they were totally to abandon their role as educators and supervisors of the national conscience they would be regarded with disdain as much as or more than if they were to seek to impose their personal views and so revise all legislative and executive policies. Moreover, our experience shows that the various segments of the population who have prevailed in a series of judicial decisions over a period of time do tend to coalesce in support of the Court.

Therefore, if the question of whether the Court gains or loses enforcement capacity by continual invalidations were one of mere behavioral speculation, the broad approach outlined above could not easily be dismissed. But, as indicated herein, the hard data of history—by no means irrefutably conclusive or totally immune from reinterpretation, but nevertheless highly persuasive—points in the opposite direction. Many invalidations have dissipated the Court's capital, and, as most recently illustrated by the Warren Court's passage, the efforts of the defenders of judicial review cannot fully compensate for what the political majority believes to be excessive judicial expenditure of that capital.

The record of past invalidations plainly suggests that the Court's educative facilities are not unlimited, and the presently available information reveals that, although the views of ordinary citizens are strongly subject to influence by public leaders, only an insignificant segment of the people fervently values the protection of individual rights. After an extensive review of various facts, Samuel Krislov found that "the American public emerges as profoundly indifferent to liberties long established and presumably noncontroversial." "[S]ome sociologists and political scientists have concluded that the Bill of Rights would be rejected by the populace if it were up for adoption today." "Over the years, a series of carefully structured studies, surveys, and polls, as well as assorted grab-bag questionnaire arrangements ascertaining the views of groups of questionable representatives, all have probed and examined the attitudes of Americans toward civil liberties. Apparently without exception, these studies record profound antiliberalism latent throughout our society.... Americans overwhelmingly favor civil liberties when asked about their attitudes in highly abstract terms. However, when queried in operational terms, without benefit of shibboleths to guide them, they give antilibertarian responses about rights that are disputed.... When CBS ran its first National Citizenship Test...[in the 1960s], a majority of *Congressmen* answered its free-speech question incorrectly; only a small minority of the general public had an accurate view of legal doctrine. A sophisticated study of young people's attitudes—based on an admittedly small sample—found only 25 percent in agreement with Supreme Court doctrine on free speech and assembly and only 10 percent with free-press decisions!"[135] A survey conducted by CBS News in 1970 produced similar results: 54 percent of over 1,100 adults sampled did *not* agree "that everyone has the right to criticize the government."[136] Seventy-six percent "believed that, even in the absence of a 'clear danger of violence,' not all groups should be allowed to organize protests against the government. Fifty-five percent felt that newspapers and other media should *not* enjoy an absolute right to publish articles that the government felt might be harmful to the national interest, even in time of peace . . . . [T]hough majorities favor the general thrust of the Fourth Amendment protection against unreasonable searches and seizures, substantial minorities do not. Bare majorities agree with the notion that an individual should not be compelled to testify against himself in court. A majority . . . believe that the police should be permitted to hold [a person suspected of a serious crime] in custody until they are able to obtain evidence against him . . . [and] simply reject the notion that a man ought not to be tried twice for the same crime."[137]

VIII. THE SIGNIFICANCE FOR INDIVIDUAL RIGHTS

A. JUDICIAL RECORD OF SUCCESS

Several matters must be clarified at this point. Much has been said herein about the brittle quality of the Court's power to have its antimajoritarian rulings fulfilled. But none of it has been meant to suggest that the Court, although meaningfully subdued in times of severe crises, has been permanently or mortally disabled. Regardless of the continual criticism and grudging and delayed acceptance of many of its judgments by the public, we have seen in chapter 2 that a great deal of what the Court has ordered has come to pass.

Nor have the Justices' efforts been futile even when popular resistance has been strong. For example, *Miranda* warnings, if not faithfully delivered on all occasions, are given many times more than was the case before 1966;[138] and this is confirmed even by the figures presented in the critical report from the District of Columbia mentioned earlier. Indeed, an empirical survey in Pittsburgh disclosed that "within one week after the *Miranda* decision the Detective Branch began complying" with its requirements.[139] The New Haven study, also referred to earlier, was conducted immediately following the *Miranda* ruling of 13 June 1966. It found that "the detectives clearly gave more adequate advise later in the summer . . . as they became more accustomed to the *Miranda* requirements; much of the noncompliance may therefore have been transitional . . . . During the two weeks of June after *Miranda* less than half the suspects received a warning which included more than half the elements of the *Miranda* advice, but by August more than two-thirds of the suspects received such a warning. More important, the number of full *Miranda* statements increased even more dramatically. No suspects received the full *Miranda* statement in June, while more than one-third of those questioned in August received the complete warning."[140] In a more recent study, public defenders in a rural area of Massachusetts reported that "the police were assisting in enforcement of the spirit of *Miranda* by making it easier for those in custody to contact lawyers."[141] In addition, within two years of *Miranda*, the Internal Revenue Service, at its own initiative, adopted a policy of providing the required warnings at the outset of all criminal tax fraud investigations.[142] Although prayer and Bible reading in the public schools has not totally vanished, it has significantly diminished.[143] One nationwide before-and-after survey revealed that the Court's decisions had reduced the number of reporting school districts with devotional Bible-reading programs from 42 percent to 14 percent.[144] Another such national study of public elementary school teachers showed that the percentage offering classroom prayers dropped from over 60 percent to 28 percent and the portion conducting Bible reading fell from 48 percent to 22 percent.[145] In contrast to the 1969 findings (set forth above) on the lack of Kentucky juvenile courts' awareness of *Gault*, a follow-up survey in 1975 "demonstrated a much higher knowledge of and compliance with *Gault* by the state's juvenile judges."[146] Finally, despite the myriad attacks from the national political branches, in retaliation of the Court's protection of individual rights, chapter 1 reveals that only a handful have been measurably successful and then only in modest degree.

B. Hostility Generated by Decisions

There is no disputing that, as a category, the Court's invalidations in defense of personal liberty have been at least as provocative of hostile response as have been its rulings on issues of federalism and separation of powers. This is evidenced by the declining public popularity of and mounting political hostility toward the Court during its increasingly protective stance in the Warren era. During a six-month period in 1962, even before the Court reached full stride in its solicitude for individual rights, it was reported that "hardly a day has gone by without some influential figure in American public life denouncing the United States Supreme Court. Twenty-five United States Senators and 75 Representatives in this period have delivered speeches in Congress attacking the Court's constitutional outlook. Hostile editorials have appeared in over 150 newspapers . . . . Police officials and state judges have attacked the justices for 'handcuffing' law enforcement. The American Bar Association has heard its outgoing president lash the Court for gravely undermining 'property rights,' 'internal security,' 'good citizenship,' and other key values of our system. Many Catholic and Protestant church leaders have criticized the justices for rulings allegedly 'secularizing' national life and 'protecting immorality' from prosecution . . . . When asked recently what businessmen thought of the Court, the general counsel of one major corporation replied: 'Well, it pays to be a Negro or a Communist if you want justice from the Warren Court. Business doesn't get it.'"[147]

Public attitude studies in the mid-1960s, although disclosing that "a reservoir of residual respect or diffuse support exists for the Supreme Court," nonetheless showed "a decrease in esteem for the Court between the years 1946 and 1966." Furthermore, the response of "elite publics" indicated that greater knowledge about the Court and its decisions generally resulted in decreased support for it.[148] More specifically, inquiries made by the Survey Research Center in 1964 and 1966 of six hundred persons who purportedly were familiar with the Court's work revealed a 71 percent critical response. In 1966, when the subjects were asked which branch they trusted more, Congress or the Supreme Court, 57 percent opted for the former.[149]

C. Relevance for Individual Rights Proposal

Nonetheless, although there has been no paucity of opinion (much of it sympathetic to judicial review) urging that the Court halt or retreat in its heightened solicitude for individual rights, that is *not* the position taken here. Rather, in continuing vigorously to exercise its power of judicial review over this class of issues, the Court is performing its vital role in American democratic society—the role for which it is peculiarly suited and for which all other government institutions are not. Just how the substantive questions should be resolved—whether the Court has been too sensitive to minority interests in disregard of majority needs, or whether it should move beyond traditional frontiers along paths sketched in chapter 2—is beyond the purview of this book. For several reasons, the Court should review individual rights questions, unabated by its judgment about whether a particular result will be subject to criticism, hostility, or disobedience.

1. Judges as Predictors

To begin with, "it is easy to misjudge or distort the impact of a Court pronouncement, and guesses about that impact are treacherous sources of precepts for Court behavior."[150] Such imponderable judicial speculation "must be anchored to social-scientific predictions which lawyers are notably unequipped to make by training, tradition, or professional experience."[151] Conceding that the public background of at least some lawyers (and surely of some Justices) ameliorates these shortcomings, nonetheless "political realism in assessing the effects of decisions and the responses of other institutions and of the public is a luxury of critical hindsight that is most problematical as a premise of adjudication"[152]—as evidenced, for example, by the long series of reapportionment cases and *Powell v. McCormack*.[153]

2. Essential Judicial Role

More important, for the Court to treat public reaction as a significant element of substantive constitutional interpretation is flatly inconsistent with the politically neutral and principled decisionmaking role that supports its antimajoritarian existence in a democratic government. Furthermore, since the minorities who call on the Court for assistance have already failed (in one degree or another) to secure their rights in the political process, the chances are often high that judicial protection will engender hypersensitive public and political reaction. Thus, for the Court to decline protection—as such eminent observers as Carl Swisher and Learned Hand have urged[154]—until popular attitudes have reached that point of consensus at which its decisions will be readily accepted is to shirk its essential duty and contradict its critical function as the government agency of last resort for the guardianship of the constitutional liberties of those without political influence.

The Court's formidable and delicate task is to consult those complex sources of historic and contemporary values that are the ingredients of sound constitutional interpretation, as well as its wisdom and conscience—and then to decide. Acceptance is not the Court's responsibility, but the obligation of the people; execution not its onus, but the duty of the political branches. There is much in the view that if the Court withdraws in fear from its basic task of seeking to safeguard individual constitutional rights, if it rejects the petitioning minority's claim on the merits (or even by summary disposition) because of apprehension of nonenforcement, it runs the serious risk of inflicting a multiple injury on these liberties. The Court not only refuses to vindicate claims in the case before it but also establishes a precedent for future government action. For example, the *Plessy* edict led to the expansion of segregation; the *Japanese Exclusion Cases* were relied on to support the McCarran Act's detention camps; the *Gobitis* decision stimulated flag salute programs; and the *Ginsberg* ruling produced a rash of juvenile obscenity laws.[155] Even if the immediate decision is ignored, judicial courage is preferable to obsequious abdication. For, although there is also the real risk that nonconformance may become an accustomed public habit, thus undermining respect for law generally as well as for future judicial invalidations, the mere articulation of cherished constitutional ideals by a Court that is "right" may carry a meaningful psychological impact that will serve the cause of liberty at a later time when popular passion has cooled.

IX. CONCLUSION

Both the Federalism Proposal that is advanced in chapter 4 (that the Court abstain from deciding constitutional questions of national power versus states' rights) and the Separation Proposal developed in chapter 5 (that the Court similarly abstain from deciding ultimate issues of constitutional authority between Congress and the President) seek to ease the commendable and crucial task of judicial review in cases of individual constitutional liberties. It is in the latter that the Court's participation is both vitally required and highly provocative. Purporting neither to immunize the Court from all hostility nor to insure acceptance of all its decisions, both proposals seek to shield the Court from categories of clashes with the populace and the politicians and thus to narrow the range of disobedience and retribution. The contention is not that the Court should avoid the federalism and separation of powers areas because all that it has done there has been "bad" (although much of it—particularly on the issue of federalism—has been in error). Rather, as chapters 4 and 5 discuss in detail, the Court should remove itself from these categories of disputes because its activity there is unnecessary to effective preservation of the constitutional scheme. Moreover, both judicial legitimations and invalidations in these areas—again, especially federalism—have expended large sums of institutional capital. This is prestige desperately needed elsewhere for, as Alexander Bickel reminded, "there is a natural quantitative limit to the number of major, principled interventions the Court can permit itself.... A Court unmindful of this limit will find that more and more of its pronouncements are unfulfilled promises, which will ultimately discredit and denude the function of constitutional adjudication."[156]

This is not to say that all or even most of the Court's federalism and separation of powers decisions have brought it trouble. Indeed, some of the federalism decisions most subject to doctrinal and practical criticism, such as those rulings that destroyed much of the ability of Congress to enforce the Civil War amendments, have been greeted with general public favor.[157] And, although we shall see that special circumstances may explain the reaction,[158] the Court's most prominent congressional-executive separation of powers decision, *Youngstown Sheet & Tube Co. v. Sawyer*[159]—which nullified President Truman's seizure of the steel mills in 1952—was widely acclaimed by the press as well as in Congress,[160] even though the President had invoked the mantle of national defense during time of war for his action.

At the risk of undue repetition, the central issue is the necessity of judicial review and the potentiality of resulting harm to the judiciary. Especially in view of the wide consensus and substantial political majority that are ordinarily required for congressional action, judicial invalidation of any federal law poses high risks for the Court. When it does so in the federalism area, it often increases the stakes because a great deal of such national legislation enacts programs and furthers policies that respond to the most broadly felt popular needs. And when the Justices rule for one political branch against the other in the separation of powers area, they frequently enter a politically charged arena from which their chances of emerging unscathed are problematic at best.

Finally, as we shall see in the following chapter, the fact is that the Court's invalidations of national authority in the name of the federalism principle have been eminently unsuccessful in terms of longevity. Indeed, putting aside the presently unforeseeable reach of the Court's most recent such venture in *National League of Cities v. Usery*, there is virtually no states' rights decision of any note that retains current meaningful force. It may be that the Court's personal liberties rulings will ultimately suffer a similar fate. Some have, but many more have not. And they are less likely to if the Federalism and Separation Proposals are heeded. To these we now turn.

Four

The Scope of National Power vis-à-vis the States

The Dispensability of Judicial Review

Federalism has been a central feature of the American polity from the nation's inception to the present day. Many of the most salient provisions of the Constitution and its amendments concern the distribution of governmental authority between the nation and its component states that defines the plan of federalism as it was originally conceived and has been periodically adjusted. Most of these constitutional ordinances describe the powers assigned to the central government; some withhold powers from the central government that would impose on the prerogatives of the states; others prohibit the constituent states from encroaching on exclusively national domains; and all seek to fulfill the clearly understood seminal principle, elaborated in the tenth amendment, that the authority of the United States is limited to its constitutionally specified delegated powers, with the residuum of governmental power reserved to the states.

This chapter concerns the appropriate role of the federal judiciary in resolving questions arising under these constitutional provisions—issues that have been continuously adjudicated over the course of our constitutional history and that have formed the basis of many of the Supreme Court's most consequential decisions.

I. CONSTITUTIONAL FRAMEWORK

Although no exhaustive listing of the constitutional provisions defining our federalism is called for, it will be helpful at the outset to identify some of the most significant clauses in the basic charter that allocate government dominion between the nation and the states.

A. GRANTS OF NATIONAL POWER

The major sources of national power are contained in Articles I, II, and IV and in a number of the amendments. Art. I, §8 grants Congress the power to lay taxes and spend to "provide for the common Defence and general Welfare," to borrow money, to regulate commerce "with foreign Nations and among the several States," to establish uniform rules for naturalization and bankruptcy, to coin and regulate the value of money, to establish post offices, to grant patents and copyrights, to constitute lower federal courts, to declare war, to raise and regulate national military forces, and to organize the militia in the states and call upon it "to execute the Laws of the Union, suppress Insurrections and repel Invasions." Art. I, §4 authorizes Congress to make rules or alter state regulations respecting the times, places, and manner of electing senators and representatives. Art. II, §2 empowers the President and Senate to make treaties. Art. IV grants Congress the capacity to effectuate the full faith and credit principle (§1), to admit new states into the union (§3), to regulate the territories and property of the United States (§3), and to guarantee to every state "a Republican Form of Government" (§4). Sections of several of the amendments empower Congress to enforce their substantive terms. Thus, Congress has the authority to implement the thirteenth amendment's prohibition of slavery, to enforce the due process and equal protection clauses of the fourteenth amendment, and to combat denials of the right to vote because of race (fifteenth amendment), sex (nineteenth amendment), failure to pay a poll tax (twenty-fourth amendment), or age (twenty-sixth amendment).

B. LIMITATIONS ON STATE POWER

The power of the central government vis-à-vis the states is further defined by a series of provisions, principally in Art. I, §10, that specifically limit state authority. Thus, the states are barred from entering into any "Treaty, Alliance, or Confederation," and from coining money or issuing bills of credit. Further, without the consent of Congress, no state may impose import or export duties "except what may be absolutely necessary for executing its inspection Laws"; or "keep Troops, or Ships of War in time of Peace, enter into any Agreement or Compact with another State, or with a foreign Power, or engage in War, unless actually invaded, or in such imminent Danger as will not admit of Delay."

C. GRANTS OF STATE POWER AND LIMITATIONS ON NATIONAL POWER

The philosophy of our federal system of divided government authority is also articulated in a number of clauses that assign powers to the states. These take several forms. Some provisions expressly stipulate state control over certain matters and, in context, imply negation of national governance. For example, Art. I, §2 declares that the qualifications of voters for members of the House of Representatives shall be those "requisite for Electors of the most numerous Branch of the State Legislature," and the seventeenth amendment sets the same qualifications in respect to senatorial elections. Further, the twenty-first amendment prohibits, if contrary to state law, "the transportation or importation" into a state of "intoxicating liquors" "for delivery or use therein." Other provisions explicitly deny national power and, in context, implicitly recognize state rule. Thus, Art. I, §9 prohibits Congress from laying direct taxes "unless in proportion to the Census"; (the sixteenth amendment modifies this bar in regard to income taxes). The second amendment forbids national infringement of "the right of the people to keep and bear arms" so as to preserve each state's control over its militia.[1] And the eleventh amendment restricts the federal judicial power from extending to suits against a state by a citizen of another state. Finally, there are several constitutional clauses that have been judicially interpreted as forbidding only national government action because, in the Supreme Court's judgment, they do not address interests sufficiently fundamental to be categorized as individual rights secure from abridgment by all levels of government, state and local as well as national. Although these provisions—the fifth amendment's requirement of grand jury indictment and the seventh amendment's guarantee of a petit jury in civil cases—may, like the eleventh amendment, raise constitutional issues implicating the scope of "the judicial power" under Article III (the subject of chapter 6), for present purposes they further illustrate the federalism regime established in the basic charter.

This somewhat detailed recitation of prominent constitutional provisions that apportion power between the nation and the states serves several purposes. First, it confirms that the central government is possessed of only limited authority, the balance resting with the states. Second, it describes—although with no effort to be thorough—the respective spheres of influence. Third, and primarily, it reveals that many important constitutional clauses may be clearly confined to the second of the three broad categories of constitutional provisions—individual rights, federalism, and separation of powers—that were earlier constructed in chapter 2.

II. IDENTIFYING THE FEDERALISM ISSUE

It is crucial to the following discussion to recognize the precise nature of the constitutional issue presented by a claim that one of the federalism provisions of the Constitution has been violated. When a litigant contends that the national government (usually the Congress, but occasionally the executive, either alone or in concert with the Senate) has engaged in activity beyond its delegated authority, or when it is alleged that an attempted state regulation intrudes into an area of exclusively national concern, the constitutional issue is wholly different from that posed by an assertion that certain government action abridges a personal liberty secured by the Constitution. The essence of a claim of the latter type—which falls into the individual rights category of constitutional issues, explored in chapter 2—is that no organ of government, national or state, may undertake the challenged activity. In contrast, when a person alleges that one of the federalism provisions of the Constitution has been violated, he implicitly concedes that one of the two levels of government—national or state—has power to engage in the questioned conduct. The core of the argument is simply that the particular government that has acted is the constitutionally improper one. To put it another way, a federalism attack on conduct of the national government contends that only the states may so act; a federalism challenge to a state practice asserts that only the central government possesses the exerted power; neither claim denies government power altogether.

III. THE FEDERALISM PROPOSAL

With the peculiar nature of constitutional issues concerning federalism being identified and many of the relevant constitutional provisions set out, the major thesis of this chapter—hereafter referred to as the Federalism Proposal—may be briefly stated: The federal judiciary should not decide constitutional questions respecting the ultimate power of the national government vis-à-vis the states; rather, the constitutional issue of whether federal action is beyond the authority of the central government and thus violates "states' rights" should be treated as nonjusticiable, final resolution being relegated to the political branches—i.e., Congress and the President.* It should be emphasized that neither this proposal nor the discussion that follows speaks to the substantive question of whether, in any given instance, the national government has overreached its del-

---

* The question of judicial oversight of state action allegedly encroaching on national prerogatives is considered in sec. VIII infra.

egated authority. Rather, the Federalism Proposal is addressed solely to the question of which branch of government should decide this constitutional issue.

IV. REPRESENTATION OF STATE INTERESTS IN THE NATIONAL POLITICAL PROCESS

We have observed that a primary justification for the Supreme Court's exercise of the power of judicial review in respect to claimed infringements of individual liberty is the teaching of theory and experience that these constitutionally secured interests are unlikely to receive sympathetic consideration in the political process. Judicial review of federalism issues cannot be similarly justified. Numerous structural aspects of the national political system serve to assure that states' rights will not be trampled, and the lesson of practice is that they have not been.

A. SENATE

Historically, the Senate, in Madison's words, was "that one branch of the legislature" that would function as "a representation . . . of the States."[2] Marshall repeatedly noted that "the States themselves, are represented in Congress,"[3] and he characterized members of the Senate as "the representatives of the state sovereignties."[4] That the Senate—a body "in which the smallest state has as much weight as the greatest"[5]—was originally intended to be a national legislative guardian against usurpation of state interests is made manifest by the Constitution's unalterable provision of equality of Senate representation for each state and the since amended provision that senators be chosen by the state legislatures. Even if the House of Representatives was "a representation of citizens"[6] rather than of states, the Senate—with its specially ordained powers over the making of treaties and the appointment of important national officials—could be depended upon to protect states' rights, for no law of the central government could be enacted "without the concurrence, first, of a majority of the people, and then, of a majority of the States."[7]

B. House of Representatives

The lower house, however, is not itself wholly devoid of mechanisms for state representation. Although not a major factor, the constitutional requirement that each state have at least one representative in the House is, nonetheless, *a* factor. The opportunities for state legislatures to influence the selection of congressmen through their authority to draw district lines that reflect political considerations is a more substantial factor, since this ability has apparently survived the Court's proscription of malapportionment.[8] Further, there is evidence that many state delegations in the House, composed of representatives from both political parties, seek to coordinate their behavior in order to serve mutual interests. Some of these state delegations often engage in bloc voting, either to achieve desired results or to establish a future bargaining position. Ordinarily, such delegations are fairly homogeneous in ideology, but when conflicts within these groups emerge, the members often make substantial efforts to act as a unit. Even within state delegations that are ideologically diverse, legislative issues of common concern are frequently discussed, although there is usually little pressure on the individual representatives to arrive at a common voting position.[9] Finally, both the Democratic and Republican leaderships in the House make special efforts in the committee assignment process to ensure fair representation from individual states, regions, and subregions,[10] and many state delegations (both homogeneous and diverse) work cohesively to obtain desirable assignments for their members.[11]

C. Electors

State legislative hegemony over members in both houses of Congress through the states' right to establish the qualifications of electors has been substantially diluted by a series of constitutional amendments and by recent federal legislation and judicial edicts that greatly expand the right to vote. But although it is no longer possible for state political chieftains to fence out significant segments of the citizenry through such devices as poll taxes and literacy tests and thus skew the electoral result, this does not mean that congressmen are now less reflective of state points of view. Rather, it simply means that the identification of state interests requires a broader survey of state opinion because, under the constitutional and statutory enlargements of the franchise, the voters who elect senators and representatives are the same voters who elect state officials.

D. SENATORS AND REPRESENTATIVES

Even stronger indication of the basic state orientation of the houses of Congress may be discovered by examining the background of their members. Madison's belief—that "even the House of Representatives, though drawn immediately from the people, will be chosen very much under the influence of that class of men, whose influence over the people obtains for themselves an election into the State legislatures"[12]—has been vindicated throughout our history. From the 1790s, usually more than three-fourths of the members of Congress have graduated from state and municipal offices. In the Senate of the Eightieth Congress, for example, nearly one-third of the senators had formerly been state governors.[13] And in the Senate of the Ninety-fifth Congress, fifteen of the senators had been governors, thirty-three others had occupied various state government positions, and fourteen more had served in local government.[14] For a variety of reasons—including the recruitment practices of local political parties (which dictate most nominations for Congress) and the electorate's hostility to "carpetbagger" office seekers—congressmen have characteristically had very long, resolute, and intimate ties to their districts.[15] Indeed, a contemporary study has revealed that "about 75 per cent of the members of recent Congresses were born in the state which they represent" and that congressmen are "less mobile than the general public and much less so than other elite groupings."[16]

It may be that these circumstances generate a parochialism and insularity of view in Congress that is subject to criticism on normative grounds. But it is significant evidence that congressmen do reflect and embody state opinions and are particularly sensitive to local concerns. And it probably goes far in explaining why national legislators generally choose to act and vote in conformity with their perceived regional interests, even when these are in conflict with the dictates of political party allegiance[17] and despite the increased reliance of a number of members of Congress on nationwide rather than local campaign support which presumably would influence them to respond to the views of special interests that are more broadly based than within the borders of a single state.

E. THE PRESIDENCY

The executive's key role in the lawmaking system also protects the states from encroachment by the national government. As a structural matter, the electoral college places the separate states directly in a nominee's path to the White House. Although the early practice of having electors chosen by state legislatures gave the states a more prominent role in presidential elections, state influence still exists, albeit to a lesser extent. Of greater impact has been the President's frequent obligation to local party organizations and state political leaders because of their substantial influence in the presidential nomination and election process.[18] Illustrative are the critical roles played by state governors in President Eisenhower's nomination and by Mayor Richard Daley of Chicago in President Kennedy's nomination and election.[19] Lyndon Johnson's late 1966 announcement of a $5.3 billion reduction in federal programs for state and local governments is another example. "Sensitive to criticism from the states, President Johnson released some of the money in February 1967, and on the eve of a conference the next month with governors he released additional amounts."[20] It is true that in the 1970s new political party rules have greatly diminished the power of state political leaders to control presidential nominations through the national conventions.[21] But candidates continue to depend on the aid of local party organizations in those states with party caucuses. And, to the extent that presidential primaries have enhanced the influence of grass-roots support, it must not be forgotten that these elections are still conducted on a state-by-state basis. Thus, at least until the establishment of national primaries, the felt obligation of presidential candidates and incumbents to be sensitive to local public officials in order to secure their nomination or renomination and reelection (or that of their preferred successor) remains.

The strongest assurance that executive action will be sensitive to states' rights derives from the President's need to maintain rapport with Congress, a body whose binding local ties have been explored in detail. President Carter's early conflict with Congress over funding of federal water projects demonstrates both congressional vigilance over the impact of executive actions on localities and the President's realization that he must treat such legislative concern delicately, if not deferentially.

Executive solicitude for states' rights can even be seen in foreign policy, where the President's "diplomatic representatives are, or are made, acutely aware of our federal character—as when they hesitate to negotiate about 'local matters,' or insist on adding 'federal-state' clauses [to treaties] that are constitutionally unnecessary but politically attractive."[22] And further examples of presidential attentiveness to state concerns may be found in such practices as the creation of a special White House unit for federal-state relations and the designation of a high-ranking administration official (in recent years often the Vice-President) to be the President's liaison with the states.

F. THE INTERGOVERNMENTAL LOBBY

The phenomenon of most recent vintage that underscores the powerful impact of state and local interests on the national political process concerns what Samuel Beer has denominated as the interplay between the "professional bureaucratic complex" (i.e., the numerous groups of federal administrative officials with scientific and technical expertise in special areas) and the "intergovernmental lobby" (i.e., "the governors, mayors, county supervisors and other officeholders, usually elective, who exercise general responsibilities in state and local governments"). In the past decade and a half, Beer observes "how rarely additions to the public sector have been *initiated* by the demands of voters or the advocacy of pressure groups or the platforms of political parties. On the contrary, in the fields of health, housing, urban renewal, transportation, welfare, education, poverty, and energy, it has been, in very great measure, people in government service, or closely associated with it, acting on the basis of their specialized and technical knowledge, who first perceived the problem, conceived the program, initially urged it on the president and Congress, went on to help lobby it through to enactment, and then saw to its administration." The intergovernmental lobby—often acting through such Washington-headquartered organizations as "the National Governors Conference, the Council of State Governments, the United States Conference of Mayors, the National League of Cities, the National Association of Counties, the International City Management Association, and the National Legislative Conference, and through alliances of them"—has engaged in "continual, almost day-to-day activity ... offering advice and pressing requests before the executive and legislative branches of the federal government." Its national political influence may be illustrated by its successful pursuit of greater federal funding with fewer conditions attached: "in the past few years the mayors, governors, county executives and others have played a major role in bringing about a shift in the character of federal aid. In 1966 categorical aid accounted for 98 percent of federal aid. By 1975 it was down to 75 percent as a result of general revenue sharing and block grants."[23]

G. IDENTIFYING THE "VIEWPOINT" OF A "STATE"

All that has been said about the accountability of the members of both national political branches to state and local concerns being accepted, it must be admitted that the task of precisely identifying a particular state's "interest" or "point of view" on any specific issue may often be difficult and fraught with ambiguity. If both of a state's U.S. senators, a majority of its delegation in the House of Representatives, and its governor all agree on a matter, then the "state's view" has most likely been accurately ascertained. But if there is a divergence of opinion among these officials, it may legitimately be asked: Who represents the "state's opinion" in the dispute?

For example, in *National League of Cities v. Usery*,[24] the attorneys general of twenty-two states (either as parties or amici curiae)—joined by the National League of Cities and the National Association of Counties—urged that amendments to the Fair Labor Standards Act (passed by Congress and signed by the President), which regulated the wages of state and municipal employees, exceeded national power vis-à-vis the states; only four state attorneys general filed amicus briefs defending Congress's action.[25] Was this law approved by the "representatives of a majority of the separate States"? The provision challenged in *Usery* was most squarely addressed in the national legislative process when a proposed Senate amendment—which voiced the sentiment of President Nixon[26]—to delete overtime coverage for police and firemen was soundly defeated by a vote of 29 to 65.[27] (No such reliable vote was taken in the lower chamber. The original House bill did not cover police and firemen but, after the Conference Committee included a modified Senate version, the House approved the complete bill by a vote of 345 to 50.)[28]

What was the position of the national representatives of the twenty-two states whose attorneys general contested the constitutionality of this provision before the Court? Both senators from seven states—California, Iowa, Massachusetts, Mississippi, Montana, New York, and South Dakota—voted to regulate the hours and wages of police and firemen. These included Democrats such as Alan Cranston, Republicans such as Jacob Javits, liberals such as George McGovern, and conservatives such as James Buckley. (In addition, in the less telling House ballot, the delegations from six of these seven states voted overwhelmingly for the bill; South Dakota's representatives were evenly divided.) The one senator (and eight representatives) from Missouri who voted were also in favor. The senators from ten of the other states split on the proposed Senate amendment. (The representatives of eight of these states—Indiana, Nevada, New Hampshire, Oregon, South Carolina, Texas, Utah, and Wyoming—supported the law by at least 2 to 1; the Maryland House delegation divided evenly; only a majority of Virginia's House members opposed it.) The one senator from Arizona whose vote was recorded cast his ballot against the national regulation (but the state's House members split). Both senators from only three of the states under consideration—Delaware, Nebraska, and Oklahoma—voted to delete the overtime coverage (yet the representatives of all three of these states backed the final bill almost unanimously).

These data, of course, are not meant to demonstrate conclusively that most of the attorneys general who made submissions to the Court in *Usery* failed to reflect their states' true positions. But the figures surely raise questions as to whether they did. At a formalistic level, it is tempting to equate a "state's interest" with the positions voiced by state and local officials rather than with the ballots cast by the state's representatives in the nation's capital. It is often heard that once the latter reach Washington they shed their regional bonds and adopt a broader national perspective. But the available data (recounted in detail in chapter 1) suggest otherwise. The canny judgment of Professor Charles Black and Representative Bob Eckhardt underlines the point: "The thing to which the interest of the Senator *must* incline is to keep his fences mended in his own State, and to do that above all, because if he fails in this, . . . he won't be living in Washington any more."[29] Even if it could be assumed that an argument advanced before the Supreme Court by a state attorney general describes the view of that state's governor (or a majority of its legislature)—and this assumption is extremely fragile in the many states in which the attorney general is elected independently—it by no means follows that that position better reflects the "opinion" of the "state" than that articulated by its representatives in Congress. That state and local officers may, because of budgetary problems, oppose a federal minimum wage for state and local employees does not necessarily mean that the "state" is opposed. Just as Madison perceived the Constitution as having been created not by the "state governments" but rather by the "people of the states"[30]—a notion that is plausibly underlined by the tenth amendment's reservation of power not merely "to the states" but also "to the people" therein[31]—so, too, it may not be the viewpoint of a state's government but that of the people of the state that is at issue. As to this, the judgment of the state's congressional representatives, politically responsible to the electorate of the entire state or to districted groups therein, may fairly be relied upon.

H. The Record of Experience

1. Historical Prediction

The early view, expressed throughout *The Federalist* by both Hamilton and Madison, was that "the State governments may be regarded as constituent and essential parts of the federal government";[32] "a local spirit will infallibly prevail...in the members of the Congress";[33] "the people of each State would be apt to feel a stronger bias towards their local governments than towards the government of the Union";[34] and "ambitious encroachments of the federal government on the authority of the State governments would not excite the opposition of a single State, or of a few States only. They would be signals of general alarm. Every government would espouse the common cause"[35] and "exert their local influence in effecting a change of federal representatives."[36]

2. Comparison of State and Federal Officials

The judgment that the voice of the states would be heard distinctly—perhaps dominantly—in the nation's capital has been that it frequently pays too great heed to the provincial as well. Observers of the American lawmaking system find that political attitudes and policy conflicts that exist in the houses of Congress are the same as those present in most state legislative halls.[37] Further, whereas a long-standing indictment of Congress has been that it frequently pays too great heed to the provincial concerns of the individual states and regions to the detriment of the needs of the nation as a whole, it has also been observed that "state officials find a large variety of values pressing upon them as they carry out their responsibilities, of which states' rights is usually a minor one."[38] Indeed, it may well be that a local legislator who opposes his state's regulating a particular subject would, as a federal lawmaker, find an identical nationwide regulation wholly acceptable because the national action would remove the competitive disadvantage to his state that its unilateral action would entail.[39]

3. Negative Quality of National Political Process

Madison's pessimistic forecast—that "measures will too often be decided according to their probable effect, not on the national prosperity and happiness, but on the prejudices, interests, and pursuits of the governments and people of the individual States"[40]—has been markedly realized. And it has been substantially reinforced by the "negative" mechanisms of the constitutional process—such as bicameralism, the committee system, and the filibuster (considered at length in chapter 1)—that allow representatives elected by minuscule numbers of citizens and senators representing an insignificant fraction of the national electorate to block the enactment of laws, as well as by the executive veto, which permits one stroke of the presidential pen to nullify the will of both legislative chambers. As a consequence, if proposed federal legislation touches the nerve of states' rights in any meaningful way, it is usually subject to extensive examination and searching scrutiny. When the political branches do decree a national solution for a problem of state concern, when—as Madison put it—they "become more partial to the federal than to the State governments, the change can only result from such manifest and irresistible proofs of a better administration, as will overcome all their antecedent propensities."[41]

4. Examples of National Solicitude for States' Rights

The immense growth of the national government's activities over the history of the American Republic cannot be denied. The familiar expansion which occurred in response to the increased complexity and number of societal problems and to the increased interdependence of the states caused by industrialization and improved transportation and communication has been profound. But the proliferation of national programs has neither led to a centralized autocracy nor resulted in the total concentration of federal power to the exclusion of the individual states. As illustrated by the prolonged constitutional debates in Congress that delayed passage of the Sherman Act for several years[42] and stalled desperately needed antilynching laws and civil rights legislation for too many more, Congress has generally paid fastidious attention to the notion that certain government powers are reserved to the states. As late as 1948, Charles Beard could write that "efforts to effect uniformity of the suffrage by national action have repeatedly been defeated in Congress, especially in the Senate, where the states are equally represented. The angry feelings aroused in both houses of Congress by attempts to abolish poll-tax qualifications on the right to vote have vividly demonstrated that the federal principle of state control over the suffrage cannot be easily broken down, if at all, by action on the part of the national government."[43]

These examples of congressional hesitancy regarding federal intrusions could easily be multiplied hundreds of times— witness Congress's refusal in 1789 to create a "Home Department" because of its belief that this might trespass on the states' authority,[44] the judicious concern for local control over education that has accompanied each proposal of federal financial aid,[45] repeated congressional rejections of President Nixon's proposals to set a national minimum for state unemployment compensation,[46] and suspension by Congress of various Environmental Protection Agency regulations in 1975 because of strong criticism by the state and local governments subject to them.[47]

Presidents as well as legislators have been solicitous of the federal system. Presidents have effectively resisted national legislation that they believed would intrude on states' rights. Examples include Andrew Jackson's rejection of the Bank of the United States, and vetoes on states' rights grounds by James Monroe of legislation extending national regulation of roads and by Franklin Pierce of a law aiding the insane.[48] Presidents have also affirmatively promoted state autonomy. For example, both Lyndon Johnson's "Creative Federalism" and Richard Nixon's

"New Federalism" emphasized the return of large areas of substantive responsibility and even larger amounts of revenue to state and local government. Federal revenue sharing, which had its genesis in the assumption by Congress of state debts following the Revolutionary War, was enacted in modern times principally to relieve the desperate financial plight of local government.[49] Revenue sharing has supplemented the traditional federal income tax policies of excluding from gross income the interest paid on state and local bonds and permitting the deduction of state and local taxes, both of which effectively are outright monetary awards to the states with no federal strings attached. Further, revenue sharing programs have built on the long-standing—although more centrally controlled—federal grant-in-aid programs for state and locally administered functions. Even Franklin Roosevelt, probably the most aggressively nationalistic President, manifested concern for preserving federalism, overruling his expert advisers to assign the administration of unemployment insurance to the states.[50] In all, there is ample support for Herbert Wechsler's persuasive conclusion that "far from a national authority that is expansionist by nature, the inherent tendency in our system is precisely the reverse, necessitating the widest support before intrusive measures of importance can receive significant consideration, reacting readily to opposition grounded in resistance within the states."[51]

This conclusion and its underlying rationale have singular pertinence to the Federalism Proposal—that the Supreme Court should not adjudicate constitutional questions of national power versus states' rights. Cases in which an act of the federal government is alleged to exceed the scope of national authority vis-à-vis the states are presented to the Court only after the federal political process has affirmatively produced the legislation—that is, only after attainment of the broad consensus that is required to overcome the inertia and negative elements of the national legislative system that permit the majority will to be stymied by only a few states' representatives. Legislation that affects states' rights must also clear the imposing hurdle of active concern for state sovereignty. As we shall see, this solicitude cannot be attributed to the threat of judicial invalidation, because, except in a few notable instances, the Court's definitions of national powers have afforded the political branches exceedingly broad discretion in this area. In contrast to the undemocratic aspect of malapportionment, which permits minority representatives to impose laws on the majority against its will, there is forceful assurance that consummated national legislation affecting states' rights has the widespread support of those affected. Under these conditions, the necessity and justification for judicial review is at its lowest ebb. Even if the Court is characterized as a disinterested arbiter between the central government and the states, since the partiality of the national political branches leans to the side of localism, ultimate resolution of federalism issues may safely be vested in Congress and the President.

5. Vitality of State and Local Government

Dire predictions to the contrary notwithstanding, and despite the prodigious grant of authority to the national political branches that has been underwritten and authenticated by the Court, American federalism is not dead or even withering. While changed circumstances over time may have lessened our devotion to Brandeis's view "that in differentiation not in uniformity, lies the path of progress"[52] (although it may well be an idea whose day has come again), the hard facts show that state and local government are currently more engaged than at any stage in our history. This has been largely ignored by those who denigrate the vitality of state and local government by focusing only on the concededly huge expansion of federal involvement. The point overlooked is that the expenditures and activities of *all* levels of government greatly increased as the American electorate became committed (at least until the late 1970s) to a continually widening public sector and to a larger investment of resources in governmentally sponsored social and economic programs. Thus, for example, in the three decades "from 1938 to 1967 the expenditures of the federal government increased a little more than eightfold, the expenditures of state and local governments a little less than eightfold.... 'Obsolete' state and local governments spend far more than the federal government for education, highways, health and hospitals, public welfare, and housing and community development.... Revenues from strictly state and local sources...were ten times greater in 1967 than in 1938.... Of about thirteen million civilians employed by government in 1969, about one in four were federal employees, more than one in five were state employees, and a bit less than half were employed by local governments.... In 1967...[state and local government] expenditures for civil functions were equivalent to 12 per cent of the gross national product, compared with 5.5 per cent for the federal government."[53]

The statistics for the 1970s are even more impressive.[54] For example, the revenues of state and local governments have become nearly as large as those of their national counterpart. Excluding federal grants-in-aid, and state utility, liquor store, and trust fund receipts, the 1975 combined local and state government revenues amounted to $182 billion compared with federal income of $225 billion.[55] On the other side of the fiscal coin, state and local expenditures, taken as a percentage of the gross national product, increased 50 percent over a twenty-three-year period, leaping from 7.4 percent of the GNP in 1954 to 11 percent in 1976. During this same period, outlays in the federal sector registered only a 21 percent increase.[56] The continuing vitality of state and local governments becomes even more apparent on examining employment figures. The number of full-time state and local employees grew from 4.1 million in 1955 to 9.3 million in 1974 (approximately one-eighth of the entire national work force)—a 125 percent increase. During the same twenty years, federal employment increased by only 19 percent and private employment by 39 percent.[57] Indeed, employment in the state-local sector has increased more rapidly than any other major sector of the economy—public or private—during these two decades.[58] By the end of 1977, the number of state and local employees had reached twelve million.

A final indication of the persisting pledge to the federalism ideal—at the state level, but analogous to that in Washington— may be seen in the progression of "home rule," a miniature system of federalism created within the states by state legislatures in order to obtain the benefits promised by localism. All these factors and developments lend strength to the proposition that, whatever the constitutional limits of national authority in this field may be, the federal political branches are fully capable of guarding against the states' being swallowed by a central monolith.

V. DEFEAT OF REGIONAL INTERESTS IN THE NATIONAL POLITICAL PROCESS

In assessing the prior discussion of state representation in the national political process, caution must be exercised to avoid exaggeration. The fact remains that "there will often be vital regional interests represented by no majority in Congress."[59] Indeed, irrespective of the "negative power" advantages held in Congress by even a single state and surely by a small group of them, the desires of certain identifiable segments of the country have been and will be periodically submerged by the force of competing numbers.

A. INSTANCES OF CONCEDED NATIONAL POWER

Tariffs are paradigmatic examples of laws that benefit some states at the expense of others. Few more illustrative examples of bitter strife along discrete geographic lines may be found than that generated by the protective tariffs promulgated by Congress in the first part of the nineteenth century. Nearly causing an early secession and civil war, the enactments produced John Calhoun's famous theory of nullification and South Carolina's authorization of armed resistance to the collection of duties within the state, which eventually led President Jackson and Congress to threaten military intervention. For our purposes, however, the important point is that given the authority specifically delegated to Congress "to regulate Commerce with foreign Nations," there can be little question but that the central government possesses the power to treat the distinct interests of certain states or regions prejudicially. Whether the national government should exercise such power may present a perplexing issue of federalism at the political level. But since there is no constitutional issue, judicial review to aid the cause of states' rights would be unavailing.

Similarly, the explicit power of Congress "to dispose of... Property belonging to the United States" convincingly immunizes from judicial scrutiny the ability of the federal political branches to favor some states over others—as was done in the Submerged Lands Act of 1953 when Congress conveyed extremely valuable coastline properties resting in the Atlantic and Pacific and the Gulf of Mexico to certain seaboard states over the objections of other less favored states.[60] National authority to acquire and establish sovereignty over a particular parcel of land within a single state, even over that state's objection, further illustrates the point.[61] And federal spending programs provide additional instances of constitutionally unimpeachable national power to affect unevenly the states' vital concerns. In the 1972 battle over federal revenue-sharing, for example, the Senate, bending to the financial interests of the more numerous smaller states, rejected an attempt to allocate a larger share of federal funds to industrial states, despite the plight of their cities.[62] It needs little further explanation to appreciate that agricultural price supports are more popular among the people in Kansas than in Connecticut and that federal subsidies for education take from the more affluent in California to pay the less fortunate in Mississippi. Since key issues of federalism such as these are committed to resolution on the political battlefield, the need for the Supreme Court to protect states' rights on subjects of identical state conflict, but where there is less clearly established national power, is hardly compelling.

B. Homogeneous versus Heterogeneous Nature of Regional Interests

Although some social and cultural differences among the people in the country may be identified by reference to state and regional boundaries, the scope of the divergence thus defined exists more plainly in its statement than in reality. Often the facile correlation of a particular state or region with a par-

ticular set of interests or a general point of view is simply errone-
ous. Rather, as Robert Dahl has shown, "the various regions of
the United States are internally very heterogeneous. So much so,
in fact, that it is exceedingly difficult to decide how to draw
regional boundaries: One must choose one set of states for one
purpose, another set for a different purpose."[63] Most genuine
disputes concerning regional interests, historically and contemporarily, revolve around economic matters: certain regions
are more heavily associated with manufacturing or the lack of it,
with unionization or the lack of it, with agriculture or the lack of
it; with cotton versus wheat, or fruits and vegetables versus
livestock; or with finance, transportation, and communication or
the lack of it. Yet, owing to the extreme economic interdependence of modern America and (as we shall see) the capa-
cious reach of the commerce clause, it is this very subject over
which the central government has probably the least disputed
authority, where the usual controversy is one of policy and wisdom rather than constitutionality or federalism. Therefore, judicial review of national regulatory power over regional disputes
would be of least value to those who cherish localism.

Apart from the general area of economics, the foremost issue of
true regional conflict—the chasm that literally split the union—
has been race. If there has been any single subject of national
political concern that has cleanly divided congressional opinion
along geographic lines and starkly put the issue of a uniform
national response as opposed to diversity among the states, it has
been the rights of the Negro. But in the 1960s, when the majority
of the states' national representatives ultimately prevailed in the
political process and decreed a monolithic solution, the Court,
relying on several sources of congressional authority, un-
reservedly upheld the national power to do so.[64] Despite the
highly uneven impact of the new federal laws on the separate
states, the issue of constitutional federalism was properly held to
rest outside the judicial process.

With national primacy clearly established on issues such as
economics and race, there is little reason to keep the Court in
reserve out of fear that Congress might enact uniform laws of

murder, divorce, inheritance, descent and distribution, or re-
cording of land titles—to mention some subjects of regulatory
concern often suggested as being within the sacrosanct province
of the states. For these are matters—like the minimum age for
voting[65]—of much less apparent homogeneous geographic conflict and in regard to which national rules would affect almost all
states fairly uniformly. (Indeed, most acts of Congress that are
challenged before the Court as invading the states' realm are of
this genre.) Here, the judgment of the political branches may be
much more safely trusted to preserve the values of American
federalism.

VI. REACH OF THE FEDERALISM PROPOSAL

Before we proceed further, it may be useful to define
the contours of the Federalism Proposal in some greater detail.
The essential contrast is between constitutional questions that
concern the scope of national power vis-à-vis the states, which
the Court should hold to be nonjusticiable, and those that concern
the scope of government vis-à-vis the individual, which, under
the Individual Rights Proposal discussed in chapter 2, should be
subject to judicial review. Under the Federalism Proposal all
questions of the reach of federal authority versus states' rights
under the delegated national powers (or prohibitions on national
power), described in sec. I of this chapter, fall into the former
classification. Thus, for example, the Supreme Court should not
have adjudicated the constitutional issues of this type in the following cases:

Bailey v. Drexel Furniture Co., 259 U.S. 20 (1922), whether Congress had power to impose a tax on enterprises employing
child labor (taxing power);
United States v. Butler, 297 U.S. 1 (1936), whether Congress had
power to pay money to farmers in exchange for their agreement to reduce planted acreage (spending power);
Hammer v. Dagenhart, 247 U.S. 251 (1918), whether Congress
had power to prohibit the interstate transportation of goods

produced in factories employing child labor (commerce power);

Woods v. Cloyd W. Miller Co., 333 U.S. 138 (1948), whether Congress had power to regulate rents after the end of hostilities in World War II (war power);

United States v. Classic, 313 U.S. 299 (1941), whether Congress had power to penalize interference with voting in state primary elections for congressmen (power respecting manner of electing congressmen);

Missouri v. Holland, 252 U.S. 416 (1920), whether the President and Senate had power to enter into a treaty to protect migratory birds (treaty power);

Coyle v. Smith, 221 U.S. 559 (1911), whether Congress had power to condition a state's entry into the Union on the state's continuing the location of its capital (power over admission of new states);

Jones v. Alfred H. Mayer Co., 392 U.S. 409 (1968), whether Congress had power to forbid racial discrimination in housing (power to enforce thirteenth amendment);

Civil Rights Cases, 109 U.S. 3 (1883), whether Congress had power to forbid racial discrimination in public accommodations (power to enforce fourteenth amendment equal protection);

United States v. Raines, 362 U.S. 17 (1960), whether Congress had power to forbid racial discrimination in voting (power to enforce fifteenth amendment);

Pollock v. Farmers' Loan & Trust Co., 157 U.S. 429 (1895), whether Congress had power to impose a national income tax (prohibition on laying of direct taxes except in proportion to the census).

These cases were chosen almost randomly for purposes of illustration and involve both judicial endorsements and invalidations of federal power. Although they cover a wide swath of traditional constitutional adjudication, they do not exhaust the category. Another constitutional question that concerns only states' rights is whether Congress, as a necessary and proper exercise of its delegated powers, may generally subject the states to lawsuits in federal courts (or before international tribunals), the states' constitutional contention being that such federal action violates their sovereign immunity secured in the eleventh amendment.[66] Yet another involves legislative authority over intoxicating liquors—the constitutional conflict pitting the powers designated to Congress to regulate and tax against the specific grant of control to the states in the twenty-first amendment.[67]

Finally, there are several additional issues of this genre that, although they are less easily related to a particular constitutional provision, nonetheless plainly involve only federalism questions and, therefore, should be left to the national political process for final resolution. The constitutional immunity of state property and activities from federal taxation and regulation is probably the most significant both in terms of quantity of litigation (taxation immunity)[68] and as a source of current controversy (regulation immunity).[69] Given (as we have seen in detail) the clarity of the states' voices in the federal government and the conceded ability of the political branches to prejudice only some states in areas of vital concern, there is no persuasive reason to put these constitutional issues to the Court—even if the federal tax or regulation is alleged to discriminate against the states as compared with persons similarly situated, or to subject some states and not others (either de jure or de facto) to the federal regime. Similarly, the constitutional question—presented in both *United States v. Belmont*[70] and *United States v. Pink*[71]—whether an executive agreement concerns a subject that lies beyond federal power and is thus reserved to the states should not be within the realm of the federal judiciary.

VII. RELATIONSHIP OF THE FEDERALISM PROPOSAL TO ISSUES OF INDIVIDUAL RIGHTS

A. DISTINCTION BETWEEN DERIVATIVE AND INDEPENDENT INDIVIDUAL RIGHTS CLAIMS

1. Derivative Rights

One element common to all the above illustrations is that claims which attack the constitutionality of the various exercises of national power concede that the challenged conduct could properly have been undertaken by state governments acting within their jurisdiction. There is no genuine constitutional claim of individual freedom from government regulation. Such an allegation may be constructed, however, perhaps premised on the dictum in *Marbury v. Madison* that "the very essence of civil liberty certainly consists in the right of every individual to claim the protection of the laws, whenever he receives an injury."[72] If the disputed actions of the federal political branches are constitutionally ultra vires the central government, the argument would proceed, then the actions are nullities and it would therefore be a violation of personal constitutional liberty to apply them to the detriment of any individual. The point may even be clothed with specific constitutional dignity by adding that the regulation of an individual's life, liberty, or property by means of a constitutionally invalid rule is a denial of due process of law. This construct is by no means an impossible one. But, unlike other approaches that equate violations of federalism with deprivations of personal liberty (which we shall examine—and reject—below), it is built more on semantics than substance. For, no matter how it is phrased, the root of the argument is that states' rights have been abridged. The personal liberty claim is merely a derivative of that primary finding. The argument concludes that transgression of a federalism principle violates civil liberty or "due process" but, without the supporting states' rights rationale, this conclusion is simply assumed. The argument—in calling for judicial review in the name of individual rights— ignores the essential difference between judicial invalidations of government action that result in augmenting the total range of individual liberty (the individual rights category) and those that result only in distributing authority to regulate personal action between the nation and states (the federalism category). If the states concededly may do to the individual what it is claimed that the federal government may not do, the issue of concern is primarily one for the states and, for reasons already discussed, may be entrusted to the states' representatives in the national political branches to decide.

2. Independent Rights

It is important, however, to recognize that true constitutional questions of personal rights may arise from action of the central government that is also and *independently* alleged to be beyond national power vis-à-vis the states. In *United States v. Darby*,[73] for example, it was contended that the Fair Labor Standards Act of 1936 (which regulated wages and hours in factories that produced goods for interstate commerce) exceeded the commerce power of Congress *and*, even if it were within that power because the matter substantially affected interstate commerce, nonetheless such regulation of personal economic freedom was a deprivation of property without due process of law. This same duet of constitutional objections was lodged against the Civil Rights Act of 1964 (which prohibited racial discrimination in public accommodations that under the Act were deemed to affect interstate commerce).[74] Similarly, in the *Belmont* and *Pink* cases, it was charged both that President Roosevelt's executive agreement with the Soviet Union respecting Russian assets within the states was an invasion of states' rights and that the Litvinov Assignment violated the fifth amendment by depriving individual creditors of property without due process of law and by taking private property without just compensation. And, in *Katzenbach v. Morgan*,[75] those attacking a provision of the Voting Rights Act of 1965 (in which Congress suspended state English literacy tests for voting only for certain groups of citizens) urged not only that the entire subject rested within the province of the states but also that, even if the national government did have general regulatory power over this aspect of the franchise, the statute's discrimination among groups of citizens violated the equal protection rights of those to whom the ballot was not extended. Analogous objections may be raised to virtually all federal enlargements of the franchise. For example, wholly apart from whether power over voting qualifications belongs to the national government or to the states, it may be alleged that, by increasing the voting ability of some persons, Congress has "restricted" or "diluted" that of others in violation of their personal constitutional rights.

The constitutional merit of the individual liberty contentions presented in these contexts is beyond the scope of discussion. What is critical is the clear distinction between them and the semantic personal rights argument examined earlier. Here, the personal rights claims are not merely derivative of or dependent on a violation of the federalism principle. Rather they present primary and independent constitutional issues. If the Supreme Court addresses the earlier argument that Congress has denied the claimant due process because it is exercising authority that is reserved to the states—and the Federalism Proposal urges that it should not—the Court need only determine whether states' rights have been abridged. But, in responding to the personal liberties contentions just advanced, the Court must decide the far more consequential question of whether all government power to take the disputed action is constitutionally forbidden.

a. Unavailability of Narrower Constitutional Decision

Acceptance of the Federalism Proposal will prevent the Court from avoiding the broader constitutional decision (of whether national action abrogates individual rights) by instead rendering the narrower constitutional holding (that states' rights have been transgressed). This seeming disadvantage is more theoretical than real, however. In most instances, the Court could only delay considering the individual rights claim. It is true that, following judicial rejection of a national program on federalism grounds, not even a single state might enact a similar program because of the competitive disadvantage to its citizens that would result. But since, ordinarily, action that one or both of the national political branches deemed sufficiently necessary would probably commend itself to at least one of the states, it is likely that the individual rights issue eventually would reach the Court.

b. Civil War Amendments Analysis

Fundamental questions concerning the Court's role in regard to issues arising under the Civil War amendments may be illuminated by the intrinsic difference between constitutional questions of states' rights, on the one hand, and individual liberties, on the other. When the Supreme Court invalidates state (or private) action under the initial sections of the thirteenth, fourteenth, or fifteenth amendments, it holds that the challenged conduct has infringed constitutionally secured personal liberty. As a general rule, these decisions may not be overturned by ordinary federal legislation;[76] rather, the results may only be modified through the extraordinary procedure of constitutional amendment or a change of view by the Court itself. Because the judiciary is the branch of the federal government that is peculiarly qualified to safeguard the constitutional liberties of individuals, this is as it should be. But these Civil War amendments have another function. Their final clauses empower Congress to enforce the personal rights created in their opening sections. Indeed, a principal purpose of these amendments—if not *the* principal purpose of their framers—was, in the words of the Hoover Commission, to effect "a revolutionary alteration in our federal system"[77] by investing Congress with a broad and flexible authority to promote civil liberties throughout the nation.[78] When Congress legislates pursuant to this extensive power and restricts state (or private) action beyond that which would be forbidden by the Court acting under §1 of each of the amendments, the usual constitutional question posed is only one of states' rights, because the congressional action is usually one that could properly be undertaken by the states themselves. Unlike judicial invalidations under the amendments' opening clauses, which can be altered only by constitutional amendment, actions of the national political branches under the enforcement clauses may be altered through the ordinary political process—i.e., by repeal or modification of the original federal statute. For the Court to change its interpretations of the first clauses of the amendments, it must confess to constitutional mistake; for the Congress to vary its decrees under the enforcement provisions, it need only admit to prudential error. These considerations strongly support the Court's present position which affords Congress extensive flexibility to define constitutional liberty under the enforcement clauses[79]—a much more spacious latitude than the Court itself assumes in reviewing state (and private) action under §1 of each of the amendments unaided by congressional legislation. Under the Federalism Proposal, the existing judicial doctrine is carried one step further: when the only constitutional issue presented by action of the national political branches is one of the states' rights (as it usually is), there should be no judicial review at all.

c. Final Illustration

The decision in *United States v. California*[80] may be usefully examined as a final illustration of the states' rights–individual rights dichotomy. The decision is of particular theoretical interest because it is slightly variant and thus does not technically involve a question of allocation of regulatory power between nation and states. The Attorney General of the United States, who possessed broad statutory authority to conduct litigation for safeguarding federal property, sought to enjoin California from leasing offshore oil lands on the ground that the central government and not the state held title. There was no disagreement that the national government had regulatory power over the property, but California contended that it had proprietary rights. Although it appeared that neither Congress nor the President had specifically asserted national ownership of the area in question, the Court, in a split decision, sided with the Attorney General. Since the "constitutional-like" issue of ultimate ownership was purely one of the rights of the state versus the nation, however, the Court *should* have treated it as nonjusticiable.[81] On the one hand, the Court could have granted—as it did grant—the requested relief on the theory that whether the United States owned the property was a matter to be resolved by the political branches, but, in the absence of their explicit consideration or determination, a judicial injunction was desirable so as to keep their options open. This approach is the same as the Court's treatment of claims that state action improperly intrudes into an area of national dominion even though the federal political branches have not spoken—an exercise of judicial authority, we shall soon see, that comports with the Federalism Proposal. Alternatively, recognizing the prevailing inertia of the national political process, the Court might well have concluded that issuance of the injunction would realistically constitute a final resolution of the dispute in favor of the central government. Thus, the political branches not having clearly laid claim to the lands, perhaps the wiser path for the Court would have been (as Justice Frankfurter suggested in dissent) to decline to lend its assistance to the Attorney General and let the matter remain as it was without judicial intervention. In any event, given the agreed-upon federal authority to regulate the property, that inquiry was in no way advanced by the Court's ruling on ownership. Seisin would only become relevant if the title-holder were to claim that public regulation amounted to a "taking" requiring just compensation. Since a state was the claimant in this case, however, under the approach advanced herein, this would *not* be an individual liberty claim but rather one of states' rights to be resolved in the political arena.

B. QUALITATIVE DIFFERENCE BETWEEN ISSUES OF FEDERALISM AND INDIVIDUAL RIGHTS

There is a distinctive qualitative difference separating constitutional issues of federalism from those of individual liberty, a dissimilarity that augurs for the variant judicial role proposed herein. The disparity does not lie in the relative difficulty or intricacy of the questions involved in either category, for both comprehend multifaceted and complex matters. Rather, the difference may be described as one between issues of practicality and issues of principle.

When government action abridges constitutionally ordained personal liberties, it seems likely that, at least in view of short-run concerns for efficient public administration and businesslike accomplishment of laudable public objectives, the commonweal would usually be better served by compromising the interests seeking judicial protection. Thus, one of the major reasons for Federalist opposition to a bill of rights was the fear that it would inhibit effective government.[82] In the main, it is only our historic ideals and special regard for the dignity of the individual that compel the collective will to subjugate its more immediate needs to the preservation of designated individual rights. In short, it is government according to principle.

Constitutional issues of federalism, on the other hand, are a distinguishable species. One of the principal purposes behind the abandoament of the Articles of Confederation and the adoption of the Constitution—if not *the* major purpose—was to establish a workable central government, one whose authority was unquestionably limited but one nonetheless with sufficient power to cope with problems which prior experience had shown the states incompetent to resolve separately and for which national action was desperately needed.[83] Assessment of the relative capabilities of the different levels of government, then, is a key step in determining whether a particular exercise of federal power exceeds the assigned boundaries. As has been emphasized at several points in this chapter, the constitutional issue is not whether there is *any* government power to fulfill the public need; it is whether the goal may be accomplished only through action of the individual states. As between the two levels of government, Madison originally saw the "impossibility of dividing powers of legislation, in such a manner, as to be free from different constructions by different interests, or even from ambiguity in the judgment of the impartial."[84] As Woodrow Wilson stated over half a century ago, the matter "cannot . . . be settled by the opinion of any one generation, because it is a question of growth, and every successive stage of our political and economic development gives it a new aspect, makes it a new question."[85] Inherent in this inquiry is whether, as a functional matter, the states are separately capable of effecting the desired result. The pragmatic, almost literally borderline question posed is thus one of comparative skill and utility—in a word, an issue of practicability.

Whatever the judiciary's purported or self-professed special competence in articulating the values and defining the scope of those constitutional clauses that declare individual rights, when the fundamental issue turns in large measure on the relative competence of different levels of government to deal with societal problems, the Court is no more inherently capable of correct judgment than its companion federal branches. Indeed, the judiciary may well be less capable, given both the highly pragmatic nature of federal-state questions and the forceful representation of the states (which are most directly affected by their resolution) in the national process of political decisionmaking. Thus, for Madison, "the roles of the two governments would not depend upon legal line-drawing but upon the political process by which they were constituted."[86]

Lest there be any misunderstanding, I am not arguing that constitutional decisions of federalism should rest with the political branches because they (especially the Congress) are better equipped than the Court to gather the underlying factual data necessary for intelligent judgment or more adept at fashioning the broad evaluations required to make wise public policy. A great many of the personal liberties questions that the Court decides—such as the nature of the threat posed by political "subversives," the ability of the accused criminal to defend without the assistance of counsel, the need for an abortion to be performed in a licensed hospital—similarly subsume large policy issues with complex and debatable factual considerations. Rather, the point is that constitutional questions of federalism differ from those of individual liberty both in terms of their distinctive, pragmatic quality and in the likelihood of their fair resolution within the national political chambers. When democratic processes may be generally trusted to produce a fair constitutional judgment, it advances the democratic tradition to vest that judgment with popularly responsible institutions.

C. ASSERTION OF STATES' RIGHTS BY INDIVIDUALS

Ironically, in the absence of the Federalism Proposal the judiciary could hold a federal enactment to be beyond national power at the behest of a private person who is affected by it, despite a majority of every state's congressional representatives having voted for the law and every state's attorney general defending it when it is challenged in the courts. This imagined case lies not very far from real ones.

The first national child labor law, invalidated by the Court on federalism grounds in *Hammer v. Dagenhart*[87] in 1918, had been approved by a Democratic-controlled Congress two years earlier by votes of 337 to 46 in the House and 52 to 12 in the Senate.

Less than a year after the *Hammer* decision, a Republican-controlled Congress, relying this time on the federal taxing power rather than the commerce clause, repeated the attempt by votes of 312 to 11 in the House and 50 to 12 in the Senate. Again, the Court found an invasion of states' rights.[88] In the 1930s, the Court, principally in defense of states' rights, struck down a federal statute regulating wages and hours of bituminous coal workers[89] despite the fact that the seven major coal producing states most directly affected by the law—Illinois, Indiana, Kentucky, New Mexico, Ohio, Pennsylvania, and Washington—came before the Court as amici curiae to support the federal enactment.

In none of these cases did any state officer question the national government's power to pass the challenged legislation. Instead, the federalism claims were raised by private persons who were subject to the federal statutes—parties who conceded that the very state governments who voiced no objection to (or indeed vigorously supported) the federal enactments, could properly impose the same regulations upon them. Under orthodox judicial doctrine, the state governments themselves are rarely permitted to judicially challenge actions of the national political branches that do not affect the states qua states but nonetheless allegedly infringe their sovereignty by imposing on private persons within their borders. It is generally held that such questions are "political, and not judicial in character."[90] Although state governments are usually allowed to present their views through amici curiae briefs, and the Court has been influenced on occasion to uphold federal power when affected states have supported it,[91] the history of judicial review in behalf of states' rights has resulted—to use Justice Jackson's pithy phrase—in a "vested *private* interest in federal impotency rather than a positive privilege of the states themselves."[92] Indeed, even the U.S. Attorney General has been permitted to question the constitutionality of a federal law on the ground that Congress exceeded its delegated powers.[93] (Since 1937 the United States may also intervene to defend the validity of federal actions that are challenged by private parties.)[94]

In view of the federal courts' proper aversion to adjudicating abstract questions of legality prior to the law's application to specific conduct, there is much to be said for the rule barring state governments from bringing lawsuits challenging federal regulations of private citizens. But this reasoning does not support the irony implicit in the companion rule that authorizes private parties to assert states' rights even when the state governments themselves have no objections whatever to the federal law. In terms of the appropriate role of the federal judiciary and in view of the states' role in the national political system, the whole matter should be left outside the judicial process.

VIII. STATE ENCROACHMENTS ON NATIONAL POWER

A. Historic Rationale for Judicial Role

To this point, the discussion of the Supreme Court's role in dealing with constitutional questions of federalism has covered only one side of the problem—the reach of federal power allegedly imposing on that of the states. Yet, so far as the past provides guidance, the prevailing view of political historians is that the predominant role envisaged for the Court in this area was to prevent state encroachments on national supremacy.[95] For Herbert Wechsler, "this is made clear by the fact that reliance on the courts was substituted, apparently on Jefferson's suggestion, for the earlier proposal to give Congress a veto of state enactments deemed to trespass on the national domain."[96] It was the fear that local regulatory and taxing ordinances might conflict with acts of Congress, usurp federal authority by unduly burdening interstate commerce, or even interfere with the property and activities of the central government itself that prompted Holmes's well-known dictum: "I do not think the United States would come to an end if we lost our power to declare an act of Congress void. I do think the Union would be imperiled if we could not make that declaration as to the laws of the several states."[97]

The rationale calling for the Court's superintendence is now both simple and familiar. Hinted at by Hamilton in *The*

Federalist No. 17,* made more explicit by Madison in Nos. 45 and 46,† and echoed by Marshall in *McCulloch v. Maryland* and by Holmes in the statement just quoted, the most thorough articulation was by Chief Justice Stone in several cases in which the Court reviewed such state legislation. On states' rights matters, "the people of all the States, and the States themselves, are represented in Congress,"[98] thus making Congress "subject to political restraints which can be counted on to prevent abuse."[99] But state and local lawmaking affecting the federal government or persons engaged in interstate activities may not be similarly trusted. State and local legislatures contain no such representatives of the central government, or of those persons outside the jurisdiction upon whom the impact of the local laws may fall. Moreover, the power of special interest groups is markedly greater in local legislative bodies than in the federal political process.[100] The phenomenon is most clearly exemplified by laws that blatantly or more subtly discriminate against outsiders to the benefit of local interests, either private or governmental. It is also presented by truly nondiscriminatory local rules that impose equivalent qualitative and quantitative burdens on insiders and outsiders alike, but, although reflecting a willingness of the state itself to pay a high price to solve a local problem, nonetheless do not express adequate appreciation or concern for the broader national interest.

B. CONTRAST WITH TRUE JUDICIAL REVIEW

Just as, under the Individual Rights Proposal, unsatisfactory political representation of the beneficiaries of constitutionally guaranteed individual rights warrants judicial review of that category of constitutional questions—and just as, under the Federalism Proposal, the thoroughly effective voice of

---

* "It will always be far more easy for the State Governments to encroach upon the National authorities, than for the National Government to encroach upon the State authorities." The Federalist, No. 17 at 70 (J. Madison ed. 1831).

† "The State governments may be regarded as constituent and essential parts of the federal government; whilst the latter is nowise essential to the operation or organization of the former." No. 45 at 201. "A local spirit will infallibly prevail much more in the members of Congress, than a national spirit will prevail in the legislatures of the particular States." No. 46 at 205.

the states in the national lawmaking system allows the Court to forgo review of that class of issues—so, too, the insufficient reflection of the national interest in the state legislative scheme justifies the Court's oversight of state action that allegedly invades or nullifies federal prerogatives.

There is another—and, for our purposes, equally important—reason for approving federal judicial oversight of state action on federalism grounds. When the Court rules on a contention that state or local laws conflict with an existing federal enactment and thus violate the supremacy clause, or that they improperly impose upon domains over which the national government is empowered (usually the areas of interstate or foreign commerce and thus violative of the commerce clause, but conceivably any other field of delegated federal endeavor such as immigration and naturalization), or that they unduly interfere with the property or activities of the central government and thus violate its implied constitutional immunity, the Court does *not* exercise the momentous power of judicial review. In such decisions, unlike its constitutional rulings on individual liberties and national power versus states' rights, the Court does not speak the final constitutional word. The federal political branches do. The Court's decisions on the federalism limits on state's actions may be revised by ordinary federal statutes. The judiciary acts only as an intermediate agency between the states and Congress. This is most obvious when the Court passes on state or local ordinances that allegedly conflict with an act of Congress. But it is equally true when, in the absence of pertinent federal legislation, the Court determines whether the challenged state action unduly imposes on a delegated but unexercised national power. In so doing, the Court performs an essentially legislative role, quite nakedly constructing policies for the particular case that are the product of the Court's own value-balancing of national versus state concerns. (Indeed, the Court not infrequently performs this very same task under the guise of the supremacy clause when it "interprets" a "relevant" federal statute whose message in relation to the state or local law before the Court is exceedingly indistinct.)

The Court may fashion its own policy determinants in the name of fulfilling some unspoken intention of Congress—such as "a Congressional purpose to leave undisturbed the authority of the states to make regulations affecting the commerce in matters of peculiarly local concern, but to withhold from them the authority to make regulations affecting those phases of it which, because of the need of a national uniformity, demand that their regulation, if any, be prescribed by a single authority."[101] Or the Court may act more openly by virtue of implicit authorization from Congress based on the long-standing practice.[102] But the fact remains that this aspect of the Court's work—determining whether state and local laws improperly control an area of national concern even in the absence of relevant federal legislation—is akin to statutory interpretation and not to judicial review. For this reason, the traditional tension between constitutional decisionmaking by the federal judiciary and the principles of majoritarian democracy is not of any real concern.

C. FUNCTIONAL JUSTIFICATION FOR JUDICIAL ROLE

Continuing judicial surveillance of alleged state encroachments on national power can also be justified on functional grounds. First, Congress has never established any regularized internal machinery for bringing to its attention the myriad of state and local rules that may arguably impose into as yet unlegislated areas of important federal interest. Under the pressure of its usual business, Congress appears to be incapable of accomplishing the job itself. Furthermore, as a structural matter, Congress seems to be especially unsuited to the task of determining on an ad hoc basis the compatibility of isolated local ordinances with the broad demands of the federal system, of gathering and applying the detailed evidence of a particular law's history and administration. This is the traditional work of adjudicative, not legislative, organs. Thus, if the courts were not to continue to review these state and local enactments, the effective final decision weighing state and federal interests would, because of the usual congressional inertia, rest with the state and local lawmaking bodies. On the other hand, despite the undisputed power of Congress to alter judicial decisions in this area, the same legislative inertia usually results in the Court's judgment being final. The preferable option between these alternatives for final value choice—the states or the federal judiciary—is quite clear. Given the national unrepresentativeness and parochial perspective of the state and local lawmaking systems, on the one hand, and the greater impartiality and sensitivity to federal needs of the courts, on the other, it should be the federal judiciary, rather than state political bodies, that exercises final judgment in our federal system.

D. POSSIBLE MODIFICATIONS OF JUDICIAL ROLE

1. Official National Representative

Although continued activity by the Court in this area is both consistent with the Federalism Proposal (as a matter of theory) and generally praiseworthy (as a matter of practice), it is not beyond improvement. It must be recognized that challenges to state or local regulatory or taxing statutes as invading federal dominion are rarely made by an official representative of the national government but rather by some private person (or corporation) that is affected by the law—the exceptional instances being when some federal agency claims immunity from a state or local requirement or tax. In terms of "standing," just as a private litigant who contends that federal action is ultra vires vis-à-vis the states is not asserting his own constitutional rights but rather is seeking to vindicate states' rights, so too the private litigant who attacks state and local laws is asserting the interest of the central government rather than his own constitutionally secured liberties.

In the former instance, the Federalism Proposal urges that, apart from any question of "standing," the underlying substantive issue of constitutionality should be treated as nonjusticiable. In the latter instance, it may be that considerations of "standing" should preclude the litigant from asserting third-party interests (those of the national political branches) even though the underlying substantive issue is adjudicable. For at least two reasons, however, the weight of the argument appears to favor a grant of standing. Because of the long-existing judicial practice, Congress may be fairly said to have implicitly authorized this method of securing the Court's protection of important federal interests; and the Court does not render a "true" constitutional decision in such cases. Nonetheless, the federal political branches might give serious consideration to formalizing a procedure—akin to that in the West German system[103]—to assure the Court the fullest possible exposition of national policy by providing for the appearance of an official federal representative in all cases in which private litigants assail state action on federalism grounds.

2. Special Federal Agency

Judicial error in engaging in its legislative-like balance of the nation's needs against local efforts to deal with pressing problems has significant consequences. If the Court errs on the side of the state, the result is no different than if the Court were not involved at all—i.e., the state judgment would be final in the absence of congressional action. But, if the Court inflates the strength of the national interest in uniform regulation (or nonregulation) and invalidates the state or local law before it, the result is politically unintended federal protection for those persons subject to the challenged ordinance—an immunity from needed and useful local regulation that will likely be permanent because of congressional inertia despite the fact that Congress may wholly approve of the state action. This may be simply written off as a necessary cost of invoking the judicial process, especially when measured against the alternative of having no review at all, thus leaving the decision with the state or local lawmaking agencies. Furthermore, it may well be that incorrect judicial rulings in favor of the private persons attacking the state action—and, for purposes of this discussion, we have seen that these are the consequential ones—are more likely to receive congressional reconsideration because of the generally greater influence possessed by the states (as compared to private persons) in the national political process.

Nonetheless, there may be merit in the establishment of some federal agency—similar to the one that Paul Freund once proposed for issues of state taxation of interstate commerce[104]—to act in the Court's stead in this entire area. Unlike the courts, such an administrative agency could enact general rules and regulations governing the subject areas as well as adjudicate particular cases. An agency would presumably possess greater expertise on the variety of complex questions—frequently economic—presented by the cases and, because of the specific nature of its duties and the political control over its personnel, it should be more familiar with both the spoken and unspoken thinking of Congress.

Intensive evaluation of this suggestion is clearly beyond the realm of consideration here. And caution must be exercised before creating yet another federal regulatory agency—no matter how theoretically attractive it is—in the hope of happily solving important problems. But there may be ancillary benefits, apart from some modest conservation of its time and energy (which would be the result of any shrinking of its jurisdiction), in divesting the Court of the duty to review state enactments on federalism grounds. In contrast to those cases in which the Court measures state action under the supremacy clause against enacted federal legislation, the situations under discussion put the Court in the position of being responsible itself (i.e., on its own motion, rather than that of Congress) for invalidating actions of important state representative institutions (albeit in a very distinct way). Since at least some decisions of this sort may generate a high degree of controversy, removing them from the judicial arena may enhance the Court's ability to perform its most critical role of protecting individual constitutional liberties. As we saw in chapter 3, the fact is that the latter task is greatly complicated by all judicial decisions that result in a hostile public attitude toward the Court.

IX. OBJECTIONS TO THE FEDERALISM PROPOSAL

A. POLITICAL BRANCHES AS JUDGES OF THE SCOPE OF THEIR OWN POWER

1. Traditional View

It is a conventional political-legal axiom—traceable to Sir Edward Coke—that no person should act as judge in his own cause or be the arbiter of the limits of his own power. Yet the Federalism Proposal advocates that the national political branches determine the scope of national authority versus states' rights. It appears flatly to contradict Hamilton's view that, as it "cannot be the natural presumption" "that the legislative body are themselves the constitutional judges of their own powers," it "is far more rational to suppose, that the courts were designed . . . to keep the [legislature] within the limits assigned to their authority."[105] This maxim, like most others, need not be without exceptions. Moreover, no matter how "unnatural" it may appear at first, it is not only rational but desirable to assign authority over discrete constitutional judgments on functional rather than axiomatic bases.

2. Contrary Authority

One need look no further than *Marbury v. Madison* to discover a branch of the national government—in that case the judiciary—acting as the final adjudicator of its own authority. And, for valuable and pragmatic reasons, to be assayed in chapter 6, the decision was wise and correct. So, too, for reasons already stated and to be advanced in this chapter, Congress and the President should be the judges of national power vis-à-vis the states.

Over the course of American history, there has been no paucity of distinguished opinions *suggesting* that each of the federal branches should make its own determinations of constitutionality and act as the arbiter of its own constitutional power. Madison wrote that "as the Legislative, Executive and Judicial departments of the United States are coordinate, and each equally bound to support the Constitution, it follows that each must, in the exercise of its functions, be guided by the text of the Constitution according to its own interpretation of it."[106] Perhaps best known is Jefferson's view that the executive and legislature should follow their own constitutional judgments, even though "contradictory decisions may arise . . . and produce inconvenience";[107] for "the judges . . . to decide what laws are constitutional, and what not, not only for themselves in their own sphere of action, but for the Legislative & Executive also in their spheres, would make the Judiciary a despotic branch."[108] Andrew Jackson stated that "the Congress, the Executive, and the

Court must each for itself be guided by its own opinion of the Constitution" and that "the authority of the Supreme Court must not, therefore, be permitted to control the Congress or the Executive when acting in their legislative capacities, but to have only such influence as the force of their reasoning may deserve."[109] Lincoln echoed this sentiment when he declared that judicial "decisions must be binding in any case upon the parties to a suit as to the object of the suit," and "while they are also entitled to very high respect and consideration in all parallel cases by all other departments of the Government," nonetheless, "if the policy of the Government upon vital questions affecting the whole people is to be irrevocably fixed by decisions of the Supreme Court, the instant they are made in ordinary litigation between parties in personal actions the people will have ceased to be their own rulers, having to that extent practically assigned their Government into the hands of that eminent tribunal."[110]

These broadly phrased opinions were, in the main, fragmentary responses to particular occasions on which the Supreme Court had acted or was expected to act contrarily to the speaker's wishes, rather than meticulously drafted comprehensive plans for the respective arbitral roles of each of the federal branches in the multitude of situations in which questions of constitutional power arise. So viewed, none is in direct conflict with the position taken herein that each context must be examined on its own and that functional considerations should govern final assignment of the power to decide.

3. Outline of a Functional Approach

In respect to some categories of issues—e.g., constitutionally secured personal liberties, as we have seen in chapter 2—it is not only suitable but necessary that the Court's word be regarded as authoritative. As to others—e.g., federal power vis-à-vis the states—it has been argued that it is appropriate to vest the political branches with the final voice. In yet other contexts, whether a particular branch should possess the ultimate responsibility of judgment—and, if so, which branch—is more ambiguous.

This is not the place for a full exploration of every potential variant, but a brief sketch may enhance our understanding of the problem. In exercising his "Power to grant Reprieves and Pardons for Offenses against the United States," it is wholly appropriate for the President to have the final say on whether the law under which the applicant was convicted was unconstitutional, irrespective of the contrary opinion of Congress and the Court. This was the principal context (specifically regarding the Sedition Law) in which Jefferson formed his views on congressional and presidential constitutional interpretation.[111] In contrast, it is totally inappropriate for the President, in pursuing his power to execute the laws, to continue to press charges under a statute that the Court has held to be invalid; indeed, completely unlike the pardon situation, this course of action should be held to be an independent violation of constitutional rights if the threat of further enforcement deters constitutionally protected activity. Further, in employing his veto power, the President should be unencumbered by the judgment of Congress and the Court that a law is constitutional. This was the situation (specifically respecting a new charter for the Bank of the United States) to which Jackson most plainly spoke.[112]

Less clear is whether the President should be able to refuse to enforce a law that he believes is unconstitutional—a view espoused by Martin Van Buren[113]—even though it has been duly enacted by Congress, perhaps over his veto, and upheld by the judiciary. Yet more uncertain—illustrated by Andrew Jackson's alleged response to the *Cherokee Nation* decision—is the legitimacy of the President's refusal to carry out a Supreme Court mandate because of his disagreement with the constitutional merit of the particular ruling. Resolution of this question must turn on a fuller recitation of the context and consequences and is beyond the scope of this book. The overriding point, however, is that it is neither unprecedented nor undesirable to rest final constitutional judgment with one or the other of the federal branches on the range of its own authority. The operational rule should depend on a pragmatic assessment of the competing factors involved.

B. EFFICACY OF JUDICIAL REVIEW FOR PRESERVING FEDERALISM

1. Destruction of State Sovereignty

a. *Control over Regulation, Taxing, and Spending*

Frequently heard and often coupled with specific hypothetical illustrations is the argument that if judicial review of alleged federal usurpation of states' rights were unavailable, Congress would not merely be able to regulate all aspects of human affairs but would also possess the unrestrained power to swallow the states whole and thus destroy federalism. On the list of horribles is that Congress might enact a statute requiring municipalities to act contrary to state-imposed restrictions[114] or demanding that states adopt or administer regulatory, taxing, or spending programs that conform to federal policies.[115] Or Congress might "undertake to abrogate a land-tax imposed by the authority of a State"[116] (or, indeed, to forbid state taxation altogether). But the argument cannot withstand realistic analysis.

Except for certain notably exceptional periods that will be mentioned later,[117] during much of our history the Court's definitions of the nation's powers have afforded the political branches exceedingly loose reins. Many of the constitutional grants of authority to Congress and the President, especially the most important ones, are phrased in expansive and expandable language—as are many of the crucial constitutional limitations on government power. And, if anything, the Court's pronouncements have enhanced their flexibility, suggesting only the slightest restrictions on federal power vis-à-vis the states. Thus, despite a recently announced limitation whose narrow and ambiguous thrust will be seen shortly to be largely inconsequential,[118] under historic and modern judicial interpretations of the commerce clause[119]—gilded by the Court's lavish construction of the necessary and proper clause[120]—Congress may not only regulate every person or commodity involved in intercourse among the states but may also reach all details of commercial transactions (and, indeed, virtually every facet of human conduct) that radiate beyond the borders of a single state. Pursuant to its taxing power, Congress is capable of effectively governing a myriad of activities even though they may be totally confined within each state's boundaries,[121] if such confinement is really possible. In furtherance of the authority to spend—augmented rather than qualified by the fertile phrase "for the general welfare"—the Court has awarded Congress a seemingly unrestrained opportunity to work its will within the states.[122] And, in passing upon the power to enter treaties—a power held jointly by the President and Senate—the Court similarly appears to have handed the political branches a potent weapon to regulate intrastate behavior.[123]

Finally, although more remains to be heard from the Court and some soundings have been discouraging to advocates of un-conditioned national power,[124] the thrust of recent decisions explaining Congress's ability to enforce the Civil War amendments has opened yet another road for national lawmaking drives.[125] The vast potential of this federal regulatory authority may be seen in the judiciary's use of §1 of the fourteenth amendment to require state and local governments to undertake such actions as levying taxes,[126] promulgating detailed school desegregation plans,[127] and adopting specified reapportionment schemes,[128] and the Court's rulings that §5 of that amendment endows the political branches with even broader power.[129]

These Supreme Court decisions, and others, demonstrate that the absence of pervasive federal control over all conduct within the states has been more the product of political than of judicial restraint. Nor should this be surprising. In contrast to the state and local orientation of the members of the political branches, the Justices—appointed with no specific regard for their geographic origins and without the tradition of senatorial courtesy—are much more inclined to view matters from a national perspective. Congress, on the other hand, has not only refrained from using its powers to anything approaching their fullest extent, but has also left virtually untapped such potentially fruitful sources as the full faith and credit and guarantee clauses. Indeed, on a number of occasions—involving such varied subjects as intoxicants and insurance[130]—Congress has reacted to judicial denials of state authority vis-à-vis the national government by restoring the power withheld by the Court. It would thus appear that, despite seemingly casual dicta to the contrary,[131] if the Court's expansive pronouncements as to the scope of national authority under its delegated powers—again, particularly the commerce clause— were to be taken seriously, even the most extreme exercises of national power hypothesized above might well have been upheld.

The rules have been changed, however, at least as to the power of Congress under the commerce clause, by *National League of Cities v. Usery*,[132] in which the Court held that federal regulation of the wages and hours of almost all state and local employees unconstitutionally overrides state sovereignty. The extent to which *Usery* qualifies the national commerce power is ambiguous because the Court variously phrased the scope of its ruling. The essence of the *Usery* rationale appears to be that the challenged provisions of the Fair Labor Standards Act were beyond the commerce power because they operated "to directly displace the States' freedom to structure integral operations in areas of traditional governmental functions,"[133] and interfered with "functions essential to [the] separate and independent existence"[134] of the states. But, as Justice Rehnquist recognized in an earlier dissent that presaged his opinion for the Court in *Usery*, this approach will "undoubtedly present gray areas to be marked out on a case-by-case basis."[135] And Justice Blackmun, a member of the five-man majority in *Usery*, accurately described the opinion as adopting a "balancing approach" that "does not outlaw federal power in [other] areas . . . where the federal interest is demonstrably greater and where state facility compliance with imposed federal standards would be essential."[136]

Most important for our purposes, however, is that the *Usery* decision is specifically limited to the reach of national power under the commerce clause and then only in connection with direct federal regulation of "the States *qua* States."[137] In this respect, *Usery* parallels the once greatly inflated, but now severely contracted, strictures on Congress's power to tax.[138] *Usery* explicitly reaffirms the extraordinarily broad authority given Congress under the commerce clause to regulate the conduct of a private person or business: "even activity that is purely intrastate in character may be regulated by Congress, where the activity, combined with like conduct by others similarly situated, affects commerce among the States or with foreign nations."[139] Further, the *Usery* Court carefully avoided deciding "whether different results might obtain if Congress seeks to affect integral operations of state governments by exercising authority granted it under sections of the Constitution such as the spending power . . . or §5 of the Fourteenth Amendment."[140] The narrow thrust of the opinion is further illuminated by the Court's concession that regulations forbidden the national government under the commerce clause by *Usery* might be validly imposed on "the States *qua* States" if Congress acted pursuant to its war power.[141] And within less than a week of the *Usery* decision the Court— again speaking through Justice Rehnquist (this time without dissent)—was willing to assume national power under §5 of the fourteenth amendment to regulate the hiring practices of the states as states by forbidding sex discrimination.[142]

Thus, *Usery* notwithstanding, the presence of judicial review would appear to afford mean solace to those who fear the national government's ability to "devour the essentials of state sovereignty."[143] If *Usery* prevents the use of the commerce power by Congress to directly require that states adopt national regulatory programs, it still permits Congress to use the commerce power to enact regulatory programs that operate directly on persons or businesses within the states. Similarly, if *Usery* prohibits direct federal limitations of maximum salaries for state employees under the commerce clause, it does not—as Justice Rehnquist has acknowledged[144]—appear to forbid Congress's recovering the excess wages from the employees under its taxing power. Alternatively, under judicially articulated doctrines unaffected by *Usery*,[145] Congress could seemingly use its spending power in respect to "the States *qua* States" to achieve desired national goals—e.g., by conditioning federal law enforcement assistance grants to the states on their payment of designated minimum wages to their police; by stipulating that state recipients of federal air pollution funds adopt specific auto or industrial emission rules; by requiring that states (or their local subdivisions) provide property tax relief in order to participate in federal revenue sharing. Thus, recent amendments to the General Revenue Sharing Act place strict conditions on recipients to assure nondiscrimination and open access to state and local decisionmaking bodies.[146] Indeed, given the massive federal financial assistance to the states—$85 billion for 1979[147]—it is difficult to conceive of virtually any state regulatory, taxing, or spending program that Congress and the President could not obtain. Finally, since *Usery* endorses national authority under the commerce clause to set minimum wages for employees of privately owned businesses, and since the Court appears to be quite ready to uphold federal power under §5 of the fourteenth amendment to affect "the States *qua* States," the narrow result in *Usery* might possibly itself be altered if Congress were to rely on the latter source of authority—i.e., under §5 "[may Congress] rectify the denial of equal protection that results from state employees' being disadvantaged vis-à-vis comparable employees in the private sector?"[148]

b. Control over Officials

The fear of national control over state and municipal officials has also often been expressed from earliest times.[149] What would happen, it is asked, if Congress decreed that any state or local officer who refused to implement or interfered with national policy could be impeached by the Senate? Or suppose that a federal statute required all state and local functionaries to be confirmed by the Senate or some other federal agency?

In fact, in modern times, issues of this general caste have reached the Supreme Court. A 1947 case involved a provision of the federal Hatch Act that state and local officers and employees "whose principal employment is in connection with any activity which is financed in whole or in part by loans or grants made by the United States or by any Federal agency" shall be forbidden from taking "any active part in political management or political campaigns." The U.S. Civil Service Commission had ordered the Oklahoma Highway Commission (whose programs were largely funded by federal money) to remove a commissioner who was also state Democratic party chairman despite Oklahoma's contention that this was a constitutional violation of its sovereignty. Although the Supreme Court gratuitously offered the dictum that "the United States is not concerned with, and has no power to regulate, local political activities as such of state officials," it rejected the state's attack. The Court reasoned that the federal government was not ordering the dismissal of any state official but only threatening the withdrawal of money. This, the Court held, was an acceptable exercise of national authority under the spending power "to fix the terms upon which its money allotments to states shall be disbursed."[150]

Whatever the ambiguous statement may mean, that "the United States...has no power to regulate local political activities *as such* of state officials,"[151] if Congress has the power to imprison state officers who frustrate interests subject to national supervision—and it most surely does under orthodox judicial interpretation[152]—then no good reason appears for believing that Congress would not also be held to have the authority to remove them from office for similar conduct. And again taking cognizance of the extremely wide range of human activity that the Court has held to be within the national province, it would seem that the Court would be prepared to uphold extensive federal regulatory authority in this area as well. Furthermore, if Congress were to legislate pursuant to the guarantee clause, could it not provide, free of any judicial condemnation, for significantly detailed control of many aspects of state government—e.g., that designated state functionaries must be elected rather than appointed (or vice versa), or that they must possess particular qualifications? A negative answer seems especially unlikely given the Court's view that issues of congressional power under the guarantee clause are "political questions," not subject to judicial review.[153]

c. Distinction between Substantive Constitutionality and Proper Arbiter

The point, it must be emphasized, is *not* that any of these exercises of national power (suppositional or real) is in fact constitutional as a matter of abstract principle. There is no necessary disagreement here with the Court's view in *Usery* that certain federal regulations of "the States *qua* States," which are otherwise fully within Congress's delegated powers (or, indeed, some national rules affecting private persons or businesses within the states), may transgress the constitutional principle of federalism, just as they may be found to offend against constitutionally secured personal rights.[154] Rather, the position is that judicial review is not the steadfast brake to be relied on to prevent the destruction of state sovereignty. As we have seen, under existing doctrine, several of the federal actions hypothesized would likely pass judicial muster on the merits; others would be altogether avoided by the Court, the final decision being relegated to the political branches. Yet others—such as the Hatch Act as well as related efforts to condition the holding of public office—raise serious questions of individual constitutional rights (under the first amendment, in the case of the Hatch Act restriction on political activity) which the Court would[155]—and, under the Individual Rights Proposal, should—adjudicate. Similarly, the imagined provisions for federal impeachment of state officials could well present personal liberty issues respecting procedural safeguards.

But the *Usery* Court's equation, for purposes of judicial review, of states' rights and individual rights as affirmative limitations on national power should be rejected, not because, as Justice Brennan argued in dissent, "there is no restraint based on state sovereignty requiring or permitting judicial enforcement anywhere expressed in the Constitution,"[156] but because, as Justice Brennan also contended, the states can and should depend on the national political branches, not the federal judiciary, for the preservation of states' rights.[157] The best evidence is probably that the most egregious of the hypothetical statutes—e.g., the national prohibition of all state taxes or the federal confirmation of all state officials—are just that: hypothetical. So, too, are the even more flagrant abuses—which actually conflict with explicit constitutional mandates for the security of the separate states—of hypothetical federal laws that prefer the ports of one state over those of another or erect a new state within the jurisdiction of an existing one. Since the influential representation of state interests in the national political system strongly assures against the passage of laws that pose dire threats to state sovereignty, the Court may confidently permit the constitutional issue to be resolved in the political arena.

2. Patent Constitutional Violations

The Federalism Proposal, it should be made clear, does not depend on the assumption that the states' position in the councils of national government provides an ironclad guarantee that no violations of states' rights will ever occur. If the federalism question is a close one, as virtually all real world ones are, then, irrespective of its "correct" answer, the political branches should be trusted to produce a reasonable and fair judgment. But should a true constitutional crisis arise, with Congress and the President joining forces in ignoring clear constitutional mandates—and these it must be remembered are the operative agencies in this regard, not minor federal bureaucrats or even state legislatures—it is probably futile to rely on the Court to right the matter.

Learned Hand's observation "that a society so riven that the spirit of moderation is gone, no court can save,"[158] echoed James Bradley Thayer's sound conclusion sixty-five years earlier that "under no system can the power of courts go far to save a people from ruin."[159] Thayer, in turn, drew on Justice Gibson's early nineteenth-century wisdom that "once let public opinion be so corrupt as to sanction every misconstruction of the Constitution and abuse of power which the temptation of the moment may dictate, and the party which may happen to be predominant will laugh at the puny efforts of a dependent power [the judiciary] to arrest it in its course."[160]

In the best of times, the people, viewing the Court as a nonrepresentative institution, ordinarily accord its invalidations of popular action an ambivalent respect. In the worst of times—and that is surely the situation when the elected representatives of the states and the people in the federal political branches determine to transgress plainly established constitutional boundaries—the Court is practically helpless. There is scant reason to believe that a people in social upheaval will heed the

Court's pronouncements of the obvious. As evidenced by our own Civil War and the continued experience of constitutional republics throughout much of the rest of the world, the game of constitutional checks and balances, no matter how bold the lettering and durable the paper, works only if the players respect the rules. For clear constitutional violations, it is only the societal checks of popular conscience and responsibility that can finally preserve American federalism by demanding that the political branches return to course.

Continuing in the realm of the imaginary, all that has been said is equally true of blatant political abridgments of constitutionally prescribed personal liberties. But there are different facts operating when states' rights are at issue. In the latter instance, there will likely be greater political resistance to the expansive national action. This reduces the likelihood both that such action will occur in the first place and that judicial review could reverse such action once it had been initiated. Encroachments on personal rights, however, ordinarily affect a less well-defined interest group and are less likely to encounter organized political resistance. Most hypothetically extreme individual rights violations would not strike at the liberty of large numbers of citizens—one such instance might be a congressional act indefinitely perpetuating the term of its members (which allegedly would conflict with the constitutional right of the people to vote)—but rather would be directed at discrete and politically defenseless minorities. Outrageous national incursions on the federalism principle would, in contrast, be imposed against the will of the majority in at least one of the constituent states, and most probably a number of others. In these circumstances, might there be a greater likelihood of popular intolerance? Might it be likely, in Hamilton's words, "that citizens . . . would flock from the remote extremes of their respective States to the places of election, to overthrow their tyrants, and to substitute men who would be disposed to avenge the violated majesty of the people"?[161] Perhaps; at least more likely for this class of constitutional violation. Therefore, whatever the forces of judicial review as a last bulwark of the Constitution, it is less necessary here.

3. Deterrent Effect of Judicial Review

Resistance to the Federalism Proposal may be based on the plausible ground—adverted to above[162]—that the record of congressional restraint in favor of states' rights is itself a function of judicial review. The argument is that, were it not for the deterrent effect of potential judicial invalidation, the national political branches would have long since engaged in the ever tempting process of self-arrogation of power or, at the very least, would have been much more generous to the central government in interpreting the breadth of its authority.[163] The logic of the premise, however speculative as an empirical matter, may not be demeaned out of hand. But available data that pervades our history not only suggests its refutation but points in the opposite direction.

a. Abdication of Political Responsibility

In numerous instances, the very presence of judicial review, hovering over congressional deliberations on proposed legislation that allegedly injures state sovereignty, has encouraged the political branches to abdicate their own constitutional responsibility, as the Court itself has recognized.[164] President Franklin Roosevelt's advice to Congress in the 1930s, that its task was only to judge the need for national action and that questions of constitutionality should be left exclusively to the province of the courts,[165] is illustrative. Other examples abound:

i) As a preface to the Civil War, "hot debate ensued over the question of the respective rights of Congress and of the Territorial and State Legislatures to establish or prohibit slavery. In the summer of 1848, Senator Clayton brought forward his unfortunate proposal for a compromise.... By this plan, Clayton argued, the whole question as to the power of Congress over slavery in the Territories would be referred to the Supreme Court for its decision.... 'Any man who ... does not desire to distract the country by a question merely political, will be able, by voting for this bill, to refer the whole matter to the Judiciary.'"[166]

ii) In urging passage of the Sherman Act in 1890 against the contention that its regulatory thrust entered ground reserved to the states, Senator Washburn asserted: "I know the sentiment of the country with regard to the question of monopolies and trusts, and I believe the people expect the Congress of the United States to make an attempt to secure some valid and satisfactory legislation. While the bill of the Senator from Ohio may not be perfect, while it may not reach every point, and may finally be declared unconstitutional, yet it is a move in the right direction."[167]

iii) In the midst of the depression, when states' rights objections were raised to the Bituminous Coal Conservation Act of 1935, "characteristic of the attitudes of Representatives favoring the bill was a comment of Mell G. Underwood, Democrat from Ohio, who declined to debate constitutionality because he was 'attempting to make this effort to assist the laboring people of the country' and was 'willing to leave that question to the proper tribunal, the Supreme Court of the United States.' Adolph J. Sabath, veteran member from Illinois, thought that a member should vote for a measure of doubtful constitutionality and then 'let the courts finally decide the matter.'"[168]

iv) When constitutional challenges were leveled against a provision in the Alaska Statehood bill in 1958 that authorized the President, subsequent to Alaska's admission to the Union, to place much of the territory under federal control, Senator Frank Church defended on the ground that citizens who might be adversely affected could always seek judicial invalidation and Senator Henry Jackson advised that "whatever doubts may exist on the subject, I believe they should be resolved in favor of constitutionality."[169]

v) In the heat of the racial upheaval in the 1960s, tenth amendment arguments in Congress against the Civil Rights Act of 1964 drew such responses as the following from Senator Paul Douglas, "Why not pass this law and let the Supreme Court make the decision as to whether or not it is constitutional?"[170] Senator Kenneth Keating believed that constitutionality "has to ultimately be decided by the Supreme Court anyway, and ... we ought to get on with our work here."[171]

vi) In 1970, when the eighteen-year-old voting rights act—the first federal statute in thirty-five years held by the Supreme Court to encroach on state authority—was under consideration in Congress, the debate "developed around three general positions. The first affirmed without question both the constitutionality of enacting 18-year-old voting by statute and the wisdom of such a congressional policy determination. The second held that unquestionably Congress was without constitutional power to lower the voting age by statute. The third position frankly admitted uncertainty on the constitutional issue, but recognized the desirability of enfranchising 18-year-olds and was willing to 'let the court decide it.'"[172]

These examples are not meant to imply that all considerations of constitutional responsibility have been forsaken in the federal political setting, or even that serious constitutional arguments were not voiced in the situations just described. As we shall see, there were such arguments. Nor is it contended that the federal laws enacted in the above cases, whatever the subsequent judicial decisions concerning them may have been, in fact abrogated states' rights. And it may well be that with or without the most demanding congressional respect for matters of constitutionality—and with or without the established possibility of judicial review—all the above federal statutes would have been enacted anyway (although at least in respect to some—e.g., the 18-year-old voting act—the congressional decision was sufficiently close as to raise real doubts). For, as we have seen, as a general matter, Congresses and Presidents have been extremely solicitous of the sovereign prerogatives of the states.

b. Aggravation Caused by Judicial Review

Nonetheless, when the above illustrations—as confirmed by a modern poll of congressmen indicating that 31 percent believe that "Congress generally should 'pass constitutional questions along to the court rather than form its own considered judgment on them'"[173]—are coupled with the nearly irrebuttable presumption of constitutionality that (as we have noted earlier) the Court has generally accorded political decisions in regard to states' rights, the presence of judicial review may tend to aggravate rather than ameliorate the enhancement of national dominion. The rationale is simple enough: if those congressmen who ignore constitutional considerations of states' rights and urge dependence for their security on the Court prevail in the legislative process, and if the Court then upholds the statute in deference to a congressional judgment of constitutionality that has never really been exercised, then judicial review is not only illusory but self-defeating. It will clearly instill confidence in those members of Congress just depicted—those with the view that constitutionality is the equivalent of what the Supreme Court will uphold—and it will encourage them to take further national steps into what were previously thought to be state preserves. There have been instances in which Congress, in the name of states' rights, withdrew federal laws that previously had been upheld by the Court. But—although it is by no means true, especially in regard to states' rights,·that Congress as a body will exercise all possible authority that may be inferred from judicial decisions*—there is a lurking tendency for Congress to follow judicial approval with more political action.[174] For even those congressmen who are most sensitive to the limits of national power and who treat the constitutional question with all due reflection cannot help being affected in some measure by judicial validation of earlier exercises of federal authority.

(1) Consequences of delay

If there is a propensity to aggrandizement of national power resulting from judicial review of states' rights issues, then serious consequences follow. Wholly apart from the fact that many arguably invalid federal laws never reach the courts at all, even in those infrequent instances in which the Court holds federal

* It has been noted that "during the 91st Congress some of the most interesting and important constitutional debates involved the proper interpretation of constitutional grants of legislative power. It would not have been surprising if Congress had assumed a broad interpretation of such constitutional grants, without questioning their limits. In fact, this turns out not to be the case. Experience with the question of Congress' power to enfranchise 18-year-old voters and the exercise of its warmaking powers shows the national legislature to be seriously concerned that the manner in which grants of power are exercised be consonant with the Constitution." Mikva & Lundy, The 91st Congress and the Constitution, 38 U. Chi. L. Rev. 449, 474 (1971).

action to be unconstitutional, the damage caused by delay is often far from remedied. No matter what the ultimate judicial pronouncement, Thayer's early belief "that the mere legislative decision will accomplish results throughout the country of the profoundest importance before any judicial question can arise"[175] has been confirmed by the events of recent history and the continually increasing delay in litigation that is now all but taken for granted.

A study of Supreme Court nullification of federal statutes calculated that, on the average, close to nine years elapsed between passage and final judgment. And, no matter how subject to qualification statistical averages may be, in the only two years that passed between enactment of the National Industrial Recovery Act in 1933 and its demise in *Schechter Poultry Corp. v. United States,* over a thousand national and regional agencies operated under it whose economic tentacles touched virtually every segment of American society, its immediate impact affecting more than four and a half million workers. Similarly, during the short life of the Agricultural Adjustment Act of 1933, overturned in *United States v. Butler* in 1935, over a billion dollars was collected and spent by the federal government, amounts impossible to redistribute accurately after the statute was invalidated.[176] These gargantuan examples are, of course, atypical. But they are not unique. President Nixon's impoundment of Clean Water Act funds in 1973 and 1974 was reversed by *Train v. New York*[177] in 1975, but the "litigation had lasted for two years. The program had been stretched out; the deadlines established by Congress were now impossible to meet. The Administration achieved its purposes even while losing in court."[178] Such events go far in affirming the contention that even accelerated judicial review usually cannot prevent major statutory impact—frequently with consequent irreparable injury, often of a substantial nature, and sometimes to massive numbers of individuals. Indeed, this phenomenon has been forthrightly recognized by congressmen who have urged the enactment of a law despite its conceded unconstitutionality because of its assured operation for the period of time before judicial invalidation.[179]

(2) Individual rights distinguished

The availability of judicial review for alleged infringements of individual rights has similarly encouraged congressional action whose doubtful validity has been explicitly recognized by its proponents. For instance, the legislative histories of both the Communist Control Act of 1954 and the District of Columbia preventive detention law of 1970 disclose an oft-stated "leave it to the courts" attitude.[180] But, for at least two reasons, the Court's activity in respect to personal liberties tends to further rather than diminish the preservation of constitutional values. First, unlike its response to the federalism category of issues, the Court, irrespective of differing judicial language, has not generally accorded a very firm presumption of constitutionality to government action affecting civil liberties; thus, it has avoided the misleading implication of judicial review and the self-generating propensity to narrow the scope of the rights at issue. More important, as we have repeatedly observed, if the Court were to relegate individual rights issues to the process of popular will, their security would be seriously endangered. In contrast, given the forceful state representation in the national legislative system, if the Court were to make clear that the final word on constitutional problems of federal versus state authority lies within that system, no constitutional void would result. Although there is surely no proving it, such a judicial stance might well result in Congress's being even more sensitive to state interests, even truer to the ideals of federalism.

C. VALUE OF JUDICIAL LEGITIMATION

Another imposing objection to the Federalism Proposal is wholly independent of the benefits that are said to flow to the American federal system from the ability of the Supreme Court to *in*validate national action that it finds to be excessive. Most fully developed by Charles Black, the position is that Court *validation* (or "legitimation") of those exercises of federal power that the Court finds to be constitutionally permissible are critically important for national unity; that public knowledge that an independent tribunal has approved political assumptions of authority adds dignity to the laws of the central government and inspires confidence that it is acting within its constitution-limited boundaries; and that the concurrence and cooperation of all three federal branches is necessary for the psychological acceptance by the people requisite to successful administration of government.[181] The Court's landmark decision in *McCulloch v. Maryland* is often cited in support of this postulate, Chief Justice Marshall's tour de force sanctioning expansive national power through his liberal interpretation of the necessary and proper clause is credited with providing the amalgam for building a single nation.

1. Validity of Premises

This conclusion may be approached at several levels. At the outset, it is important to note that its foundation has been forcefully challenged. In David Adamany's view, "there seems no question that the widely asserted legitimizing function of the Supreme Court cannot summon adequate empirical support from public opinion studies, does not square with the history of relations between the justices and the popular branches, and will not withstand a searching analysis of its assumptions."[182] Beyond this, it may be, as Philip Kurland contends, that we "have reached the stage of political evolution when 'legitimation' of congressional authority is unnecessary. There may now be consensus that there are no areas of individual behavior not subject to national governmental control . . . . Those who accept this as a political fact do not need the Court to legitimize it . . . . [T]he vast amount of national legislation and the small number of cases in which the Court affixes its stamp of approval suggest that legitimacy, acquired in this fashion, is certainly not a *sine qua non* of effective national legislation."[183]

2. Source of Public Hostility

For our purposes, however, there is a yet more telling response. Whatever the historical or contemporary advantages of judicial "legitimation" may be, the fact is that this aspect of the Court's work, particularly when it has validated exertions of national power against the plaint of states' rights, has been a prominent source of adversity for it. Charles Warren has observed that from the earliest period of our history—even within the Congress itself, which, after all, had enacted the very laws being passed upon—discontent with the Court's decisions on the limits of congressional power "arose, *not* because the Court held an Act of Congress unconstitutional, but rather because it refused to do so."[184] Thus, Jefferson's well-known hostility to the Court and judicial review stemmed not from its rejection of legislative acts but from its refusal to strike them down.[185]

Although perhaps owing to the encouragement afforded the political branches to move further against states' rights, what is yet more ironic (indeed, perverse) is that because of its approbations of national power—all of which obviously originated in and were promulgated by Congress and the President—the Supreme Court has been the branch of the national government most often denounced for the "attrition of state power" and the "downfall of the federal system." The decision in *McCulloch v. Maryland* in 1819—the keystone of those who advocate the virtue of validation—is poignantly illustrative. "It was the support which the Court gave to the wide scope of Legislative power and to the authority of Congress to charter a National Bank which inspired Jefferson and his followers with alarm."[186] The Court's act of legitimation provoked Jefferson's famous characterization of the Justices as "the subtle corps of sappers and miners constantly working underground to undermine the foundations of our confederated fabric."[187] *Congress's* Bank was anathema in many parts of the country; but it was the *Court's* decision that bore the brunt of the enmity. In Tennessee, a newspaper wrote: "This Court, above the law and beyond the control of public opinion, has lately made a decision that prostrates the state sovereignty entirely [and that] must sooner or later bring down on the members of it the execration of the community."[188] In Virginia, the state legislature called for the creation of a new tribunal to resolve constitutional issues of federal versus state power.[189]

When *Congress's* legal tender law was upheld in 1884,[190] it was said in Kentucky that the *Court* had "violated the letter and spirit of the Constitution" and had "consulted its own conception of political and economic expediency, instead of the commands of the organic law."[191] Elsewhere it was written that "the system of construction adopted in this case is one which weakens the Court itself and enlarges the power of Congress and makes a long stride in the direction of centralization."[192] Just a decade ago, after the Court declined to invalidate *Congress's* extension of the franchise to eighteen-year-olds in federal elections, the conservative press struck at the *Court* for having rewritten the Constitution by lowering the voting age.[193] Writing in 1978, Philip Kurland summarized the criticism: "throughout our history, the Supreme Court has persistently and consistently acted as a centripetal force favoring, at almost every chance, the national authority over that of the states. It made substantial contributions to the ultimate demise of federalism."[194]

The crowning injustice is the accusation—voiced by the Conference of State Chief Justices in one of the most influential attacks on the federal judiciary in recent times—that decisions legitimating the already exercised authority of the *Congress* and *President* evidence the Court's adoption of "the role of policymaker without proper judicial restraint." The conference believed it to be the unhealthy tendency of the federal *judicial* decisions—not the federal *political* decisions—"to press the extension of federal power and to press it rapidly."[195]

Perhaps there is value in having the Court serve the socially therapeutic function of being the object of vilification for those who are defeated on the political battleground (and some individual or group always is), or in permitting the Congress and executive to make the Court the ultimate receptor of the heat and hostility generated by political decisions (which, we have seen, the political branches attempted to do with slavery and other issues).[196] But when the Court validates, just as when it invalidates, it expends official and public support, certainly of those who lose before it (and some individual or group always does)—sustenance that is critical for its action in areas where judicial review is vitally needed. The fact is that popular displeasure over judicial validations of national power versus states' rights has, in the past as well as recently,[197] conjoined with and spilled over to strengthen those who oppose judicial activism in defense of personal liberties. Thus, on balance, the legitimation principle weakens the Court's ability to perform its critical role.

Of course, as a matter of theory, when the Court rejects a challenge of unconstitutionality, it in no way implies that it approves or endorses the government action it upholds. Technically, the Court decides only that the conduct is within constitutional bounds and, especially because of the powerful presumption of constitutionality generally accorded in the federalism area, the Court's rulings there usually say no more than that the national political branches had some rational or perceivable basis for their decision to exercise the delegated power. As the preceding discussion indicates, however, this is not the flavor tasted by the public or even by most officials. Judicial validation—does not the word "legitimation" imply it?—tends to be equated with judicial applause, a perception not infrequently assisted by judicial rhetoric. Thus, for example, after the Court, almost apologetically, upheld the flag salute requirement questioned by Jehovah's Witnesses, mobs attacked the religious sect's headquarters with the cry, "The Supreme Court is with us."[198]

3. Popular Misconception Respecting Nonjusticiability

The Federalism Proposal urges that the Court explicitly hold that it will not pass on constitutional questions concerning the reach of national authority versus states' rights, and one of the bases for the Proposal is that the Court's withdrawal will shield it from hostile public and official reactions. But if there is frequent misreading of the Court's validation of federal laws, will there not be a similar confusion under the Federalism Proposal, with similar consequences for the judicial image? If, despite the Court's protestations to the contrary, even denials of certiorari are often received by the people (and the press) as favorable decisions on the merits,[199] then why should a holding that the federalism issue is nonjusticiable be understood differ-

ently? Does not the overall record reveal that the public perceives deeds rather than words and that the proposed deed is a
judicial refusal to vindicate states' rights claims?

These are legitimate questions to which no wholly confident
answer may be made. Nonetheless, there is support in both reason and experience for believing that an unqualified relinquish-
ment of all responsibility for the lawfulness of these national
political decisions will be distinguishable from certiorari denials
and "legitimations." As to the former, there is in fact a good deal
more than a few grains of truth in the popular reaction to denials
of certiorari—and the Court itself has openly sprinkled the seeds
on occasion.[200] As to the latter, the two foremost decisions rendered by the Court in respect to nonjusticiable "political questions" affirm Fritz Scharpf's judgment that "even though there
may be a broad spectrum of gradations between legitimation and
nonlegitimation, the political question decision will invariably
be found at its far end: it is not intended to, and it cannot, legitimate a government measure that is challenged before the
Court."[201] The Court's intention in *Luther v. Borden*,[202] holding
the issue of which of two competing state governments was the
"lawful" one to be a nonjusticiable political question, was generally perceived accurately by the bar, Congress, the public, and
the press. "[B]oth political parties professed to be satisfied with
the decision"; and it "did much to establish confidence in the
minds of the American people in the integrity and freedom from
partisan bias of the Court as then established."[203] And, after *Cole-
grove v. Green*[204] strongly suggested that legislative malapportionment in Illinois presented a political question, the state,
rather than inferring that the Court had approved the system,
hastened to modify it because of the felt possibility that the Court
might invalidate it the next time around.[205] More recently, I
would urge that whatever criticism the Court may have engendered by refusing to adjudicate the constitutional questions surrounding the war in Indochina, it was far less than the enmity it
would have incurred had it spoken to the issues—one way or the
other. On balance, so long as the Court is sufficiently clear in its
denials of jurisdiction under the Federalism Proposal, both the

substance of the action and the motives for taking it should be properly interpreted.

D. COMPETENCE OF POLITICAL BRANCHES ON CONSTITUTIONAL ISSUES

Observers of our national government and defenders of judicial review in particular have often forcefully contended that the nonjudicial branches are simply incapable of responsible constitutional decisionmaking. Even before the first Congress convened, Hamilton wrote that "the members of the legislature will rarely be chosen with a view to those qualifications which fit men for the stations of judges; and ... on account of the natural propensity of such bodies to party divisions, there will be no less reason to fear that the pestilential breath of faction may poison the fountains of justice. The habit of being continually marshalled on opposite sides will be too apt to stifle the voice both of law and of equity."[206]

The two elements emphasized by Hamilton—the process of selection and the pressure of politics—have been frequently reiterated. That many congressmen (and Presidents, too) have not been trained as lawyers—and certainly not as constitutional specialists—casts doubt on their ability to analyze or assimilate the ingredients for rendering constitutional judgments and influences them to rely heavily on the views and interpretations of those, within and without the political system, who profess expertise. Because of the compartmentalized nature of the federal lawmaking process—set forth in detail in chapter 1—issues of constitutionality often are extensively explored only by a single committee in each chamber, and if not given serious consideration then, the matter may lie submerged throughout the remaining legislative deliberations. Since in the Congress, unlike the courts, the constitutional validity of proposed legislation is only one of a multitude of varied factors to be considered, that question frequently becomes blended with those of policy and expediency that are normally more pressing. The method of negotiation and compromise that moves the federal legislative machinery does not easily lend itself to the development of a "body of coherent and intelligible constitutional principle,"[207] and it produces the need for participants to make (and fulfill) commitments at different stages of the process without the opportunity for reflection necessary for enlightened constitutional decisionmaking. All these factors have led to conclusions such as Martin Shapiro's that "the nature of the legislative process, combined with the nature of constitutional issues, makes it virtually impossible for Congress to make independent, unified, or responsible judgments on the constitutionality of its own statutes."[208]

1. Reach of the Objection

This indictment, it should be noted, constitutes a powerful argument not only against the Federalism Proposal but also against the whole political question doctrine constructed by the Court and all of that principle's applications. Indeed, it cuts directly against any presumption of constitutionality at all, and certainly against any strong one, for the judicial presumption is premised on the belief that the political department to which decision is relegated has accorded considerations of constitutional regularity their just due.

2. Special Capacity for Federalism Issues

Further, we are concerned here with only a limited aspect of the problem—the capacity of the federal political branches to determine questions of national power vis-à-vis the states. Whatever the qualifications of elected federal officers may be for performing judicial tasks generally or rendering constitutional judgments particularly, we have seen that the tenth amendment issue has distinctive qualities. Rather than being surrounded by those technical considerations that require sophisticated judicial expertise, it is concerned more with those practical matters inherent in the growing and shifting nature of the country, questions on which the conclusions of informed politicians may be at least as creditworthy as those of distinguished jurists. That some legislators may award substantial weight to the doctrinal views of their more learned and experienced colleagues or to those of unofficial constitutional scholars, or to the judgments of committees that have heard and considered those views, is not subject to condemnation; courts are known to function along somewhat analogous lines.

Although American history has recorded many instances where partisanship and expediency rather than constitutional statesmanship have determined the fate of proposed federal legislation, as would be expected from our prior discussion, the most egregious have been in the realm of individual rights. This is illustrated by the seemingly conscious disregard of first amendment values in the congressional debates over the Alien and Sedition Acts of 1798, the Taft-Hartley Act of 1947, the Communist Control Act of 1954, and the apparently deliberate defiance of the announced right of the accused in the Omnibus Safe Streets and Crime Control Act of 1968 and the establishment of preventive detention in the District of Columbia in 1970.[209] On the other hand, although surely not all proposed national actions having a significant impact on states' rights have been thoroughly and dispassionately reviewed by Congress on constitutional grounds, it is in this category of constitutional issues that some of the most prominent illustrations are found. Witness, for example, the extensive and predominantly impartial concern for constitutionality during consideration of the Sherman Act of 1890, the Civil Rights Act of 1964, the eighteen-year-old voting bill of 1970,[210] and the proposed National No-Fault Motor Vehicle Insurance Act of 1974.[211] (The other class of constitutional issues that has received similar reflection is that of the separation of powers between the political branches—a topic to be explored at length in chapter 5. This may be exemplified by the elaborate hearings and lengthy debate in 1973 on the constitutionality, under the ineligibility clause of Art. I, §6, of appointing Senator William Saxbe to be Attorney General;[212] the systematic discussion on an issue of executive privilege during a Senate investigation following General Douglas MacArthur's dismissal in 1951, drawing on many and varied constitutional sources and finally resolved by a nonpartisan vote; and the careful consideration given to those provisions of the Reorganization Act of 1939 dealing with the ability of Congress to delegate, and to superintend that delegation, to the executive.)[213] An informative study of the handling of constitutional issues by a recent Congress reaches the same conclusion that is suggested here: "There does seem to be a discernible difference in the way Congress approaches the problem of legislating in the face of a constitutional prohibition on the exercise of governmental power—a 'Bill of Rights' prohibition—and how it reacts when the question is one of determining the extent of express grants of legislative power to Congress itself. In the former case, the attitude is often one of hostility and unwillingness to accept any alleged limitation on congressional power.... On the other hand, when Congress bases legislation on an express grant of power found in the Constitution, the extent of which is uncertain or problematical, it seems far more conscientious and careful in attempting to fathom the true limitations of its power."[214]

Neither the arguments advanced nor the data presented are intended to prove that, even in respect to states' rights, Congress has done a superlative job in assessing the constitutionality of proposed legislation, or even that it has performed that task just as effectively as has the Court. But, on a number of occasions in the past, Congress has acted at least creditably. It is true that some legislators have felt greater responsibility than others in this regard—just as some presidents, in contrast to Franklin Roosevelt's stance referred to earlier, have shown greater sensitivity to constitutional strictures than others. Witness, for example, Richard Nixon's views on Congress's capacity to lower the voting age, John Kennedy's position on federal financial aid to church-related schools, and James Madison's vetoes, four of six of which were on constitutional grounds.[215] It is also true that on occasion one house has been more conscientious than the other and that constitutional considerations have often received greater attention when policy issues have been less in dispute.[216] But, especially on questions of national versus state authority, we have seen that the political branches are well equipped to make quite respectable constitutional judgments. In a recent survey, nearly two-thirds of the federal legislators polled believed that congressmen should diligently engage in this effort.[217] The Judiciary Committees of both houses, to which most questions of constitutionality have been assigned for nearly a century, have traditionally been composed entirely of lawyers, a number of whom have earned widespread respect for their constitutional expertise.[218] And there is no paucity of resources, living and written, that may be consulted for sound constitutional advice, including the abundance of judicial views already recorded.

Furthermore, experience discloses that various techniques, such as the creation of select committees, are available to enable Congress to better its job performance. And the political branches have by no means exhausted the possible methods for improvement of procedures. In his impressive study of the topic, Donald Morgan has cataloged a number of ways in which Congress might better equip itself for the task of assuming larger responsibility—e.g., clearer identification and definition of constitutional issues by the appropriate committees, greater committee use of auxiliary expert staff and extrinsic sources and materials, and avoidance of last minute action by reviving committee hearings when constitutional questions emerge at later stages of the process.[219]

It is difficult to measure how many of such reforms have been deterred by the notion, inferrable under the present scheme of judicial review, that the Constitution "is essentially subordinate, technical, and too abstruse for any but lawyers in the courtroom and judges on the bench to discuss with sense," and "the belief that a law is not a law, but only a tentative, pressure-wrought statement of policy until judges in court subject it to judicial process and render formal judgment."[220] It is equally hazardous to predict the degree of improvement that would occur if the political branches were unqualifiedly assigned the mantle of final judgment over questions of the reach of national authority. But it is not unreasonable to speculate that some improvement would take place. On balance, given the credentials of the members of the political branches to determine the rights of the states, the ways of improving political procedures for doing so, and the damage caused to the Court's overall prestige and ability to perform its crucial role that has been occasioned by judicial review of tenth amendment claims, the Federalism Proposal should prevail.

3. Substantial Judicial Role Remains

Finally, it should be noted that the Federalism Proposal obviously does not require national legislators to perform those functions for which judges and the judicial process are peculiarly suited—such as applying law to a specifically developed set of facts, or "doing justice" in a particular case. That task remains with the courts. Moreover, it should be emphasized that resting the final constitutional *decision* with the political branches by no means disrobes the judiciary. The courts would still play a vital role in helping to shape the decision through the articulation of constitutional values and the nourishment of constitutional understanding. Federal statutes (or executive orders or treaties, etc.) are rarely so plain and precise as not to require interpretation. If, in a particular case before it, after assembling the dominant adjudicative facts and surveying the relevant data underlying the federal action, as well as traditional constitutional precepts, the Court believes that application of the enactment would or might well exceed the authority of the central government, it will virtually always be open to the Court to interpret the statute (or executive action) as being inapposite. In so doing, the Court would be following its customary procedure of assuming, in the absence of clear contrary evidence, that Congress (or the executive) either did not intend or did not consider applications of its enactments that appear to test the limits of national power.[221] This judicial stance would be especially appropriate if the record indicated either that the political branches did not reflect on the question of constitutionality or sought to mask their failure to confront that issue by using ambiguous language. The Court may continue to pay proper deference to the opinions of federal agencies as to the meaning of the statute (or executive action) before it, the usual rule being the loftier the position of the official agency in the hierarchy and the more closely involved it is with the law's administration, the greater the weight given its views. But the Court is not bound unless the pertinent political branch has itself unmistakably spoken. If so, in respect to federal power versus states' rights, the Federalism Proposal urges that that word be final.

E. INTENT OF THE FRAMERS

Another axiom of American government is that no matter how sound, laudable, or expedient a reasoned constitutional thesis may be, it must fail if it is contradicted by the clear intention of the framers. Objection based on this principle may be leveled against the attempt of the Federalism Proposal to restrict judicial review of constitutional questions of national versus state power. Such a charge would come armed with prestigious credentials.

Madison may be cited as having suggested on several occasions that the "judicial bench" was intended "as the surest expositor of...the boundaries...between the Union and its members."[222] Hamilton's already quoted statement in *The Federalist* No. 78 strongly implies that the Court would act as a barrier to national aggrandizement at state expense.[223] Even stronger assertions to this effect were made by key figures in the state ratifying conventions: in Virginia, John Marshall declared that the judiciary would void congressional attempts "to make a law not warranted by any of the powers enumerated";[224] in Connecticut, Oliver Ellsworth opined that "if the general legislature should at any time overleap their limits, the judicial department is a constitutional check";[225] in Pennsylvania, James Wilson stated that if any federal statute were to be "inconsistent with those powers vested by this instrument in Congress, the judges, as a consequence of their independence, and the particular powers of the government being defined, will declare such laws to be null and void";[226] in Massachusetts, Samuel Adams assured that the courts would invalidate national legislation that "extended beyond the power granted by the proposed Constitution."[227] In the First Congress, Representative Michael Stone remarked, without dissent, that one of the functions of the judiciary was to stop the national government from "destroying" the sovereignty of the states.[228] And, in mid-twentieth century, the point was one of the few areas of common ground between jurists of such divergent perceptions of the Court's role as Felix Frankfurter and William Douglas: the former viewed "the basic function of the Court as the mediator of powers within the federal system";[229] and the latter found that "the Constitution was designed to keep the balance between the States and the Nation outside the field of legislative controversy."[230]

Despite this impressive array of historical statements, the Federalism Proposal need not be abandoned. The original-intent axiom is itself shrouded with large uncertainties: What specifically is meant by the *"clear* intention of the Framers"? How *clear* must "clear" be? At what point does their intent contradict rather than merely cast doubt on a contemporary constitutional interpretation? How precisely is such a contradiction to be defined? Of what significance is the fact that it is a constitution intended to be permanent rather than a statute that could be easily amended, that was promulgated? Of what relevance is the change in social circumstances since 1789 (or 1868)? These are formidable and perplexing questions pervading all of constitutional law and adjudication, and they by no means exhaust those that must be addressed. But the historical evidence on the particular issue of original intent is sufficiently ambiguous to allow us to proceed without attempting the onerous task of plowing this field.

Neither Madison nor Hamilton spoke unqualifiedly. Those who have devoted their attention to the period report that Madison "was guilty, and guilty as a matter of public record, of about as complete inconsistency upon this subject as was possible";[231] and that "for the containment of the national authority Madison did not emphasize the function of the Court; he pointed to the composition of the Congress and to the political processes."[232] As for Hamilton, "in *Federalist* #33, where he discussed the necessary and proper clause, which anti-ratificationists regarded as vesting carte blanche powers in Congress, Hamilton asked who was to judge if Congress 'should overpass the just bounds of its authority.' Not once in his answer did he allude to the Supreme Court. Congress in the first instance and the people in the last would judge. How then is *Federalist* #78 to be explained?"[233] And what explanation for the eminent opinions in the ratifying conventions?

The only clear answer to these queries is that there is no clear answer. Perhaps, as has been carefully and courageously attempted, the conflicting implications of the founders' statements may be reconciled.[234] Perhaps, as has been forthrightly urged, *The Federalist* should be read with considerable skepticism, at least on this issue: "It was, in reality, a conscious partisan device...aimed at getting the Constitution adopted in the reluctant and resisting state of New York.... Thus,...it is a mistake to take at face value many of its statements on the key issue, in New York, of the division of power between the states and the national government. There can be no doubt that...*The Federalist* attempted to mollify the opposition by playing down the powers of the national government."[235] Perhaps this impetus also discloses the motive for the confident views articulated in the state conventions by those who were committed to the document by participation in its drafting. Perhaps the primary purpose of judicial review of federalism issues—and, as we have seen, there is prominent support for the proposition—was intended to assure against state incursions on national power rather than the reverse. Close reading of a number of the statements cited is quite consistent with this theory. As Samuel Huntington has written, Madison believed that "each government possessed a different 'defensive armour' which was its 'means of preventing or correcting unconstitutional encroachments' by the other. The defensive armor of the states was the political process; that of the national government was the judicial process."[236] Perhaps all of these are meandering speculations.

The most compelling justification for holding that the Federalism Proposal should not be felled by the thinking of the framers, however, is that the evidence on whether any judicial review *at all* was contemplated is short of conclusive. Although the Federalism Proposal surely does not lay claim to being a fulfillment of original intent, nor does it purport to consist with the views of even most of the scholars who have focused on the historical materials, neither should it be defeated on these grounds.

F. FEDERALISM AS A GUARANTOR OF INDIVIDUAL LIBERTY

Perhaps the most deeply rooted argument for rejecting the Federalism Proposal is that the federal system, the scheme of territorial division of power within the United States—as well as the separation of power among the three branches of the national government (a topic that will concern us in chapter 5)—was designed to preserve individual freedom and prevent government tyranny. The framers believed, the argument continues, that a powerful central monolith would become arrogant and despotic; fragmentation of authority would avoid suppression of disagreement and dissent. Years later, Lord Acton found that "the distribution of power among several States is the best check on democracy . . . . It is the protectorate of minorities and the consecration of self-government."[237] And, as stated tersely by Justice Frankfurter, "Time has not lessened the concern of the Founders in devising a federal system which would . . . be a safeguard against arbitrary government."[238]

This premise has important implications for the Federalism Proposal. If the Court's central function is to assure constitutionally ordained personal liberties, and if the federalism principle was adopted to secure individual rights, then it may be said to follow that the Court's continued review of alleged violations of states' rights is not only consistent with its critical role but demanded by it. Nor does the sensitivity of the national political process to constitutional issues of federalism wholly undermine this syllogism. For the political branches' sensitivity to the possible infringement of personal liberties when large numbers of people are affected does not, as we have seen, result in the Court's refusal to pass constitutional judgment on the issue. But the assertion that federalism was meant to protect, or does in fact protect, individual constitutional freedoms akin to those conventionally so defined has no solid historical or logical basis.

1. Tenth Amendment

The language of the Constitution itself is often cited to support the argument. If the federalism precept was intended only to guard states' rights, it is asked, why does the tenth amendment declare that "the powers not delegated to the United States ... are reserved to the States respectively, *or to the people*"? In his monumental, and equally controversial, study of the meaning of the Constitution, William Crosskey, although noting that the "reason for the inclusion of these four words in the Tenth Amendment has long been something of a puzzle,"[239] flatly concludes that "the Tenth Amendment, unlike the preceding first nine, had directly to do with 'States' Rights,' rather than the rights of individuals."[240] Meticulously parsing the language in context and carefully examining it from all relevant perspectives, Crosskey persuasively demonstrates that the two phrases "the States respectively" and "the people" do *not* "signify different persons, as has sometimes been supposed, they signify the same persons .... The meaning of the amendment is *not*, then, that a 'reservation' of powers is made *either* 'to the States respectively *or* to the people,' understanding 'the States respectively' and 'the people,' in divergent senses." Rather, "the two phrases ... were used in apposition in the amendment and are so punctuated in it."[241]

Although Crosskey has never been challenged on this point, the inquiry need not rely exclusively on his painstaking work. What has been described as "the best account of the legislative history of the Tenth Amendment,"[242] the brief filed in the Supreme Court by the United States in the case of *Mulford v. Smith*[243]—a pre-Crosskey, comprehensive study of the debates on the amendment in the ratifying conventions and the First Congress—repeatedly concludes that the amendment was designed to overcome "two fears: that the national government might assert the right to exercise powers not granted, and that the states would be unable fully to exercise the powers which the Constitution had not taken from them." "[P]erhaps the most frequently expressed purpose was to insure that the states should continue able to exercise the numerous powers which had *not* been granted to Congress." "[I]n summary, the men who proposed the Tenth Amendment seem to have been clear that the Amendment was simply declaratory of the evident proposition that Congress could not constitutionally exercise powers not granted to it, and that these powers could continue to be exercised by the states."[244] At no point does this study, whether canvassing the comments of James Madison or of Patrick Henry or of many others, in any way mention "the people" or individual rights. Madison himself demeaned the importance of the tenth amendment. He told Congress, "[The state conventions] are particularly anxious that it should be declared in the Constitution, that the powers not therein delegated should be reserved to the several States . . . . I admit [this] may be deemed unnecessary; but there can be no harm in making such declaration."[245] And despite a single dictum by the Supreme Court—that the tenth amendment's "principal purpose was not the distribution of power between the United States and the States, but a reservation to the people of all powers not granted"[246]—the overwhelming view of the Justices, including Marshall, Story, Taney, Holmes, and Stone, has been to the contrary.[247]

This virtually undisputed interpretation of the tenth amendment as being—in the words of an ardent critic of the extension of federal power—an affirmation of sovereignty not "in the people as a whole" but "in the people-as-States"[248] is fully consistent with the broad constitutional scheme mandated by the framers. The thrust of the Constitution was not to secure rights of individuals against exertions of government power but rather to distribute power between nation and states. It was the surrender of sovereignty by the states that posed the major barrier to an effective union, and it was that issue rather than personal liberties that was resolved by the great compromise. Amendments to the Constitution, which include those relatively few provisions that did establish individual rights, do not require the concurrence of "the people" but rather that of an extraordinary majority of the previously independent states. In sum, the contention that federalism secures personal liberty is simply not helped by the tenth amendment.

2. Local Government as a Protector of Freedom

A more subtle line of argument, however, appears to hold greater promise. It concedes that the federalism principle was conceived—in phrases of those at the Philadelphia

Convention[249]—because of the persisting "passion for separate sovereignty" of the states, and that this precept was reaffirmed in the tenth amendment. But, the argument continues, the reason for this historic concern for "state governments" was that they were to be relied on for the preservation of individual liberty. Decentralized decisionmaking units would assure greater individual participation in the political process and better opportunity for the selection of officials whose views reflected those of their constituents. Thus, the lower the level of effective government, the closer to the people, the greater the control each individual would have of his own destiny. Especially because of the wide religious, political, and cultural diversity of the people who were spread over the large territory of the former colonies, small groups of like-minded persons would be much more disposed than would a distant national government to impose laws that were locally desired and in harmony with local values. Through these means, freedom would be maintained.

a. Efficiency versus Freedom

This rationale merits serious attention. To begin from the perspective of history: as is unfortunately true of many assertions concerning the intentions that motivated the framers, the record in regard to *the* reason for the sanctification of the states is cloudy. Indeed, what appears to emerge most clearly is that a primary purpose (if not *the* reason) for the desire to sustain the vitality of the state governments was not so much to assure personal freedom but rather to promote the efficiency of government administration. The belief existed that, so far as the central government was concerned, there would be great difficulty in its functioning successfully over a territory that was so large geographically and so diverse culturally.[250] If the federal legislature were to attempt to devote proper attention to the myriad details presented by the concerns of each locality, there would be a wasteful dissipation of federal energy, extravagant expenditures, and an overexpansion of bureaucracy. And no matter how effective the national effort, a monolithic central government would impose added burdens of time and expense on those citizens scattered far from the capital who had to rely on it for the solution of all public problems. Moreover, a single, remote national government would more than likely possess neither the systematic knowledge of local conditions nor the flexibility required for wise administration, whereas heterogeneous state government institutions would not only function on a more manageable scale but would encourage political experimentation and innovative response to arising social needs.

This conclusion—that "the issue, then, in controversy over 'States' Rights'...[was] not an issue of liberty" but rather "an issue solely of effective government"[251]—may be seen most lucidly in Madison's unqualified statement to the Philadelphia Convention: "The great objection made [against] an abolition of the State [governments] was that the [general government] could not extend its care to all the minute objects which fall under the cognizance of the local jurisdictions. The objection as stated lay not [against] the probable abuse of the general power but [against] the imperfect use that could be made of it throughout so great an extent of country, and over so great a variety of objects.... Were it practicable for the [general government] to extend its care to every requisite object without the cooperation of the State [governments] the people would not be less free as members of one great Republic than as members of thirteen small ones."[252] Tocqueville affirmed the point half a century later in condemning a powerful centralized government as one that "relaxes the sinews of strength" and "incessantly diminish[es] local spirit."[253]

In modern times, prominent political theorists continue to urge the greater efficiency of having collective decisions made in the smallest feasible political units,[254] stressing the opportunity for those political parties out of power nationally to have laboratories for testing their policies locally. Brandeis, perhaps the most fervent twentieth-century intellectual federalist, founded his views, in Felix Frankfurter's words, "on deep convictions regarding the manageable size for the effective conduct of human affairs and the most favorable conditions for the exercise of wise judgment.... As to matters not obviously of common national concern, thereby calling for a centralized system of control, the States have a localized knowledge of details, a concreteness of interest and varieties of social policy, which ought to be allowed tolerant scope."[255] Arthur Vanderbilt, in his analysis of contemporary American national government and federalism, expressed the belief that "no government, no matter how well organized, is capable of operating efficiently on such a gigantic scale," and vividly illustrated his age-old criticism: "Approximately one half of the 3 million purchase orders issued annually by the various federal buying agencies average less than $10 in value, yet the partial cost of processing a purchase transaction is greatly in excess of $10. In other words, the overhead cost is far more than the cost of the goods themselves."[256] The Conference of State Chief Justices, in its anti–Supreme Court manifesto mentioned above, decried the decline of American federalism without reference to diminution of personal freedom: "We believe that strong State and local governments are essential to the effective functioning of the American system of Federal government; that they should not be sacrificed needlessly to leveling, and sometimes deadening, uniformity; and that in the interest of active, citizen participation in self-government—the foundation of our democracy—they should be sustained and strengthened."[257] Finally, this "government efficiency" purpose for territorial separation of power was put succinctly by the then Professor Frankfurter: "Federalism is one of the great devices to which the restless modern world turns for reconciling stability with vitality among diverse elements within a political society scattered over wide territory."[258]

b. Nature of Freedom

The foregoing recitation has not been intended to prove conclusively that individual liberty was totally outside the thinking of those who fashioned the federal scheme of government for the United States. Rather it is to indicate a dominant sentiment that federalism would promote good government. But, apart from the strongly held belief that the states were necessary for effective administration, freedom—at least of a kind—was also comprehended within the federalism ideal in the minds of many who advocated limited power for the national government. This dual purpose is evidenced by the two separate statements of

Felix Frankfurter, both set forth above, that articulate each of these goals.

But the freedom that the framers hoped would be furthered by curtailing the authority of the central government so as to assure the continued vitality of the states is of a special genre, quite different from the individual rights designated in Art. I, §§9 and 10 of the original Constitution and then supplemented by the first series of amendments. It is "freedom" somewhat elusive to define in traditional terms of "personal liberty." The purpose was not to guard the "sovereignty of the individual" from an all powerful national monolith but rather to preserve the sovereignty of states as political units. The "right of the people" was not to have some area carved out in which they would be shielded from all government incursions, but rather the right to have this area of their affairs governed only by the states. This was a collective rather than a personal right—a right that was intended not for the ultimate security of defined liberties but to insure the people's ability to choose in political units smaller than the national legislature whether and how certain of their activities would be regulated. Recalling the oppressive decisions made for them from across the Atlantic where their voices were barely heard and even less heeded, the former colonists rested their faith in the process of local government to secure their "freedom" and guard against the arbitrariness of uninformed and unresponsive majorities of strangers.[259] Thus, in the Virginia ratifying convention, Patrick Henry pointed to the state legislatures for the "care and preservation of the people";[260] and Thomas Jefferson, at his first inauguration, believed in "the support of the State governments in all their rights, as the most competent administrations for our domestic concerns and the surest bulwarks against anti-republican tendencies."[261]

c. Relevance of Federalism

It is true that, at various times when federalism was under discussion, the framers evinced a concern for "liberty" that would not be fulfilled simply through a "bias in favor of local autonomy,"[262] a process of government by officials who are responsive to local demands. The strong belief existed that, if the national government possessed only limited powers, this would assure personal liberties as conventionally defined—i.e., rights of individuals to be immune in regard to certain matters from *all* public regulation.[263] The suggestion that the federalism principle might achieve this goal is difficult to understand because in itself it concedes the right of *local* officials to regulate the affairs of the people (their "personal liberties," if you will, that are secured by the precept) as they see fit. Indeed, for Madison, at least, the method by which the federal system of government would secure individual freedom was quite the reverse. He believed that the remedy for those abuses of minorities and individual rights that had occurred under the Articles of Confederation as a result of local tyranny "lay in an improved system of republican government in which the wiser and more balanced national majority would check the arbitrary actions of local majorities . . . . [H]e declared that the Union was necessary to bring about a 'thorough reform' of the 'fluctuating policy' which had prevailed in the states and to guard the people against 'those violent and oppressive factions which embitter the cause of liberty.'"[264]

Perhaps the more conventionally articulated view of some of Madison's contemporaries that federalism would preserve individual freedom can be attributed to the inclusion of individual rights provisions in state constitutions, in contrast to the original federal Constitution's lack of literal concern for fundamental liberties. The feeling may have been that a combination of the states' bills of rights and the fact that the federal government's actions were restricted to certain areas would preserve the personal freedoms already possessed.

Whether this speculation clears the confusion is not critical for our purposes. The significant fact is that whatever the reason for the framers' concern over centralism at the expense of states' rights, they were also at least equally fearful of a national despotism—of the threat to traditionally defined rights of individuals posed by an unrestrained federal legislative authority.[265] And, even more important, there is little reason to believe that the local government process secured by the federalism precept was relied on to insure these rights. For one thing, the fear of legislative tyranny was in large measure engendered by the tendency at that time of the state lawmaking bodies to assume what was thought to be undue power.[266] For another, both Hamilton and Madison, the framers' most knowledgeable spokesmen, explicitly recognized that greater dangers to personal freedom were posed by the states than by the national government. Madison stated that "the smaller the number of individuals composing a majority, and the smaller the compass within which they are placed, the more easily will they concert and execute their plans of oppression. Extend the sphere, and you take in a greater variety of parties and interests, you make it less probable that a majority of the whole will have a common motive to invade the rights of other citizens; or if such a common motive exists, it will be more difficult for all who feel it to discover their own strength and to act in unison with each other."[267] And Hamilton agreed that "the national councils . . . will be less apt to be tainted by the spirit of faction, and more out of reach of those occasional ill-humors, or temporary prejudices and propensities, which, in smaller societies, frequently contaminate the public councils, beget injustice and oppression of a part of the community, and engender schemes which, though they gratify a momentary inclination or desire, terminate in general distress, dissatisfaction, and disgust."[268]

d. Record of Experience

Whatever undefined hope some may have held that the best promise for individual rights rested in local government units, it is the insight of Madison and Hamilton respecting political-social dynamics that has been confirmed by subsequent events. For our history has demonstrated that the smaller the population and geographic area, the greater the likelihood of dominance by a single political party or machine with a single set of mores and the greater the opportunity for aggregations of economic power to overshadow the political scene. This in turn imposes stronger pressures toward conformity, lesser incentives and larger difficulties for minorities to obtain influence, and narrower community tolerance for deviant beliefs and behavior.[269] Even the most casual survey of the *United States Reports* reveals that in every area of constitutionally designated individual liberties—whether it be speech, race, religion, the rights of the accused, or any other—the record of state and local governments has been far inferior to that of the nation. To mention two random examples: not until 1965 did the Supreme Court find federal action violative of *any* provision in the first amendment; and the Federal Bureau of Investigation, whatever its other failings, used the substance of the *Miranda* warnings for many years prior to the Court's requirement in 1966 that they be employed for the first time by state and local police. Regardless of the explanations for specific failures of local governments to protect individual rights—e.g., badly trained and poorly paid police officers are endemic in state and local governments—the hard fact may not be denied. And this state of affairs might be even worse were it not for federal judicial review of state action infringing personal liberties.

That personal liberty is neither dependent on nor enhanced by federalism has been substantiated by experience in other countries as well. Nazi Germany presents the most ignominious case of a modern federal system that utterly failed to preserve the rights of the individual, but the Soviet Union, Argentina, and Brazil also illustrate the phenomenon.[270] Alternatively, Scandinavia and England serve as examples of unitary nations in which freedom has flourished. "An obvious difficulty," Arthur Macmahon explains, "frequently blocks the use of federalism to recognize differences, to protect minorities, and to maximize government with the consent of the governed by distributing power geographically. The realization of the objective depends upon a neat concentration of national minorities. It is likely, however, that they will be present in many places and in the minority everywhere, subordinate in social prestige, economic power, and influence. When this condition exists, thoroughgoing federalism may easily result in a kind of feudalism—benevolent, perhaps, but essentially oligarchical in local domination over weaker elements. The situation may indeed be softened by various minor devices.... The main relief, however, is sought in central constitutional guarantees, centrally enforced."[271] In America, the federal Constitution, not the federal system, seeks to guarantee individual rights; and the federal judiciary, not the processes of state and local government, provides the most effective method for their enforcement.

e. Role of Judicial Review to Protect Self-Determination

But what of that special brand of "freedom" that *is* afforded by federalism: that "liberty" that is achieved through decisionmaking in small political units by locally elected officials who are peculiarly sensitive to local concerns? Should the Court not also exercise its power of judicial review in regard to allegations that the constitutional provisions protecting this feature of American political life have been abridged?

Response to these questions may be made at several levels. First, it is important to observe that the issue presented by *National League of Cities v. Usery*—the sole case in four decades in which an opinion of the Court has condemned national action as being violative of states' rights—in no way implicates the kind of "freedom" under discussion. That decision concerns federal regulation of official state functions, of "the States *qua* States," rather than national authority over the conduct of private persons within the states. Second, since the latter subject (which does involve the type of "freedom" being considered) may be regulated at the will of locally elected representatives, if the challenged congressional action has the support of a particular state's national representatives—and it must have the concurrence of at least some of these—then the people within that state have no cause to complain that their "freedom" has been wrongfully curtailed. But people in those states whose representatives opposed the relevant federal regulation, or people who level a states' rights attack against federal executive action that was never specifically put to the states' delegates in Washington, are in a different position. But for the challenged national action, the area of such people's conduct subject to the federal regulation might well be, if not altogether free of government control, at least affected in a different and more individualized way.

It may be that the peculiar qualitative nature of constitutional issues of federalism—discussed earlier—should excuse the Court from participation because the national political forum,

which is highly responsive to states' rights and the general interest in localism, has decided that no constitutional violation has
occurred. But this answer may not be found to be wholly satisfactory by the complainants because, no matter how large the
state majority favoring the federal action, different states and the
people within them may be affected by it in very different
ways—in their lives, their pocketbooks, or simply in their attitudes about national intervention. Nor is the answer
strengthened by the fact that the Court's current standard for
reviewing federalism contentions, one that virtually abdicates to
the national political process rather than carefully scrutinizing its
product, implies that the judiciary's considered view is that the
"freedoms" affected are not comparable to conventionally
defined individual rights. No matter how accurately this may
portray the Court's judgment, it assumes the conclusion being
debated.

At a different level, it may be forthrightly urged that the
federalism principle has simply outlived its usefulness. Along
with the concept of separation of powers among the federal
branches, federalism was originally designed to diffuse power in
order to make national action difficult—to enfeeble the central
lawmaking system through built-in requirements of negotiation
and compromise. But, the argument may proceed, the advantages
to the country of having a sluggish national government have
long since passed. Whatever the virtues of state and local administration may earlier have been—and Woodrow Wilson observed their deterioration as viable instruments of government
almost a century ago[272]—the growth of the nation and of the
complex nature of its problems, its transformation from a relatively stable agrarian society to one that is highly mobile and
integrated, has rendered the states incapable of effectively functioning as laboratories of social experimentation.[273] Furthermore,
whereas the states may be seen as having neglected the task of
furthering progressive and libertarian values, the record of the
national government, although far from perfect, is much better,
not only in substance but in terms of its political responsiveness
as well, as evidenced by increasing extensions of the franchise. It
is no longer the size of government per se that threatens freedom

but rather the risk that its operation will fail to abide with the constitutional mandates of liberty. To safeguard against such abuse, the Court sits.

Irrespective of the merit of the foregoing argument, competent evaluation of its content goes well beyond the boundaries of this book—and, for that matter, beyond consideration of the role to be performed by the federal judiciary in constitutional decisionmaking. And one need not rely on it to justify the Court's refusal to review constitutional challenges to the scope of national power. On balance, two principal factors, both already discussed herein, support the Federalism Proposal. First, whatever the precise quality of the special type of "freedom" that is nourished by a restrained exercise of national power, it is equally likely that the withdrawal of judicial review will result in a more fastidious concern for states' rights by the federal political branches which will assume the mantle of final decision, rather than in diminished political awareness of the virtues of limited national authority.

Second, and more important, if the ultimate question is how best to further individual constitutional liberties of *all* kinds, then removing the burden of reviewing federalism issues from the Court's shoulders is the wiser course. Perhaps in earlier days of the republic the availability of judicial review to check perceived excesses of national power vis-à-vis the states deterred acceptance of the doctrine of state interposition. Perhaps the Court's original assumption of the role of constitutional umpire of the federal system worked to strengthen its capacity to protect individual liberty.[274] As we saw in chapter 3, however, the record of time discloses that the Court's ability to defend the personal rights of minorities who have fared poorly in the political process is a fragile one, ultimately dependent on the willingness of the people to abide by the Court's antimajoritarian rulings. We have already seen in this chapter that judicial validations of federal power as against states' rights have often placed the Court at the center of a storm of controversy, thus endangering its authority in unrelated areas of constitutional adjudication. So, too, have the Court's rulings invalidating such national action expended its institutional credit and prestige.

Although the latter phenomenon is the major subject of chapter 3, several additional observations are especially pertinent here. The decision of the Supreme Court striking down the first federal income tax (described by Charles Evans Hughes in the 1920s as one of the three great "self-inflicted wounds" suffered by the Court)[275] and the subsequent series of rulings rejecting the efforts of the New Deal (which must surely be characterized as another)—all of which turned on national power versus states' rights—have been among the small handful of worst judicial disasters in terms of damage to the Court's public standing. Beyond this, the virtually undisputed judgment of history has been that these decisions, along with other federalism rulings, such as the pre–New Deal child labor cases and the intergovernmental tax immunity cases, constitute the bulk of those rendered by the Court that have been most mistaken, foolish, and destructive of progressive government.[276]

Moreover, the Court's invalidations of national authority on states' rights grounds have been strikingly short-lived. *Dred Scott's* denial of federal power to prohibit slavery in the territories succumbed to the Emancipation Proclamation in less than a decade. The *Income Tax Case* fell to constitutional amendment within two decades. The Court's extreme inflation of state immunity from federal taxation and severe contraction of national regulatory power over economic matters took longer to remedy, but both doctrines were eventually corrected by the Court itself. Its more recent venture, negating the congressionally mandated eighteen-year-old vote in state and local elections, survived for less than a year—an all-time modern record for constitutional amendment. Indeed, the presently unforeseeable reach of the *Usery* case aside, there is virtually no tenth amendment decision of any note that retains current meaningful force. This record of the failure of the Court's invalidations of national legislation on federalism grounds, along with the fact that the Court has denied most federalism challenges, strongly suggests that Congress accurately and consistently reflects the will of the states in defining the boundaries of national governmental power.

Finally, in a crucial group of post–Civil War holdings premised on the tenth amendment, the Court, by overturning federal legislation enacted under the enforcement clauses of the Civil War amendments, largely emasculated (at least at the time) the ability of the national political branches to insure racial freedom and advance the civil liberties of the politically underprivileged, blocking this cause for nearly seventy-five years. Thus, the Court not only severely damaged the fulfillment of liberty but frustrated the processes of democracy as well. The Federalism Proposal avoids all of these evils.

X. CONCLUSION

Although a fragmented inquiry into the intentions of the framers has been undertaken, no suggestion is put forward that the Federalism Proposal was originally ordained. But neither is it contradicted by the historical record or by the basic themes and values originally expressed. Indeed, it is consistent with and furthers the overriding concern for the rights of the individual. As we saw in chapter 3, the Court's political capital is finite. The Court's authority to exercise its most vital function—the protection of individual liberties—depends on the public's willingness to accept its antimajoritarian decisions. In deciding questions of the scope of national authority vis-à-vis the states, the Court needlessly risks losing the public's confidence because the constitutional interests at stake—those of the states—are forcefully and accurately represented in the national political arena. Thus, the Federalism Proposal is offered to conserve the Court's precious capital for those cases in which it is really needed—where individual, usually poorly represented and unpopular, rights are at stake.

As a bald statement, the Proposal does take a radical tone by urging the Court to reject the long-established system of judicial review over questions of states' rights. But in modern practice rather than in embedded theory, because the Court, in the main, has left decisions of federalism to the national political branches, it would change few results in concrete cases. This is not to say, however, that it would be of no real consequence.

That the Court now rarely exercises its power of review to

invalidate such national action is no guarantee that it will not revert to a mistaken policy—a turnabout already accomplished in the *Usery* decision and possibly promised on the still unsettled question of the reach of federal legislative power under §5 of the fourteenth amendment. On the other hand, if continued judicial review in this field would produce only the most infrequent invalidations, there is little justification for the Court's stamping its imprimatur on so many exercises of national power to protect against so few constitutional violations of the federalism precept. To do so would not only sap its strength to act on behalf of individual rights but, in the face of extreme national abridgments of federalism, the Court's pronouncements would, in all likelihood, be only futile, symbolic rulings.

Five

Constitutional Conflicts between Congress and the President
A Subject for the Political Process

I. INTRODUCTION

The concept of separation of powers among the three branches of the national government is one of the singular features of the American Constitution. Article I vests "all legislative Powers herein granted" in Congress; Article II vests "the executive Power" in the President; Article III vests "the judicial Power of the United States" in the federal courts; and much of the text is committed to describing the extent of the respective dominions. But, because of the inherent deficiencies of the written word and because an unyielding separation of powers was neither contemplated nor enacted, a host of fundamental questions regarding this division of authority have arisen for which the basic charter has afforded only the most ambiguous guidance or, indeed, no helpful signal at all. In contrast to constitutional matters of federalism and individual rights, relatively few of these questions have been presented for judicial resolution—particularly before the 1970s—and even fewer have ever reached the docket of the Supreme Court. But some have, and advocates seek to press many more upon it. This chapter discusses the appropriate role of the national judiciary in regard to one set of separation of powers questions—those concerning clashes of constitutional authority between the legislative and executive departments. Chapter 6 discusses the Court's proper adjudicative function in respect to alleged impositions by either or both of the political branches on the judicial power.

A. RELEVANT CONSTITUTIONAL PROVISIONS

It is useful at the outset to sketch briefly the most prominent areas of contention. The majority involve action (or inaction) by the President that arguably invades the province of Congress, but a significant number evoke the opposite charge. As observed over a century ago, "the most defective part of the Constitution beyond all question, is that which relates to the Executive Department. It is impossible to read that instrument without being forcibly struck with the loose and unguarded terms in which the powers and duties of the President are pointed out."[1] The opening words of Article II invest the President with the "executive Power." The clause is fraught with unresolved ambiguity that may either grant the chief executive independent authority or merely refer to the relatively more specific powers enumerated thereafter.[2] Art. II, §3 charges the President to "take Care that the Laws be faithfully executed." Apart from these very general phrases, the Constitution is silent as to the scope of this executive prerogative and stipulates no boundary for determining when specific presidential conduct passes from the realm of execution into that of legislation. Although the matter appears to be less uncharted in view of the language just cited, serious issues have also arisen concerning the extent of the President's discretion in carrying out the letter of congressional enactments, particularly as to whether he is constitutionally obligated to spend all appropriated funds. While Art. II, §2 defines in some detail the political branches' respective authority over the appointment of various federal officers, apart from those clauses that deal with the impeachment of judges the Constitution stands totally mute about which branch has power to remove the appointees.

In respect to the conduct of foreign relations, Louis Henkin has remarked that "the Constitution seems a strange, laconic document: although it explicitly lodges important foreign affairs powers in one branch or another of the federal government, and denies important powers to the States, many others are not mentioned."[3] Art. II, §2 designates the President as "Commander in Chief of the Army and Navy" and Art. II, §3 empowers him to "receive Ambassadors and other public Ministers"; but Art. II, §2's "Advice and Consent" proviso coordains the Senate with the authority "to make Treaties" and to "appoint Ambassadors, other public Ministers and Consuls"; and many of the powers delegated to Congress by Article I—including those "to regulate Commerce with foreign Nations," "to define and punish . . . Offenses against the Law of Nations," "to declare War . . . and make Rules concerning Captures on Land and Water," "to raise and support Armies," "to provide and maintain a Navy," and "to make Rules for the Government and Regulation of the land and naval Forces"—also encompass the topic. Thus, the issue of where ultimate authority rests for transacting the myriad affairs with other countries presents frequent and fruitful occasions for the political branches and private litigants to make conflicting assertions of primacy, of which many are "about equally intractable under all theories of constitutional power in foreign affairs."[4]

Art. II, §2 grants the President "Power to grant Reprieves and Pardons for Offences against the United States" but fails to provide for conflicts between a presidential pardon and congressionally imposed civil disabilities arising out of the criminal conviction. Despite extensive congressional powers of investigation and inquiry, Presidents beginning with George Washington have claimed that the separation of powers concept includes an executive prerogative to refuse to divulge certain information. And even such seemingly specific clauses as Art. I, §7's veto provision that "if any Bill shall not be returned by the President within ten Days (Sundays excepted) after it shall have been presented to him, the Same shall be a Law, in like Manner as if he had signed it, unless the Congress by their Adjournment prevent its Return in which Case it shall not be a Law" create prickly interpretive problems. For example, what constitutes an "Adjournment"? Does "the Congress" mean either house, or both houses, or the house in which the bill originated?

II. THE SEPARATION PROPOSAL

All these issues as well as others will concern us herein. Many have already been addressed by the Court in particular contexts. Others have not because they have never been made the subject of a specific "case or controversy." Even under the most niggardly definition of that term, however, all such issues are potentially reviewable by the judiciary because they can result in cognizable and immediate injury to individuals. In respect to such cases, no matter how they arise, and wholly apart from the substantive merits of the matter, the thesis to be urged—hereafter referred to as the Separation Proposal—is as follows: The federal judiciary should not decide constitutional questions concerning the respective powers of Congress and the President vis-à-vis one another; rather, the ultimate constitutional issues of whether executive action (or inaction) violates the prerogatives of Congress or whether legislative action (or inaction) transgresses the realm of the President should be held to be nonjusticiable, their final resolution to be remitted to the interplay of the national political process.

III. SEPARATION OF POWERS AS A GUARANTOR OF INDIVIDUAL LIBERTY

Consideration of a basic objection that may be raised against the Separation Proposal should serve as a useful prologue to its further amplification. The challenge goes to the core of the position advocated throughout this book as to the Court's central function of using its auspices to shield constitutionally ordained personal freedoms: since the separation of powers principle was perceived from the time of its origin as a keystone for guaranteeing the liberty of the people, its preservation is eminently entitled to judicial protection.

A. STATEMENTS OF THE POSITION

The argument's premise cannot be seriously disputed. Although John Locke, who more fully developed the mid-seventeenth-century thinking on the separation of powers advanced by James Harrington's *Oceana*, believed that the division of legislative and executive labor would enhance the efficiency of government,[5] he also clearly believed it to be necessary for maintenance of individual liberty. Montesquieu, whatever his misconceptions of the mid-eighteenth-century English system that inspired his extremely influential exposition, was unmistakably plain in his conviction that concentration of government powers—"that of enacting laws, that of executing the public resolutions, and that of judging the crimes of differences of individuals"—inevitably would lead to state despotism, but that their separation would point the way to "political liberty."[6] Similarly, Blackstone, who followed and refined Montesquieu's analysis, expressed the unqualified judgment that "in all tyrannical governments, the supreme magistracy, or the right both of *making* and *enforcing* the laws is vested in one and the same man, or one and the same body of men; and wherever these two powers are united together, there can be no public liberty."[7]

These were views that strongly attracted the framers and influenced the structure of the Constitution. While a number of the founding fathers—including Washington, Adams, Jefferson, Jay, and Wilson—urged acceptance of the principle on the grounds of government efficiency,[8] Madison's statement that "the accumulation of all powers, legislative, executive, and judiciary, in the same hands, whether of one, a few, or many, and whether hereditary, self-appointed, or elective, may justly be pronounced the very definition of tyranny"[9] could as well have come from Montesquieu's pen. Washington voiced the same sentiment in his Farewell Address, cautioning against "the exercise of the powers of one department to encroach upon another" because "the spirit of encroachment tends to consolidate the powers of all the departments in one, and thus to create, whatever the form of government, a real despotism."[10] John Adams wrote that "it is by balancing each of these powers against the other two, that the efforts of human nature towards tyranny can alone be checked and restrained, and any degree of freedom preserved in the constitution."[11] And Jefferson was equally confident in his opinion that concentration of powers "in the same hand [either Congress or the President] is precisely the definition of despotic government. It will be no alleviation that these powers will be exercised by a plurality of hands and not by a single one; 173 despots would surely be as oppressive as one."[12]

These conclusions have survived as articles of libertarian faith to the present time, despite the serious misgivings of many contemporary political scientists—at least prior to Vietnam and Watergate—who consider the separation of powers device an obsolete barrier to effective modern government and believe that it has actually retarded personal freedom by disabling government from acting forcefully to achieve political, economic, and social progress.[13] The most famous twentieth-century articulation is Justice Brandeis's 1927 statement, reaffirmed more recently by such philosophically opposed Justices as Frankfurter and Douglas in the *Steel Seizure Case:*[14] "The doctrine of the separation of powers was adopted by the Convention of 1787, not to promote efficiency but to preclude the exercise of arbitrary power. The purpose was, not to avoid friction, but, by means of the inevitable friction incident to the distribution of the governmental powers among three departments, to save the people from autocracy."[15]

B. PRE-REVOLUTIONARY WAR MEANING OF SEPARATION OF POWERS

The framers' purpose to use the separation of powers mechanism to guard against absolutism is firmly established historically. It by no means follows, however, that the framers intended the Court to enforce the separation of powers or that judicial review is necessary to resolve constitutional clashes between Congress and the President.

Any attempt to trace the evolutionary path leading from the historical origins of the separation of powers concept to its application in the American national governmental system rapidly becomes a muddy process. In the seventeenth century, prior to Montesquieu's elaboration, the theory's principal thrust was to separate the "Legislative" and "Executive" powers; the "Judicial" function was largely ignored. Historians report, however, that the seventeenth-century concept of the "Executive" function did not comport at all with our notion of that term. Rather, "we must see the seventeenth-century abstraction of the functions of government as a twofold one in which 'executive' was generally synonymous with our use of 'judicial,' and in fact in the latter part of the century the two words were used synonymously." The idea was that "the *legislature* must be restricted to the making of law, and not itself meddle with particular cases."[16] If so, a modern application of the theory would be an amalgamation of the political and judicial powers—a subject that is beyond the scope of discussion in the present chapter.

Among Montesquieu's major contributions to the separation principle's development were his explicit recognition of the now traditional tripartite scheme and his advocacy not only of a division of authority but, more important, of a system with effective internal checks for its maintenance. He did not, however—nor did Locke before him[17]—envision any meaningful role for the judiciary in this endeavor: "Of the three powers abovementioned the judiciary is in some measure next to nothing."[18] Rather, Montesquieu's idea of a "fundamental constitution" for his utopian system of government is fully in accord with the Separation Proposal: "The legislative body being composed of two parts, one checks the other, by the mutual privilege of refusing. They are both checked by the executive power, as the executive is by the legislative."[19]

C. The Framers' Thinking

Of course, it is not surprising that the classic, pre-American Revolution conception of the separation of powers was wholly unconcerned with the role of the judiciary, because the notion of judicial review was then virtually unknown. But neither does examination of the framers' attitudes persuasively support the view that the Court must police constitutional conflicts between the executive and legislative departments. Although the framers had no clear sense of the exact boundary between legislative and executive authority, believing instead that the contours must be fluid in order to provide the flexibility that a workable government would require, they trusted the political interplay between the two branches—rather than judicial intervention—to maintain the proper balance of legislative and executive power.

In *The Federalist,* when Hamilton, after forcefully contending that the executive possesses "all the requisites to energy," addressed the antipodal matter of the mechanisms available to withstand arbitrary exercises of presidential power—that is, "the requisites to safety"—he omitted judicial review. Rather, he referred to other "circumstances"—"the election of the President once in four years by persons immediately chosen by the people for that purpose; and from his being at all times liable to impeachment, trial, dismission from office, incapacity to serve in any other, and to forfeiture of life and estate by subsequent prosecution in the common course of law . . . . In the only instances in which the abuse of the executive authority was materially to be feared, the Chief Magistrate of the United States would, by that plan, be subjected to the control of a branch of the legislative body. What more could be desired by an enlightened and reasonable people?"[20] Madison wrote that "the several departments being perfectly coordinate by the terms of their common commission, none of them, it is evident, can pretend to an exclusive or superior right of settling the boundaries between their respective powers; and how are the encroachments of the stronger to be prevented, or the wrongs of the weaker to be redressed, without an appeal to the people themselves, who, as grantors of the commission, can alone declare its true meaning, and enforce its observance?"[21] In the First Congress, when Madison, only a week after labeling the judiciary "an impenetrable bulwark" against encroachments upon those personal liberties afforded in the bill of rights,[22] discussed the separation of powers issue, he asserted that the Constitution ordained no "particular authority to determine the limits of the constitutional division of power between the branches of the Government." "I beg to know upon what principle it can be contended that any one department draws from the constitution greater powers than another, in marking out the limits of the powers of the several departments?"[23] John Adams, who most earnestly believed that separation of powers was essential to protect individual liberty, accorded the judiciary only a subordinate role in resolving separation conflicts, and "nowhere in his writings did he ever refer to the power of judicial review."[24] Jefferson and Jackson, who were among the foremost advocates of the separation of powers concept, were equally among the strongest skeptics and harshest critics of judicial review. Further, although surely less authoritative than Hamilton or Madison on the question of original intent, it is worth observing that John Taylor of Caroline, whose influential *Inquiry into the Principles and Policy of the Government of the United States* has been described as "the most sustained and comprehensive defence of the extreme doctrine of the separation of powers to be found in either English or French," unmistakably denied the Court's authority to act as final constitutional arbiter.[25]

It is also noteworthy to observe which branch of government the framers believed would present the real threat to liberty. Although, as we shall see momentarily, the most eminent modern proponents of the separation of powers principle focus on the potential tyranny of the executive branch, this was not the major fear held by the framers.[26] Despite the colonists' recent experience recoiling from the pains of executive abuse in the mother country, both Madison and Hamilton clearly indicated that their distrust was of legislative excess.[27] For Madison, "the tendency of republican governments is to an aggrandizement of the legislative at the expense of the other departments."[28] "In republican government, the legislative authority necessarily predominates,"[29] whereas, "on the other side, the executive power being restrained within a narrower compass, and being more simple in its nature, and the judiciary being described by landmarks still less uncertain, projects of usurpation by either of these departments would immediately betray and defeat themselves."[30] Indeed, "the weakness of the executive may require . . . that it should be fortified."[31] Hamilton considered "the separation of powers not so much as a device for the sake of power-balance *per se,* but rather as a means for deconcentrating power from the legislature. While advocating possibilities for a decrease of legislative power, he demonstrated the necessity of power-concentration in the executive. And whereas 'in the legislature, promptitude of decision is oftener an evil than a benefit,' 'energy in the Executive is a leading character in the definition of good government,... essential to the protection of the community against foreign attacks;... to the steady adminis-tration of the laws;... to the protection of property....; to the security of liberty against... faction.' In order to have energy, or power, in the executive, Hamilton want[ed] its unity, duration, and an adequate provision for its support."[32] Like Montesquieu, a principal means by which Madison and Hamilton (and Thomas Paine as well)[33] sought to protect against legislative abuse was to subdivide Congress into two houses. Madison believed that "the remedy" for legislative predominance was "to divide the legis-lature into different branches; and to render them, by different modes of election and different principles of action, as little con-nected with each other as the nature of their common functions and their common dependence on the society will admit."[34] Hamilton thought that "the differences of opinion and the jarrings of the parties in that department..., though they may sometimes obstruct salutary plans,... often promote delibera-tion and circumspection, and serve to check excesses in the majority."[35]

The important message for our purposes to be gleaned from this brief glance at the founders' thinking is that the checks on legislative autocracy that they contemplated exist independently of judicial supervision of the constitutionally mandated separa-tion of powers between the President and Congress. Moreover, the founders primarily feared legislative excess and the material legislative abuse that they perceived was, in Madison's words, "the propensity... to yield to the impulse of sudden and violent passions, and to be seduced by factious leaders into intemperate and pernicious resolutions";[36] to the extent that such con-gressional errors were unconstitutional rather than merely im-provident, the judicial function would be meaningfully fulfilled by the Court's forcefully acting to protect the individual rights endangered—a role urged for judicial review throughout this book and one not in any way affected by the Separation Proposal.

D. The Modern Justification for Judicial Review: Fear of Swift and Arbitrary Executive Action

The most forceful contemporary justification for judicial review of separation of powers issues is that the President can injure individuals by abusing the executive authority and that Congress, because of institutional infirmities, cannot effectively prevent this. Intensified but by no means created by the activities of Lyndon Johnson and Richard Nixon, the argument focuses not on Congress but on the dangers of concentration of power in the single individual that occupies the presidency. Relying on Lord Acton's oft-quoted observation that "power tends to corrupt, and absolute power corrupts absolutely,"[37] many observers fear arbitrary action by a willful executive. In arguing for judicial rejection of presidential conduct that he believed to be ultra vires, Justice Brandeis expressed the essence of the view: "In America, as in England, the conviction prevailed then that the people must look to representative assemblies for the protection of their liberties."[38] And, in similar circumstances, Justice Douglas explained the underlying sentiment: "The President can act more quickly than the Congress. The President with the armed services at his disposal can move with force as well as with speed. All executive power—from the reign of ancient kings to the rule of modern dictators—has the outward appearance of efficiency."[39]

1. Limited Scope of the Argument

Several points should be established at the outset in examining the modern contention that the Court must use its authority to oppose executive overreaching of the separation of powers principle in order to serve the ends of freedom. First, the scope of the argument is limited to only a small fraction of the possible executive incursions on legislative prerogatives. Thus, it does *not* involve presidential refusals to execute congressional enactments or to provide information for legislative inquiries, or presidential pardons that conflict with congressionally imposed sanctions, or presidential vetoes that allegedly improperly deny effect to laws passed by Congress. (And these, it should be noted, comprise.the bulk—although not all—of the constitutional malversations charged against President Nixon.) Rather, the princi‑ pal type of presidential abuse that this argument envisions is affirmative government action initiated by the executive that imposes burdens on persons' lives, liberty, or property. It is best exemplified by presidential exercises of regulatory authority that the Constitution allegedly rests exclusively with Congress, such as "enacting legislation" (as was argued in the *Steel Seizure Case*) or "engaging in war" (as was charged more recently in respect to the hostilities in Indochina). Second, it must be conceded, at least in theory, that a one-person executive is capable of undertaking these kinds of actions affecting "freedom" with much less deliberation and with much greater swiftness than can the houses of Congress. Especially because of the many negative devices in the national political process (discussed at length in chapter 1) that work against the passage of laws, this presidential capacity to engage in conduct for which Congress might never be able to muster its forces exists even when the President commands a congressional majority of his own political party.

2. Nature of the Freedom Protected

Nonetheless, we must be careful to identify precisely the peculiar quality of the "freedom" that such executive action affects which, under the Separation Proposal, would not be subject to judicial review. In doing so, it is important to recognize that the crux of the constitutional issue presented by the claim that presidential action violates the separation of powers precept vis-à-vis the Congress—as well as by the contention that presidential inaction does so, or that congressional action or inaction invades the constitutional prerogatives of the President— directly parallels the issue raised by the allegation that a congressional undertaking violates the federalism principle. The

Separation Proposal would treat as nonjusticiable only the constitutional validity of presidential action that affects individual "freedom" in a way identical to what Congress could have done pursuant to its constitutionally delegated authority. On the other hand, if the presidential conduct allegedly violates individual constitutional rights—that is, those personal liberties that are secured aginst *all* governmental abridgments, presidential or congressional—then, in accord with the Individual Rights Proposal, the Court should intervene.

To illustrate: In the *Steel Seizure Case* all sides assumed that, whether or not President Truman possessed the inherent constitutional power to seize the steel mills, Congress clearly had the authority to do so. Similarly, in the major constitutional controversy over the war in Indochina, even the most vocal challengers of the power of Presidents Johnson and Nixon to order the military action that took American life, liberty, and property conceded that Congress could have engaged the military by a formal declaration of war. In other words, neither the steel manufacturers nor the war critics asserted a constitutional right to be totally free of the government action involved. Rather, they argued that they could only be so regulated by Congress. Viewed more generally, a separation of powers challenge to executive conduct urges that only the Congress may so act. In terms of "standing," the steel companies and antiwar litigants may be seen not as claiming a constitutional right of their own to be immune from all government regulation but rather asserting the interest of Congress in not having its constitutionally ordained authority usurped by the President. (As subsequent discussion will amplify, this same analysis applies to other separation of powers conflicts between the national political branches even though they affect the interests of individuals.) Under the Separation Proposal, constitutional issues in this category should be nonjusticiable.

3. Semantic Due Process Argument

A powerful argument against the Separation Proposal is that executive action in excess of constitutional authority is a nullity and that, if such invalid action works to the detriment of an individual by circumscribing the scope of the freedom he would otherwise possess he has thereby been deprived of the right of every citizen to be free from all government imposition except that taken in conformity with the law of the land. More specifically, in the *Steel Seizure Case,* the companies' claim would be that, since the President was without the inherent power of seizure, their property was appropriated without due process of law. In the Indochina war litigation, persons ordered to Vietnam would contend that, since American involvement in the war could only be declared by Congress and Congress had not done so, their liberties were being curtailed and their lives threatened in violation of the constitutional warmaking procedure guaranteed every person by the due process clause of the fifth amendment.

Although, as we shall see, in both the steel seizure and Indochina war cases true personal liberties issues were present— claims that are independent of any infringement of the separation of powers principle—the due process arguments stated are merely semantic and contain no more substance here than they did when advanced in the federalism area. Irrespective of the phraseology employed, both contentions assume congressional power to do the very things under attack. This being so, neither argument is ultimately based on any direct governmental infringement of personal constitutional liberties as conventionally defined (for which I have urged virgorous judicial review). Rather, like other separation of powers conflicts between legislature and executive, both cases depend on an initial finding that one of the political branches has encroached on the power of the other. In both, the due process arguments follow from the premise that the President exceeded his constitutional powers vis-à-vis Congress. In short, the "liberty" claims are merely derivative.

4. Adequacy of Checks and Balances

To this point, all that has been established is that the nature of the liberty at stake in the separation of powers category of constitutional issues is—like that in the federalism area—

distinguishable from the individual rights genre. The basic argument against the Separation Proposal—that since ultra vires executive actions endanger personal freedom, they should be subject to judicial review—has not been rebutted.

Although this postulate must be approached from several perspectives, the overriding consideration is plain. Whether the separation of powers designated in the Constitution was originally fashioned to secure individual liberty from national government tyranny should not be of major present significance. Nor is it important to determine whether the framers' plan was to have the Court arbitrate constitutional disputes between the national political branches (at least when traditionally cognizable individual injury resulted). Although, as noted above, there is some evidence casting doubt on the notion that the founders so intended, we have already acknowledged in chapter 2 that the entire historical setting of judicial review is clouded with ambiguity. Nor is it productive to explore the question of whether division of legislative and executive authority is necessary in a truly free government. While it is difficult to contend that England's parliamentary system (which is opposed to ours in joining the lawmaking and executive departments, but contains such similar features as effectively competing political parties and an independent judiciary) has resulted in a society markedly less protective of liberty, our Constitution clearly opts for the separation of powers. Rather, when all is said and done, the crucial issue is realistically to ascertain whether the institutionalized checks and balances that the framers indisputably devised to fortify the separation of powers—thus excluding judicial review—are themselves adequate to assure that the intended constitutional division of authority survives beyond its parchment statement. And, integrally related to this question, at least for our purposes, is functionally to determine whether the utilization of judicial review in this area will advance or retard the overall preservation of constitutionalism and individual liberty broadly contemplated by the framers and presently cherished in our society.

A principal justification for the Federalism Proposal in chapter 4 was that the constitutional restrictions on national power vis-à-vis the states would be respected wholly apart from judicial intervention because the states, who are the beneficiaries of these constitutional limitations, are vigorously represented in the federal political process. Thus, it was urged that the national political branches should be permitted to act as the ultimate arbiters of the scope of their own power in regard to states' rights. The Separation Proposal advanced in this chapter is supported by a slightly variant rationale, but one that similarly depends on a state of conditions that sharply contrast with those present when the security of individual constitutional rights is at stake. In the latter case, the political machinery is ordinarily aligned against the interests of powerless minorities whose fundamental personal liberties must ultimately be vindicated by judicial review if at all. Indeed, in the malapportionment cases, political response in behalf of the constitutional freedoms at issue was especially unlikely because it would have directly threatened the very existence of those legislative and executive officials who would have had to act. But the participation of the Supreme Court is unnecessary to police constitutional violations by one political department against the other. Each branch—legislative and executive—has tremendous incentives jealously to guard its constitutional boundaries and assigned prerogatives against invasion by the other. If either branch perceives a constitutional violation of this kind, not only will it be encouraged to respond vigorously but each department possesses an impressive arsenal of weapons to demand observance of constitutional dictates by the other. In Hamilton's simple but telling statement, each has the "necessary constitutional means and personal motives to resist encroachments of the other."[40] Without judicial review, neither Congress nor the executive will act as the final judge of its own power vis-à-vis the other. Rather both will effectively participate in defining the reach of their respective authorities—a process that promises trustworthy resolution without the expenditure of precious judicial capital.

5. Strictures on Ultra Vires Executive Action

Before examining in greater detail the mechanisms that each of the political departments may employ against the other in defending its own constitutional domain—especially those by which Congress may prevent presidential usurpations of the separation of powers principle, it is important to explore a key allegation of those who foresee significant threats to individual freedom arising from affirmative undertakings by the executive that overreach its authority. To this point, the theoretical ability of the President to impose his will easily and rapidly has been conceded. In reality, however, such arbitrary executive conduct is more readily assumed than accomplished.

Except in the rarest of circumstances, even when he is unopposed by Congress, the President is exceedingly dependent on the agreement and cooperation of a multitude of diverse persons and agencies, both governmental and private, to carry out even his modest desires and noncontroversial policies. In the words of observers of the executive establishment, there is a "far-stretching chasm between the ideal of a vigorous, creative Presidency . . . and the reality of the complicated, restraint-bound, frustrating office" it is.[41] "Probably nowhere in the world is executive leadership more hemmed in, more limited by political considerations, more vulnerable to pressures from within and without than in the United States."[42] In other words, the modern rationale for judicial review of alleged presidential abridgments of the separation of powers principle is not empirically supportable. There are numerous and varied institutional checks on ultra vires executive action and, historically, they have frequently been exercised. Not only does Congress have powerful incentives to guard its prerogatives, but the President's actions are limited by institutional inertia within the executive branch itself and by external political pressures ranging from party organizations, labor and business groups, and the press to the electorate as a whole.

a. Executive Branch

Experience has shown that the official executive bureaucracy can pose an especially recalcitrant obstacle to presidential action. This may begin even at the level of the President's own highest appointees. Throughout our history, there have been instances documenting the judgment expressed by

Charles Dawes, who served under Presidents Harding, Coolidge, and Hoover, that "the members of the Cabinet are a President's natural enemies."[43] Prominent examples are Andrew Johnson's clash with War Secretary Stanton and Richard Nixon's with Interior Secretary Hickel.

Graham Allison describes President Kennedy's obstructed efforts to have American missiles removed from Italy and Turkey: "Dean Rusk had been assigned to raise this issue with the Turkish and Italian foreign ministers during the NATO meetings at Oslo in May 1962, but when Turkish Foreign Minister Selin Samper resisted, the matter was dropped. Frustrated at this inaction, Kennedy had resorted to the most binding mechanism in the U.S. government for registering decisions on matters of national security—a National Security Council Action Memorandum (NASAM). In the third week of August 1962, a NASAM ordered removal of the missiles, and [Kennedy] personally directed George Ball (in Rusk's absence) to pay the political price and remove the missiles. Ball discussed the matter with the Turkish Ambassador in Washington and received a warning that the removal of the missiles would have most harmful effects on Turkish public opinion. So nothing happened."[44]

Arthur Schlesinger depicts how even long-time associates of President Nixon sometimes refused to abide by his directives. In 1970, after formal investigation failed to connect militant student agitators with foreign subversion, Mr. Nixon "instructed the intelligence community in a formal Decision Memorandum" to engage in surreptitious entries, plant undercover agents on the campuses, eavesdrop on Americans making international telephone calls, and remove legal restrictions on mail coverage; but "J. Edgar Hoover's opposition compelled Nixon to rescind the plan." And, "within ten days of the Watergate arrests, Nixon asked the CIA to ask the FBI to limit its investigation on the phony national-security pretext that 'an unrelated covert operation of the CIA' might be exposed. Both L. Patrick Gray, the acting director of the FBI, and General Vernon Walters, the deputy director of the CIA, were old friends of Nixon's and wanted to do what they could to help. But Gray, after holding things up for a few days, finally told Walters . . . that he 'could not possibly suppress the investigation .... He did not see why he or I should jeopardize the integrity of our organizations to protect some mid-level White House figures.' Walters himself said, 'I did not believe a letter from the Agency asking the FBI to lay off this investigation on spurious grounds that it would uncover covert operations would serve the President.... I said quite frankly that I wouldn't write such a letter.' White House pressure was hard to resist, and both Gray and Walters yielded too much to it, but there were things they knew they could not get their organizations to do."[45]

Indeed, Richard Neustadt reports that even in the steel seizure situation—one of those unusual cases of consummated presidential wishes—Commerce Secretary Sawyer thwarted President Truman's explicit post-seizure plans to apply pressure on both sides for speedy settlement: "The Secretary of Commerce spoke for business in the Cabinet. Officially and personally Sawyer had no liking for the seizure. He had not wanted to administer the mills, and he had taken the assignment with distaste. He was evidently unhappy at the prospect of his signature on wage orders and price requests committing the steel industry [as Mr. Truman had ordered him to do]. Although he did not refuse to act, he managed to immerse himself in preparations."[46]

Even greater pockets of resistance exist in the bureaucratic morass lying beneath the better-known veneer of top level officials. The distance between presidential command and policy enactment is long and complex, ordinarily requiring the President to obtain the acquiescence or support (if not the enthusiasm) of many intertwined functionaries. According to Neustadt, "the executive establishment consists of separated institutions sharing power .... Federal operations spill across dividing lines on organization charts; almost every policy entangles many agencies; almost every program calls for interagency collaboration. Everything somehow involves the President. But operating agencies owe their existence least of all to one another—and only in some part to him. Each has a separate statutory base; each has its statutes to administer; each deals with a different set of subcommittees at the Capitol. Each has its own peculiar set of clients, friends, and enemies outside the formal government. Each has a different set of specialized careerists inside its own bailiwick: . . . All agency administrators are responsible to Congress, to their clients, to their staffs, and to themselves. In short, they have five masters. Only after all of those do they owe any loyalty to each other."[47]

Allison has more recently refined this analysis. Using several models, he shows that most government action is not the product of deliberate choice but more the "independent output of several organizations" within the federal bureaucracy, each "functioning according to standard patterns of behavior" and requiring the coordination of a large number of individuals with "fractionated power" and "parochial priorities and perceptions"; ultimately, "what moves the chess pieces is not simply the reasons that support a course of action, or the routines of organizations that enact an alternative, but the power and skill of proponents and opponents of the action in question." Overall, he concludes that "in status and formal powers the President is chief. Every other participant's business somehow involves him. But his authority guarantees only an extensive clerkship. If the President is to rule, he must squeeze from these formal powers a full array of bargaining advantages. Bolstered by his 'professional reputation' and 'public prestige,' the President can use these advantages to translate the needs and fears of other participants into an appreciation that what he wants of them is what they should do in their own best interest. His bargaining advantages are rarely sufficient to assure enactment of his will, but they are his only means of ensuring an impact on governmental action."[48]

Modern executives have consistently complained about this phenomenon. Franklin Roosevelt discovered the Treasury Department to be "so large and far-flung and ingrained in its practices that I find it is almost impossible to get the action and results I want. . . . But the Treasury is not to be compared with the State Department. You should go through the experience of trying to get any changes in the thinking, policy, and action of the career diplomats and then you'd know what a real problem was. But the Treasury and the State Department put together are nothing as compared with the Na-a-vy. . . . To change anything in the Na-a-vy is like punching a feather bed. You punch it with your right and you punch it with your left until you are finally exhausted, and then you find the damn bed just as it was before you started punching."[49] Harry Truman noted that "it has often happened in the War and Navy Departments that the generals and admirals, instead of working for and under the Secretaries, succeeded in having the Secretaries act for and under them."[50]

Several examples from the Kennedy years underline the point. In 1961, after the President mandated automatic downgrading of security classifications "government security officers, fearing that reform of the system would weaken their own power, sabotaged the effort, interpreting the Kennedy order to mean that automatic downgrading did not apply to documents classified before the date of the order."[51] A year later, on a flight to Palm Beach shortly before the Cuban missile crisis, Mr. Kennedy noted that American fighter planes in Florida were "lined up wing to wing," thus posing an easy target. "After returning to Washington, he directed civil defense authorities to see that the aircraft were dispersed." During the meetings at the height of the confrontation with the Soviet Union, the Air Force assured Kennedy that this had been done. But when he then "ordered independent aerial photographs of the area," they revealed "that our aircraft were indeed still highly concentrated."[52] Yet more frightening, although Kennedy plainly instructed the Navy to draw the ultimately successful Cuban blockade much closer to the shore than originally planned, it appears that "the blockade was *not* moved as the President ordered."[53] President Nixon also experienced internal subversion: although he succeeded in delaying the trial of the Watergate burglars until after the 1972 election, "frustrated FBI agents, whose loyalty to their organization and to the truth was deeper than their loyalty to the President, began to leak the facts to the newspapers."[54]

Although recent presidents have sought to regain control through the creation and enormous expansion of the White House based Executive Office of the President,[55] the effort has been far less than successful and, in any event, as we shall see below, is directly subject to congressional budgetary authority.

As the preceding instances indicate, the concept of a monolithic executive is a myth. Even in situations involving national security, the President's will has been frustrated by recalcitrant subordinates or bureaucratic inertia. Thus, attempts by the President to exceed his constitutional authority will often be met with internal resistance and certainly will not be automatically accepted by other actors within the executive department.

b. External Groups

In addition to internal cooperation, most presidential objectives also demand the sponsorship or concurrence of various external groups for achievement. These groups include state officials, the press, party chieftains, the myriad interest groups affected such ás labor or business (or perhaps even consumers), as well as highly influential private citizens who have been labeled "the power elite" or "the new mandarins."[56] As described by Douglass Cater, "the President is challenged other than frontally from Congress. In one important area of policy after another, substantial efforts to exercise power are waged by alliances cutting across the two branches of government and including key operatives from the outside. In effect, they constitute subgovernments of Washington comprising the expert, the interested and the engaged."[57] Thus, even those commentators who have condemned the untrammeled ability of chief executives to arrive at policy decisions that are shaped not after careful deliberation but rather by little more than personal whim or idiosyncrasy, concede that "the president, though preeminent in getting things started, is often foiled in his effort to coordinate their execution."[58]

All these formidable impediments surely help explain the relatively few instances over the years of alleged usurpation of the constitutional authority of Congress by affirmative executive action. Indeed, with special significance for our purposes, they may even contribute to the historical fact that, of the two national political branches, it has not been actions of the President that have posed the greater danger to personal liberty, no matter how defined.

c. Protective Devices of Congress

Above all others, it is Congress itself that stands as the greatest barrier blocking the President from successfully taking action that the Constitution reserves to the legislature. The

broadly detailed scope of the acknowledged constitutional powers of the Congress (as compared to the executive's) equips it
with an extensive array of weapons to defend its own dominion,
and also serves to limit both the number of occasions and the
threatening quality of alleged legislative infringements on the
more narrowly perceived executive authority.

Apart from the veto power, one of whose "chief designs,"
Hamilton noted, was for a case "of an immediate attack upon the
constitutional rights of the Executive," [59] the President's principal
tools of defense (such as control of appointments and other patronage) are more subtle and less visible. That they are,
nonetheless, adequate to the task of executive self-protection
will become clear in the course of subsequent discussion. Because of the contemporary fear of presidential usurpation of congressional authority, however, the devices available to and employed by Congress to combat this merit separate consideration.

(1) Refusal to appropriate funds

The most potent congressional weapon against executive encroachment is the power of the purse. Although the precise impact that the series of congressional attempts to withhold
funds ultimately had on the final withdrawal of American forces
from Vietnam is unknown and probably unknowable, its contributing force cannot reasonably be denied. The fact is that in
1974 Congress halved the Ford administration's request for military and economic aid to defend Vietnam. "Additional requests
amounting to $522 million in 1975 were not acted upon. The
president's request for $725 million in military assistance on
April 10 in the wake of the military collapse in South Vietnam
was rejected by Congress. Only his recommendation for more
humanitarian aid was considered. The president was granted
authority, however, to use armed forces to protect Americans and
Vietnamese being evacuated from South Vietnam. In extending
this limited authority to the president, Congress implicitly asserted its right to withdraw even that much if changed conditions
so warranted." [60]

The strength of the financial power of Congress is even more
clearly demonstrated by the congressional response to the Nixon

administration's bombing of Cambodia in 1973—action defended by the executive on the basis of continued congressional appropriations (despite efforts to terminate) and on inherent presidential power to effectuate the Paris Peace Agreement with North Vietnam.[61] After President Nixon vetoed the Eagleton Amendment, which prohibited any use of funds for combat activities in Laos and Cambodia,[62] an accord between the political branches was struck: Congress authorized bombing for forty-five more days and the President agreed to sign a new bill cutting off all money after that time.[63] And there is no doubt but that Congress's firm refusal to supply material and money in 1975 and 1976 to those factions friendly to the United States in the Angola civil war put an abrupt halt to direct American involvement in that conflict.[64] Indeed, in mid-1978, President Carter loudly complained "that his hands were tied in responding to Soviet-Cuban activity in Africa," pointing specifically to the 1978 congressional appropriations ban on aid to Angola, Zambia, Tanzania, and Mozambique "as obstacles to his direction of foreign relations." Yet another provision "directed U.S. representatives at the World Bank and other international lending facilities to vote against loans to these countries as well as Uganda and four Communist countries."[65]

In many other cases, moreover, there can be little doubt that Congress's even threatening to terminate financial support had an effect. Five specific illustrations should suffice:

i) In the late 1930s, President Roosevelt sought to enlarge the executive establishment beyond the size that Congress thought was proper. "Congress was hesitant about coming to the President's aid, not because of any clear-cut notions about his individual leadership but because of an ingrained reluctance to give him troops who might be used against Congress itself. When Roosevelt tacked the National Resources Planning Board onto his Executive Office, Congress simply cut off the funds: There was to be no long-range planning around the place."[66]

ii) In the mid-1960s, President Johnson's Defense Department, having opposed the construction of additional nuclear powered guided missile ships on the ground of cost-effectiveness, refused to release funds for this purpose despite their having been twice authorized and appropriated by Congress. After several rounds of infighting, the chairman of the House Armed Services Committee (with the general support of the Joint Atomic Energy Committee) announced that, unless the contracts were awarded, he was prepared to recommend that Congress authorize no new funds for other weapons systems favored by the administration. Before any further steps were taken, President Johnson ordered the construction.[67]

iii) In 1971, when President Nixon learned that the work of the Subversive Activities Control Board, which he had helped create as a legislator two decades earlier, had dwindled to nearly zero, he granted it new powers by executive order. Congress responded by simply providing "that no funds voted to the Board could be used to carry out the executive order."[68]

iv) In 1973, President Nixon requested $1,500,000 for White House "special projects." The House accepted its Appropriations Committee's recommendation to abolish the fund "because of a White House refusal to earmark spending from the special projects category which was thought to have been the source for Watergate-related activities." The Senate restored $1,000,000 with a provision "requiring that a quarterly report on expenditures" be made. But the House members of the Conference Committee refused to accept the proviso and no funds were authorized.[69]

v) In the mid-1970s, Congress voted to end Turkey's military assistance following Turkey's invasion of Cyprus; after a series of further votes—some following presidential vetoes—a compromise emerged. President Ford agreed to the cutoff pending a settlement between Turkey and Greece and Congress delayed termination for two months to encourage the parties to move together.[70]

The presidential excess that is the object of legislative displeasure does not have to be directly related to the executive programs jeopardized by congressional fiscal retaliation. Thus, as part of the gerat "impoundment" controversy in the early 1970s—a subject that will concern us more fully below—Congress not only reduced the culprit Office of Management and Budget's 1974 request by over a million dollars,[71] but also included in the Foreign Assistance Act of 1971 a provision withholding requested foreign aid funds until President Nixon spent other monies that Congress had designated for domestic purposes.[72]

Of course, all this does not mean that this type of congressional blackmail always prevails. Indeed, the President's ability to circumnavigate legislatively imposed expenditure controls is itself substantial. For example, one commentator has observed in regard to congressional refusal to supply salaries for President Roosevelt's executive positions described above that "it was impossible to keep an accurate head count of Presidential personnel during the Roosevelt era because of the various dodges that had to be employed to get around congressional restrictions."[73] But this consideration does not detract from the fact that presidents have, in the past, found themselves hard pressed in contending with the dollar power imposed by Congress. The power of the purse remains the strongest legislative weapon against executive encroachment.

(2) Refusal to enact laws

A technique that closely parallels the legislative device of refusing to appropriate funds as a means of resisting executive incursions—one for which no detailed description is necessary—is Congress's ability to coerce the executive by simply refusing to enact presidentially sponsored legislation. A particularly germane example of this occurred in response to Franklin Roosevelt's celebrated warning to Congress in 1942 that, if Congress refused to repeal a provision of the Emergency Price Control Act, he would do so himself. Although Congress chose not to put the President to the test, it did reply shortly thereafter by withholding its approval of his proposed Third War Powers Act.[74]

(3) Refusal to confirm appointments

Similarly, Congress may combat perceived executive violations of the separation of powers by refusing senatorial consent to presidential nominations. For example, in 1959 the Senate rejected President Eisenhower's appointment of Lewis

Strauss as Secretary of Commerce in large measure because of the latter's refusal to disclose certain documents to a congressional committee several years before when he was a member of the Atomic Energy Commission.[75] And in 1973, Patrick Gray's demise as director of the FBI was directly attributable to President Nixon's gargantuan claim at the time of executive privilege for information relating to the Watergate scandal.

(4) Impeachment

Although its magnitude demands that Congress reserve the weapon of impeachment for only the most extreme situations, it is pertinent to recall that the one occasion in our history when Congress chose to use it against the President arose out of Andrew Johnson's clash with Congress over a constitutional issue of separation of powers—his power to remove a cabinet officer.[76] More recently, one of the impeachment articles adopted by the House Judiciary Committee against President Nixon concerned his constitutional dispute with Congress over executive privilege, and one of the other two articles formally proposed dealt with his Cambodia bombings alleged to be in violation of the legislative war and appropriations powers.

Congressional reliance on the tactics just described to control executive usurpation of power may reasonably be viewed as both unseemly and undesirable. It may be said that a system of government which depends upon political confrontation in order to maintain the adherence of the principal actors to fundamental postulates—that encourages Congress to secure its constitutional prerogatives from perceived presidential abuses by the usually disproportionate remedy of impeachment, or by such indiscriminately retaliatory and substantively unrelated methods that may harm public welfare as withholding needed appropriations, staying useful programs, or rejecting competent appointees—is seriously defective if not downright destructive. But history and experience suggest the contrary, however short of ideal our system may appear to be. First of all, pitched battles between the political branches arise only infrequently. And, as the bulk of the examples set forth indicate, Congress ordinarily can defend its interests from executive incursions by imposing sanctions that closely fit the offense—for example, by declining to approve a treaty if the President refuses to disclose information relevant thereto. Indeed, witness Congress's effort during the Nixon administration to compel the administration to purchase air conditioning for veterans' hospitals by making this a prerequisite to the expenditure of funds for air-conditioning facilities occupied by employees of the Office of Management and Budget and of the Executive Office of the President.[77] More important is the plain fact that our political scheme has worked—indeed, has succeeded—despite the inevitable frictions in a plan of a government rooted in the precept of the use of countervailing force between its major departments.

Moreover, at least before the tenure of President Nixon, the record demonstrates that an effective functioning of the relationship between the legislative and executive branches has been almost wholly accomplished without the participation of the national judiciary. And, although invocation of the lower federal courts to adjudicate alleged presidential violations of congressional authority became somewhat commonplace during the Nixon administration, there is no strong reason to believe that the judicial intervention acted as more than a mild palliative for the underlying distress. Rather, the developments generated by the Nixon experience that hold greatest promise for relieving future constitutional tensions between Congress and the President, and for avoiding the ad hoc use of those legislative weapons that might be counterproductive to the national interest, have been produced by the political branches themselves in the form of what Gerhard Casper has labeled "framework legislation"[78]—the War Powers Resolution of 1973[79] (enacted over Mr. Nixon's veto), the Congressional Budget and Impoundment Control Act of 1974[80] (promulgated with Mr. Nixon's pledge of "full support" and systematically observed by President Ford),[81] and the National Emergencies Act of 1976[82] (drafted in close consultation with the Ford administration and limiting a series of "open-ended grants of power" to the executive by "reasserting ultimate congressional control" over future emergencies declared by the President).[83] Nor do these innovations exhaust the opportunities for the political branches to

articulate constitutional principles to govern possible future
conflicts between them—as evidenced by recently introduced
legislation dealing with such sources of legislative-executive
antagonism as the President's power to enter into executive
agreements without the participation of Congress[84] and to withhold information from Congress on claim of executive
privilege,[85] and by Charles Black's suggestion that Congress set
guidelines prospectively defining presidential actions that
would constitute impeachable offenses.[86]

(5) Foreign affairs powers of Congress

It is often asserted that, whatever the ability of Congress to check executive domination in the domestic arena, the
President holds all the trump cards when it comes to military and
foreign affairs. It is in this area, Arthur Schlesinger maintains,
"above all, from the capture by the Presidency of the most vital of
national decisions, the decision to go to war," that "the imperial
Presidency received its decisive impetus."[87] In short, the conventional wisdom is that because of such diverse factors
as inadequate time, staff, and resources, the inaccessibility of
vital information because of the complex and sensitive nature of
such information, and the need for continuing expert attention,
Congress simply cannot equip itself to exercise any truly effective restraints in regard to international matters.[88]

Response to this contention may be made at several levels. It is
tempting to dismiss it as wholly irrelevant for our purposes on
the ground that, even granting the validity of each of its essential
premises, it shoots wide of the Separation Proposal since it in no
way implicates the Court and because, in the main, existing judicial doctrine remits otherwise adjudicable problems in this area
to the political branches. But this answer is unsatisfactory both
because of the haziness and uncertainty of the Court's pronouncements to date and, more importantly, because it begs the
very question under consideration, i.e., what role *should* the
Court play. A more effective line of attack is to concede the
basic allegations—that Congress is generally incompetent to deal
with issues of foreign policy and that only the executive branch

possesses the cumulative expertise and critical data required to pursue the nation's business with other countries—but to point out that it inevitably follows that the Court must be found at least as disabled as Congress in this respect (indeed, even more so) and therefore cannot, in any informed manner, prevent the executive from overreaching its foreign affairs powers.

The basic argument may also be met frontally, however, for its underlying premises are unpersuasive. It may be acknowledged that the pendulum between executive supremacy and legislative dominance has swung widely over the course of history—from Jackson, Lincoln, and the Roosevelts to Taylor, Fillmore, and Eisenhower. Indeed, at the very beginning Leonard White found that "by 1792 Jefferson thought the executive power had swallowed up the legislative branch; in 1798 Hamilton thought the legislative branch had so curtailed executive power than an able man could find no useful place in the government."[89] But if it is true that at some points the presidency has more closely resembled an inherited monarchy than an elected representative, even Schlesinger concedes that "it was as much a matter of congressional abdication as of presidential usurpation."[90] For "Congress can get all the staff, expertise and information it needs. What it lacks is the will to use the power it has. The fault . . . is not in their stars, but in themselves that they are underlings."[91] Although the legislators have by no means exploited all available influences on the executive,[92] when in the past they have resolutely attempted to undertake the effort they have been eminently successful both in obtaining the necessary information and then acting as a full partner with the executive in formulating and achieving policies in this realm. Abraham Sofaer reports that during the earliest Congresses the "powers over appointments, appropriations and treaties" were used "to force the presidents involved to supply more information or suffer rejection of their proposals . . . . The most notable instances in which either the House or Senate demonstrated its power to force information from the President occurred during the attempts to adopt and enforce the embargo under Jefferson . . .; in response to Madison's appointments of Gallatin and Russell as ministers (in this instance the Senate committees did not extract the desired

information, but the Senate did reject Madison's nominations)...; and when the Senate learned that John Quincy
Adams planned to send ministers to the Panama Congress."[93]

An especially revealing series of modern examples may be
found in respect to the matter of foreign aid—a subject integrally
tied to congressional power over appropriations. During the
Eisenhower administration an act of Congress provided that
specific foreign assistance disbursements should be withheld if
executive officials failed to deliver certain information to designated congressional committees or subcommittees. Mr.
Eisenhower contended that this unconstitutionally infringed on
executive control of foreign affairs. After some disagreement
between House and Senate as to the proper scope of executive
power, Congress compromised and amended the law to permit
nondisclosure only if the President personally invoked a claim of
privilege. Further confrontation was avoided during the Kennedy administration when the President instructed that requested
data be revealed to subcommittee chairmen but not to all members, a technique that the chairmen found to be satisfactory.[94]
But the controversy regained steam in the Nixon administration
when the President ordered the Departments of State and Defense not to disclose requested information dealing with its future plans for military assistance programs. The Senate Committee on Foreign Relations unanimously voted to withhold all
military aid funds until the data was forthcoming. The President
finally relented and the Secretary of State supplied the committee with his department's tentative projections.[95] During the
Kennedy years, Congress exercised its power of the purse to
restrict foreign aid to Communist-oriented countries, thereby
significantly modifying the President's foreign policy initiatives.[96] Thus, the Foreign Assistance Act of 1961 "barred or restricted: aid to Cuba, to any country which assisted Cuba, to
unfriendly and Communist countries, to the United Arab Republic, to countries that seized U.S. fishing vessels in international waters, to those that traded or permitted ships flying
their flag to trade with Cuba or North Vietnam, to those that sold
certain materials to the Communist Bloc, to countries whose
military expenditures materially interfered with their develop-

ment."[97] Perhaps in an attempt to avoid similar interference, President Johnson reportedly consulted with Congress before making certain foreign aid expenditures even when he already possessed explicit authority—"for example, on the AID program to India, where the amount was so large he felt that the Congress should have an opportunity to express itself on that point."[98]

Another example of successful congressional use of its spending power to obtain information and thereby participate in the conduct of foreign policy is the Hughes-Ryan bill of 1974, enacted because of legislative dissatisfaction with the CIA's clandestine projects. The law bars CIA expenditures for covert operations in foreign countries "unless and until" the President reports the scope of the activity "in a timely fashion" to designated legislative committees.[99] The proviso "does not legally require reports until after covert operations have begun," but CIA Director William Colby testified in 1976 that "on the day the CIA is informed that the president has signed a finding approving an operation, the CIA calls the committees' staffs to notify them that there is a finding to report at the committees' convenience." In fact, "the Senate has used the power of the purse to persuade the CIA and other intelligence agencies to give the Senate Select Committee on Intelligence *advance* notice of future covert activities" and the committee has been "fully briefed" and has "even voted on every proposed covert operation."[100]

A further illustration involves the sale of weapons to foreign nations. "By the mid-1970s, the United States had become one of the leading exporters of armaments, but Congress had had little to say about what weapons were sold to which countries." To remedy the situation, in both 1974 and 1976, Congress revised the Foreign Military Sales Act to require the executive to inform the legislators before any substantial arms transfer and to afford Congress "up to thirty days to pass a concurrent resolution disapproving the sale of major defense equipment valued at $7 million or more, as well as any arms or services of $25 million or more." As a consequence, Congress has been able "to influence the president and foreign governments to accept congressionally imposed compromises on foreign arms sales." This occurred with President Ford in 1975 respecting the missiles destined for Jordan.[101] More recently, President Carter bowed to congressional objections by agreeing to delay the sale of an airborne radar warning system to Iran, the major legislative opposition being derived "from a feeling that the Administration did not adequately consult with Congress beforehand."[102] And in mid-1978, Congress pressured Mr. Carter to include additional jets for Israel as part of his proposed arms package to Egypt and Saudi Arabia.[103]

Additional legislative involvements in affairs abroad have been recorded throughout our history—as Louis Henkin has documented with a long list of concrete instances to the end of the nineteenth century in which Congress has sought, often successfully, to set "the grand design" of this country's "foreign policy as well as the attitudes that shape day-to-day relations with other nations."[104] For example, between 1871 and 1898, the Senate "ratified *no* important treaty,"[105] and its powerful contribution a century later in connection with the Panama Canal treaty needs no elaboration. In 1954, both houses joined to forbid delivery of military goods purchased with foreign aid money to any nonratifying signatory of the European Defense Community Treaty, and in 1963 Congress legislated a ban on foreign aid to any country that nationalized American property without proper compensation.[106] Also within recent memory is the series of congressional resolutions during the 1950s stating firm legislative opposition to the admission of Communist China to the United Nations. And in the 1970s, Congress successfully linked trade concessions for the Soviet Union to its policy toward Jewish emigration.

A most prominent example of the ability of Congress to assert its strength in the field of foreign affairs may be found in the work of the Joint Committee on Atomic Energy, created in 1946 with the Atomic Energy Commission, which "soon managed to achieve a relationship to that agency which came close to serving as co-executor. The Joint Committee has helped determine the size and shape of the nation's nuclear stockpile, the nature of the weapons, the decision to produce the hydrogen bomb, the ill-fated billion dollar investment in the nuclear airplane, as well as countless other atomic matters large and small"—including development of the Polaris submarine despite executive opposition. "One prominent Committee member was prompted to declare that '... in the case of certain vital policy decisions, the urging from the Joint Committee has played so powerful a role that it can be said the Committee made the decisions, with the advice and consent of the executive branch.'... It has refused, usually with success, to accept the usual plea of Executive privilege by which certain inside information on decision making is withheld from Congress. It has regularly disregarded the procedures and budgetary controls laid down by the President. In invading the domain of the Atomic Energy Commission, it has used the same divide-and-conquer technique against the five Commissioners so often employed by the Executive against Congress .... Without the Committee's prodding, a recent study concluded, 'Almost certainly, the national investment in atomic energy would have been substantially less, and our present level of technology considerably less advanced.'"[107]

Of course, this joint committee is not typical of either the quality or quantity of legislative participation. During World War II, although Congress did employ some devices to restrain totally unbridled executive power—such as requiring periodic reports, placing time limits on some of the authority delegated, and including the proviso that the authority may be terminated at any time by joint resolution—"in general effective congressional control of the wartime establishment was conspicuous by its absence."[108] Nonetheless, President Roosevelt "did consult constantly with congressional leaders. He paid careful attention to the recommendations of Senator Truman's War Investigating Committee. He sought, and gained, congressional authorization to send military missions to friendly nations. When [Senator] Vandenberg objected to the notion that American participation in the United Nations Relief and Rehabilitation Administration should be by executive agreement, the administration agreed to submit the plan to approval by both houses through joint resolution. Above all Roosevelt was determined to give Congress a role in the making of peace ... [by bringing] members of Congress from both parties into the discussion of postwar policy."[109] At other times, the President has voluntarily sought and abided by congressional opinion regarding critical matters of foreign policy. Thus, in 1954, when the fall of Dienbienphu seemed certain, "President Eisenhower, Secretary of State Dulles, and Admiral Radford, then chairman of the Joint Chiefs of Staff, advocated aiding the French with an air strike by Navy and Air Force planes. In a secret meeting, under questioning from congressional leaders, including Majority Leader of the Senate Lyndon Johnson, it became apparent that congressional leaders were reluctant to support the action unless the administration could find allies abroad, particularly Britain. But Britain, too, was reluctant; and in the end the plan was abandoned. Even in this case, in the view of one observer, the president could probably have won congressional support 'provided he had asked for it forcefully and explained the facts and their relation to the national interest of the United States.' But he did not, and his soundings of congressional opinion evidently did prevent immediate intervention in support of the French."[110] And the lesson of World War II, sharply accentuated during the Indochina conflict when many legislators found themselves opposed to presidential actions on grounds of constitutionality as well as policy, has not gone unheeded. The Case-Zablocki Act of 1972 requires that an international agreement entered into by the executive without the Senate's formal participation be communicated to Congress within sixty days of its effective date[111] (thus enabling the legislature either to decline to appropriate funds needed for implementation or formally to disapprove the bargain). More pointedly, the War Powers Resolution of 1973, although framed with inevitable ambiguities,[112] was designed to specify the boundaries of legislative and executive authority in regard to the employment of military forces, and to assure constructive congressional participation in the process. Furthermore, former Secretary of State William Rogers offered such additional suggestions as having "the State Department's assistant secretaries in charge of each geographic region ... provide the Senate Committee on Foreign Relations with full and regular briefings on developments in their respective regions" and establishing "a joint congressional committee which could act as a consultative body with the President in times of emergencies."[113] The possibility that President Ford's action in the Mayaguez incident demonstrates that the War Powers Resolution "is more hortatory than prohibitory"[114] neither disputes the fact that the operation was supported by Congress (albeit after the event) nor refutes the lawmakers' ability to deal with the warmaking question specifically or to secure separation of powers in the area of foreign affairs generally if and when it is so inclined.

(6) Congress presented with *fait accompli*

Another argument that has been advanced to support the necessity of judicial review to prevent executive usurpations of legislative power posits a situation in which presidential action, which would never have originally commanded a majority in Congress, is so momentous as to present the legislators with a *fait accompli,* thus effectively disabling them from employing their available weapons to force rescission. The exploits of both Presidents Johnson and Nixon in connection with the hostilities in Indochina have frequently been offered as specifically illustrative. Thus, in *Massachusetts v. Laird,*[115] the state contended before the Supreme Court: "When the nation is at peace, many legislators will be most hesitant, unless the nation is physically attacked, to change the situation by authorizing a war. Consequently the President might not be able to obtain a majority in each house to vote in favor of a specific and intentional authorization of war. But if the President takes the nation into war without Congressional authorization, the practical situation will be different with respect to the burden of obtaining a majority. Many legislators, for a variety of reasons...will not vote for legislation which would cut off the use in the war of defense appropriations. Even if a majority of legislators could be amassed, the President could veto the bill and thus raise the burden much higher to the 2/3rds majority level."[116]

Before exploring this position in detail, it should be noted that the argument assumes the invalidity of the presidentially ordered military activities—an issue heatedly debated from all quarters,[117] but clearly beyond the scope of this discussion. Under the Separation Proposal, the federal courts should hold that the ultimate issue of the President's inherent constitutional power to lead the nation into a war is nonjusticiable—just as the

Supreme Court, in the *Prize Cases*,[118] should have held the question of whether President Lincoln had the constitutional authority without the approval of Congress "to institute a blockade of ports in possession of persons in armed rebellion against the Government" to be beyond judicial purview. This conclusion, at least as to the Indochina affair, is by no means a novel one. It has often been argued that foreign affairs (unlike, for example, the setting of the *Steel Seizure Case*) lie beyond the Court's ken, because there are no judicially ascertainable or manageable standards for resolution of the problem[119]—a proposition accepted by most lower federal courts but not all.[120] The Separation Proposal, however, rests on the much simpler and more objective construct that the constitutional issue presented is plainly and exclusively one of division of power between the national political departments, comprehending no genuine fundamental personal liberty claim.

(a) Actions available to Congress. The premise of the argument for judicial review set forth above is that legislators will be hesitant to deny funds necessary to support the troops in the field. Although it is subject to qualification because of the Cambodian bombing compromise and Vietnam withdrawal described earlier, this premise is generally acknowledged. But the impracticality of the appropriations tool by no means proves that Congress is powerless to reverse a course begun by the President. Wholly apart from other less direct techniques—such as refusing to fund unrelated executive programs, enact requested legislation, confirm submitted nominations, or even to censure the chief executive (as Congress did to Andrew Jackson)— Congress may seek to regain control by the simple expedient of a joint resolution stating its unqualified opposition to the executive enterprise (an action never taken by Congress during the entire Indochina controversy despite varied efforts to have it do so).*

* While Congress's repeal of the Tonkin Gulf resolution sought to deny executive power to engage in future involvements in Indochina, it was not intended to direct the President to end the war or even to remove legislative authorization for its continuance. See L. Henkin, Foreign Affairs and the Constitution 103–08, 351 (1972). Compare the troop withdrawal provision of the "Mansfield Amendment" in 1971, originally defeated in four House of Representative votes, 29 Cong. Q. Wkly. Rep. 2371 (1971), but appended in carefully circumscribed form by the

This could be supplemented by detailed legislation providing for orderly termination. In the face of congressional silence respecting the asserted demolition of its own warmaking power, and in light of the fact that "the constitutional foundations and the constitutional limits" of the President's authority to commit troops abroad "remain in dispute,"[121] it is extremely difficult to justify a judicial declaration of unconstitutionality.

This is not to contend that resting the matter with Congress will prevent the President from engaging in the challenged conduct to begin with. It is unquestionably true that no matter what Congress does—and no matter how submissive the President's reaction—tremendous irreversible consequences might occur, especially in the case of military action. Indeed, the effects of certain types of executive activities—such as the capacity to order a preemptive nuclear strike, or to "incite other nations, or otherwise plunge, or stumble this country into war"[122]—(all, by the way, carrying plausible claims of constitutional legitimacy)[123] are totally ineradicable. This is the crucial reason, it is often pointed out, that Congress, the more deliberative of the political branches, rather than the President, who may move more precipitously, was charged with the solemn duty of declaring war. But the obvious fact is that the Court's participation affords no solution. For, "since Jefferson sent the Navy against the Barbary pirates to protect American shipping, Presidents have asserted the right to send troops abroad on their own authority" on over a hundred occasions.[124] If, for example, President Johnson acted beyond his constitutional authority in dispatching 22,000 American troops to the Dominican Republic in 1965,[125] or if Theodore Roosevelt exceeded his executive power in sending the navy around the world in 1907,[126] neither a declaratory judgment nor an injunction could undo the harm any more effectively than a congressional resolution. The fact is that "never in American history [has] the Court tried in any significant way to interfere with a war in progress."[127] Nor is there any reason to believe that if the judiciary sought to do so, it could ameliorate the damages more quickly. Realistically, Congress seems capable of moving at least as rapidly. To be authoritative, judicial determination of the

Senate-House Conference Committee to a defense authorization measure that was ultimately adopted by voice vote in the House. Id. 2378.

issue would have to involve the Supreme Court, and the appellate process takes time. Even the Pentagon Papers litigation—one of the swiftest in American legal history—took sixteen days to be resolved. (This same analysis holds if the executive's constitutional improprieties are undertaken secretly, as was true of the domestic exploits of the White House :"plumbers" in the Nixon administration.)

(b) *Development of a constitutional crisis.* Suppose the President resists congressional efforts to reassume the reins. The number of hypothetical conflicts is infinite. In the argument set forth above, the possibility of a presidential veto was raised. Suppose a majority of both houses of Congress decrees that the troops should be withdrawn and the President vetoes the enactment. Or suppose that Congress explicitly authorizes certain military action; the President proceeds; Congress then determines that the President has exceeded the delegation and calls on him to desist; but the President simply ignores the request. Or suppose that Congress refuses to appropriate funds for a program that it believes usurps congressional authority, but the President nonetheless orders that checks be drawn—perhaps against money authorized for other purposes, even money that the President has previously impounded!

These are but the most modest illustrations of the escalating clashes that may arise between the political branches over the constitutional separation of powers, presenting exceedingly difficult and complex doctrinal problems. An attractive argument may be made—relying on the wisdom of *Baker v. Carr* that "the political question doctrine, a tool for maintenance of governmental order, will not be so applied as to promote only disorder"[128]—that at least here the Court should intercede to preserve our constitutional equilibrium and to avoid the unseemly conversion of a grave constitutional crisis into a street corner brawl of naked self-help that would heap scorn on both departments.[129]

(c) *Accommodation usually reached.* The fortunate fact—as has already been shown in a number of tales related above—is that the scenario just depicted is unlikely in the extreme. Although our history discloses several instances of executive defiance of the judiciary, the clear tendency of the political departments, in their relations with one another, has been to show a sensible tolerance for conflict and a tactful disinclination to push so far as to create an impasse.

The "give-and-take" on the issue of the executive's right to withhold information from legislative probes during the three decades after the Civil War affords an apt additional illustration. "Most congressional requests were honored; but when requests became too outrageous, public opinion—indeed, responsible congressional opinion—accepted presidential refusals. The presumption remained that, other things being equal, Congress would receive the information it sought. Disagreements were absorbed in the political process, and contention did not lead to a serious executive-legislative showdown. In the end the spirit of comity prevailed."[130]

President Truman's dispute with Congress in the early 1950s over which branch was empowered to determine the number of American troops to be stationed in Europe presents another instance of disagreement and accord. "Congressmen cited Congressional authority to raise armies and to spend money for the common defense, and saw troops in Europe as intimately related to its powers of war-and-peace. The President, invoking authority as Commander-in-Chief and foreign affairs powers, argued, in effect, that troops are stationed abroad not for making war but for not making war, i.e., for deterrence, or for general political influence. In the end . . . the Senate adopted what was largely a 'sense' resolution, approving the dispatch of four divisions, calling on the President to consult with both foreign affairs committees before sending troops abroad under the North Atlantic Treaty, requiring Congressional approval for any policy involving the assignment of troops abroad and for sending any additional troops, and requesting Presidential reports on the implementation of the North Atlantic Treaty. President Truman said that while he did not need Congressional approval he would consult with members of the Senate Foreign Relations Committee and the Armed Services Committee before sending troops to the North Atlantic Treaty area."[131]

The "RS 70" controversy during the Kennedy presidency continued the dominant pattern. In the early 1960s, Congress had indicated its disagreement with the Kennedy-McNamara "flexible response" defense policy (which had downgraded manned bombers in favor of guided missiles) by appropriating funds for further development of the RS-70 airplane which the Defense Department refused to spend. Representative Carl Vinson, chairman of the House Armed Services Committee, believing that Congress's constitutional authority was being flouted, announced his intention to have Congress "direct" that money be expended rather than merely renew the authorization. President Kennedy, seeking to avoid a confrontation, "persuaded the Congressman, during an informal meeting, to withdraw the objectionable language in return for letters from himself and Secretary McNamara noting that a new study of the RS-70 program would be initiated. Kennedy's letter . . . 'respectfully suggest[ed] that, in place of the word "directed," the word "authorized" would be . . . more clearly in line with the spirit of the Constitution.' Kennedy insisted upon 'the full powers and discretions essential to the faithful execution of [his] responsibilities as President and Commander in Chief . . . .' Yet he recognized that the Constitution's implicit intent that 'a spirit of comity govern relations between the executive and legislative,' while making 'unwise if not impossible any legislative effort to "direct" the Executive on matters within the latter's jurisdiction, . . . also makes it incumbent upon the Executive to give every possible consideration in such matters to the views of the Congress.' . . . The companion letter from the Secretary of Defense contained a reassurance that the Secretary desired to work with the Armed Services Committee and Congress 'in the spirit in which a Government of divided powers such as ours must . . . in order to function successfully.' . . . The next day Chairman Vinson rose in the House and, to the disappointment of the many who had hoped for a pitched battle, recommended the substitution of 'authorized' for 'directed.'"[132]

Other examples emerge in the rancorous skirmishes between President Nixon and Congress over presidential impounding and executive privilege—a period during which the spirit of political accommodation fell close to its nadir. As to impoundment, although continuing to refuse to release funds appropriated at the end of the Ninety-second Congress for a variety of programs—and to defend his constitutional power to do so—Mr. Nixon capitulated on the matter of aid to "impacted" school districts (those containing major federal installations) when it became clear that the Ninety-third Congress not only had the votes to reauthorize the funds but, since the money was to go to almost four hundred congressional districts, to override a presidential veto as well.[133] About the same time, the Secretary of Agriculture announced that he was terminating all low interest loans under the Rural Electrification Act. When two congressional attempts to mandate total restoration of the program failed to pass, a compromise was struck: the legislative appropriation bill omitted a compulsory spending proviso in exchange for Secretary Butz's pledge that at least $105 million would be made available for REA loans.[134] Thereafter, "when the Administration failed to implement the program, Congress threatened to prevent payment of certain salaries and expenses for persons responsible for the delay. The threat was withdrawn after Congress received assurance from OMB Director Ash that he would recommend and support implementation of the program."[135]

As to executive privilege, when Henry Kissinger was nominated as Secretary of State, the President opposed "complete disclosure of the initiation, conduct, and results of the 'bugging' done in an effort to trace the sources of leaks" that had plagued the administration. But "an informal arrangement was worked out giving a few members of the Senate Foreign Relations Committee access to the information, and they made a report."[136] Similarly, when "the President invoked executive privilege to prevent White House aide Peter Flanigan from testifying before the Senate Judiciary Committee on his knowledge of the Justice Department's controversial settlement of the ITT merger case," the committee delayed confirmation of Richard Kleindienst as Attorney General "until the President permitted Flanigan to testify. The President acceded to the Senate's demand and allowed Flanigan to appear under special ground rules which set limits to senatorial inquiry."[137] In an earlier encounter concerning Mr. Flanigan, the Senate Committee on Foreign Relations sought to obtain greater executive accountability as to the making of foreign economic policy by the then-proposed White House

Council of International Economic Policy. "SCFR at first refused to authorize appropriations to run CIEP in fiscal year 1973 unless the President would submit Director Peter Flanigan's name for confirmation and thereafter permit him to testify regularly before Congress . . . . Consequently, the Administration tried to bypass SCFR by routing the CIEP authorization request through the more pliant Senate Banking, Housing, and Urban Affairs Committee . . . . The bill passed the Senate in the form requested by the Administration . . . but when it appeared that SCFR had jurisdiction over the CIEP authorization, Senate passage was reversed." Finally, SCFR compromised by "giving CIEP a one year authorization and leaving open for reconsideration in 1973 the issue of Senate confirmation of the CIEP Director. This resolution was facilitated by a promise of CIEP Director Peter Flanigan to . . . [provide] informal briefings" to the committee.[138] Further, during the opening rounds of Watergate, the President greatly contracted his expansive claim regarding the absolute right of his aides not to testify before Senator Ervin's committee investigating the Watergate affair when public criticism mounted and it soon became plain—through its refusal to consent to his nomination of Patrick Gray and its suggestion that recalcitrant witnesses would be held in contempt—that the Senate meant to stand firm.

Shortly after assuming office, President Ford clearly established his view that executive privilege was not "the absolute right that many of his predecessors believed it to be."[139] But by late 1975, battle lines were drawn with the House Select Intelligence Committee. The first clash arose when, after the committee publicly divulged secret information about certain United States intelligence failures, the President refused to give the committee access to other documents unless it agreed to various conditions, including his deleting sensitive information. The issue appeared to be headed to the House Floor with Chairman Otis G. Pike threatening to seek a contempt citation against CIA Director William E. Colby for refusing a subpoena of documents relating to the Tet offensive in Vietnam. The matter was defused when the committee obtained full information in exchange for its promise not to disclose it without White House approval.[140] A somewhat related incident escalated even further: the committee cited Secretary of State Henry Kissinger for contempt when he refused to turn over State Department files involving covert operations of the CIA between 1962 and 1972. The committee pressed along this path despite President Ford's invocation of executive privilege and order to Kissinger to withhold the material because it contained "highly sensitive military and foreign affairs assessments" as well as advice to former Presidents Kennedy, Johnson, and Nixon. After Chairman Pike retorted that the incumbent administration could not assert executive privilege for its predecessors, intensive negotiations between the combatants produced an accord: several committee members and staff received an oral briefing at the White House and Pike announced that, "substantial compliance" having been made, the contempt action against Kissinger was "moot."[141]

Less dramatic, but equally revealing illustrations of the usual spirit of conciliation that accompanies constitutional struggles between the political branches may be found in the Nixon and Ford State Departments' offers to Congress to fashion detailed procedures for consultation on international agreements entered into by the President without formal Senate approval.[142] And, overall, additional empirical evidence may be found in the paucity of litigated cases, at least until the 1970s, in which issues of ultimate constitutional power concerning division of authority have arisen.

As Arthur Schlesinger "saw the executive branch in action" under President Kennedy, it "was haunted by a fear and at times an exaggerated fear of congressional reaction. The notion that the executive goes his blind and arrogant way, saying damn the torpedoes, full speed ahead, is just not true. I would say a truer notion is that the executive branch cowers day and night over the fear and sometimes quite an exaggerated and irrational fear of what the congressional response is going to be to the things it does."[143] Although this may describe an atypically deferential executive attitude, even the most willful occupants of the White House have manifested a healthy respect for Capitol Hill. For example, one might point to the fact that in perhaps the most extravagant assertion of executive power in our history—

Franklin Roosevelt's claimed authority to disregard a provision of standing law—the President's message to Congress carefully and repeatedly pleaded for legislative cooperation. Further, in 1940, when Roosevelt wished to comply with Winston Churchill's "life and death" plea for "the loan of forty or fifty of your older destroyers" to help the Royal Navy hold the English Channel, although he was informed by "eminent lawyers" within and without his administration that he had constitutional power to make the transfer, he did so only after consulting with congressional leaders as well as the Republican nominees for President and Vice-President—and then relied partially on statutory authority after which Congress soon gave "its implicit sanction."[144] Within seventy days of President Lincoln's authorization of the military to suspend the writ of habeas corpus, and immediately on Congress's convening in special session to cope with the emergency,[145] he submitted a resolution of the entire issue "to the better judgment of Congress." In doing so, Lincoln followed the lead of President Jackson who, in 1831, sought congressional approval after he had dispatched a naval carrier to protect American shipping off the coast of South America, and of President Wilson who, in 1914, requested legislative support after he ordered troops to Mexico to secure the lives of American citizens.[146] Nor should it be forgotten that—as President Carter most recently grounded his voluntary wage and price guidelines exclusively in legislative delegation[147]—throughout the Indochina controversy, both President Johnson (in respect to Vietnam) and President Nixon (in respect to Cambodia as well) almost always sought to rely on congressional concurrence, if not explicit authorization or ratification of one kind or another.[148] This is best illustrated by both administrations' frequent invocation of the Tonkin Gulf resolution (which, it should be noted, was specifically solicited by Mr. Johnson as a prologue to his increasing American participation) and by Mr. Nixon's repeated references (after the Tonkin resolution was repealed at his request) to continued congressional appropriations (in the face of minority opposition) as affirming his winding down of our military involvement.[149] Indeed, at the end, President Ford, although seemingly possessed of independent authority, sought specific congressional permission for his plan for the American evacuation of Saigon.[150] Finally, irrespective of its impact on the final outcome of the constitutional tug of war over Indochina, the sensitive and productive debate concerning the separation of powers at the time of the well-known Cooper-Church amendment in 1970 demonstrates the high degree of mutual tolerance that the political branches may exhibit even on matters of most heated controversy. In the view shortly thereafter of one Democratic legislator who was strongly antagonistic to executive activity in Indochina, "while the spirit of the Cooper-Church limitation is offended more than a little by extension of the war into Laos, the White House rhetoric emphasizes the President's meticulous compliance with congressional directives."[151]

(d) *Unlikelihood of successful judicial action.* If, however, despite the long history of political accommodation, Armageddon is reached, if a clash between the political branches reaches the stage of pitched battle as has been hypothesized, if one or both of the branches feel impelled to proceed in the face of all battalions the other can muster, or if either Congress or the President engages in conduct that we may assume is flagrantly beyond its constitutionally assigned power, then there is scant reason to believe that the Court will succeed in halting the march. For such a crisis will arise only in extreme circumstances—usually in the case of perceived "emergency." When Lincoln, without congressional authorization, blockaded the ports of the Confederacy, he did so to "save the life of the nation." Just as he refused to honor Chief Justice Taney's writ in *Ex parte Merryman*—and just as Jefferson ordered that Justice Johnson's mandamus against his embargo be disregarded[152]— there is every reason to believe that Lincoln would have ignored an adverse decision in the *Prize Cases*. This inflammatory juncture having been reached, it is too late to argue that judicial abdication will mean that "provisions in the Constitution are of no more than hortatory significance."[153]

It may be that in some few instances of this sort a President who is embroiled in bitter controversy with Congress (or vice versa) and who has deliberately defied Congress's views will succumb when the weight of the Court's neutrality and prestige is interposed. Richard Nixon's capitulation in the Watergate tapes cases may be argued to be illustrative. But it must not be forgotten that Mr. Nixon's compliance with the ruling of the court of appeals on the subpoena obtained by Archibald Cox occurred only after the President's plan for Senator John Stennis to act as arbitrator failed because of the "firestorm" engendered by the "Saturday night massacre" and that whether he would abide by the Supreme Court's decision on Leon Jaworski's subpoena was in serious doubt to the very end. Once suggesting that he would accede only to a judicial ruling that was "definitive," Nixon later withdrew even that commitment, both in his own public statements and by his counsel's representations before the Court itself.[154] Indeed, it has been reported that after the Court issued its order, the President argued for several hours that he should ignore it.[155] What his final course would have been had his standing with the electorate at the time not been so precarious— Gallup, Harris, and Roper polls consistently showed growing popular majorities favoring Nixon's removal for withholding data sought by various officials[156]—and, perhaps more important, without the threat of punishment for defiance of the Court that he would likely suffer in the impeachment proceedings then in motion,[157] will never be known. But the Nixon experience was unique in that all the operative factors favored the Court. And it closely paralleled the Court's other most successful opposition to an assertion of presidential authority—President Truman's steel seizure—which, as we have noted, also enhanced the Court's prestige. "When that case came to the Justices, public opinion was hostile to the Truman administration (only 23% of the public expressed support for Truman); there was broad Congressional opposition to the economic burdens of the Korean War at that point and to the seizure of the steel industry without Congressional sanction. Furthermore, the way in which the President's lawyers had argued his case in the early stages of the litigation collided with public beliefs in 'limited government' principles."[158]

More commonly, if the clash between the political branches is so painful, the convictions so deeply held, and the consequences so momentous, it is much more doubtful that the Justices will prevail. And, for these same reasons the potential cost—in terms of assuring in the future that constitutional provisions for individual rights are of "more than hortatory significance"—is simply too great. The odds are too short that the Court's institutional credit would be seriously jeopardized by its role in such a political battle irrespective of which way it decides. According to Alan Westin, ever since *Marbury* the Court has consistently adhered to an unwritten rule "when reviewing politically charged and controversial presidential actions: . . . When the political situation is too dangerous for the Supreme Court (e.g., if a ruling against the President is likely to be disobeyed by him or to produce serious reprisals against the Court's powers or prestige), the Court . . . [has found] a way to duck the issue or to deflect it, leaving its immediate resolution to the larger political process."[159] The Separation Proposal forbids the Court's following such a path of unprincipled expedience—if in fact it has—for, as adumbrated in chapter 3,[160] such a course is not only generally beyond the predictive capacity of the Justices but is also wholly at odds with the politically neutral posture that supports the Court's antimajoritarian role in our system of government.

Moreover, by clearly withdrawing the availability of a judicial forum, the Court may well remove an existing disincentive to political settlement. The extent to which the large number of lawsuits—some filed by members of Congress themselves— diverted the legislative branch from coming to grips with the constitutionality of the war in Indochina cannot be accurately measured.[161] But the phenomenon may be quite plainly evidenced by events arising out of those two prominent rifts between the political branches in recent times that have been the subject of full judicial review. After President Truman's seizure of the steel mills, a number of senators from both parties argued against congressional response on the ground that the issue would be resolved by the Supreme Court. And during the impeachment proceedings against President Nixon, several members of the House Judiciary Committee—both opponents and defenders of the President—specifically withheld their support of the impeachment article dealing with his refusal to disclose information to Congress on the ground that the issue was for the courts.

(7) Successful executive action that burdens individuals

The fact is that the President cannot accomplish very much for very long in the absence of congressional concurrence. But despite the formidable number and quality of weapons at the legislature's disposal, there is no disputing that situations do arise when the President may act precipitously to impose his will and succeed, at least in the short run, in the teeth of congressional opposition. But these moments are extremely rare. In his classic study of presidential power, Richard Neustadt concludes that this opportunity occurs only when a combination of five distinct factors exists: there must be assurance that the President himself has spoken rather than some subordinate; there must be no ambiguity as to his meaning; his command must be widely publicized so as to foreclose the opportunity of reluctant officials to ignore it; those who receive the President's order must have control over everything needed to carry it out; there must be general acceptance of the constitutional legitimacy of his authority. "How often is that combination likely to occur? How much, then, can a President rely on sheer command to get him what he wants? It takes but a glance at the examples in this chapter to suggest the answers: not very often and not very much."[162]

It is the last feature—the constitutional validity of the executive action—that bears directly on the Separation Proposal and therefore merits further consideration. Its perceived presence by no means assures effectuation of the President's will, but its absence will almost always doom the effort. As documented by the "debacles of each of the imperial presidencies"—those of Lyndon Johnson and Richard Nixon—major decisions of questionable constitutional legitimacy, particularly when undertaken unilaterally by the chief executive, are "politically costly," "draw unfavorable attention to the President," and are "emphatically open to the kind of backlash that Neustadt had in mind—especially because decisions of this sort are not shared with other leaders, with the result that the blame for them is not shared."[163] Therefore, if, despite the great incentives and effective techniques that Congress enjoys to prevent executive invasion of its domain, the legislature fails to react to the President's move and (as shall be explored further below) the electorate remains quiescent, it is wholly reasonable to assume, without a judicial word having been spoken, that no constitutional violation has occurred.

Several factors beyond the persuasive matter of constitutional acquiescence support the conclusion that political accommodation rather than judicial expertise may be trusted to resolve this separation of powers issue. As noted earlier, the Constitution's delineation of the division between legislative and executive authority is highly uncertain at best and often totally unrewarding. Moreover, the blurred line that separates the respective spheres of the political branches—which are jointly obliged to create and implement effective solutions for novel and pressing societal problems as they emerge—must inevitably be a shifting one, responding to continual modifications in the social and economic environment. Furthermore, the most consequential presidential actions, those "legislative-like" ones most likely to inflict government burdens on individuals, will ordinarily be undertaken in "emergency" circumstances, when the clarity of the dividing line is at its dimmest. For these reasons, there is much to Justice Jackson's assertion that "it is hard to conceive a task more fundamentally political than to maintain amidst changing conditions the balance beween the executive and legislative branches of our federal system."[164]

The possibility exists that the executive may impose regulatory authority on individuals without evoking legislative response, not because Congress has consciously determined that the executive action lies within the constitutionally proper sphere, but because, owing either to well-known inertia or the press of other business, Congress does not view the matter as sufficiently important or the persons subject to it influential enough to prod reaction. Here, it may be argued, "politically impotent minorities," unable to move Congress to assert its interest in

their behalf, must depend on judicial review to curb the ultra
vires executive order and to vindicate their "rights" if any
redress at all is to be forthcoming.

This contention, in conflict with the Separation Proposal, is
neither illogical nor irrelevant. But its real world force must be
severely qualified. To begin with, it assumes that, in some
abstract sense, the executive action violates some historically
intended or contemporarily ideal constitutional separation of
powers—a breach that would go unrepaired without the Court's
intervention. But for reasons just discussed, this is an uneasy
assumption. That Congress has failed to defend its prerogatives
is impressive, albeit not dispositive, evidence of its perception
that the challenged executive undertaking, no matter how substantively insignificant, does not fall far outside the limits of
permissible presidential power. Indeed, since under existing
judicial doctrine the Court has been willing to adjudicate the
issue, the fact (as subsequent discussion will disclose) that there
is virtually no reported case conforming to this description additionally indicates its unlikelihood.

Furthermore, the peculiar nature of the "rights" involved
bears reemphasis. They are not within those fundamental personal liberties that are immune from all government restraint.
Rather, they are "rights" that Congress could, if it wished, regulate at will. Although it does not necessarily follow that Congress has affirmatively acquiesced in their regulation here because it has not chosen to unburden these "rights" by opposing
the President, its silence does suggest that Congress might easily
be led to burden them in the course of enacting legislation. The
humble status of these "rights," in contrast to traditionally
defined personal liberties, is also evidenced by the long series of
Supreme Court decisions—reviewing alleged abridgments by
the *states* of the division of authority concept—in which the Supreme Court has refused to hold that the fourteenth amendment,
or the guarantee clause, or any other constitutional provision
imposes any "restriction upon the form of a State's governmental
organization as will permit persons affected by government action to complain that in its organization principles of separation
of powers have been violated."[165] In weighing all these consid-

erations as well as the cost of judicial review over this category of constitutional issues, the Separation Proposal should prevail.

d. Check of the Electorate

The ultimate political weapon against consequential separation of powers violations—and, more particularly, a safeguard against truly threatening executive abuse—is recourse to the electorate itself. It is important to note that, as a historical matter, the central reason for the distrust of executive power—a fear, as Brandeis's earlier quoted statement reveals, that rests at the base of the modern argument for judicial review to secure individual "freedom"—was the lack of the executive's political accountability. The early separation of power theorists sought a way to contain the control of the aristocracy and to enhance the policymaking ability of those government institutions that were responsive and answerable to the people.[166] This goal is satisfied in the American presidency. In large measure, the method of selecting the President, his dependence on the entire populace, and his concern not simply for his own reelection but also for his party's interest in electing his successor and its congressional candidates (whom empirical studies reveal depend significantly on the electorate's judgment of presidential performance)[167] undermine an essential premise of the contemporary argument that judicial review of separation of powers issues is necessitated by the President's insulation from electoral control. In the informed and astute judgment of Robert Dahl, "a president who defies Congress cannot succeed in his defiance unless he and his policy have more support in the influential publics of the nation than the congressmen he opposes. A president who persists in opposing *both* the Congress *and* a large fraction of articulate opinion is headed for certain defeat, one way or another."[168] This reality is confirmed by George Reedy's experienced observation that "a president whose political leadership is unchallenged can do just about anything," but "a president whose political leadership has suffered from erosion is virtually helpless."[169] Thus, there is much to be said for the view that if public opposition is not forthcoming, the constitutional issue of whether a division of authority has been breached is not worthy of an expenditure of the Court's limited capital. As Arthur Schlesinger urges, "the effective means of controlling the Presidency" rests "less in law than in politics . . . . [T]he American President [rules] by influence; and the withdrawal of consent, by Congress, by the press, by public opinion, could bring any President down."[170]

Of course, this is not to contend that every alleged presidential usurpation of legislative authority that engenders popular disapproval will either cause him to alter his course or produce his demise. But, especially if the matter is of sufficient moment, as Lyndon Johnson would testify in respect to Indochina, it is likely to, unless the President can persuade the public otherwise. David Mayhew has observed that both "the voicing of public opinion" and "the congressional uprising during the Tet offensive of 1968" led President Johnson "to stop escalating the Vietnam War."[171] Arthur Schlesinger has opined that "above all, probably," it was "the prospective loss of the impending Wisconsin primary to Senator Eugene McCarthy" that "eventually persuaded [Johnson] that he could go down the road no farther."[172] The force of the citizenry's voice is interestingly confirmed by an event of later vintage. During President Nixon's "Christmas bombing" of North Vietnam in December 1972 and January 1973, the *New York Times* editorialized that "the President took this step without seeking authority from Congress or the American people. He ignored the fact that the majority that re-elected him did so with the clear expectation that a negotiated peace was 'at hand.'" Yet, on the very same day on the very same page of the *International Herald Tribune* where the editorial also appeared, Rowland Evans and Robert Novak wrote that "Mr. Nixon has been studying secret White House polls showing almost two-thirds of the country either backed his bombing . . . or did not care."[173] In contrast, by the summer of 1973, when Congress at last spoke against the bombing of Laos and Cambodia and President Nixon then capitulated, it is interesting to observe a contemporary Gallup Poll showing that the American public opposed the bombing by a two to one count and that almost six-sevenths of the persons responding believed that the President should obtain congressional approval before taking additional military action in Southeast Asia.[174] Further, at the end of 1973, when Congress overrode the President's veto of the War Powers Act, the Gallup Poll disclosed that the public favored the substance of the bill by a vote of five to one.[175] Finally, there is little doubt that the lopsided popular majorities recorded at the end, which favored his impeachment and removal from office,[176] played a tremendous, if not determinative, role in forcing Mr. Nixon's resignation.

(1) Congressional investigation as a stimulus

The extensive power of congressional investigation—itself a potent, albeit indirect, weapon to harness executive excess in matters both foreign and domestic[177]—may stimulate public sentiment and produce enormous pressure. For example, as Arthur Schlesinger has noted, "the Senate Foreign Relations Committee opened up a national debate where one had really not existed before. The educational job performed by the senators on Vietnam has been quite extraordinary."[178] Additional evidence may be gleaned from the early stages of Watergate—Republican hierarchs became concerned months after the break-in, not so much because of "the lengthening list of gamy revelations as the growing realization that they could pose a threat to GOP election fortunes in 1974 and 1976. Shattering the widespread assumption that the nation was indifferent to the Watergate issue, The Wall Street Journal had already published a poll showing that 91 per cent of voting-age citizens were aware of it—and that one in five independent voters and two out of eleven Republicans said it might turn them against the GOP."[179]

(2) Jeopardy to President's total program

Furthermore, the whole of a President's program and policies may be endangered by voter displeasure with just one or a few of his actions because both his congressional support and the opposition are strongly influenced by his overall standing. The President's prestige is a fragile commodity. Dahl's 1972 scholarly assessment comes fairly close to describing the evolving events during Watergate: "His slightest mistakes are ruthlessly exploited—usually exaggerated—by the opposition; the least breath of scandal is turned against him; and if he claims

the benefits of good times when they occur during his administration, he is also a handy target for resentment when the economy declines or things go badly in international politics (which
sooner or later, they do.)"[180]

In sum, the President is constrained by the executive bureaucracy, external political groups, a Congress that is usually jealous
of its constitutional authority, and, ultimately, by the electorate
itself. In combination, these forces can be adequately trusted to
resist executive action that unconstitutionally invades legislative
prerogatives. If they effectively check presidential usurpation,
judicial review would be superfluous. If they decline to react
adversely to allegedly ultra vires presidential behavior, it is
wholly reasonable to assume that no true constitutional violation
has occurred. And if they seek to halt what they perceive to be an
unconstitutional executive incursion and fail, there is little reason to believe that the Court will succeed when they have not.

E. Consequences of Judicial Involvement

Finally, if it is fear of presidential abuse of power—
whether generally usurping the authority of Congress or more
specifically imposing on the interests of individuals—that trig-
gers the call for judicial involvement (and that is its modern
impetus), then, in the plausible judgment of distinguished
observers, history teaches that the Court's participation has, on
balance, been counterproductive. Rather than curtailing executive aggrandizement, many judicial holdings and dicta have, in
Philip Kurland's words, "licensed the executive branch to secure
the dominant voice in our society."[181] There is solid evidence
tending to substantiate this conclusion. Kurland points to three
"judicially created constitutional doctrines" as being "major
contributors to the notion of the imperial presidency": the articulation of national power over foreign affairs reposed
essentially in the executive,[182] the grant to the federal government of "hegemony over all affairs of the citizens and residents
of this nation . . . despite the existence of the states,"[183] and the
endorsement of wholesale congressional transfer of its domestic

and foreign power to the President.[184] Other rulings by the Justices that have vested inherent constitutional powers in the executive may be added—such as the decision that the President is the sole judge of the existence of such an imminent danger of invasion or insurrection as to justify the defensive use of federal troops,[185] the approval of the President's unilateral capacity in proper circumstances to enter into agreements with other countries,[186] the endorsement of executive lawmaking power even within the nation's borders during wartime,[187] and the grant to the executive branch of independent authority to initiate action in certain instances of major domestic importance.[188] "The judicial attitude" toward the President's prerogative as commander-in-chief, Arthur S. Miller contends, "is more than abstention; it verges at times upon the courts being an arm of the executive when violence, foreign or domestic, erupts."[189] Indeed, it may well be that the long-term significance of the Court's pronouncement in *United States v. Nixon* will not be its specific holding that ordered the President to comply with the special prosecutor's subpoena, but rather its broader legitimation of the executive's constitutional privilege in appropriate cases to withhold information from the other branches of government. Adherence to the Separation Proposal would have avoided most, if not all, of these judicial declarations enhancing presidential dominion.

IV. CONTOURS OF THE SEPARATION PROPOSAL

Although conventional judicial doctrine assumes that, if presented with a traditionally perceived case or controversy, the federal courts will unhesitatingly adjudicate questions of constitutional conflict between Congress and the President—a position at odds with the Separation Proposal—only a handful of Supreme Court decisions (and, until recently, not too many more lower federal court cases) have in fact done so. A detailed consideration of these relatively few rulings and their factual settings will help to define the contours and implications of the Separation Proposal.

A. The Steel Seizure Case

1. Absence of Nonconstitutional Issues

Youngstown Sheet & Tube Co. v. Sawyer[190]—the most prominent of these decisions, involving President Truman's seizure of the steel mills to avert a strike that would have halted the production of steel needed for the Korean war effort—is an appropriate point of departure. It should be noted at the outset that the President, unable to locate a statutory source of authority to defend his seizure, sought instead to justify it by relying on the inherent constitutional power of the executive. Thus, the Court's ruling, enjoining his Secretary of Commerce, was unlike the legion of judicial decisions holding that executive officials, acting under presidential mandate, have exceeded their province. In virtually all of the latter cases, neither the President nor his executive branch subordinates contended that the power to engage in the challenged action flowed directly from the Constitution. Rather, the exclusive claim was that the executive's authority was delegated by Congress.[191] Thus, in the lower court in *Youngstown,* government counsel defending the seizure could accurately point out that "there is not one single instance in which the courts have enjoined executive power where it was based upon the Constitution and not upon statute."[192]

The Separation Proposal in no way affects the dominant line of cases—typified by such celebrated rulings against executive misconduct as *Greene v. McElroy*[193] and *Harmon v. Brucker*[194]—that afford judicial relief "to one who has been injured by an act of a government official which is in excess of his express or implied powers."[195] Nor does it touch the related group of decisions that invalidated the activities of subsidiary executive agencies on the ground that they had extended beyond the President's direction.[196] None of these cases involves any constitutional question whatever. In all of them, since the President, either explicitly or implicitly, concedes that the only source of his authority is Congress, the cases concern only issues of statutory interpretation. Decisions may be found that hold that courts should abjure from questioning the executive's interpretation of the scope of its congressionally delegated power, thus placing the burden "on the Congress to pass such remedial legislation as may obviate any injustice brought about."[197] (A related contention, in the context of the presence of a dependent constitutional issue, will be considered shortly.) But when the case comprehends nothing beyond ordinary determination and application of legislative intent—a task that is probably the most common function of courts in all legal systems—there is no warrant for judicial abstention.

2. The President's Constitutional Authority to Engage in Lawmaking: Theories of Presidential Power

The constitutional issue in *Youngstown* was whether President Truman's seizure order—which had all the trappings of a legislative enactment and was operative within the nation's borders at a time when it was not a "theater of war"—fell within the aggregate of his authority under those provisions in Article II stating that "the executive Power shall be vested in a President," that "he shall take Care that the Laws be faithfully executed," and that he "shall be Commander in Chief of the Army and Navy"; or whether it was a naked exercise of "legislative Powers" in usurpation of Article I's grant to Congress. It is important to note that the Solicitor General, who represented the President in the Supreme Court, did not contend that the President had such "legislative-like" power superior to that of Congress, even in time of "national emergency"—although the Assistant Attorney General who appeared in behalf of the President in the district court claimed at least this much in oral argument,[198] a position publicly repudiated by Mr. Truman himself within several days.[199] Rather, the thrust of the Solicitor General's argument—as evidenced by his lengthy denial that the Taft-Hartley Act precluded the emergency action taken[200] and by the fact that President Truman had plainly advised Congress immediately after the seizure that he would abide by its decision (which was never forthcoming)—was that, under the above-mentioned clauses of Article II, the President had inherent authority "to avert crises during time of war or national emergency"[201] only so long as that authority was neither previously denied nor subsequently disaffirmed by Congress.

This conception of executive power was similar to Theodore Roosevelt's so-called stewardship theory of the presidency and unlike William Howard Taft's very restrictive but equally well-known theory of presidential authority. President Taft believed that "the true view of the Executive functions is...that the President can exercise no power which cannot be fairly and reasonably traced to some specific grant of power or justly implied and included within such express grant as proper and necessary to its exercise. Such specific grant must be either in the Federal Constitution or in an act of Congress passed in pursuance thereof. There is no undefined residuum of power which he can exercise because it seems to him to be in the public interest."[202] In contrast, the first President Roosevelt "declined to adopt the view that what was imperatively necessary for the Nation could not be done by the President unless he could find some specific authorization to do it. My belief was that it was not only his right but his duty to do anything that the needs of the Nation demanded unless such action was forbidden by the Constitution or by the laws."[203]

With the exception of the government's argument in the district court in *Youngstown*, the most unrestrained view of executive power—that authorizing unilateral legislative-like actions irrespective of contrary congressional enactment—appears rarely if ever explicitly to have been asserted in litigation by any President. For example, in *United States v. United States District Court*, where the President pleaded a constitutional prerogative to use electronic surveillance in internal security matters without prior judicial approval, counsel for the executive branch conceded at oral argument that Congress had ultimate power to limit the enterprise;[204] indeed, the executive's basic justification for its conduct was statutory authorization. And when, in *Zemel v. Rusk*,[205] the Secretary of State—although relying primarily on congressional delegation of authority—claimed inherent executive power to regulate the issuance of passports, it was never suggested that the State Department could do so in the face of a legislative negative.

Presidents have extrajudicially claimed the more unbounded view of presidential power on at least several occasions of honestly perceived national emergency. Most plainly illustrative is Franklin Roosevelt's quite unmistakable threat to repeal a statutory provision during World War II if Congress did not. Although Abraham Lincoln, after suspending the statutorily authorized writ of habeas corpus in 1861, then submitted the matter for dispositive congressional resolution, his 1863 statement—"that measures otherwise unconstitutional might become lawful by becoming indispensable to the preservation of the Constitution through the preservation of the nation"[206]—at least suggests unrestricted presidential power. Another articulation of this position perhaps may be found in the words of Harry Truman, written several years after the *Youngstown* decision (although, as with Lincoln, his precise intention remains somewhat doubtful because of ambiguities lurking in the later statement and his more modest views earlier expressed): "Whatever the six justices [in the majority] of the Supreme Court meant by their differing opinions about the constitutional powers of the President, he must always act in a national emergency . . . . The President, who is Commander in Chief and who represents the interest of all the people, must be able to act at all times to meet any sudden threat to the nation's security. A wise President will always work with Congress, but when Congress fails to act or is unable to act in a crisis, the President, under the Constitution, must use his powers to safeguard the nation."[207]

3. Application of the Separation Proposal

a. Absence of Relevant Congressional Legislation

When the executive branch defends its undertaking of legislative-like action that allegedly encroaches on Congress's dominion on the ground that it is directly empowered to do so by the Constitution, the Separation Proposal advises that the Court should treat the constitutional issue as nonjusticiable no matter what the executive's particular theory of presidential power happens to be. The application of the proposal is least complicated

when the executive's position—like President Truman's in
Youngstown, the executive branch's counsel in *U.S. District
Court,* and Theodore Roosevelt's described above—is that its
constitutional authority operates only in the absence of congressional denial or disaffirmance. Under these circumstances, if
those opposing presidential action point to no conflicting legislative enactment but instead rely exclusively on the contention
that the President has exceeded his power vis-à-vis Congress, the
Court should simply accept the presidential assertion of constitutional authority and carry out his mandate accordingly, irrespective of the consequences to the individuals subject to the
challenged action. If Congress is displeased with the course of
events, it is fully capable of employing political processes to
undo the effects of the executive action by substituting its
judgment—in which the President has already agreed to abide.

This model (as we shall see shortly) does not describe the
situation in *Youngstown* because there the steel companies argued that Congress had deliberately forbidden a presidential
seizure. But it does comprehend several other familiar cases in
which—usually implicitly, but on occasion explicitly—executive
action has been sought to be justified on this basis. For instance,
in the renowned case of *In re Debs*[208]—in which the United
States sued in federal court to prevent union officials from
obstructing interstate railway and mail transportation—as well as
in the widely publicized more recent decision in *United States v.
Brand Jewelers, Inc.,*[209] the government obtained an injunction
against private individuals despite the fact that no act of Congress had expressly declared the conduct in which they had engaged to be unlawful. In effect, the executive was itself "enacting" law as well as "enforcing" it. Although the *Debs* Court
never clearly framed the constitutional issue accurately—that is,
in terms of executive versus legislative power, talking instead
about the overall power of the "national government"—the result upholding the injunction was consistent with the Separation
Proposal. But the Court's rationale was not. Since there was no
dispute that *Congress* had the power to make the enjoined conduct unlawful, the Court should not have addressed the issue of
whether, as a matter of substantive constitutional interpretation,
the executive had overstepped its bounds in doing so. Rather,

because there was no suggestion that Congress disagreed with the President's initiative, the Court should have held the issue to be nonjusticiable and granted the injunction accordingly. We will subsequently consider the proper course of action for the judiciary when one political branch seeks a court's assistance to affect individuals and the other political branch allegedly has dictated the opposite result. This was not the case in *Debs*, however; hence if Mr. Debs were ever found to have violated the injunction, appropriate penalties should have been assessed regardless of any claim on his part that the executive had engaged in lawmaking.

The case of *In re Neagle*[210] is subject to similar analysis. There, the Attorney General, without express statutory authority had assigned Neagle, a federal marshal, to protect a Supreme Court Justice. When Neagle killed an assailant in the course of this duty, he was arrested by the state. He then sought a federal writ of habeas corpus under a congressional statute that authorized the writ for persons imprisoned "for an act done or committed in pursuance of a law of the United States." The Court could have confined itself to the question of whether Congress intended to extend habeas corpus to this type of situation and thus need not have addressed any constitutional issue whatever. But all the Justices, focusing on the word "law" in the statute, spoke to the ultimate constitutional problem and, by split vote, held that the writ should issue since the Attorney General's assignment was within the boundaries of Article II and did not poach on the authority of Congress. Under the Separation Proposal, the result was correct, but the constitutional issue, if it had to be reached, should have been treated as nonjusticiable.

Apart from the relatively few litigated cases, most instances of presidential action—both actually undertaken and realistically possible—that observers suggest infringe congressional power fall under the heading of "legislative-like" executive mandates that appear to be neither explicitly authorized nor contradicted by statute. To mention just a few examples:

President Roosevelt's proclamation of a bank holiday suspending all banking transactions within the country for four days;[211] President Truman's executive order setting forth detailed substantive and procedural provisions for the investigation of all applicants for employment in all executive departments and agencies and for the removal of "disloyal" personnel;[212]

Executive orders by Presidents Roosevelt, Truman, Eisenhower, Kennedy, and Johnson forbidding racial discrimination by federal government contractors, including various government sanctions (such as termination) and requiring specific employer procedures (such as equal opportunity programs);[213]

President Kennedy's executive order directing relevant federal officials to "take all action necessary" to prevent racial discrimination in any housing in any way related to federal agencies and providing elaborate machinery for enforcement;[214]

President Johnson's detailed price-wage guidelines providing that violators could not qualify as suppliers of the federal government,[215] his executive order subjecting foreign investments to strict limitations and controls,[216] and his Department of Health, Education, and Welfare's guidelines to effect public school desegregation that threatened to terminate federal funds to recalcitrant districts;[217]

President Ford's executive order restructuring the nation's intelligence apparatus,[218] creating "two new governmental units—the Committee on Foreign Intelligence, established to supervise and manage the government's intelligence activities, and the Intelligence Oversight Board, to monitor the performance of intelligence operations"[219]—both responsible to the President.

On the basis of past experience, it is most likely that, if the propriety of any of these regulations were to be attacked in the course of litigation, the executive department would—as did President Nixon in respect to his general import duty surcharge[220] and President Ford in regard to his license fees for oil imports[221]—depend exclusively on some statutory authorization for their validity. If so, as observed above, the Separation Proposal is inapplicable. Or it may be that the Court would be led to find, as in *Youngstown*, that the challenged executive promulgation has been precluded by some congressional enactment—a circumstance that will concern us forthwith. But if the case comes within neither of these alternative contexts, and the extremely difficult and largely uncharted question of whether the action falls within the President's power to "take Care that the Laws be faithfully executed" rather than within Congress's "legislative Power" is presented, then the Court should hold the issue to be nonjusticiable and proceed with the case in ordinary course.

Nor is the force or application of the Separation Proposal deterred by the unreal but familiar "parade of horribles"—such as executive promulgation of a detailed tax law or industrial code or, if Congress had not enacted the existing authorization,[222] independent presidential use of armed troops to enforce laws in the face of Article I's provision that "Congress shall have Power To . . . provide for calling forth the Militia to execute the Laws of the Union." The more extravagant the imagined presidential assertion, the less likely it will come to pass, the more assured will be the congressional response, the less apt a judicial order will be obeyed, and the more probable the Court will be damaged.

b. Presence of Relevant Congressional Legislation

We turn now to the *Youngstown* decision itself, in which those attacking the executive action contended that it conflicted with, and therefore was precluded by, an act of Congress. The Separation Proposal does not interfere with the Court's adjudication of this issue—one exclusively of statutory interpretation and not of constitutionality. Indeed, careful examination of the six separate opinions written by the six prevailing Justices in *Youngstown* reveals that, despite far-ranging dicta as to the scope of the President's constitutional power, the Court *majority* decided no more than this statutory matter. Although joining in Justice Black's "opinion of the Court," Justices Frankfurter, Jackson, Burton, and Clark, in their individual concurring opinions, all pointedly rested their judgment on the ground that, in the Taft-Hartley Act, Congress—having designated procedures for executive use in dealing with emergency labor problems, and having considered and rejected seizure as an available technique—intended that seizure not be employed.

Justices Black and Douglas also specifically found this to be true,[223] but leapt beyond this to hold additionally that, apart from prior congressional disapproval of seizure, President Truman's takeover was an act of "lawmaking" which exceeded his constitutional power. The four concurring Justices clearly did not subscribe to the relatively rigid interpretation of the constitutional separation of powers put forward by Justices Black and Douglas; some among the four Justices directly disowned it and others differed somewhat from it and among themselves. Thus, the majority's result in holding the President's action invalid as well as its *rationale*—that Congress had previously negated seizure as a remedy—does not stand as a precedent against the Separation Proposal. Rather, the assumption by all nine members of the Court that the question of the President's ultimate constitutional power was justiciable and their discourse concerning the extent of this authority make *Youngstown* an obstacle to the adoption of the Separation Proposal.

The three dissenters, Chief Justice Vinson and Justices Reed and Minton, properly explored the issue of whether Congress had meant to deprive the President of the seizure device. But, having concluded that it did not so intend, they should have stopped at that point, treated the issue of presidential power to be nonjusticiable—instead of finding on the merits that President Truman's action comported with Article II—and voted to dissolve the injunction.

When, as in *Youngstown*, the President claims inherent constitutional power to engage in legislative-like conduct but concedes that this power exists only in the absence of previous denial or subsequent disaffirmance by Congress, the Separation Proposal plainly does not foreclose the Court from deciding the statutory question of whether the legislature, in fact, has done so. Apart from the Separation Proposal, however, there is substantial merit in the view that, in the context described, even this nonconstitutional issue might be judicially avoided. In almost all recorded instances of questioned executive action, we have seen that constitutionality was not put in issue; the executive instead has relied on statutory authorization alone to justify its conduct. In these rather commonplace circumstances, there is no compelling reason for the courts to abandon their traditional function of statutory interpretation. It will normally only be in especially important instances, however, that the President will be moved to assert an independent constitutional power to defend action that he has undertaken—usually times of particular stress or perceived national emergency. Because of the highly charged nature of the surrounding factual context that may be ordinarily anticipated and the correspondingly fragile quality of the Court's institutional position, it may well be that the preferable judicial posture is to accept the executive department's view of expressed congressional intent and thus force Congress to speak for itself if it disagrees with the executive's reading of existing statutes or disapproves of the President's action.

If Congress responds, the matter should be closed since the President has stipulated—as did Mr. Truman at the time of the steel seizure—that he will respect the word of Congress. And there is every reason to believe that Congress will be heard from if it is not content with what the President has done. It is true that legislative silence after a typical judicial declaration of a law's meaning in no way proves that Congress acquiesces in the accuracy of the interpretation. Because of indifference or the usual press of business, Congress may neither know of the decision nor feel that the subject is important enough to engage itself in the burdensome task of mustering the forces necessary for change.[224] But the matter now being considered is by no means routine; rather, a presidential assertion of independent constitutional authority will be an occasion of great moment—indeed, much more so than most of the incidents that have incited Congress to express its disagreement with another branch's construction of legislative will. This may be illustrated by the steel seizure itself, which was the subject of heated debate in both houses from the day it was announced. In less than two weeks, the Senate approved an amendment to a pending appropriations bill that forebade use of any of those funds by the President to effectuate the takeover.[225] But with a judicial ruling known to be forthcoming, there was no need for Congress to assume final responsibility. (Indeed, not only did the Court's assumption of jurisdiction over the steel seizure act as deterrent to an effective legislative response, but it also removed the incentive for a private settlement of the collective bargaining dispute which had then been imminent.)[226]

This is not to deny that the extreme controversiality of the matter might place a stranglehold on the political process, thus preventing a majority of the legislators from expressing their true sentiment. But if the issue is both so delicate and sensational as to immobilize Congress from asserting its own jealously held constitutional prerogatives, then that may provide all the more reason for the Court to stand aside. For although it is possible that a ruling on the merits will augment the Justices' institutional position, as it did in *Youngstown,* the opposite consequence is more likely. In sum whether this is an area of nonconstitutional adjudication from which the Court should abstain, so as better to fulfill its critical antimajoritarian function in American society, warrants serious consideration.

B. INDEPENDENT INDIVIDUAL RIGHTS ISSUES

The *Steel Seizure Case* also affords an illustration of the distinction—central to the Separation Proposal—between the separation of powers category of constitutional issues and that of constitutionally guaranteed personal liberties. The discussion of *Youngstown* to this point has concerned the former, because the steel companies conceded that Congress could have done the very thing for which they were attacking the President, and they did not contend that the Constitution granted them a right to be free from all such government conduct. Originally, however, an issue of the latter type was present in the case: whether the seizure constituted "private property be[ing] taken for public use," which, the fifth amendment stipulates, cannot be done by *any* organ of the national government "without just compensation." This issue—clearly a proper, indeed crucial, subject of judicial review under the Individual Rights Proposal—was removed from center stage by the Solicitor General, who explicitly conceded that the seizure, although within the President's inherent constitutional power, was a taking "subject to the payment of just compensation."[227] Having done so, he was able to argue correctly that the takeover of the steel mills involved no abridgment of constitutionally secured individual rights.[228]

In the specific setting of the *Steel Seizure Case,* if the Court had concluded that Congress had not denied the President's authority of seizure, then, pursuant to the Separation Proposal, in addition to upholding the executive action, if it agreed that a "taking" had occurred, it should have ordered compensation if and when the claim was properly presented. Whether the President's action was "legal" or "lawful" in some abstract sense—a problem that appeared to trouble Justices Black and Douglas[229]—should be irrelevant. The Court, having *accepted* the presidential assertion of constitutional authority—although *not* placing its official imprimatur upon it—should seek to assure the individual right to just compensation afforded by the Constitution. Under the Tucker Act, Congress has provided the appropriate route, granting "the Court of Claims ... jurisdiction to render judgment upon any claim ... founded ... upon the Constitution,"[230] and, as the Court has held, "if there is a taking, the claim is 'founded uopon the Constitution' and within the jurisdiction of the Court of Claims to hear and determine."[231] Furthermore, other decisions have awarded just compensation for "takings" despite the fact that the government official involved acted without statutory authority.[232]

This does not discount the possibility that Congress may, for reasons of pique or otherwise, withhold the funds necessary for compensation or withdraw its consent to suit in instances such as these. But that does not erase the constitutional deprivation; it accentuates it. Such a legislative posture is simply an example of Congress's refusing to abide by the Court's determination that constitutionally guaranteed individual rights have been abridged. Indeed, just as if Congress refused to appropriate funds to remedy a judicially declared impairment of contract, the refusal itself might amount to an independent violation of personal liberty: a deprivation of property without due process of law. History suggests[233] and the Court has stated that "just compensation is provided for by the Constitution and the right to it cannot be taken away by statute."[234] The Court can do no more than seek to secure this individual right—as well as others—to the best of its ability. In the case of an executive taking whose compensation will not be funded by Congress, the Court may, as in *United States v. Lee*,[235] order ejectment, or it may award damages against the trespassing officials themselves. But, as is true of many judicial rulings in behalf of personal liberties, effectuation may be stymied by the political departments.

Two more recent, and much noticed, decisions of the Supreme Court have also presented distinct issues of both separation of powers and individual rights, although, consistently with the Separation Proposal, in neither case did the Justices, save one, adjudicate the division of authority question. In *New York Times Co. v. United States*,[236] the Nixon administration sought to enjoin the *New York Times* and the *Washington Post* from publishing the celebrated "Pentagon Papers." The executive branch contended that, although no act of Congress authorized such an injunction, the government's right to obtain one "stems from two interrelated sources: the constitutional power of the President over the conduct of foreign affairs and his authority as Commander-in-Chief."[237] In a brief per curiam opinion, the Court refused the injunction. Each of the six majority Justices wrote separately. Only Justice Marshall rested on the *Youngstown* rationale: since "on at least two occasions Congress has refused to enact legislation that would have made the conduct engaged in here unlawful and given the President the power that he seeks in this case," it would "be utterly inconsistent with the concept of separation of powers for this Court" to accede to his request for an injunction. The other five members of the majority implicitly accepted the thrust of the Separation and Individual Rights Proposals by moving to the issue of personal liberty. Justices Black, Douglas, and Brennan ruled unambiguously that an injunction would constitute a prior restraint forbidden by the first amendment, as did Justice Stewart in an opinion joined by Justice White. But Justice White also authored an opinion, in which Justice Stewart concurred, emphasizing both the absence of statutory authorization for an injunction and the existence of numerous criminal penalties which had been enacted by Congress that were "potentially relevant" to the newspapers' conduct. Despite this "*Youngstown*-like" approach, however, Justice White's view was *not* that these factors meant that the presidentially demanded injunction would usurp the power of Congress under Article I; rather, his conclusion appeared to be that, under the first amendment, since Congress "has apparently been satisfied to rely on criminal sanctions," the government "has not satisfied the very heavy burden that it must meet to warrant an injunction against publication in these cases, at least in the absence of express and appropriately limited congressional authorization for prior restraints in circumstances such as these." Whether, as Justice White suggests, the Court's substantive interpretation of the scope of constitutionally guaranteed personal liberties should be influenced by whichever political branch has undertaken to affect them is (as stated in chapter 2) beyond the scope of this book. What is important to observe, however, is that the inquiry is a legitimate one under the Individual Rights Proposal and is not precluded by the Separation Proposal.

United States v. United States District Court also involved a Nixon administration claim of constitutional prerogative: to engage in electronic surveillance without prior judicial approval. The Court, after first concluding that the pertinent statutes neither granted nor denied the executive assertion, then turned "to the constitutional powers of the President." Two paths of inquiry were available: first, whether this "legislative-like" action invaded the Article I prerogatives of Congress; and second, whether failure to secure a warrant abridged the fourth amendment's personal right against "unreasonable searches and seizures." In accordance with the Separation Proposal, the Court abjured the former and, consistently with the Individual Rights Proposal, addressed itself exclusively to the latter.

The prolonged constitutional debate over the war in Indochina offers a final example of challenged executive action that may present both a separation of powers issue and a bona fide individual rights claim independent of the separation claim. We have seen that it is not enough for a member of the armed forces who is ordered to the battle site to contend that he has a personal right under the due process clause not to be commanded to engage in an "illegal" war, for if the "illegality" argument depends on the war not having been declared by Congress, the issue is really one of separated powers. But a soldier's position that the barbarity of the war is such that his forced participation will subject him to punishment before an international tribunal for "war crimes" violative of the Geneva and Hague conventions—and thus denies him due process of law—raises a genuine personal liberty claim.[238] Whatever its substantive merit, it denies *all* government power in respect to the conduct being assailed. It can be remedied only by cessation of that conduct, not merely by the constitutionally proper branch doing what the other has already done.

Thus, the Separation Proposal in no way affects the Court's authority—under the Individual Rights Proposal—to decide issues of *direct* injury to constitutionally guaranteed personal liberties. The Justices should treat as nonjusticiable any claim that an individual was injured by an unconstitutional executive action if Congress constitutionally could have so acted. On the other hand, if a person contends that he was injured by an unconstitutional executive action that *neither* branch constitutionally could have taken, the Court should decide the claim.

C. President's Removal Power

1. Scope of the Problem

Apart from the *Steel Seizure Case*—and its underlying constitutional problem of whether particular executive action constitutes "lawmaking" in excess of presidential authority under Article II—the most notable Supreme Court decisions concerning the constitutional separation of powers between the political branches have been *Myers v. United States*[239] and *Humphrey's Executor v. United States*.[240] The substantive constitutional question involved—the respective authority of Congress and the President to remove from office persons who are employed in the numerous executive agencies and departments—is unaddressed in the basic document and has been debated since the origins of the republic. In the First Congress, a bill by Madison, proposing the creation of a Department of Foreign Affairs and providing that its chief officer was subject to removal by the President, sparked broad discussion as to which of the two national branches was so empowered by the Constitution. The final ambiguous resolution seemed to favor the executive.[241] The issue reappeared in *Marbury v. Madison* in which Chief Justice Marshall suggested that the President was powerless to revoke an appointment that had been congressionally authorized for a designated term.[242] But it was not until Myers, a postmaster who was removed by order of President Harding—despite a statute providing that postmasters "shall be appointed and removed by the President with the advice and consent of the Senate"—sued for his salary that the matter was presented for full-blown judicial consideration.

In *Myers*, the Court not only upheld the President's contention that this statutory provision unconstitutionally invaded the domain of Article II but appeared to announce the sweeping doctrine that the presidential power of removal extended absolutely to all "executive officers of the United States appointed by him." This principle was modified in *Humphrey's Executor*. Humphrey had been appointed to the Federal Trade Commission by President Hoover for a term of seven years. The Federal Trade Commission Act permitted removal by the President only "for inefficiency, neglect of duty, or malfeasance in office." When Humphrey was dismissed by President Roosevelt within two years because of policy differences, he brought an action for his compensation. The Court now ruled that the President's constitutional power of removal was limited to "executive officials," rather than members of "quasi-legislative or quasi-judicial agencies" who "act in discharge of their duties independently of executive control." Thus, Congress had not exceeded its constitutional bounds by imposing on the authority of the President.

2. Application of the Separation Proposal

Under the Separation Proposal, in neither of these cases should the Court have addressed the constitutional separation of powers contentions. Rather, in both instances, the Court should have accepted the presidential claim of constitutional power to remove and proceeded accordingly. Thus, the result—though not the rationale—in *Myers* comports with the proposal. Nor, in this respect, need *Humphrey's* be seen as in conflict. The Court's judgment in that case awarded unpaid salary which is not inconsistent with judicial acceptance of the executive's constitutional assertion. It is undisputedly within the power of Congress to authorize funds for the payment of any federal employee who has been removed from office, regardless of the reason. Thus, even in *Myers* the Court could have ordered compensation to the postmaster, if it had discerned a congressional intention to provide it, without in any sense rejecting the President's constitutional authority to declare the position vacant. Direct confrontation between the two political departments would only arise if, in the face of such a presidential assertion of power, Congress specifically mandated that the individual be retained in office. Hypothetical, diametrically opposed stances of this kind will be considered shortly. But the problem has never been presented in any actual removal case—the usual remedy sought is money damages[243]—and in all other removal cases decided by the Supreme Court, the President did not assert that he had a constitutional power of removal but rather relied exclusively on statutory authorization.[244]

3. Individual Rights Issues

As noted above, it was in the context of a claim to hold office that, in *Marbury v. Madison,* having found that President Jefferson's refusal to deliver Marbury's commission as justice of the peace violated the law by which Congress had authorized the commission, Chief Justice Marshall uttered his famous dictum that "the very essence of civil liberty" demands that when an individual "receives an injury" because his "right has been violated" "the laws of his country [must] afford him a remedy."[245] This edict, too, may be satisfied under the Separation Proposal. If an individual has been given a statutory "right" to hold federal office, then Congress may provide a complete remedy for its violation through executive removal by authorizing compensation. If Congress chooses not to do so, then (unless we are to engage in a circular game of semantics) it must be concluded—as the Court, in effect, has held[246]—that the individual has not been granted a "right."

Regardless of congressional actions, it is possible for the Court to find that the dismissal of a government employee contrary to statute abridges an individual *constitutional* right, such as the due process protection against retroactive impairment of contract—a conclusion that would assume a right of redress if *either* Congress or the President caused his removal. In this case, as earlier discussed, the Court should order compensation regardless of prior congressional provision of funds. This critical difference between a removal contested because of a violation of the separation of powers principle and one challenged as abridging a constitutionally guaranteed personal liberty is exemplified by a number of cases raising issues within the latter category— advancing such contentions as denial of the sixth amendment right to confront and cross-examine adverse witnesses[247] or the more general fifth amendment right of procedural due process.[248]

4. Submission of Issue to Judiciary by the Political Branches

One further aspect of the *Myers* case merits attention. Although it was initiated by a private party, at the Court's invitation, Senator George Wharton Pepper appeared as amicus curiae and argued Congress's point of view; the Solicitor General represented the President. The subsidiary nature of Myers's interest in the matter was highlighted by Senator Pepper's opening statement that "this is an issue between executive power and legislative power; and the question is where the Constitution has vested the power to prescribe terms of removal—whether in the Congress, as I contend, or in the President, as I think the Solicitor General must contend."[249] Thus, in a meaningful (if not literal) sense, the case may be viewed as one in which both political departments "voluntarily" decided to "submit" a difficult and uncharted constitutional disagreement for orderly resolution by the judiciary. As Senator Pepper put it: "Here we have a constitutional 'no man's land.' It lies between the recognized lines of executive prerogative and of legislative power. The question is, who may rightfully occupy it? And the decision of this Court in this case will be of enormous significance in helping to clear up the question as to who may enter in and possess that area which up to date has been debatable."[250] The *Pocket Veto Case*[251] (which shall concern us below) may be subject to a similar characterization, the Attorney General representing the President and a committee of the House of Representatives appearing as amicus curiae and advancing the interests of Congress.

At least in these circumstances, and given a genuine case or controversy, it may be forcefully argued that the Court should decide the constitutional question presented on the merits rather than remit the principal contestants to the political battlefield. Despite the appeal of this position, the Court should abstain in accord with the Separation Proposal. We have discussed the penchant of politicians in all respect and deference to pass difficult and provocative matters to the Court only to respond to an adverse decision—and it needs no restatement that the ruling sought here will reject the views of one of the political branches—with hostility and intimidation. The ability of the particular issue of removal to arouse political wrath is vividly evidenced by the impeachment of President Johnson and the fact that President Roosevelt's loss in the *Humphrey's* case, according to his Solicitor General, "irked him even more than the treatment afforded New Deal legislation."[252] In short, the stakes are too high and the issue is wholly capable of satisfactory resolution outside the halls of the judiciary.

D. EXECUTIVE PRIVILEGE AND THE SEPARATION OF POWERS

Under the Articles of Confederation, the Continental Congress, having created whatever executive departments there were, possessed unqualified access to their working papers. Since the Constitution's establishment of an independent executive, however, no subject implicating the division of authority between the two political branches has been more frequently or vigorously disputed than the collision of the congressional right to obtain information with the President's asserted privilege to withhold it. A long list of Presidents from George Washington to Jimmy Carter, believing that disclosure would not be "in the public interest," have declined, either personally or by direction to subordinates, to comply with legislative requests to submit written documents or oral testimony. Other Presidents who have asserted executive privilege include Thomas Jefferson, James Monroe, Andrew Jackson, John Tyler, James Polk, Millard Fillmore, James Buchanan, Abraham Lincoln, Ulysses Grant, Rutherford Hayes, Calvin Coolidge, Herbert Hoover, Franklin Roosevelt, Dwight Eisenhower, and Gerald Ford. Three chief executives—Grover Cleveland, Theodore Roosevelt, and Harry Truman—were condemned in congressional resolutions for refusing to divulge information on a claim of executive privilege, and Richard Nixon almost suffered impeachment therefor.

There is no intention here of evaluating the widely divergent constitutional interpretations of the substance of the executive privilege doctrine. Views on the matter range from an assertion of virtually unlimited presidential immunity for all communications by all executive branch employees (most expansively voiced during the Army-McCarthy hearings by President Eisenhower and at one stage of Watergate by President Nixon)[253] to a wholly unqualified congressional "right to know."[254] The problem has been surveyed in depth and the oft-stated views emanating from the political branches themselves as well as from constitutional scholars have been collected elsewhere.[255] Rather, the pertinent inquiry for our purposes is the proper adjudicatory function of the national judiciary. Despite the frequency with which the ultimate constitutional issue has been posed in pristine form and although *state* courts had rendered opinions as to such conflicts between governor and legislature,[256] until 1974 no federal court had ever passed judgment on the respective constitutional prerogatives of President and Congress.[257] Under the Separation Proposal, the federal judiciary should not. Even if the constitutional issue is central to the decision of an undisguised case or controversy affecting tangible individual interests, and wholly part from the difficulties of fashioning workable judicial criteria for its resolution,[258] so long as the matter analytically concerns only the constitutional separation of powers between the political branches, its disposition should be left to political accommodation.[259]

1. United States v. Nixon

United States v. Nixon,[260] although containing the seeds for a Supreme Court adjudication contrary to the Separation Proposal, is not inapposite. The case arose when Leon Jaworski, the Watergate Special Prosecutor, caused a subpoena to be issued to President Nixon that required the President to surrender tapes and documents in his possession that Mr. Jaworski wished to use in the scheduled criminal trial of six presidential assistants. In ruling that, "as against a subpoena essential to enforcement of criminal statutes," the President's constitutionally supported claim of "general privilege of confidentiality" must yield to the "primary constitutional duty of the Judicial Branch to do justice in criminal prosecutions," the Supreme Court in no way resolved a constitutional clash between the President and Congress. Rather, the Court carefully based its decision on the conflict between "the Art. II powers of the President" and the "function of the courts under Art. III," holding that "the legitimate needs of the judicial process" outweigh the "presumptive privilege for Presidential communications."

The Court advanced two major justifications in support of its conclusion that to uphold the claim of executive privilege would "gravely impair the role of the courts under Art. III." First, it contended that by ordering "that all relevant and admissible evidence be produced," it would fulfill "the manifest duty of the courts to vindicate" the fifth amendment right to due process and the sixth amendment rights to compulsory process and confrontation of the defendants in the criminal prosecution from which the subpoena arose. If the case had involved claims by the defendants that these personal constitutional rights would be violated by the President's nondisclosure, then (as will be discussed shortly) under the Individual Rights Proposal, the issue should have been adjudicated. But, in *Nixon*, it was the Special Prosecutor who was seeking the evidence. The rights of the accused would surely not have been abridged by denying evidence to the prosecution to bolster its case against them.

The Court stated its second argument, to sustain its view that disclosure was necessary to preserve its authority under Article III, as follows: "The ends of criminal justice would be defeated if judgments were to be founded on a partial or speculative presentation of the facts. The very integrity of the judicial system and public confidence in the system depend on full disclosure of the facts, within the framework of the rules of evidence. To ensure that justice is done, it is imperative to the function of courts that compulsory process be available for the production of evidence needed either by the prosecution or by the defense."

The point is not free from difficulty. Prosecution of crime is ordinarily an executive, not a judicial, enterprise. Indeed, the *Nixon* Court itself concedes that "the Executive Branch has exclusive authority and absolute discretion to decide whether to prosecute a case." Although courts are vitally concerned with what evidence may be *admitted* in a criminal trial, it conventionally is the executive that determines what evidence is sought to be *introduced*.

Nonetheless, the Court's position is not without some force. The grand jury, which had already returned an indictment in the case, is traditionally considered an "appendage of the court."[261] The indictment having been filed, it could not be dismissed without judicial consent.[262] At trial, the court itself may summon witnesses.[263] In the peculiar circumstances of this prosecution, which involved shocking charges of corruption by the President's close advisers and in which President Nixon himself had been named as an unindicted coconspirator, the very integrity of the judicial system and public confidence in the system might well have been impaired—and the federal judiciary perceived "as an independent agency of whitewash"[264]—if "critical and

admissible evidence had been withheld by the President to insure a verdict of 'acquittal' which might otherwise be utterly
unwarranted."[265]

Whether *Nixon* correctly held that the "judicial Power" of Article III would have been constitutionally infringed by a contrary
decision is beyond the scope of discussion. As we shall see in
chapter 6, the Court properly held *this* separation of powers
issue to be justiciable.

The constitutional issue of separation of powers that *Nixon*
clearly neither addressed nor resolved—and which the Separation Proposal urges should be beyond judicial purview—centers
on the issue of Mr. Jaworski's authority to challenge the President's refusal to disclose the information demanded in the subpoena. The President contended that since his decision was
"final in determining what evidence is to be used in a given
criminal case," the "matter was an intra-branch dispute between
a subordinate and superior officer of the Executive Branch and
hence not subject to judicial resolution."

The Special Prosecutor's mandate was contained in a unique
regulation issued by the Attorney General. It granted the Special
Prosecutor complete control of investigation and prosecution of
offenses arising out of the Watergate scandal, including the authority "to contest the assertion of 'Executive Privilege.'" It
further provided that "in exercising this authority, the Special
Prosecutor will have the greatest degree of independence that is
consistent with the Attorney General's statutory accountability
for all matters falling within the jurisdiction of the Department of
Justice," and that, "in accordance with assurances given by the
President to the Attorney General that the President will not
exercise his Constitutional powers to effect the discharge of the
Special Prosecutor or to limit the independence that he is hereby
given, the Special Prosecutor will not be removed from his
duties except for extraordinary improprieties on his part and
without the President's first consulting the Majority and the
Minority Leaders and Chairmen and ranking Minority Members
of the Judiciary Committees of the Senate and House of Representatives and ascertaining that their consensus is in accord with
his proposed action."

In response to the President's contention, Mr. Jaworski might have fashioned an argument along the following lines: The Attorney General's authority to conduct criminal litigation for the United States and to appoint subordinates to aid him therewith derives from statutes enacted by Congress[266] pursuant to its power under Art. II, §2. The regulation, in which the Attorney General delegated the authority to the Special Prosecutor to pursue Watergate offenses, was issued pursuant to those statutes. Thus, the Special Prosecutor served subject to statutory, not presidential, authority—a fact underlined by this extraordinary regulation's proviso that, on the President's own word, the Special Prosecutor would not be removed without the consensus of designated congressional leaders. Conceding that the Special Prosecutor is an officer of the executive branch, "it is well accepted that Congress may impose on [such] officers powers and duties to make decisions and carry out programs which are not subject to the President's control."[267] Since the statutorily authorized regulation has never been amended or revoked by an official properly empowered by Congress to do so, the President is bound by it. Therefore, President Nixon's attempt to rescind Mr. Jaworski's authority to contest the claim of executive privilege infringed on the power of Congress.

Although, at least at one point, the Special Prosecutor appeared to approach this line of argument,[268] he explicitly disclaimed invoking the contention "that the regulations creating a Special Prosecutor's office . . . reflect a statutory regime imposed by the Legislative Branch."[269] If he had, and if the President had replied—as he did in a different context—that "the ultimate authority over all executive branch decisions is, under Article II of the Constitution, vested exclusively in the President,"[270] then under the Separation Proposal the Court should have held the issue to be nonjusticiable. In the context of the Nixon case, for reasons to be assayed below,[271] the Court should have then accepted the President's view and gone on to determine whether it conflicts with other constitutional principles that were properly adjudicable.

The Nixon Court's rationale for upholding the Special Prosecutor's authority to contest President Nixon's claim of executive privilege is somewhat opaque in terms of constitutional power. The Court adopted both parties' characterization of the issue as being one of an "intra-branch dispute," thus never confronting the potential legislative-executive separation of powers problem outlined above. Also following the lead of the Special Prosecutor's brief, the Court considered the matter under the heading of "Justiciability"; whether or not this caused the issue to be "buried and lost, subsumed in the mere determination of the Special Prosecutor's standing to sue and the justiciability of his claim,"[272] the Court at least partially obscured its substantive ramifications.

The Court's reasoning was brief. It began by stating that "the mere assertion of an 'intra-branch dispute,' without more, has never operated to defeat federal jurisdiction." It ended by ruling that the setting of the case assured "that concrete adverseness" necessary to bring it "within the traditional scope of Art. III power." In between these unimpeachable edicts, the Court first recounted the history of the Attorney General's regulation empowering the Special Prosecutor and then held that "so long as this regulation is extant it has the force of law"—relying on *United States ex rel. Accardi v. Shaughnessy*,[273] *Service v. Dulles*,[274] and *Vitarelli v. Seaton*.[275] Under these cases, the *Nixon* opinion proceeds, although "it is theoretically possible for the Attorney General to amend or revoke the regulation defining the Special Prosecutor's authority . . . he has not done so" and "so long as this regulation remains in force, the Executive Branch is bound by it."

The unanswered question is the *constitutional* basis for this conclusion. The three cases cited do indeed hold that so long as a cabinet officer's regulation remains operative he is bound to observe it even though he could achieve a result contrary to it if he were first to amend it. But the rule of these decisions does not rest on the Constitution. As accurately observed by Justice Frankfurter, the precept is a "judicially evolved rule of administrative law."[276] In none of these cases did the Court address either the question of whether the "executive Power" enables a member of the President's cabinet to ignore his own regulation or whether his doing so abridges any constitutional right of individuals adversely affected thereby.

It may well be that the complainants in those cases—one challenging deportation, the others dismissal from government employment that allegedly contravened existing regulations—could persuasively contend that their personal rights to due process had been violated. Indeed, if Special Prosecutor Jaworski had been fired in breach of the Attorney General's regulation in *Nixon*—as his predecessor had been—he would have had a sufficient personal interest to contend that his individual right to due process had been similarly infringed.[277] But such a due process claim on Jaworski's part in the *Nixon* case itself is extremely tenuous at best and was neither advanced by him nor decided by the Court.

In *Nixon*, however, the President—unlike the cabinet officers in *Accardi, Service,* and *Vitarelli*—explicitly defended his position by invoking Article II, arguing that his constitutional authority afforded him plenary control over the Special Prosecutor. Since the Court apparently conceded that the President could have his way either by instructing the Attorney General to rescind the regulation or, failing that, by appointing a more cooperative Attorney General to do so, then what constitutional provisions forbade the President from employing the means he chose—that is, asserting his will through counsel in these proceedings—to accomplish the result? It may be that the Court, albeit implicitly and perhaps unconsciously, held that, under the extraordinary circumstances of this case, President Nixon's effort to restrict the Special Prosecutor's independence was an attempt to do indirectly what he had promised the nation (and Congress)[278] he would not do directly, and therefore simply exceeded (or abused) his power under Article II. If so, there being no resolution of a legislative-executive conflict, there is no incompatibility with the Separation Proposal.

Nonetheless—wholly apart from the substantive merit of this explanation for the *Nixon* Court's ruling[279]—there is much to be said for the view that, with no individual constitutional rights issue at stake, the Court should have treated the President's assertion of power as nonjusticiable, and then, having accepted that premise, proceeded to measure it against the contention that such exercise of authority in this instance collided with Article III. For the rationale, examined above,[280] that lends support to the *Nixon* decision's articulated constitutional ruling is equally applicable here.

2. Nixon v. Administrator of General Services

Nixon v. Administrator of General Services[281] presents greater difficulties for the Separation Proposal. In upholding the facial validity of a congressional enactment that directed the Administrator to take custody (and to have government archivists screen) all papers, documents, memorandums, transcripts, and tape recordings that former President Nixon had accumulated during his terms of office, all the Justices addressed the question of whether Congress had unconstitutionally intruded on executive autonomy. This is contrary to the Separation Proposal. But the case presented a peculiar problem. The statute that was challenged as being violative of the division of powers precept was atypical—indeed, unique—in that it did not regulate the presidency as such by directly affecting official actions of the incumbent. Thus, unlike the legislation in the *Myers* and *Humphrey's* cases, the law did not restrict the chief executive's power to remove a subordinate officer; nor, as would an act of Congress forbidding all executive agreements without some legislative concurrence, did this statute hamper the President's ability to conduct foreign relations. Nor did this law—which was signed by President Ford and supported in the litigation by President Carter—apply to all presidents, or even to all persons who had been president; rather, it concerned only former President Nixon. Given this set of circumstances, the normal incentives and assurances of political self-interest that underlie the Separation Proposal—which advocates that when Congress allegedly interferes with the proper functioning of the President the Court should hold the constitutional issue to be nonjusticiable and rely on the political process for a fair and trustworthy resolution—are considerably weakened.

Nonetheless, the Court should not have decided the separation of powers question. To the extent that congressional action of this kind may actually injure the office of the presidency or impair the effective discharge of executive duties, the incumbent can be counted on to use the vast arsenal of protective devices at his disposal to guard against it. For example, in this case if President Ford, who held office at the time of the bill's enactment, felt that archival scrutiny of his predecessor's materials would "stand as a veritable sword of Damocles over every succeeding President and his advisors,"[282] then he could have vetoed it; if President Carter had so believed, then he could have directed Mr. Nixon—as he may instruct any existing or former official of the executive branch—to assert executive privilege and then defend this position as the Separation Proposal contemplates. For, unlike the fifth amendment's privilege against compelled self-incrimination which protects distinct interests of the individual against government oppression, the purpose of the constitutionally derived executive privilege of nondisclosure is to secure the institution of the presidency against invasion by its sister branches of government.[283]

This does not ignore the "political and historical reality"[284] that "there is at least some risk that political, and even personal, antagonisms could motivate Congress and the President to join in a legislative seizure and public exposure of a former President's papers without due regard to the long-range implications of such action for the Art. II functions of the Chief Executive."[285] But, especially when such action is directed against only one person, or even a handful of prior officeholders, the value of judicial review will be substantially preserved under the Individual Rights Proposal through constitutional provisions such as the bill of attainder prohibition or the equal protection clause. Indeed, wholly apart from the substantive merits of the Court's ruling (which is beyond the scope of our consideration), the bill of attainder issue was invoked and properly adjudicated in the instant case, as were Mr. Nixon's additional individual liberties claims that archival review of his personal communications and the records of his political activities abridged his right of privacy and freedom of association.

3. Executive Privilege and Individual Rights

Before leaving the subject of executive privilege, it is important to recognize that the constitutional issue may arise—and, in fact, has often arisen—in the context of a genuine claim of infringement of personal constitutional liberty. (In addition, this potential exists when the assertion of privilege is legislative rather than executive—for example, an immunity argued by a house of Congress or one of its committees in response to a subpoena for documentary evidence gathered during the course of an investigation, often in closed session.)[286] These cases do *not* involve a direct contest between the President and Congress or an individual seeking to resist the infliction of injury by asserting the constitutional power of one political department against the other. Rather they concern a clash between the executive (or legislative) interest in secrecy and the independent personal rights of an individual before the court. Although it may well be that the "public interest"—however that is to be ascertained and measured—in executive disclosure is greater when Congress demands the information than when an individual seeks it in litigation, the Separation Proposal permits judicial intervention in the latter instance but not in the former because individual constitutional rights, unlike the Congress's constitutional interests, are not well protected by the political process. (Whether the judiciary should also determine the existence or scope of an alleged constitutional privilege of the President [or Congress] when the individual's need for the information does not reach constitutional proportions[287] is beyond the subject of discussion.)

a. Criminal Prosecutions

The issue may be presented in a number of adjudicative contexts. One occurs when a defendant in a federal criminal prosecution contends that the government's withholding of certain information (such as the identity or background of an adverse witness, or a communication between certain government officials) so prejudices his opportunity to defend as to constitute a deprivation of fifth amendment procedural due process or the sixth amendment right of confrontation and cross-examination. If the Court agrees that conviction under these circumstances would abridge the personal constitutional right,[288] and if the prosecution's claim of privilege is clearly alleged—by the President himself or by a delegee that the Court agrees is properly authorized—to rest on the Constitution (rather than on some statutory or common law basis),[289] then the Court could proceed along one of several courses. It could decline to make an inquiry into the nature of, or necessity for, the government's claim of privilege (even when the immunity is grounded merely in a statute or the common law rather than in the Constitution), and remedy the defendant's constitutional injury by simply dismissing the prosecution or—if it satisfies the security of the individual constitutional rights—by resolving the specific issue related to the nondisclosure in the defendant's favor.[290] This may accurately be characterized as indirect coercion on the executive. But the Court may not permit its process to be employed in the executive's behalf to impose criminal sanctions against an individual unless the personal guarantees afforded by the Constitution are met.

The *Nixon* decision's aversion to a criminal prosecution's being "totally frustrated"[291] may well be read, however, as requiring the judiciary to assess the particular claim of executive privilege. Although the *Nixon* Court confined its analysis to the resolution of the conflict between the President's authority under Article II and the "judicial Power" of Article III—an issue, it should be observed, that is potentially present in all the situations now being considered—the Court's rationale would seem to be no less applicable when the constitutional provision in competition with the executive claim of power is one securing personal liberty. Thus, if the executive's claim for secrecy is based on nothing more than a "generalized privilege of confidentiality" respecting executive branch communications, as it was in *Nixon,* it would seem, at a minimum, that the "constitutional need for relevant evidence in criminal trials" would call for an in camera judicial examination of the allegedly privileged information. The *Nixon* Court spoke of "a presumptive privilege for Presidential communications." Although the meaning of this presumption requires further judicial elucidation in other contexts, *Nixon* appears to say that, rather than "a weighing of the public interest protected by the privilege against the public interests that would be served by disclosure in a particular case,"[292] this presumption gives way so long as the evidence is "relevant and admissible" (and "not otherwise procurable").[293] Indeed, in these circumstances, *Nixon* may even demand—as members of the Court have strongly suggested in the analogous context of a habeas corpus proceeding[294]—that through its contempt power the Court seek directly to compel production from the executive official in possession.

If, however, the executive's refusal to disclose is based on a "need to protect military, diplomatic or sensitive national security secrets," *Nixon* points in the opposite direction. True, a "footnote near the end of Chief Justice Burger's opinion assimilates claims of military and diplomatic secrets to those of general confidentiality for the purposes of the availability of an in camera procedure."[295] But, in the text, the Court reaffirms the view of *United States v. Reynolds*,[296] that if the government satisfies the Court "that there is a reasonable danger that compulsion of the evidence will expose military matters which, in the interest of national security, should not be divulged," then the Court should not even examine the material in camera, much less order its production, no matter how important to the defendant. In these circumstances, the personal rights of the accused must be vindicated by the remedies referred to above.

b. Civil Litigation

Where the United States is the plaintiff in a civil suit, a similar analysis should obtain. If the government wishes to restrict an individual's liberty by means of an injunction or secure his property by claiming damages but, at the same time, refuses to submit information needed by the individual defendant, then if in the Court's judgment the government's refusal to disclose is constitutionally based and the handicap to the defendant is so great as to amount to a denial of due process, the Court may—

without questioning either the constitutional validity or the public necessity of the assertion of executive privilege—render judgment for defendant or resolve the related substantive issue in his favor. An existing Federal Rule of Civil Procedure and a once proposed Federal Rule of Evidence spell out a number of alternatives.[297] This approach relieves the judiciary of the imposing burden of examining the sensitive information itself and evaluating the government's claim of need for secrecy—and thus sidesteps the risk of confrontation between judicial and executive branches. It rests the final constitutional decision as to privilege with the political department yet, at the same time, safeguards against violation of individual constitutional rights. Whether, in the context of a civil suit rather than a criminal prosecution, the Court should (or must) employ the alternate procedure called for by the *Nixon* decision is as yet uncertain. But, as discussed above, that method as well as the one just described will satisfy the Court's obligation to intervene in behalf of constitutionally secured personal liberties.

Of the two approaches outlined, only the procedure advanced in *Nixon* is pragmatically available in the context of purely private civil litigation when one party seeks to obtain information from the government and the government resists on a properly asserted constitutional claim of privilege. In theory, the Court could automatically accept the government's reply and, if it then determined that the encumbrance thereby imposed on the private litigant resulted in a denial of due process,[298] award monetary damages against the government. This parallels the judicial remedy for an assertion of executive privilege against a civil plaintiff's discovery attempt when he is suing the government. But, wholly apart from historical notions of sovereign immunity that would separate these cases from those in which the government is the moving party, the practical fiscal impact of such a course may call for its rejection.

Rather, in these situations, the Court must sagaciously and prudently enter the fray, for, at base, personal constitutional rights and not simply the competing interests of the political branches of government are at stake. The Court must carefully appraise the facts underlying the government's plea—probably employing the device of in camera inspection—and, engaging in the traditional weighing process used when individual liberties are in issue, must finally determine whether the individual's interest is overcome by the diplomatic or military need for government secrecy or by whatever other state interest is advanced in justification.[299] The Court may hold that the government should prevail and, in doing so, may conclude that, because evaluation of its claim for privilege is so sensitive and complex as to be judicially unmanageable, the constitutional issue should be treated as a "political question" to be decided by the political branches. But this type of "nonjusticiability" determination is very different from that suggested by both the Separation and Federalism Proposals. In deferring to the political branches in the present context—one involving alleged deprivation of personal constitutional rights independent of a separation of powers infringement—the Court is not relegating the constitutional question to the political branches because, at bottom, it is their respective interests that are at play and thus the political process may be trusted for fair resolution. Rather, although the Court does not formally place its imprimatur on the substantive conclusion that the government interest in secrecy outweighs the competing constitutional freedoms of the individual, the Court should recognize that it effectively does so by entrusting personal interests to a system that affords little assurance that they will be sympathetically considered.

If, on the other hand, the Court rules against the government's assertion of privilege and holds that nondisclosure would violate due process, the Court must then choose an appropriate remedy for noncompliance with its divulgence order. When the government is a party to the litigation (as defendant in the setting being considered), the Court may simply rule against it on the issue in the case related to the evidence withheld. But when the United States is not a party, how should the Court proceed? Until 1978, there was no recorded instance of a federal court using its contempt power to compel an officer of the executive branch to produce evidence.[300] Perhaps the Court will continue to avoid such potentially dangerous confrontations—which might be readily escalated by a President who, having ordered a subordinate not

to disclose, could simply pardon the subordinate from the strictures of the contempt—by instead, in this narrow situation,
awarding monetary damages against the government in fulfillment of the individual's constitutional right. As a matter of wise
policy, whether this is preferable to contempt falls beyond the
scope of discussion here. But, once it determines that government action (or inaction) violates personal constitutional rights,
under the Individual Rights Proposal, the Court must seek recti-
fication in some way.

E. Directly Conflicting Assertions of Power between the Political Branches That Affect Individual Interests

Most of the major decisions that we have considered—*Youngstown, U.S. District Court, Zemel v. Rusk, Debs,
Neagle, New York Times,* and the *Nixon* cases—did not present
the Court with directly conflicting assertions of constitutional
power by each of the political departments. Although the *Myers*
and *Humphrey's* cases did, we have seen that they did not ultimately require the Court, after treating the constitutional claims
as nonjusticiable, to decide the cases by effectively vindicating
the position of one branch and submerging that of the other.
Discussion of the Separation Proposal's application to hypothetical variants in the *Nixon* decisions did concern such a problem. Only a very few actual cases of this kind have ever arisen,
but a fertile imagination may readily conceive a very long
string—especially in regard to the matter of executive privilege.
Dispatch of the real cases is relatively uncomplicated, but the
imagined ones may present exceedingly intricate difficulties.

1. Executive Assignment of Statutory Authority

To begin with an example of the former group, a
number of cases have arisen—some reaching the Supreme
Court—in which an act of Congress designates a particular
executive officer to enforce its provisions but a presidential order
assigns the task to another officer.[301] Individuals to whom the

statute has been applied have resisted, sometimes successfully, on the ground that the presidential transfer is invalid. In most of these cases, the executive has relied exclusively on statutory authority[302]—an occasion in which the Separation Proposal is inoperative. But if the question is put whether the "executive Power" includes this authority (and has therefore been infringed by the statute) or whether it does not (thus making the executive order violative of Congress's constitutional prerogatives), the Court should hold the issue to be nonjusticiable. Under the Separation Proposal, the Court should accept the executive's conduct as valid and, since the litigant's only constitutional claim is one of separation of powers, uphold enforcement of the statute against him.

2. Pardon and Commutation Power

Another set of cases involves the President's constitutional "Power to grant Reprieves and Pardons." In *Ex parte Garland*,[303] a post–Civil War act of Congress conditioned the practice of law in the federal courts on the applicant's taking an oath that, among other things, he had not borne arms against the United States. Garland, who had been a Confederate sympathizer, sought admission to the federal bar. Although he was unable to take the prescribed oath, Garland had received a "full pardon" from President Johnson. Under the Separation Proposal, the Court is in no way prevented from interpreting the intention of both the statute and the pardon to determine whether they are compatible. If the case cannot be resolved on that basis, however, and if the issue is then posed whether the President's pardon power overrides Congress's regulatory power or vice versa, the Court should treat the issue as nonjusticiable rather than discuss it on the merits as the Court did in *Garland*. That judicial excursus in favor of the pardon was dicta, however, and *Garland* therefore does not stand as a precedent against the Separation Proposal. The *Garland* Court finally held that, irrespective of the pardon, the statute constituted a bill of attainder and ex post facto law, and thus abridged personal liberties secured by the Constitution.

If we assume, in *Garland,* that there was no infringement of individual constitutional rights, adoption of the course of action urged by the Separation Proposal does not reveal whether or not the Court should order Garland to be admitted to the bar—a result that we have now assumed has been mandated by the President's pardon yet forbidden by the congressional statute. In those unlikely circumstances of irreconcilable conflict between the political branches that impose on the immediate interests of individuals, the Court should seek to limit the impact of its unavoidable involvement as much as possible. The Court should attempt to dispose of cases otherwise properly before it in a manner that best approximates the result that would be produced without its participation as an original matter. In this process of striving to preserve the status quo, the Court should resolve any doubts against employing its authority to impose restrictions against the individual on behalf of either Congress or the executive. Thus, in the suppositional extension of the *Garland* case that we have posited—Garland not having taken an oath that Congress has stipulated power generally to require—the Court should refuse Garland's petition. Although Garland would not be admitted to the bar, the Court would not have imposed the limitation. Rather, the Justices—by refusing to side with either Congress or the President—would simply allow Congress's restrictions to stand. This, in short, is the result that would occur in the absence of judicial involvement.

Several other hypothetical situations, rooted in actual cases implicating the pardon power, may be used as further illustrations. If Congress were clearly to provide that property, seized as belonging to an enemy, should be returned only if its owner proves that he committed no offense, and if a conceded offender bases his claim on a presidential pardon that undeniably was intended to permit his reacquisition of the property, the Court should hold the conflicting constitutional power assertions to be nonjusticiable and—since, apart from the pardon, Congress is plainly empowered to confiscate enemy property—refuse to order its return.[304] But if Congress were to provide that persons with prior convictions should receive increased punishment for subsequent offenses, and if a person who is now convicted presents a presidential pardon for an earlier offense that unmistakably purports to immunize him from the effect of the statute, the Court—although abstaining from resolution of the constitutional power clash—should *not* impose the greater sentence.[305] Judicial preservation of the status quo and the Court's disinclination to employ its authority to impose burdens on individuals that are unobtainable without its auspices distinguish this case from the enemy property situation set forth above.

The recent case of *Schick v. Reed*[306] affords another illustrative springboard. After being convicted of murder by court-martial, Schick was sentenced to death pursuant to a statute that authorized either capital punishment or life imprisonment (with the possibility of parole). President Eisenhower commuted the sentence to life imprisonment, but with no eligibility for parole. Schick subsequently challenged the condition on the ground that, since it was not authorized by statute, the President had engaged in lawmaking and thus exceeded the pardon power granted by Article II. Since this part of Schick's argument conceded that Congress could have imposed the no-parole condition without violating his individual constitutional rights, then, under the Separation Proposal, the Justices, rather than addressing the separation of powers issue (as they did), should have simply accepted—but not endorsed—the executive's assertion of constitutional authority and dismissed Schick's contention. But since the Court did ultimately reject Schick's claim, the result comports with the Separation Proposal.

The same analysis should obtain if, unlike the situation in *Schick,* Congress had explicitly (or implicitly) forbidden the imposition of a life sentence with no chance of parole. (This arguably was the case in *Hoffa v. Saxbe,*[307] which concerned President Nixon's commutation of James Hoffa's sentence on condition that he refrain from holding a position of union leadership despite Congress's previous refusal to enact such a disqualification.)[308] It may well be, as *Schick* acknowledged,[309] that just as some legislatively imposed conditions on parole may abridge personal liberties secured by the Constitution, so, too, certain strings attached to a presidential pardon may also impinge on individual rights.[310] Thus, if the terms of a reprieve actually ag-

gravate the punishment that Congress has set forth for the offense, there are constitutional prohibitions on the actions of all
government agencies that may be called into play.[311] Indeed, it
may well be that, at least in certain circumstances, denying defendant the choice of either accepting or rejecting the executive
grant of clemency might violate his constitutional rights.[312] In
the absence of a claim of this sort, however, the Court should
preserve the status quo by rejecting the plea of the recipient of a
conditional presidential pardon whose sentence as commuted
could validly have been designated by Congress. If Congress
disapproves of the result, it may, of course, alter it by appropriate
legislation.

3. Executive Privilege Hypotheticals

Cases, mostly imaginary, within the context of a claim
of executive privilege afford a final set of examples that fall across
the full spectrum. If, as has actually come to pass,[313] a congressional committee were to seek enforcement of a subpoena
against an executive officer who has declined to disclose information under direct order of the President, the Court should
hold the constitutional issue to be nonjusticiable and refuse the
injunction. (An equivalent case would be presented if, pursuant
to the unambiguous statement of Congress, the Administrator of
General Services sought a judicial order that the incumbent chief
executive hand over his presidential papers and the President
resisted by claiming that this contradicted his constitutional
executive privilege.)

Similarly, if, pursuant to an existing federal statute,[314] Congress were to certify to the appropriate United States Attorney (or
to the Attorney General) that an executive officer, for the same
reason, has refused to testify before or deliver documents to a
congressional committee—and if Congress in some unlikely way
were to manage to persuade this presidentially appointed prosecutor to bring criminal contempt charges (perhaps after a change
of administration), the Court should refuse to convict. (These
events would be more likely, of course, with the presence of a
congressionally created special prosecutor.) The analysis paral-

lels that in the increased punishment illustration above. (An analogous situation would be posed if Congress were to create a defense to a statutory crime—for example, no person shall be convicted of draft evasion if his refusal to submit is based on the conduct of executive sponsored hostilities without a formal declaration of war—but the President continued to prosecute on the ground that this provision infringed his constitutional powers. If the executive branch, having been rebuffed by the courts, were to rely on self-help to seize and imprison the unwilling draftee, then the Court should be open to the latter's petition for release on the ground that his summary detention without any judicial participation abridges his individual right against deprivation of liberty without due process of law.)[315]

Finally, if Congress were to take the matter into its own hands by having its sergeant at arms arrest and incarcerate the recalcitrant executive officer who was relying on a presidentially directed claim of privilege, and if the official sought habeas corpus, the Court—if it had only the constitutional issue of separation of powers before it, rather than some independent procedural due process claim which challenged the long-assumed congressional authority to imprison contemnors for the duration of the legislative session[316]—should decide that the case is nonjusticiable and deny the writ. This leaves matters as they were before the Court's process was invoked; the official was originally incarcerated without the Court's participation. Although it must be conceded that this result smacks of injustice, such a case is highly unlikely to arise. While both the Senate and House in the past have used this technique to hold private citizens in contempt for refusing to cooperate with legislative investigations,[317] in the persuasive judgment of Joseph Bishop, despite serious sounding threats from sundry legislators, "Congress has never in the past been willing to push matters to the point of dispatching the Sergeant at Arms to cleave a path through the Secret Service cordon and seize the person of the President, or even one of his subordinates. Not even Theodore Roosevelt, at his most pugnacious, [or, it may be added, Richard Nixon, at his most obdurate] could succeed in provoking the Senate into such extreme measures. It is more than likely that Congress never will resort to them."[318]

Our history instead reveals that one side or the other will desist. Thus, when the Senate threatened to imprison an executive officer in Theodore Roosevelt's time for refusing to deliver certain data, Arthur Schlesinger reports that "T.R. with great relish ordered the papers to the White House and challenged the Senate to come and get them."[319] It never did. On the other hand, Philip Kurland recounts two encounters during Watergate in which the executive submitted: "[I]mmediately after Alexander Butterfield had told the Select Committee's staff of the existence of the White House tapes, he proposed to take off for Russia on Federal Aviation Administration business. When he was told that his testimony was wanted immediately before the committee in full session, he replied that he could not come because of this previous engagement. Thereupon Senator Ervin sent him a message: 'Tell Mr. Butterfield that if he is not here this afternoon I will send the sergeant at arms to fetch him.' Wherefore Butterfield was voluntarily present to tell the world the story of the existence of the White House tapes, a story that ultimately led to the first resignation of an American president.

"Senator Ervin had earlier responded in a similar tone when President Nixon told his White House staff that they should not attend the hearings at the behest of the committee. Then, too, the putative witnesses backed down when Ervin announced he would cause them to be arrested by the sergeant at arms, if necessary. Fortunately, it was not necessary. The self-help of a Senate sergeant at arms is a puny force against executive branch soldiery. As Senator Baker was said to have observed, the sergeant at arms couldn't get beyond the White House gates if he had to."[320]

If the most extreme circumstances were, indeed, to come to pass with the individual held in the Capitol jail, and, with the knowledge that judicial resolution was unavailable, the political branches still reached no accommodation, then the likelihood of a court order obtaining the prisoner's release is even scantier than it was in *Ex parte Merryman*. Although a political impasse of this kind is virtually unimaginable, if it did occur, the Court should abstain. Even if the conflict between the President and Congress burdens an individual, the clash is nonetheless between the two branches, not between the individual and government as a whole. Under the Separation Proposal, the resolution of all constitutional interbranch disputes is entrusted to the political branches themselves.

F. FOREIGN AFFAIRS

The matter of the nation's conduct of foreign relations has provided a particularly fruitful source of conflict between the two political departments as to their respective constitutional power. It contains many illustrations, both in litigated cases in which individual interests have been affected by national regulatory action as well as outside the judicial arena, of constitutional issues falling clearly within the separation of powers category. Even accepting the expansive realm that the Court has, on several occasions, stated as being constitutionally granted to the President in the maintenance of the country's military and international affairs,[321] legitimate questions arise whether action that is undertaken by the executive alone transgresses the boundaries of Congress's domain.

1. Executive Agreements

Several such instances have concerned the constitutionally unmentioned executive agreement—employed as early as 1817 by President Monroe and used to initiate such major ventures as Secretary of State Hay's famous Open Door Policy for the Far East under President McKinley. The Supreme Court has never ruled on the issue of whether such pacts, entered into by the President alone, poach on the Senate's constitutional prerogatives—although some Justices have adverted to the matter[322]—and, on one occasion, only the most faithful and energetic adherence to the precept of avoiding unnecessary constitutional decision enabled the full bench to stop short of doing so.[323] An especially poignant instance, never litigated, occurred when Theodore Roosevelt—after the Senate failed to ratify a proposed treaty with the Dominican Republic that he had sent to the Capitol—simply incorporated its terms into an executive protocol.[324]

Under the Separation Proposal, no matter how persuasive the substance of the argument may seem,[325] the ultimate constitutional question should be held to be nonjusticiable. So, too, should such issues as whether the President or Congress is authorized to terminate a treaty (as did President Carter himself with respect to Taiwan), or to acquire realty for the nation (as did President Jefferson alone with the Louisiana Territory),[326] or to dispose of property belonging to the United States (as did President Carter and the Senate by the Panama Canal Treaty),[327] or to determine the rules of governance for American territories,[328] or to confiscate enemy property within the country's borders in time of war.[329] The supporting reasons require no further reiteration.

2. Legislative Veto

No area has provoked more presidential assertions of congressional usurpation of the executive's constitutional power than that of foreign affairs. For example, in 1950, President Truman expressed the view that a legislative directive to make specified loans to Spain unconstitutionally invaded his domain and thus elected to treat the statute's mandatory language as simply authorizing him to make the loans.[330]

At least until recently, however, most of the battles have been fought over the constitutional propriety of the "legislative veto," a device equally applicable to matters of exclusively domestic concern. The mechanism takes various forms. It may require a resolution of both houses of Congress—or of one house, or even of a single committee, subcommittee, or chairman—before previously authorized executive or administrative action may take effect; or it may provide that earlier delegated action of the executive branch or of an independent regulatory agency may be implemented only if it is not disapproved by such a resolution within a designated period of time after it has been specifically

proposed by the President or the administrative agency; or a
statute may provide that the effect of delegated action may be
terminated by joint resolution.[331] Employed increasingly by
Congress, legislative vetoes have been attached to nearly two
hundred statutes, the majority coming since 1968.[332] And the
impact of legislative vetoes promises to grow—as illustrated in
the field of foreign affairs by recent efforts to subject almost all
executive agreements to congressional review,[333] and in the
domestic arena by a seriously considered current proposal that
would authorize legislative rejection of "any rule or regulation to
be used in the administration or implementation of any law of the
United States or any program established by or under such a
law."[334]

The charge of unconstitutional interference with executive
prerogative has been voiced since the time of President Wilson.[335] Franklin Roosevelt opined that a provision for repeal of
his authority under the Lend-Lease Act of 1943 by concurrent
resolution of both houses unconstitutionally impinged on the
President's veto power which could otherwise be used against
any bill that would rescind an earlier statute.[336] Presidents Nixon
and Ford both vetoed bills containing "concurrent resolution"
provisions because they believed the bills to be unconstitutional.[337] Presidents Truman, Eisenhower, Kennedy,
Johnson, and Nixon all contended that the "committee veto" was
a clear infringement of the "executive Power"—Truman,
Eisenhower, and Johnson each rejected bills for this reason;[338]
Kennedy and Johnson treated the provision as merely a legislative request for information;[339] and Nixon stated simply that he
would disregard it.[340] President Ford spoke similarly; in signing
a bill containing a "one-house veto" provision, he explained that
it was "a nullity."[341] Finally, in his first year in office, President
Carter began by signing bills containing legislative veto clauses
while expressing serious doubts about their constitutional compatibility with his veto power and his authority to execute the
laws; later in 1977 he disapproved one measure on the ground
that its legislative veto provision invaded his constitutional prerogatives and accepted another while stating his intention to
treat its legislative veto as a "report and wait" directive;[342] by

mid-1978, Carter "served notice on Capitol Hill . . . that he considers the legislative veto unconstitutional and that he doesn't feel legally bound to comply when Congress takes that route to overturn acts of his administration."[343]

This area of controversy also affords additional evidence of the tendency of the political departments to shun ultimate confrontations. For example, on two occasions, President Eisenhower threatened to ignore committee veto clauses until they were judicially approved. In one of these instances, Congress retreated by replacing the provision; in the other, the Defense Department complied with Congress's mandate despite the President's protestations.[344] When, as indicated above, Presidents Kennedy and Johnson sought to read the offending provision liberally but the House appropriations subcommittee interpreted the statute as written and, pursuant thereto, voted to disapprove several contemplated foreign aid projects, the Agency for International Development abandoned them.[345] And, despite President Carter's strongly stated recent posture on the matter, at the same time his chief domestic adviser reported "that 'as a matter of comity' the White House would continue to abide by legislative vetoes under the Arms Export Control Act, which allows Congress to block weapons sales by action of both houses"; indeed, the President himself "stopped short of saying that he would ignore congressional vetoes," indicating instead that he was only "trying to dissuade Congress from attaching such provisions to future bills" by observing that the "inclusion of such a provision in a bill will be an important factor in my decision to sign or to veto it."[346] Finally, the practice of "reprogramming" appropriated funds which has grown up between the Department of Defense and certain congressional committees—by which executive officials regularly confer with committee members to gain approval for shifting money between projects within a budget account[347]—further illustrates the amicable interbranch cooperation that can take place in this area of constitutional contention.

Several cases in the federal courts have raised the constitutional separation of powers questions, but, as yet, apart from a dictum by Justice White,[348] a divided opinion of the Court of the Claims,[349] and the view of one judge of the United States Court of Appeals for the District of Columbia Circuit,[350] there has been no authoritative judicial pronouncement. A wide range of constitutional objections has been leveled against the legislative veto. The basis of one of these—that the device improperly transfers congressional power to fractional parts of the legislature—is discussed at the end of this chapter. Another objection—that the mechanism usurps the judiciary's traditional function of defining the scope of statutorily delegated authority—is the subject of chapter 6. But the major challenges to the practice, by which Congress has sought to enhance the accountability of the executive and administrative process while at the same time continuing to delegate rulemaking responsibility quite broadly, concern division of power between the political branches.[351] Under the Separation Proposal, these issues—although subtle, intriguing, and hotly debated—should be held to be nonjusticiable.

3. Individual Rights Issues

Closely analogous to the matter of executive privilege, constitutional issues that are independent of the separation of powers and plainly fall within the category of individual rights have often arisen in criminal, quasi-criminal, and civil cases implicating the nation's conduct of military and foreign affairs. Here again, under the Individual Rights Proposal, the Court's approach should be wholly different from that urged in regard to the class of issues just discussed. In the context of a federal criminal prosecution in which the defendant alleges an abridgment of personal constitutional liberty—exemplified by such cases as *Reid v. Covert,*[352] *Wilson v. Girard,*[353] and the "war crimes" hypothetical constructed earlier[354]—the Court must itself, in the course of exercising its power of judicial review, determine whether the government interest is substantial enough to overcome the individual constitutional rights claim. Thus, in *Reid,* the Court upheld the contention of an army wife living on a military base abroad that her trial by court-martial for murder of her husband would violate her constitutional right to trial by jury. In *Girard*, the Court rejected the claim of a soldier stationed abroad that his trial in the courts of the country in which he was located for a crime against a citizen of that country violated due process. The Court apparently believed that a ruling in Girard's favor "would have thrown a major roadblock into the arrangements for stationing American troops on foreign soil and substantially interfered with the powers of Congress and the president to handle both foreign and military affairs."[355] Whether the result of the Court's weighing process in these cases was substantially correct or desirable is beyond consideration here—but the process itself is plainly called for by the Individual Rights Proposal.

a. Judicial Deference to Political Judgments

In the course of this process, the Court may on occasion—perhaps in the "war crimes" case—believe that the government's claim of critical importance for its challenged conduct, or the underlying facts needed to evaluate the claim, are so inherently entwined with large and complex matters of foreign policy as to fall realistically beyond the realm of intelligent judicial comprehension. If so, the Court may conclude that it must forthrightly accept the government's position that the individual's claim of constitutional liberty must succumb—and it may affix the "political question" label to this course of action. But, as was observed in reviewing this judicial characterization in the setting of executive privilege, wholly apart from the merits of this decision, it should be recognized for what it is—an effective ratification of a final political decision in rejection of a bona fide assertion of personal liberty and not a nonjusticiability determination of the kind that has been discussed throughout.

(1) Exclusion and deportation of aliens

This analysis may be vividly illustrated by the long line of "quasi-criminal" cases dealing with the exclusion and deportation of aliens. The Court has made it clear from the beginning that the national government's power over noncitizens is "an incident of sovereignty" and has held as a matter of its own constitutional interpretation that aliens seeking entry or resisting

deportation have no substantive constitutional rights whatever.[356] Wholly apart from the correctness of this interpretation,
the Court's unmistakable exercise of its power of judicial review
in these cases is not in conflict with the Separation Proposal.

The Court's position on the question of whether such aliens
are entitled to a certain minimum procedural due process has,
however, been somewhat less consistent. As to deportation, the
Court has established that some such procedural rights do
exist.[357] As to exclusion, however, the Court has *said* on a
number of occasions that "whatever the procedure authorized
by Congress is, it is due process as far as an alien denied entry is
concerned,"[358] again indicating the Court's own judgment on the
merits of this constitutional personal liberty claim. But Fritz
Scharpf's careful study of the cases shows that, from the early
1900s on, "while most cases continued to go for the government
on their merits, the Court seems to have assumed . . . that the
Fifth Amendment required a minimum of procedural due process even for the exclusion decision, and that to this extent judicial review was available to the alien."[359] Nonetheless, owing to
several extremely harsh decisions in the 1950s that denied entry
to aliens without a hearing,[360] Scharpf concludes that "the
majority position becomes tenable only if understood as a decision to accept without examination the Congressional determination of the Fifth-Amendment issue," that is, "as an application of the political question doctrine."[361] He offers a similar
explanation for several deportation decisions[362] that he finds
"indefensible as determinations of the [substantive] constitutional issues raised."[363]

Scharpf is probably right in describing what the Court *did* in
these cases and it may be helpful to characterize its actions as
falling under the broad "political question" heading. But the
hard fact is that the Court's opinions spoke to the merits of the
personal liberty claims. And this is as it should be, especially
because these litigants as a class are a paradigm of a politically
impotent minority. No matter how the Court's doctrine may be
analyzed or phrased, the judiciary should realistically bear final
responsibility for the decision. Although the Court may ultimately decide as a normative matter that certain action of the

political branches that rejects constitutional personal liberty claims should not be subject to judicial scrutiny—as it did in *Ludecke v. Watkins*[364] in permitting the summary deportation of an enemy alien—the Court should not do so under the misapprehension that these constitutional claims will ordinarily receive the same treatment in the political process as do considerations of federalism or separation of powers.

(2) Civil litigation

In the area of civil litigation in which the United States is a party, the case of *Chicago & Southern Air Lines, Inc. v. Waterman Steamship Corp.*[365]—in which the Court held that it would not examine the basis, no matter how allegedly arbitrary, for presidential grants and denials, pursuant to the Civil Aeronautics Act, of overseas route licenses to American air carriers—exemplifies the extreme deference the Court may pay to political decisions touching foreign policy even though individual constitutional rights may be at issue. The Court reasoned that "the President, both as Commander-in-Chief and as the Nation's organ for foreign affairs, has available intelligence services whose reports are not and ought not to be published to the world. It would be intolerable that courts, without the relevant information, should review and perhaps nullify actions of the Executive taken on information properly held secret. Nor can courts sit *in camera* in order to be taken into executive confidences. But even if courts could require full disclosure, the very nature of executive decisions as to foreign policy is political, not judicial. Such decisions are wholly confided by our Constitution to the political departments of the government, Executive and Legislative. They are delicate, complex, and involve large elements of prophecy. They are and should be undertaken only by those directly responsible to the people whose welfare they advance or imperil. They are decisions of a kind for which the Judiciary has neither aptitude, facilities nor responsibility and which has long been held to belong in the domain of political power not subject to judicial intrusion or inquiry."[366] Perhaps the Court was right in all particulars. Or perhaps it should, at a minimum, have required the President to assure that he had in fact exercised the judgment called for, or to articulate the reasons for his action, thus enabling the Court to reject any that it found to violate individual constitutional rights. But those issues go to the substance of such constitutional rights—in this context, to the scope of judicial superintendence that their security requires— and *not* to whether judicial review should operate at all. It is the latter condition with which the Separation Proposal is concerned.

The case of *Hijo v. United States*[367] is of particular interest in identifying the precise contours of the Separation Proposal in the context under discussion. Plaintiff corporation's vessel had been commandeered by the military during the Spanish-American War and returned when the Senate ratified the peace treaty with Spain. Conceding that it was not entitled to just compensation under the fifth amendment during time of war, plaintiff nonetheless claimed that it was entitled to compensation for that period after hostilities ended and the peace protocol signed but before Senate ratification. The Court was thus called upon to interpret the limits of the personal right embodied in the just compensation clause. But—as measured by the Individual Rights Proposal—in properly addressing this question, the Court improperly further undertook to decide a separation of powers issue, stating that "the President had not the power to terminate the war by treaty without the advice or consent of the Senate . . . and the war did not end by treaty until then, and all the use made by the government of the vessel was justified by the rules of law and international law, without compensation." The decision on the individual rights issue—that compensation does not accrue until ratification of the peace treaty—may have been correct. But the dictum regarding the respective constitutional powers of the executive and legislative branches was unnecessary for purposes of decision and beyond the Court's proper function under the Separation Proposal.

Wholly private litigation may also afford instances in which the security of individual constitutional rights may be tempered by judicial deference to political decisions respecting foreign affairs. For example, if a foreign government expropriates property

within its boundaries that belongs to one person and conveys it
to another, under the traditional American property law rule, the
buyer would take the property as a bona fide purchaser.[368] But if
the foreign government in our case has not been accorded diplomatic recognition by the United States, despite its undisputed
de facto status, the original owner may claim that the property
was not expropriated but feloniously obtained. In response, the
buyer may argue that for the Court to ignore the reality of the
foreign government's existence for some abstract reason of
foreign policy and thereby deny his defense against the original
owner constitutes a government deprivation of property without
due process of law. The Court may find for the original owner by
strictly adhering to the precept that "what government is to be
regarded here as representative of a foreign sovereign state is a
political rather than a judicial question, and it is to be determined by the political department of the government."[369] Or
it may reject this principle and find for the buyer. Or it may
generally honor the precept, but still rule for the buyer by finding
some exception to avoid what it considers to be a harsh result.[370]
But whatever it does, it should recognize what it is doing—and
that is making its own determination of whether the foreign
policy considerations overcome the force of the asserted constitutional liberty interest. A similar judicial determination is contained within the strongly established but often criticized
doctrine that the federal courts will immunize a foreign government from suit for damages by an injured plaintiff if the
Department of State suggests that rendering the defendant liable
would "embarrass the executive arm of the Government in conducting foreign relations."[371]

G. PRESIDENT'S VETO POWER

Several decisions of the Supreme Court have adjudicated constitutional questions of whether the President has
properly exercised his veto power in respect to acts passed by a
majority of both houses of Congress—and thus whether the purportedly vetoed statute was an operative law or not. In all these

cases, the Court has upheld the President's assertion of power and thus the results, albeit not the rationales, comport with the Separation Proposal under which the Court should have held these issues to be nonjusticiable. Brief review of these cases, as well as two recently decided in the lower courts adversely to the President, should afford some notion of the nature of the issues involved in the area and demonstrate that they concern only the proper division of authority between the political branches, rather than possible violations of constitutionally guaranteed personal rights.

The *Pocket Veto Case*[372]—referred to earlier[373]—is the first and most prominent. The issue was whether the President's failure to sign a bill passed within ten days of the end of an *initial session* of Congress (the legislators returning home for five months), rather than within ten days of final "Adjournment," constituted a proper veto. The limited and indirect constitutional interest of the private litigant, who would have benefited from the bill's enactment into law, is obvious. In situations of this kind, the alleged defect may be only technical in nature, curable by the President's merely returning the bill (assuming he could within ten days) with his objections, although this would then permit the veto to be overridden. More important, if Congress believes that its constitutional power to legislate has been too casually dealt with by the President, its remedies are numerous. The most straightforward—although, because of the cumbersomeness of the legislative process, less easily done than said—is simply to re-enact the bill when Congress reconvenes, an action not undertaken in any of the litigated situations. For the future, Congress may avoid the issue altogether simply by timing its presentment of a bill to prevent any dispute from arising, or Congress may deal with the problem more broadly by legislatively defining "adjournment" for these purposes,[374] or by providing for the receipt of presidential veto messages when it is not convened, or by employing the technique—reportedly used by early Congresses and engaged in frequently by state legislatures[375]—of avoiding all recesses by technically remaining in session while conducting no business.

Moreover, Congress may seek presidential modification of any objectionable pocket veto policy by threatening to abandon an existing practice that is directly related. The present understanding is that when the President is out of the country, Congress will delay "presenting" bills to him until his return, thereby affording him an unhurried opportunity to veto if he wishes.[376] And if the President contends that he is constitutionally "presented" with a bill only when it is delivered to him personally, Congress may accept this view but then bunch the presentation schedule of enacted bills so as greatly to increase the President's burden of careful consideration. There is no need further to continue the scenario. The opportunities for political accommodation mentioned barely scratch the surface. But even these few forcefully suggest that judicial intervention is unnecessary.

Examination of the other cases reveals that they are subject to the same analysis. In 1974, a federal court of appeals sustained Senator Edward Kennedy's challenge to a pocket veto by President Nixon in which the ten-day period expired during a five-day congressional recess for Christmas.[377] And in 1976, a federal district court upheld the senator's attack on the president's pocket veto during a twenty-nine-day intersession adjournment.[378] The courts' distinction of the *Pocket Veto Case* may be persuasive, but the dispensability of judicial review is identical. In *Wright v. United States*,[379] the President had vetoed a bill and returned it to the Secretary of the Senate (where the bill originated) at a time when the Senate was in temporary recess; although no congressional objection was heard, a private party (again the bill's beneficiary) contended that the veto was improper. And in *Edwards v. United States*,[380] the President signed a bill within ten days of its presentation but after Congress had adjourned. In a case brought in the Court of Claims involving the statute, for some undisclosed reason, the court certified the question of the validity of this action to the Supreme Court despite the fact that no one seemed to be disputing it. The executive branch as well as the plaintiff agreed that it was proper, as did the chairman of the House Judiciary Committee, who appeared as amicus curiae. Separation Proposal or no, it would have been ironic indeed for the Court to have ruled adversely.

H. President's Refusal to Execute Laws

Whether the President is unexceptionally obligated by the Constitution to enforce all laws enacted by Congress, or whether—as Chief Justice Marshall phrased it in *Marbury v. Madison*—"the executive possesses a constitutional . . . discretion"[381] to refuse to so act even when this would adversely affect private interests, is another issue that comes within the separation of powers category. With one possible exception—to be reviewed below—in every Supreme Court decision in which an individual has sought to compel the execution of a federal statute, the executive branch has resisted solely on the ground that Congress had authorized discretionary execution. These cases, involving only matters of statutory interpretation, are unaffected by the Separation Proposal. But if the executive were to frame its justification in terms of constitutional prerogative, the Court should hold that the issue is nonjusticiable.

To begin with an unusual example: Suppose that an individual who was clearly intended to be the beneficiary of a congressionally enacted tariff on certain goods sued to force collection and the President, acknowledging the law's clarity, nonetheless refused to order payment on the ground that the tariff abridged the constitutional rights of those upon whom it was imposed. Whether the President has "standing" to assert the constitutional rights of others presents a nice question beyond the scope of consideration. Putting this issue aside, if the President were to contend that the "executive Power" itself authorizes his stance, under the Separation Proposal the Court should treat this issue as nonjusticiable. Thus, in *Marbury v. Madison*, if President Jefferson had argued—as he apparently complained after the fact[382]—that delivery of Marbury's commission was actually a component of the act of appointment, which was concededly within his constitutional discretion, then the Court should have accepted this position without passing on its validity.

1. The Kendall Case

The most prominent decision on the subject is *Kendall v. United States ex rel. Stokes*.[383] Kendall, the Postmaster General, disputed Stokes's claim for wages for carrying the mail. Congress then authorized the Solicitor of the Treasury to resolve the matter. The Solicitor ordered payment but Kendall continued to disagree. Stokes then appealed to President Jackson, who referred the controversy to Congress "as the best expounder of the intent and meaning of their own law." The Senate resolved that Stokes be paid; the House of Representatives did not address the issue. With Kendall still standing firm, Stokes sought a writ of mandamus in federal court. Kendall argued that "it is doubted whether, under the Constitution of the United States, it confers on the Judiciary Department of the Government, authority to control the Executive Department in the exercise of its functions, of whatsoever character." The writ issued and, in the Supreme Court, the Attorney General restated the essence of Kendall's position—*not* that the President was constitutionally empowered to disregard the will of Congress in enforcing a law, but rather that the judiciary should keep hands off the matter: "What we say is, that where Congress pass a law for the guidance and government of the executive, in matters properly concerning the executive department, it belongs to the President to take care that this law be faithfully executed . . . . If, therefore, the executive be clearly satisfied as to the meaning of such a law, it is his bounden duty to see that the subordinate officers of his department conform with fidelity to that meaning; for no other execution, however pure the motive from which it springs, is a faithful execution of the law. In a case of this kind, one which thus concerns the proper executive business of the nation, we do indeed deny the power of the judiciary to interfere in advance, and to instruct the executive officer how to act."

The Court, in affirming the mandamus, dismissed this contention and, because of some statements in the course of its opinion that may fairly be read as addressing the executive's constitutional power respecting the enforcement of laws, the decision may be viewed as a rejection of the Separation Proposal. But it need not be. Despite the broader discussion, the Court was careful to point out that the President had not claimed the constitutional prerogative to forbid the execution of laws enacted by Congress, "but on the contrary, it is fairly to be inferred, that such power was disclaimed. He did not forbid or advise the

Postmaster-General to abstain from executing the law, and giving the credit thereby required, but submitt[ed] the matter in a message to congress." Thus, with no constitutional question before it concerning the scope of the President's power vis-à-vis Congress—but only the issue of the reach of the judicial function (a matter beyond the Separation Proposal that will be considered in the following chapter)—the Court appears to have held no more than that its jurisdiction plainly extends to determining whether Congress intended that Stokes be paid.

2. Impoundment

The problem concerning the President's constitutional obligation to fulfill the letter of congressional mandates that has been most vehemently debated is that of the executive's authority to impound funds that Congress has authorized to be spent. The kindling appears to have been laid as early as the time that Thomas Jefferson refused to build a frigate that he deemed to be unnecessary. Sparks were ignited both in Woodrow Wilson's dictate that "Congress has the power and the right to grant or deny an appropriation . . . but once an appropriation is made . . . [it] should be administered . . . by the executive branch,"[384] and in the withholding of money appropriated for sundry domestic purposes by Ulysses Grant, Warren Harding, Calvin Coolidge, and Herbert Hoover. And fire first clearly emerged in the early 1940s as a result of Franklin Roosevelt's "effort to defer public works projects he considered nonessential in view of the war emergency. Congress continued to appropriate funds for these projects and the President did not wish to veto entire appropriation bills. Accordingly, he directed the Bureau of the Budget to place the funds for these projects in reserves unavailable for expenditure by the agencies."[385] Since then, Harry Truman refused to spend money authorized by Congress for the air force in excess of his request, Dwight Eisenhower retained various aircraft and missile appropriations, and John Kennedy withheld funds for the B-70 bomber program. In the mid-1960s Lyndon Johnson declined to construct legislatively approved nuclear powered guided missile ships and "impounded $5.3

billion of funds provided for highways, housing, education and other domestic programs in order to reduce inflation."[386] The flames reached unprecedented heights under Richard Nixon, who, by some estimates, impounded as much as $25 billion that had been legislated for a wide variety of domestic programs.[387] Although in the two cases that reached the Supreme Court in which the issue was raised,[388] the Nixon administration defended its actions exclusively on the basis of statutory authority, several recent lower federal court decisions have demonstrated that the ultimate constitutional question may be posed by a tangible case or controversy.[389]

There is no intention here to canvass the merits of the substantive question, which has been thoroughly explored elsewhere.[390] Nor need anything more be said to show that the constitutional conflict over impoundment is purely one of congressional versus presidential power. As we have seen, the political branches recently have sought to resolve the conflict through an amicable accord after acrimonious contention over the issue.[391] For the reasons submitted throughout, the federal courts should hold the issue to be nonjusticiable.

I. DELEGATION OF POWER BETWEEN THE POLITICAL BRANCHES

Delegation of power from one of the political branches to the other is the final topic for consideration under the Separation Proposal. The judiciary has never questioned the constitutional ability of the President to delegate his authority to subordinates within the executive department. Nor has it ever suggested that the President's custom of "senatorial courtesy"—"resulting for practical purposes in appointments by the senators (or occasionally by majority members of the House), of officials whose duties are within the bounds of a single state"[392]—constitutes an undue delegation of his appointment power to Congress.[393] And the Judges' Bill of 1925, in which Congress delegated its authority to regulate the Supreme Court's appellate jurisdiction by conferring a vast discretion on the Justices themselves to decide whether the great majority of cases brought to them will secure their review, has gone unchallenged for over fifty years. But in several twentieth-century decisions, the Supreme Court has held that duly enacted congressional statutes, concededly authorizing the President to undertake action, were unconstitutional on the ground that the failure of Congress to articulate its policy and objective and to specify adequate standards by which the executive department was to achieve that objective resulted in such an unlimited delegation of legislative power as to be beyond Congress's constitutional capacity.[394] The delegation doctrine persists in theory—at least five different members of the Warren and Burger Courts have cast votes to invalidate acts of Congress because of its violation[395]—and has been accorded some scholarly approval.[396]

In terms of practical results, however, the doctrine, as applied to the respective powers of Congress and the President—in contrast to delegations that affect individual rights from one or both political branches to subordinate bodies[397] (a topic outside the separation of powers category)—is now moribund. Since the mid-1930s, the most vague and uninstructive "standards" have passed judicial muster; executive agencies charged with the duty of regulation in a certain area have been told no more than that they should act in the public interest, and Congress has articulated no intelligible principle as to matters of basic policy or details of implementation.[398] Although some earlier decisions (involving congressional delegation to the states) suggested otherwise,[399] the Court has even held that Congress—at least in the field of foreign affairs—may delegate its authority to define criminal offenses.[400] In related doctrinal areas, the federal courts have approved the most spacious congressional delegations— including the legislation of crimes—to the judiciary itself (such as under the Sherman Act), to the states[401] (despite some initial hesitancy),[402] as well as to private parties.[403] Indeed, in the sole federal court decision since 1936 holding a congressional delegation to the executive branch—authorizing the Federal Home Loan Bank Board to reorganize or liquidate federal savings and loan associations—to be unconstitutional the Supreme Court reversed, ruling that the complete absence of standards could be cured by the delegee through resort to custom and usage.[404]

Harking back to John Locke, the judicial aversion to undue delegation is premised on the political philosophy that fundamental policy decisions should only be made and governmental burdens should only be imposed by broadly based assemblies that are responsible to the people.[405] That precept, it should be recalled, was one of the major pillars upon which the argument for judicial review of executive action that allegedly violates congressional power was constructed. One reason for its rejection there—equally applicable here—was that the executive branch in the American system of government *is* politically accountable. But that is but the most modest justification for judicial abstinence in respect to the delegation problem. The more compelling point is that Congress *has* exercised its judgment in these instances. Both political branches have registered their concurrence that action should proceed in the designated manner.

Private parties who challenge executive activities that Congress is indisputably empowered to undertake assert that the Court should protect Congress from ceding its own power despite the fact that Congress has consciously done so. It may be that some legislative decisions to shift the task of formulating basic policy to an executive agency will be undertaken because Congress believes that it cannot itself obtain the consensus required for action and that such delegations will result in the promulgation of rules that Congress is not itself institutionally equipped to establish—that, as J. Skelly Wright has said, Congress will have "done through the back door what it could not accomplish in direct, democratic fashion."[406] But Congress's judgment here that some rule is better than none at all, or that its own organic weaknesses promise that the administration will produce a result more in keeping with the public welfare,[407] is surely no less democratic than its occasional decision, through deliberately ambiguous statutory language, to transfer the final resolution of politically delicate problems to the judiciary,[408] an organ of government whose popular base is clearly weaker than that of the executive branch. Nor does it differ from Congress's charging the federal courts to fashion "federal common law" in fields in which it believes that judicial legislation would be preferable to its own. Indeed—although for historic reasons concerning the allocation of government power, the analogy is far from perfect—the fact is that when Congress leaves subject areas to local regulation by not imposing its own uniform rule despite the power to do so, it is effectively delegating national legislative authority to the states; and, unlike congressional delegations to the executive, it often does so silently and inattentively rather than affirmatively and purposively.

Perhaps in all of these instances of congressional delegation—including those to the executive—the wiser legislative course calls for more studied consideration and precise articulation of policy goals. And there is much to be said, especially in cases in which the delegee's action appears to be unenlightened or oppressive, for the Court's adopting the posture of resolving all uncertainties against an executive agency's claim of legislative authority, thus forcing Congress to face the problem itself.[409] Further, the judiciary may employ other methods—such as statutory interpretations, judge-made administrative law, and, ultimately, application of constitutionally secured personal liberties—to oversee the integrity of a delegee's decisionmaking process, as well as to insure individual fairness and other aspects of formal justice.[410] But if Congress intentionally and unmistakably delegates its power—whether it be to enact taxes or declare war—and if no individual constitutional rights are in issue, the Court should remit to the political process the question of Congress's constitutional authority to do so.

The contention is not that the Court's constitutional superintendence in the delegation area—especially because it has been so rarely exercised—has done great harm either to the Court or to effective national government. It may even be argued that the continued formal survival of the delegation doctrine has prodded Congress to engage in more careful deliberation and draftsmanship. But that is neither an efficient nor an appropriate use of the Court's fragile and easily expended power of judicial review. For whatever may be said about congressional impotence in defending against presidentially initiated dominance—and we have seen that congressional ability there is imposing—Congress has powerful incentives to secure its own authority. Experience indicates that when Congress affirmatively cedes its power, it usually does so cautiously and deliberately—as illustrated by its compressive response in 1957 to President Eisenhower's request for military authorization in the Middle East[411] and its immediate correction of the *Panama Refining* decision by legislatively incorporating the substance of President Roosevelt's executive order that the Court had nullified. Moreover, if Congress's delegated authority is abused, the available techniques for correction are manifold. As described by Kenneth Davis, Congress and its committees "may require reports, ask questions, make suggestions, apply pressures, manipulate appropriations, threaten legislation withdrawing or altering power, publicize faulty administrative judgments, and through any or all of these weapons it may retain the ultimate control over administrative policies."[412] Although this judgment may be optimistic in light of available legislative resources,[413] Congress's ability to remedy delegations that it views as having been exercised unwisely may be illustrated in the mid-1970s by its redefinition of presidential authority to sell wheat to the Soviet Union.[414] In all, Congress is well equipped to secure its due without judicial review.

Many of the reasons for judicial abstention in regard to constitutional issues of delegation are also pertinent (though somewhat less forceful because of the danger in inferring approval from silence) in those instances—a number of which, such as *Debs* and *Neagle,* have already been discussed—in which one of the political branches engages in conduct that is allegedly within the constitutional dominion of the other but the "offended" branch cannot be found to have voiced any objection whatsoever. The analysis is wholly applicable when both political branches affirmatively approve action which a private party subsequently asserts unconstitutionally usurps the prerogatives of one of the branches. This was the ironic situation in the *Wright* and *Edwards* cases when the Court addressed the question of the President's power to sign and veto acts of Congress. But these are not the only times that the Court has entertained the claim on the merits.

In *Shoemaker v. United States*,[415] petitioner resisted condemnation of his property by the park commission of the District
of Columbia on the ground that the commission members had
been designated in a statute—*that had been signed by the
President*—rather than appointed by the President, thus infringing the executive power. In *Brown v. Walker*,[416] a statute
authorizing the executive to grant immunity from prosecution
was challenged on the ground that it invaded the President's
pardon power—again despite the fact that the law had been approved by the President and its force only became operative
when the President chose to afford the immunity. And, in *La
Abra Silver Mining Co. v. United States*,[417] the Court passed on
the question of whether congressional action *requested by the
President* usurped the exclusive province of the executive
branch. Since, in these cases, the Court sustained the constitutionality of the challenged actions, the results are not inconsistent with the Separation Proposal. Nonetheless, the Court
should have treated the issues as nonjusticiable.

One part of the recent celebrated decision in *Buckley v.
Valeo*,[418] however, does clash with the Separation Proposal. The
Court held that the provision of the Federal Election Campaign
Act of 1971 that two members of the Federal Election Commission be designated by the President, two by the Speaker of the
House, and two by the president pro tempore of the Senate (all
appointees to be confirmed by both houses of Congress) usurped
the President's Article II power to appoint "officers of the United
States." The Court ruled, at the behest of private parties (though
joined on this point in the litigation by a brief filed in behalf of
the executive branch), that, despite the President's concurrence
in the enactment of the law, the statute improperly delegated his
authority to Congress. The question presented—as was also true
of a recently adjudicated district court case[419] that concerned the
President's power to make temporary appointments without
congressional authorization or Senate confirmation—dealt only
with the respective constitutional prerogatives of the political
branches. Whether or not, as an abstract matter, the Justices
properly interpreted the historical intent of the appointments
clause, the Court should have held the issue to be nonjusticiable.

V. IMPACT OF THE SEPARATION PROPOSAL

Having reviewed the relevant decisions at length, we have seen that—in those cases in which one of the political branches has itself challenged the constitutional authority of the other or, as is more often true, defended its own—adoption of the Separation Proposal would change virtually no *result* thus far reached by the Supreme Court. Moreover, in respect to such cases, since it is applicable only in those instances when either the President or Congress asserts ultimate constitutional power against the other, the proposal would, if history is a guide, only infrequently be employed, for such claims have seldom been made in the context of litigation. Nor, in all likelihood, would judicial acceptance of the proposal significantly encourage the political branches to reach more often for what would become their crowning argument in court. We have seen that, so far as constitutional conflicts between Congress and the President are concerned, the dangerous political risks associated with exaggerated claims of power have usually caused each branch to be respectful of the other's prerogatives, and that when they have not—and judicial resolution seemed to be unavailable—both have been encouraged to reach accommodation through the political process. Neither of these conditions should be significantly affected by application of the Separation Proposal. For example, if, in the *Steel Seizure Case*, the President were to have asserted final constitutional power and the Court were to have accepted—but not placed its imprimatur upon—that claim, there is every reason to believe that Congress would have responded rather than acquiesced. And if the matter at issue is not significant enough to engage the attention of the competing political branch, then, similarly it is unlikely that it will initially cause the other to fire its ultimate weapon in the course of litigation.

It must be acknowledged, however, that the Separation Proposal will, on rare occasion, force the Court more quickly to decide whether government action abridges individual constitutional rights. This may be illustrated by those decisions involving persons who were denied passports, pursuant to State

Department regulations, because they were associated with disfavored groups or wished to visit restricted areas. The rejected applicants contended that the regulations were not authorized by Congress and, in any case, violated their individual constitutional right to travel. In *Kent v. Dulles*,[420] the Court agreed with the first point and ruled in the applicants' favor. Although the Court's opinion did contain one sentence—stating that the right to travel may only be regulated "pursuant to the lawmaking functions of the Congress," citing *Youngstown*—the case involved only statutory interpretation because the State Department relied solely on congressional authority. *Kent*, therefore, would be unaffected by the Separation Proposal. In *Zemel v. Rusk*,[421] however, the State Department appended the rarely asserted defense that the executive possessed inherent constitutional authority, in this case to regulate passports. Thus, to decide the case, whether by conventional process or under the Separation Proposal, the Court had no alternative but to reach *some* constitutional issue. Apart from the Separation Proposal, the Court could have ruled against the government without reaching the individual liberty question by holding that the State Department's regulations were neither authorized by Congress nor within the executive's constitutional power. (In fact, only Justice Black took this route. The majority upheld the passport denial, thus rejecting *all* the constitutional arguments. Justices Douglas and Goldberg found for the individuals, ruling in favor of *both* of their constitutional challenges.) Under the Separation Proposal, the Court must accept the executive's claim of power and must therefore proceed to decide the broader personal liberty question—similar to the course the Court has often taken in such cases as *Ex parte Garland, New York Times*, and *U.S. District Court*—of whether the government as a whole may constitutionally impose such regulations.

VI. CONCLUSION

This disadvantageous feature of the Separation Proposal becomes operative only in highly qualified circumstances. When balanced against those occasions in which it permits judicial avoidance of *all* constitutional decision and the concomitant risk of injury to the Court's institutional prestige, the proposal should prevail. It is true that the traditional criteria for determining nonjusticiable political questions are unsatisfied here. No language in the Constitution clearly commits separation of power issues between Congress and the President for resolution outside the judicial sphere, and it may well be that there are adequate criteria for decision and available remedies for enforcement. Nonetheless, since, as a functional matter, the political branches are fully capable of protecting their own vital constitutional interests, the Court will better secure its own critical constitutional role in our system by forcing them to do so.

Six

Political Regulation of Judicial Authority
A Matter for Court Review

I. INTRODUCTION

The Separation Proposal, advanced in chapter 5, deals with the Court's appropriate role in constitutional boundary clashes between Congress and the President. But such controversies do not exhaust the range of constitutional issues that fall within the earlier designated category of separation of powers at the national level. An obvious subclassification remains: fundamental conflicts between the political branches, on the one hand, and the federal judiciary, on the other.

A. JUDICIAL TRANSGRESSION OF POLITICAL POWER

What function the Supreme Court should perform in respect to one of this question's two sides—alleged judicial infringements of the authority vested in the legislative and executive departments—has already been implicitly resolved in the course of previous discussion. By approving judicial review of actions of the national political branches (and of state and local agencies as well) that allegedly abridge personal liberties, and by concluding that the Court must serve as final constitutional arbiter for this group of issues, the Individual Rights Proposal tacitly rejects the oft-voiced charge that the Court's exercise of review transgresses the division of national power decreed by the Constitution and usurps functions delegated to Congress and the President. Indeed, the Federalism and Separation Proposals as well—although they ultimately urge that the Justices decline to decide the constitutional questions that fit within their respective categories—nonetheless rest final determination of the matter with the Court itself. This underlines (albeit somewhat backhandedly) the notion that the federal judiciary has supreme *power* to decide constitutional questions. This approach is consistent with the conventional view under which the Supreme Court has not hesitated to authoritatively adjudicate the question of whether actions by federal judges—e.g., indefinitely suspending a criminal sentence mandated by statute[1]—overstep the "judicial power" and invade the province of the political branches.

B. POLITICAL TRANSGRESSION OF JUDICIAL POWER

The principal concern of this chapter is the proper scope of the Court's competence in regard to the other half of this separation of powers subclassification: purported abrogations of "the judicial power" by enactments of the political branches. Those that will be most extensively considered take two general forms. On the one hand, Congress may be accused of improperly enlarging the purview of the national judiciary by statutorily conferring jurisdiction on the federal courts over matters that are not proper for judicial cognizance—e.g., subjects that do not present "Cases" or "Controversies," or that fall outside the specific areas stipulated in Art. III, §2. Or legislation may be challenged as expanding either the original or appellate jurisdiction of the Supreme Court beyond the constitutionally designated allocation. On the other hand, Congress may be charged with unduly restricting the capacity of the federal courts. For example, Congress might create administrative bodies or "legislative courts" (whose members do not possess Article III's guarantees of life tenure and undiminished compensation that are designed to assure an independent judiciary), grant them adjudicatory power over matters within federal judicial purview, and make their decisions either final or subject to limited review by Article III courts. A federal statute might effect analogous consequences by divesting the federal courts of jurisdiction over certain types of cases, thereby limiting such actions to the state courts and restricting appeals therefrom to the national judiciary. Or legislation dividing the Supreme Court into several panels, or delegating certain aspects of its decisionmaking authority to a subsidiary body might be challenged as violative of Article III's investiture of "the judicial power of the United States" in "one supreme court." [2]

A third category of political regulations that arguably offend provisions of Article III consists of those laws that may be perceived as affecting the federal courts' general independence or their capacity to function effectively and administer justice. For example, if Congress were to establish procedures for the reassignment, suspension, or removal of federal judges under certain designated conditions, they might be attacked as inconsistent with the guarantee of judicial independence secured in Art. III, §1.[3] Or, if the national political branches were to deny the judiciary all authority to regulate those persons who practice before it,[4] set unduly rigid time limits for the decision of cases, require (as President Jefferson successfully demanded) that Supreme Court Justices reassume extensive duties sitting on the circuit courts of appeal,[5] or impose other rules of procedure or evidence that drastically interfered with the judicial decisionmaking process[6]—some of which (as we have seen in earlier chapters)[7] could also be urged as contravening provisions of the fourth through eighth amendments which may or may not be applicable to litigation in the state courts—such laws might be said to overstep the constitutional lines dividing political from judicial power.[8] This third category of issues will not be significantly discussed herein.

II. THE JUDICIAL PROPOSAL

The major thesis of this chapter—referred to hereafter as the Judicial Proposal—is that the Supreme Court should pass final constitutional judgment on questions concerning the permissible reach and circumscription of "the judicial power."

A. BROAD CONTOURS

Several preliminary observations may be helpful. As we will see in greater detail below, many purported political encroachments on judicial prerogatives—particularly those that improperly restrict "judicial power," e.g., by apportioning adjudicatory duties to non–Article III bodies—may concomitantly create a genuine claim of abridgment of constitutionally secured personal liberties, an issue that is subject to judicial review by virtue of the Individual Rights Proposal. But even if the Court rejects the individual rights claim on the merits, under the Judicial Proposal, the broader separation of powers issue remains for its consideration. An appealing argument can be made that if an act of Congress neither threatens individual rights nor endangers the independence of the judiciary or the integrity of the judicial process in the ways sketched above, then there is no special reason why the sole question of whether it comports with Article III's delineation of "the judicial power" should not be finally resolved by the political branches. For example, only rarely if at all will an asserted legislative expansion of federal (or Supreme Court) jurisdiction present a colorable charge of violation of individual freedom—not even of the "derivative" or "semantic" type examined in our earlier discussion of federalism and separation of powers between Congress and the President. In *Marbury v. Madison,* for example, the Supreme Court held that Congress's assignment of original jurisdiction to the Court "to issue ... writs of mandamus ... to ... persons holding office under the authority of the United States" exceeded the contours established in Article III. Marbury did not argue, and could not seriously have contended, however, that the challenged provision of the Judiciary Act of 1789[9] infringed—directly or indirectly, primarily or derivatively, or otherwise—any constitutionally ordained individual guarantee. Nor does it appear that the statute's distribution of judicial authority would interfere with the overall ability of the federal courts to perform their duties properly. Nonetheless, for both functional and historical considerations that will be developed below, even though the constitutional problem is solely one of separation of powers, when any unadulterated question of political abrogation of the federal judiciary's authority arises—and some such apparent questions may not survive closer analysis—the Judicial Proposal urges that the Court intervene and permit litigants' standing to raise the constitutional interests of a third party (i.e., the judicial branch).

B. FUNCTIONAL JUSTIFICATIONS

The essence of the rationale underlying chapter 5's Separation Proposal—which urged judicial withdrawal from constitutional disputes between Congress and the President—was that, owing to abundant weaponry and patent self-interest, the political branches had both the incentive and capability of securing their own salient constitutional interests. The Court's participation was, therefore, found to be unnecessary to safeguard that segment of the constitutional separation of powers at the national level. This functional rationale is not applicable, however, to the issue of political expansions or constrictions of federal judicial authority that seemingly conflict with Article III. Since the federal judicial branch is not formally politically represented in the national legislative halls, Congress's natural tendency is to be relatively insensitive to the spirit (if not the letter) of the constitutional licenses and limits of judicial authority—at least when they appear to obstruct the accomplishment of important legislative goals. Thus, institutionally excluded from the national political process, the Court must resort to the judicial process to protect its interests.

The Judicial Proposal does proceed from the same functional analysis as its companion proposals respecting individual rights, federalism, and separation of powers, by recognizing the distinctive ability of the Justices (in contrast to elected officials—lawyers and laymen alike) to define the proper boundaries of judicial power. Such a task calls for special knowledge of judicial history, tradition, capacity, and mission rather than for practical judgments concerning the optimum distribution of governing authority (as between nation and states or legislature and executive) to fulfill the complex social and economic needs of American society. Although all categories of constitutional issues require appraisal of these or analogous elements in respect to which the expertise and sensitivity of the three branches of national government differ in varying degrees, the judiciary is uniquely equipped to evaluate all these factors for questions arising under Article III.

Finally, the Judicial Proposal is premised on the pragmatic thesis that the Court should speak the last constitutional word only when realpolitik strongly indicates that earlier utterances by its coordinate branches are relatively undependable in securing adherence to constitutional precepts.

C. CONSISTENCY WITH TRADITIONAL VIEWS

From the perspective of original design, judicially developed doctrine, and the current of scholarly comment (both within and without the mainstream), the Judicial Proposal—at least in naked statement—stands four-square with tradition. Indeed, although there is no intention here to root the Judicial Proposal exclusively in the soil of history, forceful arguments have been made by eminent legal historians that, at least so far as judicial review over the acts of the coordinate national departments was concerned, no wider grant of authority was ever meant to be awarded the Court.[10] This view relies not only on the expressed thinking of the framers—as exemplified by Madison's statement that Article III's extension of the Supreme Court's jurisdiction to "Cases ... arising under this Constitution" was "limited to cases of a Judiciary Nature"[11]—but on the course of judicial response as well. Even before *Marbury*, only three years after passage of the First Judiciary Act in the first reported instance of federal judicial invalidation of national legislation, the ground for decision was that the challenged act of Congress, by making judicially mandated settlements of pension claims subject to revision by the political branches, had sought to impose duties of a nonjudicial nature on Article III courts.[12] Since, as already observed, the unconstitutional element of the federal statute overturned in *Marbury* itself was of the same genre, the strict holding of this fountainhead of judicial review—if not the far-reaching language of Chief Justice Marshall's opinion—may be read to stand for no broader proposition. Indeed, it was not until *Dred Scott* in 1857 that the Court struck down congressional legislation on grounds other than collision with the national judicial function delineated in Article III.

D. ILLUSTRATIONS OF PRIOR DECISIONS

Whatever the merit of the theory that judicial review was historically meant to be confined solely to self-defensive declarations of unconstitutionality—and it has been vigorously disputed by equally learned constitutional scholars,[13] as well as rejected on functional grounds by the Individual Rights Proposal herein—the belief that it at least encompassed the matter has been unqualifiedly and unhesitatingly confirmed by the Court on numerous occasions since *Marbury*. Recitation of a few additional cases in which the Court considered the validity of congressional contractions and expansions of judicial authority may be useful in fleshing the skeletal outlines of the subject under consideration:

i) *United States v. Klein*, 80 U.S. 128 (1872), held that a federal statute that required the Supreme Court, after it had properly assumed jurisdiction of certain appeals, to dismiss them for want of jurisdiction if designated facts appeared, "passed the limit which separates the legislative from the judicial power" by compelling the Court to decide a central fact in all pending cases of this kind in favor of one of the parties.[14]

ii) *American Insurance Co. v. Canter*, 26 U.S. 511 (1828), held that a federal statute that created a "legislative court" (with judges of limited tenure and some duties of a nonjudicial nature) in an American territory, did not contravene Article III even though it empowered this court to decide controversies within the limits of that provision.

iii) *Crowell v. Benson*, 285 U.S. 22 (1932), held that a federal statute which provided that designated factual findings of an administrative agency (respecting whether and to what extent an employee had been injured in a dispute that was conventionally adjudicated by courts) "shall be final" if they are "supported by evidence" did not usurp the "judicial power of the United States."[15]

iv) *United States ex rel. Toth v. Quarles*, 350 U.S. 11 (1955), held that a federal statute that subjected ex-servicemen to trial by court-martial for offenses committed abroad while they were in the armed forces "encroaches on the jurisdiction of federal courts set up under Article III."[16]

v) *Keller v. Potomac Electric Power Co.*, 261 U.S. 428 (1923), held that a federal statute that granted the Supreme Court appellate jurisdiction to revise an administrative commission's finding as to the value of public utility property exceeded the judicial power by authorizing the Court to engage in a "legislative function."[17]

vi) *Hobson v. Hansen*, 265 F. Supp. 902 (D.D.C. 1967), appeal dismissed, 393 U.S. 801 (1968), held that a federal statute that required the judges of the United States District Court for the District of Columbia to appoint the members of the District of Columbia Board of Education, did no violence to "the doctrine of separation of powers."[18]

Whether these rulings were substantively correct is inconsequential for our purposes. Rather, at the risk of belaboring the point, they are notable because they reflect the unwavering judicial conviction—tersely expressed by Justice Frankfurter—"that the Court has deemed itself *peculiarly* qualified, with due regard to the contrary judgment of Congress, to determine what is meet and fit for the exercise of 'judicial power' as authorized by the Constitution."[19] This conclusion has been approved by virtually every scholarly observer of the Court's role in American government, no matter what his ultimate appraisal of the proper function and scope of judicial review, and is therefore perhaps the least controversial proposition concerning the overall subject. And, despite the often unconditionally professed aversion to the idea in the abstract (or other contexts), its proponents straightforwardly call for the federal judiciary to act as final arbiter of its own constitutional power. The Judicial Proposal, unencumbered by any seeming contradiction with the axiom against any person or institution serving as judge in its own cause, does likewise.

III. POLITICAL RESTRICTIONS OF JUDICIAL AUTHORITY

The congruence between the Judicial Proposal and orthodox constitutional doctrine is substantial but not perfect. Some detailed consideration of its application in several familiar problem areas should serve to clarify its contours and illustrate its relationship to its sister propositions.

A. Relationship to Individual Rights Proposal

This inquiry may most profitably be undertaken in regard to laws, enacted pursuant to various congressional regulatory powers, that assertedly constrict the lawful constitutional reach of the federal courts. The most common variety are statutes that establish legislative courts or similar non–Article III bodies and assign them either completely or substantially final adjudicative duties over matters to which "the judicial power" extends. The *Canter, Crowell,* and *Quarles* cases (briefly described above), which concerned legislatively created territorial courts, administrative agencies, and military commissions respectively, illustrate the types of non–Article III adjudicative bodies that are most usually employed. Other such congressional provisions— only slightly variant and not wholly imaginary—might authorize specified federal executive officers, upon making certain factual determinations, to summarily seize private property[20] or revoke previously granted privileges,[21] or might empower international tribunals to impose civil responsibilities or criminal sanctions on American citizens for conduct engaged in within the United States.[22] Or the political branches might simply vest state courts with exclusive (or nearly unreviewable) adjudicatory authority over matters within the purview of Article III.

In addition to the fact that all these instances would raise justiciable issues under the Judicial Proposal, they could also present colorable claims of deprivation of personal liberty that would be reviewable by virtue of the Individual Rights Proposal. The most elemental contention would be that neither criminal penalties, quasi-criminal disabilities, civil liabilities, nor any other sanctions that are mandated by federal law may be consigned for resolution to non–Article III adjudicative councils in the absence of procedures guaranteeing a "fair trial" prior to deprivation of liberty or property—i.e., at a minimum, due process requires adequate notice of the issues, a reasonable opportunity to present and confront evidence and witnesses, and some form of hearing by an impartial tribunal. If the matter may be characterized as either a "criminal prosecution" or "a suit at common law"[23] concerning "the liability of one individual to another,"[24] it may be further argued that, under the sixth or seventh amendments, there is a constitutional right to jury trial.

It is important to recognize that issues of the particular nature just described may fall *exclusively* within the category of individual constitutional rights—i.e., these constitutional objections could be wholly cured simply by Congress's providing, or the Court's requiring, that the requisite elements of fairness be incorporated in all adjudicatory proceedings before the legislatively designated tribunals.[25] But even these changes would not substantively foreclose other meritorious constitutional challenges—although determining whether they fit within one or the other of the classifications that have been fashioned (personal liberty or usurpation of the federal judiciary's function), or some amalgam of both, is less readily discernible. This is not a matter of significant concern for our purposes, however, because the subtle distinctions that must be drawn do not bear on the ultimate question of justiciability—since judicial review is available under both the Individual Rights and Judicial Proposals—but further pursuit of the inquiry should illuminate the relationship between the two.

A persuasive argument with some firm doctrinal moorings may be made that, irrespective of Congress's providing, or the Court's mandating, the full panoply of procedural safeguards in the administrative proceeding (or regardless of their existence in the state judicial system), at least *some* measure of review or supervision by Article III courts—at least in respect to *some* issues—is constitutionally required. The case of *Yakus v. United States*[26] affords a useful point of departure. In upholding a federal district court conviction for violation of an Emergency Price Control Act regulation whose legality and constitutionality Congress had stipulated might be challenged only in a separate administrative proceeding, the Court made clear that its affirmance rested on the fact that the administrator's decision was subject to review in Article III courts (first the Emergency Court of Appeals and then the Supreme Court itself): "There is no constitutional requirement that ... [the chance for testing the validity of a regulation be had] in one tribunal rather than another, so long as there is an opportunity to be heard and for judicial review which satisfies the demands of due process, as is the case here." Thus, at a minimum, *Yakus* fairly stands for the proposition—albeit in dictum—that the Constitution forbids Congress from invoking the judicial branch's authority to impose criminal sanctions without also permitting the defendant the right to question the validity of the law defining the offense in some Article III court.

Apart from the discrete issue presented in *Yakus* of the prerequisites for the political branches' use of Article III courts to enforce its edicts (a matter to which we shall return) several facets of the decision merit attention for our purposes. First, the Court, especially in the statement quoted above, pointedly suggests that, as earlier phrased by Justice Brandeis, "under certain circumstances, the constitutional requirement of due process is a requirement of judicial process."[27] Does this go so far as to mean that, in some instances at least, there is a constitutionally ordained *individual right* to some form of hearing before a federal court established in accordance with Article III—i.e., that the terms "judicial review" (in *Yakus*) and "judicial process" (by Brandeis) cannot be fulfilled either by a legislatively created administrative body, or by a state court whose judges need not, under the Constitution, be awarded the privileges of life tenure and compensation security that Article

III guarantees their federal counterparts? Is the *Yakus* opinion to be understood as pronouncing that Congress could not, consistently with *due process,* have provided for exclusive and final enforcement of Emergency Price Control Act regulations in *state courts*—including adjudication of all claims as to their legality under the statute, their constitutionality, and the constitutionality of the statute as well?

As should soon be apparent, these queries intertwine a series of complex problems. And even if the issues are properly segregated, the answers are neither clear nor simple. Although the matter is not beyond historical dispute,[28] the Court has been uniformly of the view—at least since the mid-nineteenth century—that, under Article III, Congress "possess[es] the sole power of creating . . . [inferior federal courts] and of investing them with jurisdiction either limited, concurrent, or exclusive, and of withholding jurisdiction from them in the exact degrees and character which to Congress may seem proper for the public good."[29] Nonetheless, it is not beyond the pale to argue—as a federal court did, not too long ago—that Congress "must not so exercise that [withholding] power as to deprive any person of" individual liberties designated in other clauses of the Constitution.[30] And even if total withdrawal of the opportunity for a lower federal court hearing does not abridge any constitutionally secured personal right, it may be that denial of the availability of all review in the Supreme Court does.

The argument that appellate review by the Supreme Court—or at least *some* consideration by *some* Article III body—is a matter of constitutional entitlement, i.e., it is an individual right secured by the basic charter, is strongest when the underlying dispute itself concerns constitutional issues. Examples, real and hypothetical, of such instances, coupled with various kinds of limitations on access to the federal courts, are abundant. In *Yakus,* the defendants—convicted for violating a maximum price regulation—contended that the regulation deprived them of property without due process of law. In the much heralded *Ben Avon* and *St. Joseph Stock Yards* cases,[31] the litigants—challenging rates set by state and federal administrative officials—asserted that the values placed on their property were so low as to constitute takings without just compensation. In the landmark decision of *United States v. Lee*,[32] the plaintiffs—requesting ejectment against federal officers who had taken possession of their property—alleged that the seizure violated their rights to due process and just compensation. In *Ng Fung Ho v. White*,[33] the habeas corpus petitioners—resisting summary deportation on the ground that they were American citizens—presented the issue of whether their individual constitutional rights were abridgèd by the nonreviewable executive decision that they were aliens. Similar problems would be raised if Congress were to foreclose an Article III hearing on the question of who is a member of "the land or naval forces" so as to be subject to court-martial jurisdiction,[34] or decree that state court determinations of whether verbal or written communications are "obscene" (under the test propounded by the Supreme Court) must thereafter be treated as "final and nonreviewable."[35]

The foregoing illustrations—although very sparingly described—deliberately cover a broad and varied swath. Some (such as the last several) involve denial of a hearing altogether in Article III courts; others (such as *Ben Avon* and *St. Joseph Stock Yards*) concern only restrictions on the intensity or scope of review; *Yakus* puts the special problem—that I will address more fully below—of bifurcated opportunity. In one set, the principal adjudicating bodies are administrative agencies or executive officials; in another, they are the state courts. In regard to the underlying constitutional issues, a few (e.g., *Ben Avon*) implicate what may be fairly characterized as pure questions of "fact"; some (e.g., *Yakus*) turn more on questions of "law"; yet others (e.g., the obscenity case) raise "mixed" questions of law and fact. And assuming, as Brandeis did,[36] that the distinction is a meaningful one, one group invokes liberties of the person; the other, property rights.

None of these distinctions—nor their authenticity or materiality—need be further explored here, for such pursuits address matters of substantive constitutional law. Whether, for example, the fifth amendment right of just compensation permits nonreviewability of state court determinations of relevant questions of fact; whether the first amendment freedom of speech demands de novo review of mixed questions of law and fact; whether the nearly absolute fourteenth amendment citizenship right allows federal judicial deference to critical administrative findings; whether fifth amendment substantive due process prevents Congress from directing that deprivation of property claims may only be advanced through narrowly defined channels; whether any individual rights claim is wholly satisfied if the non–Article III adjudicative body is a state court whose members enjoy the same insulation from political influence as the federal judiciary; whether effective vindication of some constitutional provisions requires special federal remedies such as injunctive or declaratory relief; or whether, if the participation of an Article III court is mandated to secure some constitutional provision, this may be fulfilled by nothing more than discretionary consideration of a petition for certiorari by the Supreme Court, thus making the strength of the individual right quite modest indeed[37]—in sum, whether and to what extent, in cases such as these, federal judicial process is a component necessary for the protection of the underlying constitutional ordinance itself—are ultimately functions of interpreting the content of each of the above-mentioned constitutional provisions. The important point for our purposes is that each of the substantive constitutional clauses just discussed falls within the category of individual constitutional rights. Thus, the contention that some degree of consideration by an Article III court is required itself raises an issue of abridgment of constitutionally ordained personal liberty, and it follows that it is subject to judicial review under the Individual Rights Proposal.

B. RELATIONSHIP TO FEDERALISM PROPOSAL

This is not true in regard to all underlying controversies that present constitutional issues. For example, let us assume an act of Congress that provides that "all businesses whose operations affect commerce" must pay a minimum wage; that all enforcement proceedings shall be brought before an administrative agency (or in the state courts); that the administrative agency (or state court) shall determine, on a case by case basis, whether the business before it "affects commerce"; and that this finding shall be "final." Even if we further quite plausibly assume that the question of whether a business "affects commerce" is one of constitutional dimension, the presence of *this* constitutional question should not cause the issue of whether Congress constitutionally can prevent an Article III court from reviewing the agency's or state court's resolution of the commerce question to be subject to judicial review. Since the underlying constitutional problem is one of congressional power vis-à-vis the states, under the Federalism Proposal its final resolution should be lodged with the national political branches. It follows that this judicially unreviewable political authority includes the decision to delegate its application in specific instances to subsidiaries of Congress's choice.

This hypothetical federal minimum wage statute is reminiscent of the famous case of *Crowell v. Benson*.[38] One question before the Court was whether the Federal Longshoreman's and Harbor Workers' Compensation Act, promulgated pursuant to "the general authority of the Congress to alter or revise the maritime law which shall prevail throughout the country," did (or could) vest the administrative agency before which cases were to be adjudicated with unreviewable power to determine the existence of the facts on which its jurisdiction was based— whether the injury occurred upon the navigable waters of the United States and whether a master-servant relationship existed. These conditions were "indispensable to the application of the statute, not only because the Congress ha[d] so provided explicitly . . ., but also because the power of the Congress to enact the legislation turn[ed] upon the existence of these conditions." Conceding the accuracy of the latter point, the presence of this constitutional question—consistent with our analysis of the minimum wage law—should not make the issue of agency finality in *Crowell* subject to judicial review. For, despite the fact that Congress's legislative power over admiralty and maritime affairs finds its source in Article III, the underlying constitutional problem is one of states' rights. In contrast to the usual constitutional issues that are rooted in Article III—dealing with the scope of the federal judicial prerogative—this particular issue concerns the proper allocation of national versus local regulatory power rather than the effective and efficient operation of the judicial branch. For these reasons—traditional doctrine notwithstanding[39]—the Federalism Proposal urges that the issue be treated as nonjusticiable with the consequence that details surrounding its interpretation should similarly be held to be beyond the Court's purview. (The Court in *Crowell* was correct in hearing the case, however, as we will see. The Judicial Proposal urges that the Court treat as justiciable claims that an action of the political branches encroaches on the constitutional judicial authority. In *Crowell*, the justiciable issue was whether Congress constitutionally could divest the federal judiciary of jurisdiction to review the agency's factual determinations.)

The preceding discussion has sought to illuminate the relationship of the Individual Rights and Federalism Proposals to instances in which the national political branches have excluded or limited the participation of the federal judiciary in respect to controversies that come within the scope of federal judicial power. Before following this legislative path beyond those disputes that themselves involve underlying constitutional issues—thus moving further from the pertinence of all but the Judicial Proposal—a brief detour is appropriate to examine a few problems (the first of which involves a political expansion rather than a constriction of federal judicial authority) analogous to those raised by the minimum wage and *Crowell* cases.

1. Eleventh Amendment

The eleventh amendment prevents the "judicial power of the United States" from extending to "any suit in law or equity" against a state. Questions normally arise under this provision when a state that is sued in the federal courts pursuant to an act of Congress contends that the jurisdictional statute contravenes states' rights secured by the eleventh amendment.[40] Since the amendment defines "the judicial power of the United States," and since the state is asserting its own constitutional interests, it would appear naturally to follow from the Judicial

Proposal—which permits "judicial power" issues to be resolved by the Supreme Court even at the behest of those who are not the direct beneficiaries of the constitutional separation of political and judicial functions—that the state's claim is justiciable. But the Federalism Proposal again calls for the Court to hold otherwise. The constitutional issue raised may be whether the eleventh amendment is simply inapplicable to any congressionally authorized federal court action against the states,[41] or whether certain powers of Congress supersede (or pro tanto repeal) the amendment's limitation,[42] or some variation of these propositions. No matter how the constitutional problem is framed, however, it is exclusively an issue of federalism, which ultimately should be determined by the national political process in which (as we saw in chapter 4) the states' interests are forcefully represented. This is in contrast to the *Crowell* situation which involved both the scope of Congress's legislative power over admiralty and maritime affairs in opposition to that of the states (a federalism problem) as well as the ability of the national political branches to divest the federal judiciary of certain of its traditional duties (a possible "judicial power" problem, that will further concern us shortly).

In interpreting legislation that authorizes federal jurisdiction, the Court may decide to inject its own understanding of the constitutional values underlying the eleventh amendment. For example, it may refuse to hold that a generally worded jurisdictional statute evinces a congressional intention to include the states as parties defendant, or it may require that the political branches unmistakably cover the states before it will find them amenable to suit in federal court.[43] But if the Justices are satisfied—by whatever standard of statutory interpretation they choose—that Congress meant to bring the states within the purview of the federal judiciary, then, under the Federalism Proposal, the Court's constitutional task is done.

Although most eleventh amendment issues may thus be placed in the federalism category, a few unusual ones do require independent evaluation by the Court. If—as occurred in *Chisholm v. Georgia*[44]—a person were to bring suit against a state in the Supreme Court by invoking its self-executing original jurisdiction, and if for some reason the Court chose not to exercise its discretion to decline to hear the case, then, since no act of the political branches has resolved the constitutional issue of states' rights, under the Judicial Proposal the Court would itself determine the constitutional scope of its jurisdiction. Analogously, if a person were to sue state officials (or the state itself) in federal court alleging deprivation of constitutionally protected personal liberty that may be effectively corrected only by a particular federal remedy (such as money damages),[45] then, under the Individual Rights Proposal, the Court must resolve the tension between the substantive constitutional provision and the eleventh amendment.

C. RELATIONSHIP TO SEPARATION PROPOSAL

Another interesting question—nearer to *Crowell* because it potentially implicates both "judicial power" issues and constitutional questions falling within an independent classification—would arise if a legislative court were to be established by executive order.[46] Persons brought before such a court could raise two discrete constitutional challenges: first, that the court's jurisdiction comprehends disputes that may be adjudicated only in Article III courts; and second, that the creation of non–Article III courts requires an exercise of legislative power beyond the constitutional authority of the President. Although the former constitutional problem is plainly subject to the Court's consideration under the Judicial Proposal, it should by now be equally clear that the Separation Proposal renders the latter nonjusticiable.

The interrelation between the Judicial and Separation Proposals may be additionally illuminated by the case of a presidential pardon to a person for conduct that has caused him to be held in contempt, either criminal or civil. In chapter 5 we concluded that constitutional disputes regarding the compatibility between the President's pardon power and Congress's regulatory authority should be treated—along with other constitutional boundary clashes between the executive and legislative branches—as nonjusticiable. The instant case is distinguishable, however, be-

cause it involves a question of executive versus *judicial* authority. The argument once forcefully voiced by a federal judge—that
"the power to punish for contempts is inherent in, and essential
to, the very existence of the judiciary" and that "if the President
is allowed to substitute his discretion for that of the courts in this
vital matter, then truly the President becomes the ultimate
source of judicial authority"[47]—demonstrates that a constitutional question of singular concern to the judicial department is at stake. Thus, as with the issue of the extent to which the
President is constitutionally immune from judicial process,[48]
whatever its disposition on the merits, the Judicial Proposal rests
ultimate resolution of the pardon question with the Court.[49]

D. Participation of Article III Courts as an Individual Right

The digression just taken was intended to provide a
more fully rounded picture of the interaction between the Judicial Proposal and its companion propositions. We return now to
the main track: congressional enactments that restrict or deny the
traditional authority of Article III courts. We have seen that statutes of this kind are reviewable under the Individual Rights
Proposal if the underlying question involves personal liberty.
But, if the controversy or the issue that Congress either relegates
for final decision to non–Article III bodies or makes only modestly reviewable in the federal courts concerns some other category of constitutional problem, or is simply one of statutory
interpretation or run-of-the-mill adjudicative fact, and if the tribunal affords the requisites of procedural fairness, then it becomes substantially more difficult to place the matter within the
Court's province through any but the Judicial Proposal. It must
be acknowledged—as we shall observe—that no litigant is
foreclosed from asserting that, irrespective of the nature of the
underlying dispute, some form of federal court hearing is a matter of individual constitutional entitlement. But—as we shall also
see (and, admittedly, the discussion will hint strongly at the
merits)—the argument is fairly difficult to sustain.

1. State Courts

The principal analogic obstacle is that if no federal question is involved state courts are indisputably conceded to hold final adjudicatory authority over issues of both fact and law in cases properly before them. Unless the state litigation presents a problem that is contained within the jurisdictional boundaries of Article III—and most disputes at state law do not—the rule that the state judicial system's finding of facts and constructions of laws are unreviewable in any federal court has never been thought to abridge individual rights secured by the Constitution. Since questions of ordinary adjudicative fact and statutory interpretation that arise in the enforcement of laws enacted by Congress are essentially no different, at least in terms of the fashion in which they need be resolved and the manner in which their resolution affects individual behavior and interests, there is no persuasive reason to believe that their final or presumptive disposition by non–Article III state tribunals generates any superior claim of infringement of personal liberty.

2. Federal Legislative Courts and Administrative Agencies

Similar analysis may be applied to the constitutional issue presented when a judge of a federal legislative court, who has neither life tenure nor compensation security, presides— either by statutory authorization,[50] designation of the Chief Justice,[51] or recess appointment of the President[52]—in what would otherwise be an Article III criminal or civil trial. It may be forcefully contended that the absence of the judicial independence that Article III judges possess denies the litigants a constitutionally mandated individual freedom. The stirring words of Hamilton—that "inflexible and uniform adherence to the rights of the Constitution, and of individuals, which we perceive to be indispensable in the courts of justice, can certainly not be expected from judges who hold their offices by a temporary commission"[53]—lend graphic support to the view that the impartial and fearless administration of justice required for the se-

curity of a person's life, liberty, or property is badly subverted
when federal judges may be subjected to political pressures
and reprisals that Article III forbids. And, within recent times,
Justice Harlan opined that this issue "relates to basic constitutional protections designed in part for the benefit of
litigants."[54]

Nonetheless, the argument suffers what may be a fatal weakness. It has been long agreed that Congress need not create
lower federal courts at all and—apart from those cases that the
Constitution assigns to the Supreme Court's self-executing original jurisdiction—may instead rely on the state courts for initial
adjudication of all matters comprehended within "the judicial
power." Since it is essentially uncontested that this practice,
which, indeed, was the predominant one for the first hundred
years of the nation's history, violates no individual right, it would
seem to follow that congressional reliance on federally appointed
judges without life tenure rather than similarly situated state
judges—or on nationally established legislative courts or administrative agencies rather than tribunals set up by the states—
could evoke no stronger claim of infringement of personal liberty. But a nonfrivolous distinction can be drawn. It may be
plausibly contended that, especially in regard to enforcement of
federally created crimes or fulfillment of other nationally promulgated policies, judges and other adjudicative officials who
are directly subject to congressional nonrenewal, removal, or salary reduction would be significantly more susceptible to congressional pressure and substantially less inclined to detached
performance than their state counterparts.[55] And the argument
that individual freedom thereby becomes threatened is enhanced if all opportunity for appellate review in an Article III
court is also withdrawn.

Whether the Court should interpret the due process clause to
recognize the merits of this plea—or hold that Congress violates
the fifth amendment's guarantee of equal protection by affording
litigants in some cases complete trappings of Article III while
relegating others to state courts or "lesser" federal tribunals[56]—is
beyond the scope of consideration here. Whatever the force of
the personal liberty position just sketched, however, there is

trenchant reason (and voluminous authority) to support the conclusion that important constitutional issues are present, not of
individual rights but rather concerning "the strong interest of the
federal judiciary in maintaining the constitutional plan of separation of powers."[57] When the political branches attempt to denude or delimit the authority of Article III courts over questions
of fact or matters of law—be they constitutional or nonconstitutional—by vesting their final, presumptive, or original
settlement of the issues in federal legislative courts, administrative agencies, or Article III courts presided over by non–
Article III judges, a well-founded argument may frequently be
made that the law illegitimately shrinks the coverage of "the
judicial power" defined in the Constitution.

E. Issues concerning Scope of the Federal Judicial Power

Although substantive exploration of these questions in
any detail lies beyond our concern,[58] a few brief comments are
appropriate. For example, even though it is conceded that
Congress may assign all cases and controversies within the jurisdiction of Article III tribunals to state courts for initial determination, it by no means necessarily follows that Congress may similarly delegate such matters to non–Article III federal bodies. We
have already observed, in discussing trials conducted by federal
legislative judges, that a tenable issue of personal liberty may
arise in the latter situation that is plainly nonexistent in the
former. Some observers believe that the inquiry should stop
here. In Justice Brandeis's view, for example, "if there be any
controversy to which the judicial power extends that may not be
subjected to the conclusive determination of administrative
bodies or federal legislative courts, it is not because of any prohibition against the diminution of the jurisdiction of the federal
district courts as such, but because, under certain circumstances,
the constitutional requirement of due process is a requirement of
judicial process." Indeed, he strongly disbelieved that "Article
III has properly any bearing upon the question."[59] But it seems
that the more cogent objections to such congressional measures

focus not on the individual's right of due process but rather on that aspect of the constitutional division of power designed to preserve the integrity and vigor of the judicial branch. A congressional decision to bypass the national judicial system authorized by Article III in favor of state courts established through a preexisting and independent government order may be both explicable and justifiable because of values grounded in historical tradition and compromises struck in forging the union. But it is quite another matter for Congress to circumvent the constitutionally contemplated plan for federal courts by fashioning a comprehensive national adjudicatory system that is to function almost totally outside the requirements of Article III. At some stage, irrespective of such action's effect on individual rights, the political branches may be found to have overstepped the scope of their regulatory power and to have sapped the intended vitality of their coequal and coordinate judicial partner. Although the precise perimeters of the judicial power vis-à-vis the authority of the political branches—which the Justices have shifted considerably over time[60]—is immaterial for our purposes, the task of defining those limits should ultimately fall to the Court for reasons that have already been stated.

We previously concluded that the Federalism Proposal prevents the Court from deciding the constitutional question of whether factual or statutory determinations of a designated non–Article III adjudicatory body result in a violation of states' rights. But it does not follow that the Court should abjure from ruling whether Congress's refusal to permit fuller consideration by Article III courts of the underlying factual and statutory issues offends the constitutional separation of powers at the national level. Under the Judicial Proposal, the matter is subject to judicial review not because, at base, a fundamental question of national versus state authority is at stake, but rather despite the existence of this constitutional question. The earlier discussion (in sec. III, B) of the hypothetical federal minimum wage statute and the *Crowell* case illustrates this point. In both instances, Congress had ordered that questions of fact (or interpretations of law), that seemingly were crucial in fixing the reach of national power vis-à-vis the states, should be finally (or presumptively) resolved by federal legislative tribunals (or state courts). On one hand, the Federalism Proposal would treat as nonjusticiable the issue of the proper allocation of national versus local regulatory authority. On the other hand, however, the Judicial Proposal strongly urges the Court to use its most potent weapon—judicial review—to guard against encroachments by the political branches on the federal judicial power.

This abbreviated excursion into the substantive realm of "the judicial power" may end near to where we earlier began. The question that we have been generally exploring—whether Congress's grant of certain adjudicative authority to non–Article III bodies transgresses either individual rights or the separation of powers—has been considered in isolation from a related question previously noted: the consequence of seeking to enforce an order of those tribunals through the auspices of an Article III court. Even if we assumed—for analytic purposes only—that Congress constitutionally could assign judicial functions to non–Article III bodies, pressing issues surface when the further ingredient is added. Whatever their ultimate resolution on the merits, it may be persuasively urged that the political branches unconstitutionally invoke judicial authority by conscripting Article III courts to effectuate the decisions of other government agencies while simultaneously restricting their ability to examine the bases—factual or legal—on which these judgments rest.[61] And, for our purposes, it is important to note that this argument is wholly independent of any issues of violation of personal liberty. Indeed, once it is assumed that Congress constitutionally can provide for exclusive disposition of certain matters by non–Article III tribunals, it seems plainly to follow that no stronger individual rights claim arises simply because enforcement of the disposition is sought in an Article III court. This point may be forcefully underlined by reference to the *Yakus* decision. It may be conceded that the criminal defendants' procedural due process contention was without merit, given their earlier opportunity to challenge the validity of the regulation under which they were prosecuted in the Emergency Court of Appeals—an Article III court. Nonetheless, the issue remained whether Congress improperly interfered with the judicial function by providing for conviction in another Article III court and denying that court the ability to consider the defense of invalidity in that enforcement proceeding.

IV. POLITICAL EXPANSIONS OF JUDICIAL AUTHORITY

The discussion to this point primarily has concerned purported constrictions of "the judicial power" by the national political departments. As was observed in the opening pages of this chapter, however, these represent but one of the two principal ways in which the stipulations of Article III may be offended. Under the Judicial Proposal, the federal judiciary also holds ultimate authority to determine that certain legislative conferments of jurisdiction either (1) invalidly augment the judicial province that is carefully described in Article III or (2) otherwise unconstitutionally undermine the critical role historically contemplated and contemporarily demanded of the Supreme Court in American government.

A. CONFLICT WITH TERMS OF ARTICLE III

The first type of congressional enactments, those that would cause the judicial branch to exceed the limits of its adjudicatory power delineated by the language of Article III, may be generally described with relative ease—as we have already seen in sec. I, B. At least in some cases, however, specific resolution of whether a law in fact oversteps the lines may be more difficult—as has been demonstrated by the criticisms[62] of Chief Justice Marshall's peremptory disposition in *Marbury v. Madison* of §13 of the Judiciary Act of 1789 (a statute of the genre under discussion). The matter may be sufficiently illustrated for our purposes by noting that, irrespective of the wishes of the political branches, both the Judicial Proposal and firmly entrenched orthodox doctrine hold that the federal courts should refuse to rule on any question that is not presented by a constitutionally prescribed case or controversy. Although the phrase is by no means self-defining, one clear example of failure to fulfill its terms is presented by a request from either Congress or the President (or from a private party) that the Court offer nonbinding advice as to the constitutionality of a proposed course of action not yet undertaken by either of the political branches.[63]

B. CONFLICT WITH COURT'S ESSENTIAL ROLE

Legislative grants of the second kind of adjudicatory authority referred to above—those that empower federal courts to render obligatory judgments in truly adversary disputes that constitute unquestioned cases or controversies, whose subject matter and contestants undisputably fall within the literal coverage of Article III, that raise no issue of misallocation between the original and appellate jurisdiction of the Supreme Court but which jeopardize the Court's role in our governmental scheme—call for fuller consideration. If the Court finds, in the principled exercise of judgment—further elucidation of which will concern us shortly—that its resolution of a constitutional question would impair the performance of its essential function in our constitutional system, then it should abstain from decision.

A moment's reflection discloses that, for reasons already surveyed at length in the preceding chapters, those constitutional questions that the Federalism and Separation Proposals urged the Court to treat as nonjusticiable fit within this latter group. It may be argued—employing the Court's language in *Baker v. Carr*—that by "a delicate exercise in constitutional interpretation" these matters fall beyond the judicial realm because of "a textually demonstrable constitutional commitment of the issue to a coordinate political department."[64] But this tends more to affirm a conclusion than to explain its bases. The clauses of the Constitution that allocate power between the national government and the states and that divide authority between Congress and the President no more plainly reveal, either by text or intent, which institution of government should determine the constitutionally proper balance than does Article IV's proviso that "the United States shall guarantee to every State in this Union a Republican Form of Government" or Article V's procedures for amending the Constitution. And while the Court has ruled that

both the guarantee clause and Article V raise nonjusticiable constitutional issues,[65] they no more obviously concern matters
"committed by the Constitution to another branch of government"[66] than do most other clauses of the Constitution that have
been traditionally subject to judicial interpretation. Nor, in my
view, do the other criteria set forth in the Court's landmark essay
on the political question doctrine in *Baker v. Carr* fully explain
or persuasively justify the Justices' refusal to adjudicate certain
constitutional questions that have reached the Court which
otherwise comport with the explicit terms of Article III or that
would similarly come before the Court under the Federalism and
Separation Proposals. Rather, the functional considerations that
have provided the basis of our evaluation throughout this book
should determine whether the Court should refrain from deciding a constitutional issue on grounds of nonjusticiability.

1. Technique of Statutory Interpretation

Urgent objection—relying on Chief Justice Marshall's
oft-repeated dictum in *Cohens v. Virginia* that "we have no more
right to decline the exercise of jurisdiction which is given, than
to usurp that which is not given"[67]—may be raised to the view
that the Court should refuse to resolve constitutional questions
despite their presence in a case that undeniably satisfies the
explicit language of Article III and that apparently comes within
a congressional grant of jurisdiction. One method of avoiding this
protest is for the Court to narrowly construe the seemingly encompassing language of the jurisdictional statute as not commanding the decision of constitutional issues when the Justices
find, on the basis of principled criteria, that their resolution
would undermine the Court's performance of its central constitutional role. This technique—more often available than actually employed[68]—would rest on the credible and beneficial
proposition that, although "jurisdiction under our system is
rooted in Article III and congressional enactments . . . [and] is not
a domain solely within the Court's keeping,"[69] the Court should
be hesitant to attribute an intention to the political branches that
requires the Court to engage in the delicate process of con-

stitutional adjudication despite the Justices' belief that it would be inappropriate or wasteful for the Court to do so. This approach may be used to explain, and to blunt the criticism of, the Court's dismissing appeals in cases such as *Poe v. Ullman*[70] which come to it from the state courts under the facially obligatory jurisdiction of 28 U.S.C. §1257(2). In *Poe*, the Justices might well have explicitly held that, although the case met all of the literal requirements of Article III and the jurisdictional statute, Congress should not be read as ordering the Court to exercise its fragile and antimajoritarian power of judicial review—with all the attendant short- and long-term costs to its institutional position—when there was no realistic threat of deprivation of appellants' individual constitutional rights. Thus, the principled reason for the Court's refusal to decide the appeal would not be that the matter was nonjusticiable but that it lacked that "immediacy which is an indispensable condition of constitutional adjudication."[71]

2. Unmistakable Authorization of Jurisdiction

This suggested ground for nondecision would, of course, be unavailable if a clearly articulated legislative intent forbade a limiting construction of the jurisdictional statute. Such a situation could arise, for example, if the political departments, embroiled in a dispute concerning their respective constitutional powers over a matter such as executive privilege or impoundment of appropriated funds, were to enact a special jurisdictional provision submitting the controversy for judicial resolution. (It may be recalled, as we observed in chapter 5, that this is not far from what actually happened in *Myers v. United States* and the *Pocket Veto Cases*—and, indeed, effectively occurred in the conflict between President Nixon and the special Watergate committee chaired by Senator Ervin.)[72] Although the issue has arisen in lower federal court litigation,[73] whether the federal judiciary may refuse an explicit statutory mandate to decide a constitutional question within a case that satisfies all of the explicit elements in Article III has never been definitively resolved by the Supreme Court. To put it another way, the Court has never determined—when faced with a controversy that is sufficiently concrete, developed, and adverse to fulfill the explicit requirements of Article III—whether the political question doctrine is rooted in the Constitution or is simply a judicial construct that exists at the sufferance of the political branches. Nor, in the context of a similarly evolved case, has the Court ever ruled whether Congress may compel it to abandon certain other judicially created bars to adjudication that parade under such labels as "ripeness" or "standing" and to pass judgment on a substantive constitutional issue.

In considering whether a political directive to decide is binding on the Court, it is tempting to distinguish the Court's precept against resolution of nonjusticiable constitutional questions from its disinclination to address otherwise justiciable constitutional questions when it believes they are presented prematurely or asserted by a person other than the beneficiary of the constitutional provision. All the Court need do in respect to nonjusticiable questions, as we have seen, is to hold as a matter of constitutional interpretation that their resolution is committed to the political branches and that, as a consequence, no ordinary act of Congress may supersede the command of the fundamental charter. This approach is obviously inapplicable in regard to matters of ripeness and standing since it is conceded that the underlying constitutional questions are ordinarily adjudicable. We have already rejected the "demonstrable constitutional commitment" rationale as a means of sustaining the Court's refusal to decide nonjusticiable questions. Instead, the Court should use a more pragmatic analysis as a guide for holding that certain constitutional decisionmaking would unnecessarily endanger its critical function. Although the topic, because of the extensive independent discussion it requires, lies beyond the manageable confines of this book, the same utilitarian considerations should govern the Court's approach in respect to cases (or specific issues within them) that it finds improvident to decide owing to problems of ripeness or standing—even in the teeth of an obligatory conferral of jurisdiction.

That Congress and the President may have deliberately chosen—either by a generally worded jurisdictional statute or a specific grant of authority—to consign the question for judicial disposition should not be determinative. If the rationale were that the Court should abjure resolution of nonjusticiable questions because of a constitutional commitment of the matter to one or both of the political departments, then such a submission to the Court might be viewed as a constitutionally impermissible delegation. But that has not been the analysis for judicial abstention urged here. And we have earlier observed that even announced political acquiescence prior to the Court's judgment provides no sure immunity from subsequent attack; indeed, in many instances, the very reason for the bequest has been to shift the focus of popular hostility. Moreover, if one of the political branches only grudgingly consents or actively opposes the Court's dominion over the matter (as when the President either refuses to sign or vetoes Congress's jurisdictional enactment), then the likelihood of ultimate damage to the judiciary is exacerbated. By employing the propounded criteria and staying its hand in the manner suggested, the Court may exercise a principled prudence that should enable it to avoid uneconomic and potentially hazardous dissipation of its energy, thus more firmly securing its essential role in American government.

3. Pertinent Constitutional Provision

The opening words of Article III provide a fair constitutional peg. To justify its deliberate refusal to decide some constitutional questions at all times and other constitutional questions at some times, to abstain from ruling on certain constitutional issues in resolving some cases and sometimes (when the case is incapable of being disposed of otherwise) to refrain from adjudicating altogether, the Justices should hold that political edicts to the contrary infringe "the judicial power of the United States." Like all other constitutionally enumerated powers (as affirmed by *United States v. Nixon*)[74] this clause implies those accessory powers necessary to its effective discharge, and final interpretation of its meaning belongs to the Supreme Court.

In only a relatively few instances has the Court declined to resolve disputes (or to decide constitutional issues within them necessary to their disposition) that have reached it with no apparent defects under the literal jurisdictional prerequisites of Article III and statutory law (or conventional precepts against premature adjudication). And none of the handful in which the Justices have so abstained contains an opinion for the Court that explicitly rests on "the judicial power" justification for nondecision. But several cases lend support. For example, in *Luther v. Borden*,[75] the plaintiff sought damages for trespass against officers of the "charter government" of Rhode Island who, when the state was under martial law, forcibly entered his house to arrest him for supporting the rebellious government. In affirming a verdict for the defendants, the Court rejected plaintiff's argument that it should hold that the rebellious government, rather than the charter government, "was the lawful and established government."[76] In considering the guarantee clause of Article IV, the Court employed the "constitutional commitment" rationale, ruling that "it rests with Congress to decide what government is the established one in a State. For as the United States guarantee to each State a republican government, Congress must necessarily decide what government is established in the State before it can determine whether it is republican or not.... It rested with Congress, too, to determine upon the means proper...to fulfill this guarantee."[77] In denying its authority to review the validity of a presidential summons of the militia under the guarantee clause, however, the Court observed that "if the *judicial power extends so far*, the guarantee contained in the Constitution of the United States is a guarantee of anarchy, and not of order."[78] And in finally vindicating its abstinence, the Court concluded that "while it should always be ready to meet any question confided to it by the Constitution, it is equally its duty not to *pass beyond its appropriate sphere of action*, and to take care not to involve itself in discussions which properly belong to other forums."[79]

Perhaps the most forceful testimony may be gleaned from the several eighteenth-century opinions in *Hayburn's Case*.[80] Congress had provided that disabled Revolutionary War veterans file pension claims in federal court. The judges were to determine the proper amounts to be awarded and were to so certify to the Secretary of War, who, in turn, was to place the names on the pension list unless he "shall have cause to suspect imposition or mistake." Although the matter never reached the Supreme Court, five of the then six Justices, sitting on three different circuit courts, rendered judgments that they could not perform the assigned task despite the seeming presence of adverse parties and the undisputed existence of a concrete federal question ripe for determination. The obstacle—in the language of one of the opinions—was that the Secretary of War's authority for "revision and control we deemed radically inconsistent with the *independence of that judicial power* which is vested in the courts."[81] Whatever the soundness of this particular ground for nondecision, more important for our purposes was the further reasoning offered in all the opinions that the federal judiciary could refuse to accept jurisdiction specifically conferred. In the most frequently cited passage, Chief Justice Jay and Justice Cushing agreed "that neither the *Legislative* nor the *Executive* branches, can constitutionally assign to the *Judicial* any duties, but such as are properly judicial, and to be performed in a judicial manner."[82] The Court has often relied on this proposition in declining to rule on matters that it finds not to present a true case or controversy.[83] Similarly, Justices Wilson and Blair found they could not proceed in this instance "because the business directed by this act is not of a *judicial nature*. It forms no part of the *power* vested by the Constitution in the courts of the United States."[84] And, finally, Justice Iredell specifically invoked the pertinent constitutional phraseology; although acknowledging the "implicit and unreserved obedience" owed by the federal judiciary to the political branches in respect to assignment of jurisdiction, he concluded "that at the same time such courts cannot be warranted, . . . by virtue of that part of the Constitution delegating *Judicial power*, . . . in exercising . . . any power not in its nature *judicial*, or if *judicial*, not provided for upon the terms the Constitution requires."[85]

Most recently, in *Ohio v. Wyandotte Chemicals Corp.*[86]— denying leave to Ohio to file a complaint against several chemical companies for contaminating Lake Erie—the Court, although never referring to "the judicial power" clause of Article III, articulated a rationale for declining to exercise a seemingly mandatory jurisdiction that, by analogy, squarely sustains the approach proposed here. The Court stipulated at the outset that it was "beyond doubt" that the complaint revealed "the existence of a genuine 'case or controversy'"[87] satisfying all formal requisites of the Court's original jurisdiction. Moreover, the majority conceded that "it may initially have been contemplated that this Court would always exercise its original jurisdiction when properly called upon to do so."[88] Nevertheless, the Court abjured decision, advancing pragmatic and functional criteria closely paralleling those that we have been considering throughout—"principally, as a technique for promoting and furthering the assumptions and value choices that underlie the current role of this Court in the federal system."[89] Emphasizing "this Court's paramount responsibilities to the national system"[90] (analogous to the Court's essential role in securing individual constitutional liberties) and noting that "much would be sacrificed, and little gained, by our exercising original jurisdiction over issues bottomed on local law"[91] (as is also true in its resolving the constitutional issues of federalism and separation of powers that I have argued the Court should treat as nonjusticiable), "it seems evident to us that changes in the American legal system and the development of American society have rendered untenable, as a practical matter, the view that this Court must stand willing to adjudicate all or most legal disputes that may arise between one State and a citizen or citizens of another even though the dispute may be one over which this Court does have original jurisdiction."[92] Just as the Court is no better equipped than the political branches to resolve certain kinds of constitutional issues, so, too, the Court in *Wyandotte* laid "no claim to special competence in dealing with the numerous conflicts between States and nonresident individuals that raise no serious issues of federal law."[93] Finally, the Court's concluding remarks for refusing to decide aptly summarize much of the basis for the nonjusticiability rationale advocated here: "(1) declination of jurisdiction would not disserve any of the principal policies underlying the Article III jurisdictional grant and (2) the reasons of practical wisdom that persuade us that this Court is an inappropriate forum are consistent with the proposition that our discretion is legitimated by its use to keep this aspect of the Court's functions attuned to its other responsibilities."[94]

Whether "the judicial power" clause of Art. III, §1 is ultimately the most appropriate and effective vehicle for judicial self-defense against the various political devices of the "Exceptions and Regulations" clause of Art. III, §2, that (as we have seen in chapter 1) Congress can employ to diminish the Court's authority—e.g., curtailing its appellate jurisdiction, abolishing its terms, requiring a unanimous vote for a declaration of unconstitutionality—is not our concern. But I believe that enough has been said to demonstrate that its force may be sufficient to permit judicial invalidation of congressional efforts to require the Court to render judgments that the Justices find would subvert the Court's central role in our constitutional system. Congressional enactments of this sort may burden the Court quantitatively (as would a statute mandating Supreme Court appellate jurisdiction in all cases between citizens of different states or original jurisdiction in all cases with federal questions in which a state is a party) or qualitatively (as would forced resolution of those issues that the Court believes nonjusticiable). In either event, the Court should retain the power to decide that it has no power to decide.

4. Consistency with Congress's Authorized Control of Jurisdiction

Vesting this ultimate constitutional authority in the judiciary by no means denies the plainly documented historical intention and explicit constitutional language according the political branches significant control over the Court's jurisdiction. Neither does it conclude—as Gerald Gunther berated Alexander Bickel for urging—that "there is a *general* 'Power to Decline the Exercise of Jurisdiction Which Is Given,' that there is a *general* discretion not to adjudicate though statute, Constitution, and remedial law present a 'case' for decision and confer no discretion."[95] Nor does it afford the Supreme Court an unfettered license to abstain from constitutional decision on an "opportunistic" or "hot potato" theory[96]—an approach of "judicial impressionism"[97] to "accommodate the stern demands of principle to the perceived needs of expediency"[98] by employing its "instincts for political survival"[99] so as to escape "prickly issues" and "contentious questions" that strike the "hypersensitive nerve of public opinion."[100] For these unconfined standards and particular criteria are not only totally lacking in the doctrinal integrity that requires our antimajoritarian judiciary to perform principled constitutional adjudication, but their use also amounts to a gross abdication of the Court's profound obligation in exercising its power of judicial review—that of seeking to secure individual constitutional liberties in the face of hostile popular attitudes and actions. Rather the thesis advanced here is that the Court should hold that "the judicial power of the United States" does not extend to the resolution of constitutional questions that the Court—through the use of the functional, but substantively neutral and nonopportunistic, factors that have been previously explored at length—finds to be unnecessary for the preservation of genuine personal constitutional freedoms and subject to fair and effective resolution in the national political process.

It must be conceded that this aspect of the Judicial Proposal—which entitles the Court (pursuant to Art. III, §1) to articulate and enforce constitutional limitations on the legislative authority (designated in Art. III, §2) to regulate its jurisdiction—materially affects the distribution of constitutional power among the national branches of government. But it is highly important to recognize the peculiar quality of the judicial assumption of power at issue. Viewed realistically, it is a judicial authority not to enhance the Court's power but rather to confine it, a course not of self-arrogation but rather one of self-denial—a capacity of the judiciary to refrain from exerting influence not wholly dissimilar (though the analogy is far from perfect) to whatever discretion the executive has to decline to enforce laws, or even to the unquestioned ability of the legislature to refuse to enact them (though here the analogy may be stretched beyond permissible limits).

Finally, it is especially meaningful to contrast the relatively modest nature of the practice urged here with the more frequently debated constitutional policy respecting legislative control of "the judicial power"—that of Congress's authority under the "Exceptions and Regulations" clause to restrict the Supreme Court's appellate jurisdiction. In chapter 1 we briefly reviewed the series of persuasive arguments that have found substantial judicial power to resist political encroachments enacted pursuant to this provision. As there indicated, the merits of these various constitutional interpretations is beyond the scope of our consideration. For present purposes, however, it is extremely important to note that their thrust empowers the Court to maintain its substantive constitutional role and to inject its influence over governmental policy despite concrete political sentiment to the contrary. Their acceptance must overcome the central historic purpose—as explained by Justice Frankfurter —of affording a formal political check against what might be felt to be judicial dominance: "There was a deep distrust of a federal judicial system . . . in the Constitutional Convention . . . . [S]ince the judges of the courts for which Article III made provision, not only had the last word (apart from amending the Constitution) but also enjoyed life tenure, it was an essential safeguard against control by the judiciary of its own jurisdiction, to define the jurisdiction of those courts with particularity. The Framers guarded against the self-will of the courts . . . by marking with exactitude the outer limits of federal judicial power."[101] Whatever the past or present force of these concerns may be in respect to the Court's ability to invalidate congressional contractions of federal jurisdiction, they are signally inapt in regard to the legitimacy of the Justices' refusal to abide by what they find to be inappropriate and potentially destructive expansions of the power of judicial review.

Notes

Preface

1. Howe, Split Decisions, N.Y. Rev. of Books 17 (July 1, 1965).
2. Kelly, Clio and the Court: An Illicit Love Affair, 1965 Sup. Ct. Rev. 119, 122 & n.13.

One   The Supreme Court and the Political Branches

1. See the recitation of these views in R. Dahl, A Preface to Democratic Theory 34–35 (1956) (hereafter cited as R. Dahl, Preface). See also Ely, Constitutional Interpretivism: Its Allure and Impossibility, 53 Ind. L.J. 399, 405–11 (1978).
2. H. Mayo, An Introduction to Democratic Theory 70 (1960); see also McCleskey, Judicial Review in a Democracy: A Dissenting Opinion, 3 Houston L. Rev. 354, 357 (1966); A. Ranney & W. Kendall, Democracy and the American Party System 54–55 (1956).
3. See, e.g., 7 The Writings of Thomas Jefferson 75 (H. Washington ed. 1861); 10 The Writings of Thomas Jefferson 89 (P. Ford ed. 1892–99).
4. R. Dahl, Preface 35.
5. Id. 31.
6. R. Scigliano, The Supreme Court and the Presidency 9–10 (1971).
7. C. Black, The Occasions of Justice 75 (1963).
8. Bishin, Judicial Review in Democratic Theory, 50 S. Cal. L. Rev. 1099, 1132 (1977).
9. Rostow, The Supreme Court and the People's Will, 33 Notre Dame Law. 573, 577 (1958).

10. The phrase is Charles Reich's in The New Property, 73 Yale L.J. 733, 774 (1964).

11. See, e.g., W. Kendall, John Locke and the Doctrine of Majority Rule 134–35 (1959).

12. The point is considered further in chap. 2.

13. Auerbach, The Reapportionment Cases: One Person, One Vote—One Vote, One Value, 1964 Sup. Ct. Rev. 1, 52 (footnotes omitted).

14. Rostow, 33 Notre Dame Law. at 576.

15. Cf. Miller, Some Pervasive Myths about the United States Supreme Court, 10 St. L. U. L.J. 153, 159 (1965).

16. AFL v. American Sash and Door Co., 335 U.S. 538, 555–56 (1949) (Frankfurter, J., concurring).

17. L. Hand, The Bill of Rights 73 (1958).

18. 2 J. Burgess, Political Science and Comparative Constitutional Law 365 (1891).

19. C. Curtis, Lions under the Throne 323 (1947).

20. A. de Tocqueville, Democracy in America 115 (Mentor ed. 1956).

21. M. Shapiro, Freedom of Speech: The Supreme Court and Judicial Review 17 (1966) (hereafter cited as M. Shapiro, Freedom of Speech).

22. Id.

23. See generally Bishin.

24. See Chroust, Law: Reason, Legalism, and the Judicial Process, 74 Ethics 16 (1963).

25. M. Shapiro, Law and Politics in the Supreme Court 46 (1964).

26. R. Dahl, Preface 131.

27. For a mathematical demonstration of control by 25 percent of all voters plus one additional voter under simple majority voting, see J. Buchanan & G. Tullock, The Calculus of Consent 220–22 (1962).

28. Cf. generally A. Downs, An Economic Theory of Democracy (1957); V. Key, The Responsible Electorate (1966).

29. R. Dahl, Pluralist Democracy in the United States: Conflict and Consent 455–56 (1967) (hereafter cited as R. Dahl, Pluralist Democracy).

30. See, e.g., Dexter, The Representative and His District, in New Perspectives on the House of Representatives 3 (R. Peabody & N. Polsby eds. 2d ed. 1969); A. Campbell, P. Converse, W. Miller & D. Stokes, The American Voter (1960); Miller & Stokes, Constituency Influence in Congress, 57 Am. Pol. Sci. Rev. 45 (1963). See generally V. Key, Public Opinion and American Democracy (1967); Rothman, Individualism, Indecision and Indifference, 35 Marq. L. Rev. 219 (1952); C. Hardin, Presidential Power and Accountability 148–52, 174–76 (1974).

31. See the study and report of the Ass'n of the Bar of the City of New York, Congress and the Public Trust 10–15 (1970) (hereafter cited as Congress and the Public Trust); D. Mayhew, Congress: The Electoral Connection 57–59 (1974).

32. See Nelson, The Effect of Incumbency on Voting in Congressional Elections, 1964–1974, 93 Pol. Sci. Q. 665 (1978).

33. R. Dahl, Pluralist Democracy 134 (citing Miller & Stokes 52).

34. D. Spitz, Democracy and the Challenge of Power 79 (1958).

35. Wesberry v. Sanders, 376 U.S. 1, 18 (1964).

36. See Malbin, Compromise by Senate Eases Anti-Filibuster Rule, 7 Nat. J. 397 (1975).

37. See Congress and the Public Trust 7–12.

38. N. Polsby, Congress and the Presidency 111 (3d ed. 1976). See generally J. Manley, The Politics of Finance: The House Committee on Ways and Means (1970).

39. Fenno, The Internal Distribution of Influence: The House, in The Congress and America's Future 52, 64–65 (D. Truman ed. 1965).

40. N. Polsby 167.

41. R. Fenno, Congressmen in Committees 195–96 (1973).

42. N. Polsby 170–71.

43. See generally R. Fenno; Jones, The Agriculture Committee and the Problem of Representation, in New Perspectives on the House of Representatives 155 (R. Peabody & N. Polsby eds. 2d ed. 1969).

44. N. Polsby 140.

45. G. Galloway, The Legislative Process in Congress 289 (1953).

46. D. Cater, Power in Washington 149–52 (1964). See generally R. Fenno, The Power of the Purse (1966).

47. D. Cater 17–19. See also Jones 155.

48. R. Davidson & W. Oleszek, Congress against Itself 32, 37 (1977).

49. See generally Truman, Federalism and the Party System, in Federalism: Mature and Emergent 115 (A. Macmahon ed. 1955).

50. See generally Polsby, Two Strategies of Influence: Choosing a Majority Leader, 1962, in New Perspectives on the House of Representatives 268–69 (R. Peabody & N. Polsby eds. 2d ed. 1969); Peabody, Party Leadership Change in the United States House of Representatives, 61 Am. Pol. Sci. Rev. 675 (1967).

51. N. Polsby 149.

52. Hopkins, Congressional Reform: Toward a Modern Congress, 47 Notre Dame Law. 442, 501 (1972).

53. D. Cater 9–10.

54. Gore, The Conference Committee: Congress' Final Filter, The Washington Monthly, June, 1971, at 43.

55. See, e.g., D. Truman, The Governmental Process (1951).

56. See generally R. Bauer, I. Pool & L. Dexter, American Business and Public Policy: The Politics of Foreign Trade (1963).

57. See generally M. Bernstein, Regulating Business by Independent Commission (1955); S. Lazarus, The Genteel Populists 90 (1974).

58. E. Griffith, Congress, Its Contemporary Role 127 (1956). See also J. Freeman, The Political Process: Executive Bureau—Legislative

Committee Relations (1965); Neustadt, Politicians and Bureaucrats, in The Congress and America's Future 102 (D. Truman ed. 1965).

59. M. Shapiro, Freedom of Speech 23. See generally T. Lowi, The End of Liberalism, ch. 3 (1969); G. McConnell, Private Power and American Democracy (1966).

60. M. Shapiro, Freedom of Speech 25.

61. Kommer, Professor Kurland, The Supreme Court, and Political Science, 15 J. Pub. L. 230, 242 (1966).

62. See D. Mayhew 126–27.

63. B. Eckhardt & C. Black, The Tides of Power 139 (1976).

64. See D. Mayhew 130–31; C. Hardin 125–27.

65. R. Dixon, Democratic Representation: Reapportionment in Law and Politics 10 (1968).

66. See S. Lazarus 16–18, 62–65, passim.

67. Auerbach 65.

68. D. Spitz 74.

69. Id.

70. See Pomper, From Confusion to Clarity: Issues and American Voters, 1956–68, 66 Am. Pol. Sci. Rev. 415 (1972). See also V. Key, The Responsible Electorate 7–8 (1966).

71. R. Dahl, Pluralist Democracy 248. See generally id. 243–57.

72. D. Spitz 74.

73. See Congress and the Public Trust 12–15; G. Galloway, Congress at the Crossroads 320–21 (1946); Miller & Stokes 45.

74. McLaughlin, What Has the Supreme Court Taught? 72 W. Va. L. Rev. 326, 335 (1970).

75. The Federalist, No. 71, at 303 (C. Beard ed. 1959).

76. Rostow, The Democratic Character of Judicial Review, 66 Harv. L. Rev. 193, 208 (1952).

77. See The Federalist, No. 56.

78. Miller & Stokes 55.

79. D. Mayhew 15–16 (footnotes omitted).

80. Erikson, The Electoral Impact of Congressional Roll Call Voting, 65 Am. Pol. Sci. Rev. 1018, 1023 (1971).

81. Abramowitz, Name Familiarity, Reputation, and the Incumbency Effect in a Congressional Election, 28 W. Pol. Q. 668, 673, 683 (1975).

82. See id. 677.

83. See Glazer, Is Busing Necessary? 53 Commentary 39, 41 (Mar. 1972).

84. See, e.g., D. Mayhew 32–37, 70–72; J. Kingdon, Congressmen's Voting Decisions 59–60 (1973); Ingram, The Impact of Constituency on the Process of Legislating, 22 W. Pol. Q. 265 (1969); Miller & Stokes 45. See generally S. Bailey & H. Samuel, Congress at Work 112–26 (1952); G. Galloway, The Legislative Process in Congress 198–215 (1953); V. Key, American State Politics 152 (1956); D. MacRae, Dimensions of

Congressional Voting 278 (1958); D. Truman, The Congressional Party (1959).

85. Congress and the Public Trust 33.

86. Id.

87. D. Mayhew 71.

88. Id. 71–72.

89. Dexter 22.

90. See G. Reedy, The Twilight of the Presidency 146–47 (1970).

91. See 31 Cong. Q. Wkly. Rep. 501–04 (1973); 31 Cong. Q. Alm. 930–33 (1975). See generally Eckhardt, The Presumption of Committee Openness under House Rules, 11 Harv. J. Leg. 279 (1974).

92. 31 Cong. Q. Alm. 931.

93. Hopkins & Oleszek, Ninety-fifth Congress: Legislative Reform in 1977, 64 A.B.A.J. 341, 344 (1978).

94. Miller & Stokes 54–55. See also Dexter 3.

95. M. Green, J. Fallows & D. Zwick, Who Runs Congress? The President, Big Business, or You? 95 (1972).

96. See Weissberg, Collective vs. Dyadic Representation in Congress, 72 Am. Pol. Sci. Rev. 535 (1978).

97. Miller & Stokes 51–52.

98. Id. 50.

99. See Verba et al., Public Opinion and the War in Vietnam, 61 Am. Pol. Sci. Rev. 317 (1967).

100. See Davidson, Congress in the American Political System, in Legislatures in Developmental Perspective 129 (A. Kornberg & L. Musolf eds. 1970).

101. R. Dahl, Pluralist Democracy 135.

102. Brenner, Congressional Reform: Analyzing the Analysts, 14 Harv. J. Leg. 651, 660 (1977).

103. See generally J. Robinson, The House Rules Committee (1963).

104. See D. Mayhew 154–55.

105. See Hopkins, Congressional Reform Advances in the Ninety-third Congress, 60 A.B.A.J. 47, 48 (1974).

106. See B. Eckhardt & C. Black 152.

107. N. Polsby 133.

108. D. Cater 148. See generally J. Manley.

109. See D. Cater 26–48.

110. 2 U.S.C. §190a(a) (1970).

111. See 31 Cong. Q. Alm. 30 (1975); Hopkins & Oleszek, 64 A.B.A.J. at 345.

112. See 31 Cong. Q. Wkly. Rep. 69, 136, 279 (1973); Hopkins, 47 Notre Dame Law. at 481–83; 31 Cong. Q. Alm. 26 (1975); 35 Cong. Q. Wkly. Rep. 279 (1977); Rohde, Committee Reform in the House of Representatives and the Subcommittee Bill of Rights, 411 Annals 39 (1974); Hopkins & Oleszek 345.

113. See 31 Cong. Q. Alm. at 32–34; 33 Cong. Q. Alm. 10 (1977).

114. R. Davidson & W. Oleszek 271.

115. See R. Dahl, Pluralist Democracy 288.

116. See Peabody 687–89.

117. This explanation was suggested to me by Nelson W. Polsby. See also Fenno, in The Congress and America's Future at 63.

118. D. Mayhew 100–101. See also Huitt, Democratic Party Leadership in the Senate, in Congress: Two Decades of Analysis 136, 140 (R. Huitt & R. Peabody eds. 1969): "The constituency has a virtually unqualified power to hire and fire. If the member pleases it, no party leader can fatally hurt him; if he does not, no national party organ can save him."

119. Legislative Reorganization Act of 1970, Pub. L. No. 91–510, §125(b) (3), 84 Stat. 1140, 1159–60 (Oct. 26, 1970).

120. See Hopkins, The Ninety-third: An Authentic Reform Congress, 61 A.B.A.J. 37, 40 (1975); Hopkins & Oleszek 344.

121. See Jacqueney, Public Interest Groups Challenge Government, Industry, 6 Nat. J. 267 (1974).

122. See Brenner 655–56.

123. See, e.g., Miller & Stokes 50. See also S. Rice, Quantitative Methods in Politics, ch. 14 (1928).

124. A. Bickel, The Least Dangerous Branch 18 (1962).

125. R. Dahl, Preface 132.

126. A. Bickel 19.

127. See N. Long, The Polity 70–71 (1962).

128. See Kirkpatrick, Representation in the American National Conventions: The Case of 1972, 5 British J. of Pol. Sci. 265 (July 1975).

129. W. Keech & D. Matthews, The Party's Choice 8, 215 (1977). Cf. id. 97–105.

130. Compare generally N. Polsby & A. Wildavsky, Presidential Elections 166–72 (1964) with N. Peirce, The People's President (1968).

131. See, e.g., C. Black, The People and the Court 209–12 (1960); J. Buchanan & G. Tullock 260–62.

132. The subject will be treated in detail in chap. 3.

133. The eleventh amendment in 1795—overruling Chisholm v. Georgia, 2 U.S. 419 (1793); the first section of the fourteenth amendment in 1868—overruling Dred Scott v. Sandford, 60 U.S. 393 (1857); the sixteenth amendment in 1913—overruling Pollock v. Farmers' Loan & Trust Co., 157 U.S. 429 (1895); the twenty-sixth amendment in 1971—overruling Oregon v. Mitchell, 400 U.S. 112 (1970).

134. See generally R. Scigliano 96; H. Abraham, Justices and Presidents: A Political History of Appointments to the Supreme Court 31 (1974).

135. See Kahn, Book Review, 63 Calif. L. Rev. 827, 836 (1975).

136. See R. Scigliano 125–60; Wasby, The Presidency before the Courts, 6 Cap. U. L. Rev. 35, 69 (1976).

137. Prize Cases, 67 U.S. 635 (1863).

138. 75 U.S. 603 (1870).

139. See C. Fairman, Reconstruction and Reunion 1864–88, vol. VI of History of the Supreme Court of the United States 713–38 (P. Freund ed. 1971).

140. Knox v. Lee, 79 U.S. 457 (1871).

141. See generally C. Fairman 738–75; Ratner, Was the Supreme Court Packed by President Grant? 50 Pol. Sci. Q. 343 (1935); E. Corwin, The President: Office and Powers 289 (4th ed. 1957).

142. See L. Tribe, American Constitutional Law 449 & n.18 (1978).

143. See J. Burns, Roosevelt: The Lion and the Fox 315 (1956).

144. See Ex parte McCardle, 74 U.S. 506 (1869).

145. See Wiscart v. Dauchy, 3 U.S. 321, 327 (1796); United States v. More, 7 U.S. 159, 173 (1805); Durousseau v. United States, 10 U.S. 307 (1810); Barry v. Mercein, 46 U.S. 103, 119–21 (1847); Daniels v. Railroad Co., 70 U.S. 250, 254 (1865); Ex parte McCardle, 74 U.S. 506 (1869); The Francis Wright, 105 U.S. 381 (1881); see also Yakus v. United States, 321 U.S. 414, 472–73 (1944) (Rutledge, J., dissenting).

146. Van Alstyne, A Critical Guide to Marbury v. Madison, 1969 Duke L.J. 1, 32–33.

147. R. Berger, Congress v. The Supreme Court 285–96 (1969); Merry, Scope of the Supreme Court's Appellate Jurisdiction: Historical Basis, 47 Minn. L. Rev. 53 (1962); Brant, Appellate Jurisdiction: Congressional Abuse of the Exceptions Clause, 53 Ore. L. Rev. 3 (1973).

148. Van Alstyne, A Critical Guide to Ex parte McCardle, 15 Ariz. L. Rev. 229 (1973).

149. Ratner, Congressional Power over the Appellate Jurisdiction of Federal Courts, 109 U. Pa. L. Rev. 157 (1960). Cf. Hart, The Power of Congress to Limit the Jurisdiction of Federal Courts: An Exercise in Dialectic, 66 Harv. L. Rev. 1362 (1953).

150. 1 W. Crosskey, Politics and the Constitution in the History of the United States 610–18 (1953).

151. Wechsler, The Courts and the Constitution, 65 Colum. L. Rev. 1001, 1006–07 (1965).

152. See Ex parte Yerger, 75 U.S. 85 (1869) (holding that the act of Congress upheld in Ex parte McCardle closed only one of the existing avenues of appeal to the Supreme Court).

153. See W. Murphy, Congress and the Court 245–46 (1962).

154. McCleskey 364.

155. See R. Scigliano 36–50.

156. R. McCloskey, The American Supreme Court 23 (1960).

157. Abraham, Machtkampf: The Supreme Court of the United States in the Political Process, 13 Parl. Affairs 424, 428 (1960) (emphasis in original).

158. Id. 430.

159. See C. H. Pritchett, Congress versus the Supreme Court 133 (1961).

160. See, e.g., W. Murphy 246–47. For further discussion, see chap. 3, sec. VI, D.

161. The phrase is Chief Justice Stone's in The Common Law in the United States, 50 Harv. L. Rev. 4, 25 (1936).

Two   The Individual Versus Government

1. 5 The Writings of James Madison 269 (Hunt ed. 1904).

2. Grey, Do We Have an Unwritten Constitution? 27 Stan. L. Rev. 703, 717 (1975).

3. 5 U.S. 137 (1803).

4. Fletcher v. Peck, 10 U.S. 87 (1810); Martin v. Hunter's Lessee, 14 U.S. 304 (1816).

5. 5 U.S. at 165–66.

6. Luther v. Borden, 48 U.S. 1 (1849).

7. Compare, e.g., C. Beard, The Supreme Court and the Constitution (rev. ed. 1938) and R. Berger, Congress v. The Supreme Court (1969) with 2 W. Crosskey, Politics and the Constitution in the History of the United States, chap. 29 (1953).

8. "[I]n little more than a dozen years, Madison took contradictory positions on at least three questions related to interpretation of the Constitution. First, he asserted judicial review would work, and that it wouldn't. Second, he claimed that the three federal departments were co-equal in interpreting the Constitution, and that the judiciary was pre-eminent. Third, he argued that the general government was the only logical agency of interpretation, and that the states had to be the final judges of the meaning of the Constitution." Ketcham, James Madison and Judicial Review, 8 Syr. L. Rev. 158, 160 (1957). See also Levy, Judicial Review, History, and Democracy: An Introduction, in Judicial Review and the Supreme Court 1 (L. Levy ed. 1967); The Constitution of the United States of America: Analysis and Interpretation 624–26 (N. Small ed. 1964).

9. See, e.g., 1 C. Warren, The Supreme Court in United States History 83–84 (rev. ed. 1928).

10. See C. Black, The People and the Court 23–25 (1960); Hazard, The Supreme Court as a Legislature, 64 Corn. L. Rev. 1, 5 (1978).

11. A. Bickel, The Least Dangerous Branch 3–14 (1962). See also Corwin, Marbury v. Madison and the Doctrine of Judicial Review, 12 Mich. L. Rev. 538 (1914).

12. See Cooper, Book Review, 85 Harv. L. Rev. 702 (1972).

13. Rostow, The Supreme Court and the People's Will, 33 Notre Dame Law. 573, 576 (1958).

14. See Cooper v. Aaron, 358 U.S. 1 (1958).

15. See Berger v. New York, 388 U.S. 41 (1967); Katz v. United States, 389 U.S. 347 (1967).

16. See generally D. Morgan, Congress and the Constitution 249–50 (1966).

17. R. Dworkin, Taking Rights Seriously 143 (1977).

18. 6 Works of John Adams 63 (C. Adams ed. 1851).

19. Lewis, Historic Change in the Supreme Court, in The Supreme Court under Earl Warren 73, 81 (L. Levy ed. 1972).

20. Bishin, Judicial Review in Democratic Theory, 50 So. Calif. L. Rev. 1099, 1125 n. 86 (1977).

21. L. Lusky, By What Right? 35 (1975).

22. 1 Annals of Congress 457 (1834).

23. 5 U.S. 137, 170 (1803).

24. A. Bickel, The Supreme Court and the Idea of Progress 37 (1970).

25. Warren, Fourteenth Amendment: Retrospect and Prospect, in The Fourteenth Amendment 212, 228 (B. Schwartz ed. 1970).

26. West Virginia State Board of Education v. Barnette, 319 U.S. 624, 638 (1943).

27. N.Y. Times, Feb. 25, 1959, p. 25, col. 1.

28. See Olmstead v. United States, 277 U.S. 438 (1928), holding that telephonic messages are not within the fourth amendment's protection against unreasonable searches and seizures, followed by §605 of the Federal Communications Act of 1934, generally prohibiting the use of intercepted communications.

29. See United States v. White, 401 U.S. 745 (1971) and Lopez v. United States, 373 U.S. 427 (1963), holding that the fourth amendment does not forbid such consensual monitoring of conversations, followed by Internal Revenue Service regulations (I.R.S. Manual §652.22) prohibiting them without appropriate authorization.

30. See Miranda v. Arizona, 384 U.S. 436 (1966), holding that special warnings must be given by police officers only in connection with "custodial" interrogation, followed by an Internal Revenue Service policy (I.R.S. News Rel. No. 897, Oct. 3, 1967) requiring agents investigating the possibility of criminal tax fraud to advise persons, even though not in custody, of their privilege to remain silent and to retain counsel.

31. See Bartkus v. Illinois, 359 U.S. 121 (1959) and Abbate v. United States, 359 U.S. 187 (1959), holding that successive federal-state or state-federal prosecutions of the same person for the same conduct do not violate the fifth amendment's prohibition against double jeopardy, followed by the enactment of an Illinois statute (Ill. Rev. Stat. Ch. 38, §601.1 (1959)) and an announcement by the Attorney General of the United States (Dept. of Justice Press Release, Apr. 6, 1959) setting policy against such sequential prosecutions.

32. See Zurcher v. Stanford Daily, 436 U.S. 547 (1978), holding that the first amendment freedom of the press does not forbid the issuance of a search warrant to obtain evidence from a newspaper office—even

though there was no emergency need to protect life or property, the evidence was not contraband, and the newspaper was not suspected of criminal activity—followed by the enactment of laws in a number of states restricting such use of search warrants. See, e.g., Cal. Penal Code §1524 (c) (1978).

33. See Branzburg v. Hayes, 408 U.S. 665 (1972), holding that the first amendment freedoms of speech and press do not afford newsmen a privilege to withhold the names of sources and information from grand juries, followed by the enactment or expansion of "newsmen's shield laws" in a number of states affording either an absolute or qualified privilege. For a collection of such statutes, see Note, The Newsman's Privilege after Branzburg: The Case for a Federal Shield Law, 24 U.C.L.A. L. Rev. 160, 167 n.41 (1976).

34. See discussion in chap. 4, sec. IX, B, 3, a.

35. See Lewis, The Supreme Court and Its Critics, 45 Minn. L. Rev. 305, 317–18 (1961).

36. See S.2097, 89th Cong., 1st Sess. (1965); S.3, 90th Cong., 1st. Sess. (1967).

37. United States v. Rabinowitz, 339 U.S. 56, 69 (1950) (dissenting opinion).

38. L. Jaffe, Judicial Control of Administrative Action 475 (1965).

39. See generally J. Peltason, Fifty-eight Lonely Men (1961); Wisdom, The Frictionmaking, Exacerbating Political Role of Federal Courts, 21 Sw. L.J. 411 (1967).

40. United States v. Carolene Products Co., 304 U.S. 144, 152 n.4 (1938).

41. Id.

42. See 2 W. Crosskey 1004; A. Bickel, The Least Dangerous Branch 6–7.

43. See Duncan v. Louisiana, 391 U.S. 145 (1968). But cf. Apodaca v. Oregon, 406 U.S. 404 (1972); Johnson v. Louisiana, 406 U.S. 356 (1972).

44. San Antonio Independent School District v. Rodriguez, 411 U.S. 1, 34 n.74 (1973).

45. Hart, Foreword: The Time Chart of the Justices, 73 Harv. L. Rev. 84, 99 (1959).

46. A. Cox, The Role of the Supreme Court in American Government 113 (1976).

47. Bork, The Supreme Court Needs a New Philosophy, 78:4 Fortune 138, 170 (Dec. 1968).

48. Wellington, Common Law Rules and Constitutional Double Standards: Some Notes on Adjudication, 83 Yale L.J. 221, 284 (1973).

49. R. Dworkin 126, 149.

50. Mueller & Schwartz, The Principle of Neutral Principles, 7 U.C.L.A. L. Rev. 571, 587 (1960).

51. 1 J. Bryce, The American Commonwealth 273 (1913).

52. C. Curtis, Lions under the Throne 335 (1947).

53. Sandalow, Judicial Protection of Minorities, 75 Mich. L. Rev. 1162 (1977).

54. Ely, Foreword: On Discovering Fundamental Values, 92 Harv. L. Rev. 5 (1978).

55. United States v. Carolene Products Co., 304 U.S. 144, 152 n.4 (1938).

56. A. Goldberg, Equal Justice: The Warren Era of the Supreme Court 46–47 (1971).

57. Frantz, Two Kinds of Judicial Review, 19 Law. Guild Rev. 75, 76 (1959).

58. Frantz, The First Amendment in the Balance, 71 Yale L.J. 1424, 1447 (1962).

59. See generally H. Lasswell, Politics: Who Gets What, When, How? (1958).

60. See S. Benn & R. Peters, The Principles of Political Thought 412–13 (1959).

61. Fiss, Groups and the Equal Protection Clause, 5 Phil. & Pub. Aff. 107, 154–55 (1976).

62. Id. 174–75.

63. See Abraham, Civil Rights and Liberties: Some Fundamental Considerations, 41 Soc. Sci. 131 (1966).

64. Cf. C. Black, Structure and Relationship in Constitutional Law (1969).

65. See, e.g., Vlandis v. Kline, 412 U.S. 441 (1973).

66. Compare, e.g., R. Berger, Government by Judiciary (1977) with, e.g., Ely, Constitutional Interpretivism: Its Allure and Impossibility, 53 Ind. L.J. 399 (1978) and Murphy, Constitutional Interpretation: The Art of the Historian, Magician, or Statesman? 87 Yale L.J. 1752 (1978).

67. See generally Sandalow.

68. Ely, Constitutional Interpretivism 448.

69. H. Commager, Majority Rule and Minority Rights 47 (1950).

70. R. Dahl, Pluralist Democracy in the United States: Conflict and Consent 166 (1967).

71. R. Dahl, Democracy in the United States: Promise and Performance 204 (2d ed. 1972) (hereafter cited as R. Dahl, Democracy).

72. Frank, Review and Basic Liberties, in Supreme Court and Supreme Law 109, 139 (E. Cahn ed. 1954). See also Ulmer, Judicial Review as Political Behavior: A Temporary Check on Congress, 4 Admin. Sci. Q. 426 (1960).

73. Funston, The Supreme Court and Critical Elections, 69 Am. Pol. Sci. Rev. 795, 809 (1975) (emphasis in original).

74. See generally S. Wasby, The Impact of the United States Supreme Court 32–42 (1970) (hereafter cited as S. Wasby, Impact of Court).

75. Id. 32.

76. S. Krislov, The Supreme Court and Political Freedom 166 (1968).

77. Wright, The Role of the Supreme Court in a Democratic Society—Judicial Activism or Restraint? 54 Corn. L. Rev. 1, 7–8 (1968).

78. S. Wasby, Impact of Court 142.

79. D. Berman, It Is So Ordered: The Supreme Court Rules on School Desegregation 5 (1966).

80. Levy, Introduction, in The Supreme Court under Earl Warren 3, 21 (L. Levy ed. 1972).

81. S. Wasby, Impact of Court 37.

82. See pp. 65–66.

83. Cummings v. Missouri, 71 U.S. 277 (1867); Ex parte Garland, 71 U.S. 333 (1867).

84. H. Hyman, Era of the Oath 115 (1954).

85. Russ, The Lawyer's Test Oath during Reconstruction, 10 Miss. L.J. 154, 165 (1938).

86. H. Hyman 116–18.

87. See Dietze, Hamilton's Federalist—Treatise for Free Government, 42 Corn. L.Q. 307, 310, 511 (1957).

88. H. Maine, Popular Government 248 (1885).

89. See generally W. Lockhart, Y. Kamisar & J. Choper, Constitutional Law: Cases—Comments—Questions 521–29 (4th ed. 1975).

90. R. McCloskey, The American Supreme Court 151 (1960).

91. United States v. Lovett, 328 U.S. 303 (1946).

92. Kunz v. New York, 340 U.S. 290 (1951); Saia v. New York, 334 U.S. 558 (1948); Thomas v. Collins, 323 U.S. 516 (1945).

93. Craig v. Harney, 331 U.S. 367 (1947); Pennekamp v. Florida, 328 U.S. 331 (1946); Bridges v. California, 314 U.S. 252 (1941).

94. Terminiello v. City of Chicago, 337 U.S. 1 (1949).

95. United States v. Ballard, 322 U.S. 78 (1944).

96. Nat'l Comm'n on Law Observance and Enforcement, Report on Lawlessness in Law Enforcement, No. 11 at 4 (1931).

97. Brown v. Mississippi, 297 U.S. 278 (1936).

98. Rochin v. California, 342 U.S. 165 (1952).

99. Reck v. Pate, 367 U.S. 433 (1961).

100. U.S. Comm'n on Civil Rights, Book 5: Justice 17 (1961) (footnotes omitted).

101. O. Stephens, The Supreme Court and Confessions of Guilt 15 (1973).

102. Holtzoff, The Right of Counsel under the Sixth Amendment, 20 N.Y.U.L.Q. Rev. 1, 8 (1944).

103. 304 U.S. 458 (1938).

104. 312 U.S. 275 (1941).

105. 310 U.S. 88 (1940).

106. 310 U.S. 106 (1940).

107. 312 U.S. 321 (1941).

108. Padway, History in the Making, 48 American Federationist 22 (Apr. 1941).

109. See Bakery & Pastry Drivers & Helpers Local 802 v. Wohl, 315 U.S. 769 (1942); Hotel & Restaurant Employees' Int'l Alliance Local 122 v. Wisconsin Employment Relations Board, 315 U.S. 437 (1942); Allen-Bradley Local No. 1111 v. Wisconsin Employment Relations Board, 315 U.S. 740 (1942); Carpenters and Joiners Union Local 213 v. Ritter's Cafe, 315 U.S. 722 (1942).

110. See, e.g., Garner v. Teamsters Union Local 776, 346 U.S. 485 (1953); Youngdahl v. Rainfair, Inc., 355 U.S. 131 (1957); San Diego Bldg. Trades Council v. Garmon, 359 U.S. 236 (1959).

111. See Teller, Picketing and Free Speech, 56 Harv. L. Rev. 180, 185–90 (1942).

112. Padway, Shackling Labor by Legislation, 47 American Federationist 10 (Aug. 1940).

113. See D. Manwaring, Render unto Ceasar: The Flag Salute Controversy 26–28 (1962).

114. See Lovell v. City of Griffin, 303 U.S. 444 (1938); Schneider v. State, 308 U.S. 147 (1939).

115. D. Manwaring 20.

116. Id. 28.

117. Id. 187.

118. Id. 190.

119. West Virginia State Board of Education v. Barnette, 319 U.S. 624 (1943), overruling Minersville School Dist. v. Gobitis, 310 U.S. 586 (1940).

120. D. Manwaring 242.

121. Id. 250.

122. Id. 242.

123. Id. 20.

124. U.S. Comm'n on Civil Rights, Book 1: Voting 21 (1961).

125. Smith v. Allwright, 321 U.S. 649 (1944).

126. V. Key, Southern Politics in State and Nation 619 (1949).

127. Id. 625.

128. Weeks, The White Primary: 1944–1948, 42 Am. Pol. Sci. Rev. 500 (1948).

129. Id. 503.

130. Strong, The Rise of Negro Voting in Texas, 42 Am. Pol. Sci. Rev. 510, 512 (1948).

131. Weeks 505.

132. Id. 506.

133. U.S. Comm'n on Civil Rights, Book 1: Voting 22.

134. Id. 21.

135. 305 U.S. 337 (1938).

136. 339 U.S. 629 (1950).

137. 339 U.S. 637 (1950).

138. Konvitz, The Courts Deal a Blow to Segregation, 11 Commentary 158, 162 (1951).

139. Comment, Constitutional Law—Equal Protection of the Laws—Segregation of Negroes in Public Schools, 24 So. Cal. L. Rev. 74, 82 (1950).

140. 1 Southern School News 13 (Sept. 3, 1954).

141. See Kelly, The School Desegregation Case, in Quarrels That Have Shaped the Constitution 243, 256 (J. Garraty ed. 1964).

142. Id. 256.

143. R. Harris, The Quest for Equality 139 (1960).

144. See Briggs v. Elliott, 98 F. Supp. 529, 531 (E.D.S.C. 1951).

145. See Argument: The Oral Argument before the Supreme Court in Brown v. Board of Education of Topeka, 1952–55 at 83, 89 (L. Friedman ed. 1969) (hereafter cited as Argument).

146. See Leflar & Davis, Segregation in the Public Schools—1953, 67 Harv. L. Rev. 377, 421 n.144 (1954).

147. See N.Y. Times, Apr. 22, 1951, p. 58, col. 3.

148. The source of the discussion that follows is Federal Security Agency (Office of Education), Statistical Summary of Education, in Biennial Survey of Education in the United States, vols. 46–54.

149. 1 Southern School News 5.

150. The task will be to examine the effects of many more Supreme Court decisions upholding individual rights than is appropriate for inclusion in this book.

151. Argument 244.

152. J. Casper, The Politics of Civil Liberties 169 (1972).

153. U.S. Comm'n on Civil Rights, Public Education 292 (1964).

154. A. Bickel, The Supreme Court and the Idea of Progress 137.

155. See Yudof, Equal Educational Opportunity and the Courts, 51 Tex. L. Rev. 411, 468–69 (1973).

156. A. Lewis, Portrait of a Decade 5, 8–9 (1964).

157. Karst, Foreword: Equal Citizenship under the Fourteenth Amendment, 91 Harv. L. Rev. 1, 21 (1977).

158. The phrases come from the Brown opinion, 347 U.S. at 494.

159. L. Lomax, The Negro Revolt 73–74 (1962).

160. E. Cleaver, Soul on Ice 3 (1968).

161. Carter, The Warren Court and Desegregation, 67 Mich. L. Rev. 237, 247 (1968).

162. Id. 246.

163. 388 U.S. 1 (1967).

164. See Applebaum, Miscegenation Statutes: A Constitutional and Social Problem, 53 Geo. L.J. 49, 50 (1964).

165. The repealing states were Arizona, Colorado, Idaho, Indiana, Maryland, Montana, Nebraska, Nevada, North Dakota, Oregon, South

Dakota, Utah, and Wyoming. See Applebaum 50 n.12; Note, Miscegenation: An Example of Judicial Recidivism, 8 J. Fam. L. 69, 70 (1968); 388 U.S. 1, 6 n.5.

166. Perez v. Lippold, 32 Cal.2d 711, 198 P.2d 17 (1948).

167. See Applebaum 50; Zabel, Interracial Marriage and the Law, 216:4 Atlantic Monthly 75, 77 (Oct. 1965).

168. Alabama, Arkansas, Delaware, Florida, Georgia, Kentucky, Louisiana, Mississippi, Missouri, North Carolina, Oklahoma, South Carolina, Tennessee, Texas, Virginia, and West Virginia. 388 U.S. 1, 6 n.5.

169. See Applebaum 55–56; 388 U.S. 1, 2–3.

170. Applebaum 53 n.41.

171. Id. 53.

172. See, e.g., State v. Miller, 28 N.C. 224, 29 S.E.2d 751 (1944) (length of sentence not stated); 31 Newsweek 25 (Jan. 19, 1948) (6 month sentence in Virginia).

173. 388 U.S. 1, 3.

174. Applebaum 54.

175. See 52 Newsweek 20 (Dec. 22, 1958).

176. See cases and authorities cited in Applebaum 54–55; 8 J. Fam. L. at 71–72.

177. See 43:15 U.S. News & World Report 110 (Oct. 11, 1957).

178. McLaughlin v. Florida, 379 U.S. 184 (1964).

179. See Seidelson, Miscegenation Statutes and the Supreme Court, 15 Cath. U. L. Rev. 156, 156–57 (1966).

180. 8 J. Fam. L. at 72.

181. 55:15 U.S. News & World Report 63 (Oct. 7, 1963).

182. Mapp v. Ohio, 367 U.S. 643 (1961).

183. See J. Wilson, Varieties of Police Behavior 231 (1968); Reiss & Bordua, Environment and Organization: A Perspective on the Police, in The Police: Six Sociological Essays 25, 39 (D. Bordua ed. 1967).

184. Amsterdam, Perspectives on the Fourth Amendment, 58 Minn. L. Rev. 349, 379 (1974).

185. See, e.g., Spiotto, Search and Seizure: An Empirical Study of the Exclusionary Rule and Its Alternatives, 2. J. Leg. Studies 243 (1973).

186. See Note, On the Limitations of Empirical Evaluations of the Exclusionary Rule, 69 Nw. U. L. Rev. 740 (1974); Canon, The Exclusionary Rule: Have Critics Proven That It Doesn't Deter Police? 62 Judicature 398 (1979).

187. Oaks, Studying the Exclusionary Rule in Search and Seizure, 37 U. Chi. L. Rev. 665, 667 (1970).

188. Canon, Is the Exclusionary Rule in Failing Health? Some New Data and a Plea against a Precipitous Conclusion, 62 Ky. L.J. 681, 698 (1974).

189. La Fave, Improving Police Performance through the Exclusionary Rule, Part I: Current Police and Local Court Practices, 30 Mo. L.

Rev. 391, 395 (1965). See generally D. Horowitz, The Courts and Social Policy 220–54 (1977).

190. W. La Fave, Arrest—The Decision to Take a Suspect into Custody 428 (1965). See also Canon, 62 Judicature 398. But see Schlesinger, The Exclusionary Rule: Have Proponents Proven That It Is a Deterrent to Police? 62 Judicature 404 (1979).

191. D. Horowitz 230.

192. Katz, The Supreme Court and the States: An Inquiry into Mapp v. Ohio in North Carolina, 45 N.C.L. Rev. 119, 134 (1966). See Canon, Testing the Effectiveness of Civil Liberties Policies at the State and Federal Levels, 5 Am. Politics Q. 57 (1977).

193. S. Wasby, Small Town Police and the Supreme Court 113–14 (1976) (hereafter cited as S. Wasby, Small Town Police).

194. J. Skolnick, Justice without Trial 224 (1966).

195. Canon, 62 Ky. L.J. at 698. See also Kamisar, Public Safety v. Individual Liberties: Some "Facts" and "Theories," 53 J. Crim. L. C. & P. S. 171, 179–81 (1962).

196. La Fave, Improving Police Performance through the Exclusionary Rule, Part II: Defining the Norms and Training the Police, 30 Mo. L. Rev. 566, 594 (1965). See also S. Wasby, Small Town Police 107–08.

197. Murphy, The Problem of Compliance by Police Departments, 44 Tex. L. Rev. 939, 941 (1966).

198. See id. 941–42; Specter, Mapp v. Ohio: Pandora's Problems for the Prosecutor, 111 U. Pa. L. Rev. 4 (1962).

199. Amsterdam 431.

200. 372 U.S. 335 (1963).

201. Brief for Petitioner at 29, Gideon v. Wainwright, 372 U.S. 335 (1963).

202. 316 U.S. 455 (1942).

203. See Kamisar, The Right to Counsel and the Fourteenth Amendment: A Dialogue on "The Most Pervasive Right" of an Accused, 30 U. Chi. L. Rev. 1, 19 (1962) (hereafter cited as Kamisar, Right to Counsel).

204. Id. 20.

205. S. Wasby, Impact of Court 8.

206. G. Mitau, Decade of Decision 161 (1967).

207. See p. 109 infra.

208. See Blumberg, The Practice of Law as Confidence Game: Organizational Cooptation of a Profession, 1:2 Law & Soc. Rev. 15 (June 1967).

209. 369 U.S. 506 (1962).

210. See McNeal v. Culver, 365 U.S. 109 (1961); Uveges v. Pennsylvania, 335 U.S. 437 (1948).

211. 369 U.S. at 513, 516.

212. See Ass'n of N.Y.C. Bar & Nat'l Legal Aid Ass'n, Equal Justice for the Accused 98–111 (App.) (1959) (hereafter cited as Equal Justice), as updated by McNeal v. Culver, 365 U.S. 109, 119–22 (App.) (1961) and

Kamisar, Right to Counsel 14–21 (22 of 37 states); id. 67–74 (App. I) (3 of 8 states).

213. See Equal Justice 49 (New Jersey).

214. See Van Alstyne, In Gideon's Wake: Harsher Penalties and the "Successful" Criminal Appellant, 74 Yale L.J. 606 n.5 (1965).

215. See Medalie, Zeitz & Alexander, Custodial Police Interrogation in Our Nation's Capital: The Attempt to Implement Miranda, 66 Mich. L. Rev. 1347, 1371–72 (1968).

216. 351 U.S. 12 (1956).

217. 372 U.S. 353 (1963).

218. See, e.g., E. Brownell, Legal Aid in the United States 83 (1951); Kadish & Kimball, Legal Representation of the Indigent in Criminal Cases in Utah, 4 Utah L. Rev. 198, 214 (1954); Boskey, The Right to Counsel in Appellate Proceedings, 45 Minn. L. Rev. 783 n.1 (1961); L. Silverstein, Defense of the Poor: The National Report 7–8 (1965); Report of the Attorney General's Committee on Poverty and the Administration of Federal Criminal Justice 134 (1963).

219. See, e.g., Brief for Petitioners at 21–25, Griffin v. Illinois, 351 U.S. 12 (1956).

220. 351 U.S. 12, 33 (Harlan J., dissenting).

221. Wilkes, Post-Conviction Rights of Indigent Criminal Defendants: State Interpretations of Griffin v. Illinois, Apps. I 1–20, II 21–23, II 26–28 (Institute of Judicial Administration 1959).

222. L. Silverstein 139.

223. Wilkes.

224. L. Silverstein 139.

225. Israel, Criminal Procedure, The Burger Court, and the Legacy of the Warren Court, 75 Mich. L. Rev. 1319, 1424 n.438 (1977).

226. See, e.g., Schware v. Board of Bar Examiners, 353 U.S. 232 (1957); Sweezy v. New Hampshire, 354 U.S. 234 (1957); Gibson v. Florida Legislative Investigation Committee, 372 U.S. 539 (1963); De Gregory v. Attorney General, 383 U.S. 825 (1966); Cramp v. Board of Public Instruction, 368 U.S. 278 (1961); Baggett v. Bullitt, 377 U.S. 360 (1964); Elfbrandt v. Russell, 384 U.S. 11 (1966); Keyishian v. Board of Regents, 385 U.S. 589 (1967); United States v. Brown, 381 U.S. 437 (1965); United States v. Robel, 389 U.S. 258 (1967); Bond v. Floyd, 385 U.S. 116 (1966); Tinker v. Des Moines School District, 393 U.S. 503 (1969); Aptheker v. Secretary of State, 378 U.S. 500 (1964); Brandenburg v. Ohio, 395 U.S. 444 (1969); Watts v. United States, 394 U.S. 705 (1969).

227. See, e.g., Edwards v. South Carolina, 372 U.S. 229 (1963); Cox v. Louisiana, 379 U.S. 536 (1965); Brown v. Louisiana, 383 U.S. 131 (1966); Gregory v. City of Chicago, 394 U.S. 111 (1969); Shuttlesworth v. City of Birmingham, 394 U.S. 147 (1969).

228. See Engel v. Vitale, 370 U.S. 421 (1962); School District of Abington Twnshp. v. Schempp, 374 U.S. 203 (1963).

229. See Torcaso v. Watkins, 367 U.S. 488 (1961).

230. S. Wasby, Impact of Court 234.

231. See J. Casper 122 n.51.

232. See id. 183–84.

233. See Frederickson & Cho, Legislative Apportionment and Fiscal Policy in the American States, 27 W. Pol. Q. 5 (1974); Hanson & Crew, The Effects of Reapportionment on State Public Policy Out-Puts, in The Impact of Supreme Court Decisions 155 (T. Becker & M. Feeley 2d ed. 1973) and studies cited therein.

234. Bishop, The Warren Court Is Not Likely to Be Overruled, in The Supreme Court under Earl Warren 93, 98 (L. Levy ed. 1972).

235. Dorsen, The Court of Some Resort, 1 Civ. Lib. Rev. 82 (Winter-Spring 1974).

236. L. Tribe, American Constitutional Law v (1978).

237. L. Levy, Against the Law 439 (1974).

238. S. F. Chronicle, Oct. 18, 1978, p. 36, col. 1.

239. See, e.g., Harris v. New York, 401 U.S. 222 (1971); Michigan v. Tucker, 417 U.S. 433 (1974); Oregon v. Hass, 420 U.S. 714 (1975); Michigan v. Mosley, 423 U.S. 96 (1975); Beckwith v. United States, 425 U.S. 341 (1976).

240. See, e.g., United States v. Calandra, 414 U.S. 338 (1974); United States v. Robinson, 414 U.S. 218 (1973); Schneckloth v. Bustamonte, 412 U.S. 218 (1973); United States v. Janis, 428 U.S. 433 (1976); Stone v. Powell, 428 U.S. 465 (1976); Zurcher v. Stanford Daily, 436 U.S. 547 (1978); United States v. Ceccolini, 435 U.S. 268 (1978); Rakas v. Illinois, 439 U.S. 128 (1978).

241. Kirby v. Illinois, 406 U.S. 682 (1972); Ross v. Moffitt, 417 U.S. 600 (1974).

242. For fuller exploration, see Israel.

243. 437 U.S. 385 (1978).

244. 436 U.S. 499 (1978).

245. 429 U.S. 245 (1977).

246. 420 U.S. 103 (1975).

247. 433 U.S. 1 (1977).

248. 407 U.S. 297 (1972).

249. 426 U.S. 610 (1976).

250. 407 U.S. 25 (1972).

251. 408 U.S. 471 (1972).

252. 411 U.S. 778 (1973).

253. 422 U.S. 806 (1975).

254. 435 U.S. 475 (1978).

255. See Kamisar, Right to Counsel.

256. See, e.g., Herring v. New York, 422 U.S. 853 (1975); Geders v. United States, 425 U.S. 80 (1976); Bounds v. Smith, 430 U.S. 817 (1977); Brewer v. Williams, 430 U.S. 387 (1977).

257. See Evans v. Abney, 396 U.S. 435 (1970); Moose Lodge v. Irvis, 407 U.S. 163 (1972); Jackson v. Metropolitan Edison Co., 419 U.S. 345 (1974); Hudgens v. NLRB, 424 U.S. 507 (1976); Flagg Bros., Inc. v. Brooks, 436 U.S. 149 (1978).

258. See Gordon v. Lance, 403 U.S. 1 (1971); Whitcomb v. Chavis, 403 U.S. 124 (1971); Abate v. Mundt, 403 U.S. 182 (1971); Mahan v. Howell, 410 U.S. 315 (1973); Gaffney v. Cummings, 412 U.S. 735 (1973); Salyer Land Co. v. Tulare Lake Basin Water Storage District, 410 U.S. 719 (1973); Richardson v. Ramirez, 418 U.S. 24 (1974).

259. See Miller v. California, 413 U.S. 15 (1973); Paris Adult Theatre I v. Slaton, 413 U.S. 49 (1973); United States v. Reidel, 402 U.S. 351 (1971); United States v. Thirty-seven Photographs, 402 U.S. 363 (1971); United States v. 12 200 Ft. Reels of Film, 413 U.S. 123 (1973); Hamling v. United States, 418 U.S. 87 (1974); Ward v. Illinois, 431 U.S. 767 (1977); Smith v. United States, 431 U.S. 291 (1977); Young v. American Mini Theatres, Inc., 427 U.S. 50 (1976).

260. See Bishop v. Wood, 426 U.S. 341 (1976); Paul v. Davis, 424 U.S. 693 (1976).

261. 412 U.S. 783 (1973).

262. 412 U.S. 755 (1973).

263. 414 U.S. 524 (1974).

264. See also Hadley v. Junior College District, 397 U.S. 50 (1970); City of Phoenix v. Kolodziejski, 399 U.S. 204 (1970); Chapman v. Meier, 420 U.S. 1 (1975). Compare Rosario v. Rockefeller, 410 U.S. 752 (1973) with Kusper v. Pontikes, 414 U.S. 51 (1973).

265. 408 U.S. 229 (1972).

266. 418 U.S. 153 (1974).

267. 422 U.S. 205 (1975).

268. 420 U.S. 546 (1975).

269. 424 U.S. 669 (1976).

270. 419 U.S. 565 (1975).

271. 436 U.S. 1 (1978). See also Bell v. Burson, 402 U.S. 535 (1971).

272. See Francis v. Henderson, 425 U.S. 536 (1976); Stone v. Powell, 428 U.S. 465 (1976); Wainwright v. Sykes, 433 U.S. 72 (1977).

273. See Laird v. Tatum, 408 U.S. 1 (1972); United States v. Richardson, 418 U.S. 166 (1974); Schlesinger v. Reservists Committee to Stop the War, 418 U.S. 208 (1974); O'Shea v. Littleton, 414 U.S. 488 (1974); Warth v. Seldin, 422 U.S. 490 (1975).

274. See Younger v. Harris, 401 U.S. 37 (1971); Hicks v. Miranda, 422 U.S. 332 (1975); Huffman v. Pursue, Ltd. 420 U.S. 592 (1975); Juidice v. Vail, 430 U.S. 327 (1977); Trainor v. Hernandez, 431 U.S. 434 (1977).

275. As to standing, see Doe v. Bolton, 410 U.S. 179 (1973); Arlington Heights v. Metropolitan Housing Dev. Corp., 429 U.S. 252 (1977); Singleton v. Wulff, 428 U.S. 106 (1976); Craig v. Boren, 429 U.S. 190 (1976); Carey v. Population Services Int'l, 431 U.S. 678 (1977); Duke Power Co. v. Carolina Environmental Study Group, Inc. 438 U.S. 59

(1978). As to enjoining state proceedings, see Wooley v. Maynard, 430 U.S. 705 (1977). Cf. Steffel v. Thompson, 415 U.S. 452 (1974); Doran v. Salem Inn, Inc., 422 U.S. 922 (1975).

276. Washington v. Davis, 426 U.S. 229 (1976). See also Mayor of Philadelphia v. Educational Equality League, 415 U.S. 605 (1974).

277. See, e.g., United States v. O'Brien, 391 U.S. 367 (1968). But see, e.g., Griffin v. County School Board, 377 U.S. 218 (1964).

278. Arlington Heights v. Metropolitan Housing Dev. Corp., 429 U.S. 252 (1977).

279. See Dayton Board of Educ. v. Brinkman, 433 U.S. 406 (1977); Austin Independent School District v. United States, 429 U.S. 990 (1976); School District v. United States, 433 U.S. 667 (1977); Pasadena Board of Educ. v. Spangler, 427 U.S. 424 (1976).

280. Milliken v. Bradley, 418 U.S. 717 (1974).

281. Swann v. Charlotte-Mecklenburg Board of Educ., 402 U.S. 1 (1971).

282. Keyes v. School District, 413 U.S. 189 (1973).

283. United States v. Scotland Neck Board of Educ., 407 U.S. 484 (1972); Norwood v. Harrison, 413 U.S. 455 (1973); Milliken v. Bradley, 433 U.S. 267 (1977).

284. Hills v. Gautreaux, 425 U.S. 284 (1976).

285. See United States v. Kras, 409 U.S. 434 (1973); Ortwein v. Schwab, 410 U.S. 656 (1973); Hurtado v. United States, 410 U.S. 578 (1973); Maher v. Roe, 432 U.S. 464 (1977).

286. Boddie v. Connecticut, 401 U.S. 371 (1971).

287. Lubin v. Panish, 415 U.S. 709 (1974); Bullock v. Carter, 405 U.S. 134 (1972).

288. Tate v. Short, 401 U.S. 395 (1971); Williams v. Illinois, 399 U.S. .235 (1970).

289. Lindsey v. Normet, 405 U.S. 56 (1972).

290. See generally W. Lockhart, Y. Kamisar & J. Choper 815–22.

291. See, e.g., Cole v. Richardson, 405 U.S. 676 (1972); United States Civil Service Comm'n v. National Ass'n of Letter Carriers, 413 U.S. 548 (1973); Broadrick v. Oklahoma, 413 U.S. 601 (1973); Arnett v. Kennedy, 416 U.S. 134 (1974). But see Papachristou v. Jacksonville, 405 U.S. 156 (1972); Gooding v. Wilson, 405 U.S. 518 (1972); Smith v. Goguen, 415 U.S. 566 (1974); Lewis v. City of New Orleans, 415 U.S. 130 (1974); Doran v. Salem Inn, Inc. 422 U.S. 922 (1975); Erznoznik v. City of Jacksonville, 422 U.S. 205 (1975).

292. See Rosenfeld v. New Jersey, 408 U.S. 901 (1972); Brown v. Oklahoma, 408 U.S. 914 (1972); Lewis v. City of New Orleans, 408 U.S. 913 (1972); Papish v. Board of Curators, 410 U.S. 667 (1973).

293. See Healy v. James, 408 U.S. 169 (1972).

294. See Smith v. Goguen, 415 U.S. 566 (1974); Spence v. Washington, 418 U.S. 405 (1974); Wooley v. Maynard, 430 U.S. 705 (1977).

295. Elrod v. Burns, 427 U.S. 347 (1976).

296. Buckley v. Valeo, 424 U.S. 1 (1976).

297. First Nat'l Bank v. Bellotti, 435 U.S. 765 (1978).

298. McDaniel v. Paty, 435 U.S. 618 (1978).

299. Wisconsin v. Yoder, 406 U.S. 205 (1972).

300. Branzburg v. Hayes, 408 U.S. 665 (1972).

301. Pell v. Procunier, 417 U.S. 817 (1974); Houchins v. KQED, 438 U.S. 1 (1978).

302. New York Times Co. v. United States, 403 U.S. 713 (1971).

303. Nebraska Press Ass'n v. Stuart, 427 U.S. 539 (1976). See also Oklahoma Pub. Co. v. District Court, 430 U.S. 308 (1977).

304. Landmark Communications, Inc. v. Virginia, 435 U.S. 829 (1978). See also Cox Broadcasting Corp. v. Cohn, 420 U.S. 469 (1975).

305. Miami Herald Publishing Co. v. Tornillo, 418 U.S. 241 (1974). See also Columbia Broadcasting System, Inc. v. Democratic Nat'l Comm., 412 U.S. 94 (1973).

306. Dionisopoulos, New Patterns in Judicial Control of the Presidency: 1950's to 1970's, 10 Akron L. Rev. 1, 30 (1976).

307. See Skinner v. Oklahoma ex rel. Williamson, 316 U.S. 535 (1942).

308. See Griswold v. Connecticut, 381 U.S. 479 (1965).

309. 410 U.S. 113 (1973). See also Doe v. Bolton, 410 U.S. 179 (1973); Planned Parenthood of Central Missouri v. Danforth, 428 U.S. 52 (1976); Colautti v. Franklin, 439 U.S. 379 (1979).

310. Eisenstadt, 405 U.S. 438 (1972); Carey, 431 U.S. 678 (1977).

311. 431 U.S. 494 (1977).

312. 434 U.S. 374 (1978).

313. 422 U.S. 563 (1975).

314. Graham v. Richardson, 403 U.S. 365 (1971); Sugarman v. Dougall, 413 U.S. 634 (1973); In re Griffiths, 413 U.S. 717 (1973); Examining Board of Engineers v. Otero, 426 U.S. 572 (1976); Nyquist v. Mauclet, 432 U.S. 1 (1977). But cf. Foley v. Connelie, 435 U.S. 291 (1978).

315. Craig v. Boren, 429 U.S. 190 (1976). See also Reed v. Reed, 404 U.S. 71 (1971); Frontiero v. Richardson, 411 U.S. 677 (1973); Weinberger v. Wiesenfeld, 420 U.S. 636 (1975); Stanton v. Stanton, 421 U.S. 7 (1975); Califano v. Goldfarb, 430 U.S. 199 (1977).

316. Weber v. Aetna Casualty & Surety Co., 406 U.S. 164 (1972); Gomez v. Perez, 409 U.S. 535 (1973); New Jersey Welfare Rights Org. v. Cahill, 411 U.S. 619 (1973); Trimble v. Gordon, 430 U.S. 762 (1977). But see Mathews v. Lucas, 427 U.S. 495 (1976).

317. See Valentine v. Chrestensen, 316 U.S. 52 (1942).

318. Virginia State Board of Pharmacy v. Virginia Citizens Consumer Council, 425 U.S. 748 (1976); Linmark Associates, Inc. v. Willingboro, 431 U.S. 85 (1977); Carey v. Population Services Int'l, 431 U.S. 678 (1977); Bates v. State Bar, 433 U.S. 350 (1977).

319. Lockett v. Ohio, 438 U.S. 586 (1978); Bell v. Ohio, 438 U.S. 637 (1978); Roberts v. Louisiana, 431 U.S. 633 (1977); Coker v. Georgia, 433 U.S. 584 (1977); Woodson v. North Carolina, 428 U.S. 280 (1976); Roberts v. Louisiana, 428 U.S. 325 (1976); Furman v. Georgia, 408 U.S. 238 (1972). But cf. Gregg v. Georgia, 428 U.S. 153 (1976); Proffitt v. Florida, 428 U.S. 242 (1976); Jurek v. Texas, 428 U.S. 262 (1976).

320. See text at footnote 150 supra.

321. 407 U.S. 25 (1972).

322. See Brief for Petitioner at 17, 23, 25, 26–27, Argersinger v. Hamlin; S. Krantz, C. Smith, D. Rossman, P. Froyd & J. Hoffman, Right to Counsel in Criminal Cases 694–701 (1976).

323. See Brief for Petitioner at 18, 21, 26, Argersinger v. Hamlin.

324. Id. 11.

325. See generally Goldberg & Hartman, Help for the Indigent Accused: The Effect of Argersinger, 30 N.L.A.D.A. Briefcase 203, 205 (1972).

326. See Brief for Petitioner at 11–28, Argersinger v. Hamlin; S. Krantz et al. 694–701.

327. See Portman, Gideon's Trumpet Blows for Misdemeanants— Argersinger v. Hamlin, The Decision and Its Impact, 14 Santa Clara Law. 1, 14 (1973).

328. See id. 18; Note, Dollars and Sense of an Expanded Right to Counsel, 55 Ia. L. Rev. 1249, 1260 (1970).

329. Portman 13.

330. 440 U.S. 367

331. 372 U.S. 335 (1963).

332. See Brief for Petitioner at 11, Argersinger v. Hamlin.

333. State v. Borst, 278 Minn. 388, 154 N.W.2d 888 (1967).

334. See Comment, Right to Counsel: The Impact of Gideon v. Wainwright in the Fifty States, 3 Creighton L. Rev. 103, 133 (1970).

335. See S. Krantz et al. 694–701.

336. See Scott v. Illinois, 440 U.S. 367, 386–88 (1979) (Brennan, J., dissenting).

337. ACLU, Legal Counsel for Misdemeanants, Preliminary Report 1 (1970).

338. President's Commission on Law Enforcement and Administration of Justice, Task Force Report (hereafter cited as President's Commission): Corrections 27 n.1, 186–87 (1967).

339. U.S. Dep't of Justice, Sourcebook of Criminal Justice Statistics—1976, p. 703 (1977).

340. See D. Stanley, Prisoners among Us 106 (1976) (23% of parolees); President's Commission: Corrections 62 (35%–45% of parolees); President's Commission: The Courts 56 n.28 (108,000 of 459,000 adult probationers); U.S. Dep't of Justice 748, 750, 760 (1977) (25% of state male

parolees; 21% of state female parolees; 29%–40% of federal parolees); ABA, Survey of Parole Revocation Procedures i (1973) (10,000 of 44,000 parolees).

341. Sklar, Law and Practice in Probation and Parole Revocation Hearings, 55 J. Crim. L. C. & P. S. 175 (1964).

342. Cohen, Due Process, Equal Protection and State Parole Revocation Proceedings, 42 U. Colo. L. Rev. 197, 198 (1970).

343. Morrissey v. Brewer, 408 U.S. 471, 488 n.15 (1972).

344. O'Leary & Nuffield, Parole Decision-Making Characteristics: Report of a National Survey, 8 Crim. L. Bull. 651, 668 (1972) (emphasis added).

345. 408 U.S. 471 (1972).

346. 411 U.S. 778 (1973).

347. ABA 2.

348. See O'Leary & Nuffield 668–69, 679 (App.); Van Dyke, Parole Revocation Hearings in California: The Right to Counsel, 59 Calif. L. Rev. 1215, 1220–21 (1971).

349. O'Leary & Nuffield 671. See also O'Leary & Hanrahan, Law and Practice in Parole Proceedings: A National Survey, 13 Crim. L. Bull. 181, 197 (1977). The data collected earlier on probation revocation hearings, although much less detailed, was not dissimilar. See Sklar 192–93.

350. ABA 1.

351. ABA 3–7, 10.

352. ABA 7.

353. See Fisher, Parole and Probation Revocation Procedures after Morrissey and Gagnon, 65 J. Crim. L.C. & P.S. 46 (1974).

354. See O'Leary & Hanrahan 197–202.

355. O'Leary & Nuffield 671, 673. See also O'Leary & Hanrahan 197; Van Dyke 1221; Note, Parole Revocation in the Federal System, 56 Geo. L.J. 705, 719 (1968); Annot., 33 A.L.R.3d 272–82 (1970). These figures were substantially confirmed in the 45 state survey undertaken shortly after Morrissey was handed down. See ABA 19.

356. See O'Leary & Nuffield 673.

357. 389 U.S. 128 (1967).

358. See Sklar 189, 192; L. Silverstein 143 (1965).

359. See D. Stanley 114–15.

360. See Comment, The Impossible Dream? Due Process Guarantees for Calif. Parolees & Probationers, 25 Hast. L.J. 602, 630 (1974); Lee & Zuckerman, Representing Parole Violators, 11 Crim. L. Bull. 327 (1975); Fisher 57.

361. O'Leary & Hanrahan 199, 202.

362. See, e.g., Lee & Zuckerman.

363. Lee & Zuckerman 331.

364. O'Leary & Nuffield 674.

365. See Comment, Due Process for Parolees, 53 Ore. L. Rev. 57, 78 (1973).

366. See O'Leary & Hanrahan 201, 203.

367. See Comment, The Prisoner's Right to a Statement of Reasons for Parole Denial, 24 Buf. L. Rev. 567, 580 (1975). See also O'Leary & Hanrahan 204.

368. D. Stanley 113.

369. Gregg v. Georgia, 428 U.S. 153 (1976).

370. 408 U.S. 238 (1972).

371. See M. Meltsner, Cruel and Unusual: The Supreme Court and Capital Punishment 292–93 (1973).

372. Id. 293.

373. See Dobbert v. Florida, 432 U.S. 282, 309 (1977) (Stevens, J., dissenting).

374. Commonwealth v. O'Neal, 339 N.E.2d 676, 694 n.2 (Mass. (1975).

375. 428 U.S. 280 (1976).

376. 108:2 Time 35 (July 12, 1976).

377. 438 U.S. 586 (1978).

378. Id. 616–17 (Blackmun, J., concurring). See, e.g., Jordan v. Arizona, 114 Ariz. 452, 561 P.2d 1224 (1976), vacated and remanded, 438 U.S. 911 (1978).

379. NAACP Legal Defense Fund, Death Row, U.S.A. (June 20, 1978).

380. People v. Davis, 43 N.Y.2d 17, 400 N.Y.S.2d 735, 371 N.E.2d 456 (1977), cert. denied, 435 U.S. 998 (1978); Pennsylvania v. Moody, 476 Pa. 223, 382 A.2d 442, cert. denied, 438 U.S. 914 (1978).

381. NAACP Legal Defense Fund.

382. 433 U.S. 584 (1977).

383. See H. Bedau, The Courts, the Constitution, and Capital Punishment 112 (1977).

384. See U.S. Bureau of Prisons, National Prisoner Statistics, Bull. No. 45, Capital Punishment 1930–1968 at 1 (1969).

385. Bedau, New Life for the Death Penalty, 223 Nation 144; 146 (Aug. 28, 1976).

386. Note, Civil Commitment of the Mentally Ill, 87 Harv. L. Rev. 1190, 1202–04 (1974).

387. Stone, Mental Health and Law: A System in Transition 43 (1976); 87 Harv. L. Rev. at 1193 n.3.

388. See Steinzor, Kenneth Donaldson's Fight for Freedom, 41:4 The Progressive 48, 50 (Apr. 1977) (NIMH statistics indicate "that out of 1,600,000 live-in patients...at least 480,000 were involuntarily committed"); 87 Harv. L. Rev. at 1193 n.3 (of 404,000 patients admitted in 1972, 41.8% were involuntarily committed); Note, Involuntary Civil Commitments, 29 Baylor L. Rev. 187 (1977) (almost 50% of admissions

to Texas state mental hospitals in 1975–76 were involuntary); Brief of New Jersey as Amicus Curiae at 2, O'Connor v. Donaldson, 422 U.S. 563 (1975) (approximately 60% in New Jersey); Brief of Ohio as Amicus Curiae at 1, O'Connor v. Donaldson (at least 50% in Ohio).

389. 87 Harv. L. Rev. at 1203 n.11.

390. Id. 1203–04.

391. Id. 1385–86.

392. 422 U.S. 563 (1975).

393. Id. 573.

394. 87 Harv. L. Rev. at 1198 n.17.

395. 422 U.S. 563, 564.

396. See State ex rel. Hawks v. Lazaro, 202 S.E.2d 109, 121 (W. Va. 1974).

397. 87 Harv. L. Rev. at 1378 n.6.

398. 422 U.S. 563, 568–69.

399. Id. 576.

400. Id. 573.

401. Id. 574 n.10.

402. Interview with Alan Stone, Chairman for Judicial Action of the American Psychiatry Ass'n, N.B.C. Today Show (July 8, 1975).

403. 87 Harv. L. Rev. at 1230.

404. N.Y. Times, June 27, 1975, p. 1, col. 5.

405. 106 Time 44 (July 7, 1975).

406. See Kopolow, A Review of Major Implications of the O'Connor v. Donaldson Decision, 133 Am. J. Psych. 379, 380 (1976); Steinzor 50.

407. Steinzor 50.

408. Dixon v. Attorney General, 325 F. Supp. 966 (M.D. Pa. 1971); Lessard v. Schmidt, 349 F. Supp. 1078 (E.D. Wis. 1972), remanded, 414 U.S. 473, order on remand, 379 F. Supp. 1376 (1974), remanded, 421 U.S. 957 (1975), order reinstated on remand, 413 F. Supp. 1318 (1976); Bell v. Wayne County Gen. Hosp., 384 F. Supp. 1085 (E.D. Mich. 1974); Lynch v. Baxley, 386 F. Supp. 378 (M.D. Ala. 1974); Doremus v. Farrell, 407 F. Supp. 509 (D. Neb. 1975); Stamus v. Leonhardt, 414 F. Supp. 439 (S.D. Iowa 1976).

409. See Code of Ala. §22–52–10 (enacted 1975); Mich. Comp. Laws Ann. §330.1401 (amended 1975); Neb. Rev. Stat. §83–1009 (enacted 1976); Pa. Stat. Ann. tit. 50, §7301 (enacted 1976); Wis. Stat. §§51.01.(12) (b), 51.20 (enacted 1975).

410. 87 Harv. L. Rev. at 1203.

411. See, in addition to statutes listed above, Conn. Gen. Stat. Ann. §17–179 (amended 1977); Ida. Laws §66–329(i) (amended 1974); Ind. Code §16–14–9.1–10 (amended 1975); Kan. Stat. Ann. §59–2902 (amended 1976); Ky. Rev. Stat. Ann. §202A.080(6) (enacted 1976); Mont. Rev. Codes Ann. §§38–1302(14); 38–1305(7) (amended 1975); Nev.

Rev. Stat. §433.194(2) (enacted 1975); 1977 N.M. Laws, chap. 279, §11(c); Va. Code Ann. §37.1–67.3 (amended 1976); W. Va. Code Ann. §§27–1–12, 27–5–4 (amended 1974).

412. Allerton, An Administrator Responds, in Paper Victories and Hard Realities: The Implementation of the Legal and Constitutional Rights of the Mentally Disabled 17, 18 (V. Bradley & G. Clarke eds. 1976).

413. Id.

414. See 87 Harv. L. Rev. at 1198–1200.

415. Note, Overt Dangerous Behavior as a Constitutional Requirement for Involuntary Civil Commitment of the Mentally Ill, 44 U. Chi. L. Rev. 562, 563 (1977).

416. 410 U.S. 113 (1973).

417. See Note, Abortion: The Five-Year Revolution and Its Impact, 3 Ecol. L.Q. 311, 313 (1973).

418. See 3 Ecol. L.Q. at 317–18.

419. See id. at 313–14, 345.

420. See Comment, Roe! Doe! Where Are You? The Effect of the Supreme Court's Abortion Decisions, 7 U.C.D.L. Rev. 432, 440–41, 445 (1974); Moyers, Abortion Laws: A Study in Social Change, 7 San Diego L. Rev. 237, 241 (1970).

421. See 3 Ecol. L.Q. at 314, 345.

422. See id. at 314, 346.

423. See id. at 315, 346.

424. 410 U.S. 179 (1973).

425. 428 U.S. 52 (1976).

426. See Note, Abortion Statutes after *Danforth:* An Examination, 15 J. Fam. L. 537, 556–58 (1976–77).

427. See 15 J. Fam. L. at 548–49.

428. 439 U.S. 379 (1979).

429. See 15 J. Fam. L. at 563–66; Alan Guttmacher Institute, Abortion 1974–1975: Need and Services in the United States, Each State and Metropolitan Area 122–23 (1976) (hereafter cited as Guttmacher Institute).

430. Tietze, The Effect of Legalization of Abortion on Population Growth and Public Health, in Guttmacher Institute 110, 111; Guttmacher Institute 7.

431. Center for Disease Control, HEW, Abortion Surveillance 1976 at 1 (1978).

432. See Louisell & Noonan, Constitutional Balance, in The Morality of Abortion 220, 241–43 (J. Noonan ed. 1970); Lucas, Federal Constitutional Limitations on the Enforcement and Administration of State Abortion Statutes, 46 N.C.L. Rev. 730 (1968).

433. See Tietze 110.

434. See Chicago Sun-Times, The Abortion Profiteers (Special Reprint 1978).

435. Tietze 111.

436. See Pakter & Nelson, Abortion: New York City, 3 Family Planning Perspectives 5, 10 (July 1971).

437. See State of California, Department of Health, Therapeutic Abortion Reports, 1968–1976.

438. Louisell & Noonan 231.

439. See id. 231–32.

440. See Tietze 112 (Table 1).

441. Center for Disease Control 9.

442. Id. 48.

443. See 3 Ecol. L.Q. at 338–39.

444. See Cates, Legal Abortion: Are American Black Women Healthier Because of It? 38 Phylon 267 (1977).

445. See Forrest, Tietze & Sullivan, Abortion in the United States, 1976–1977, 10 Fam. Plan. Perspec. 271 (1978).

446. See Lamm & Davison, Abortion Reform, 1:4 Yale Rev. L. & Soc. Action 55, 56 (1971); Tietze 111.

447. Forrest et al. 275–76.

448. 3 Ecol. L.Q. at 341.

449. See studies cited in 7 U.C.D.L. Rev. at 441 n.47.

450. Niswander, Medical Abortion Practices in the United States, 17 Case W. Res. L. Rev. 403, 412 (1965).

451. Center for Disease Control iv.

452. Forrest et al. 273 (footnote omitted).

453. Center for Disease Control iv.

454. See Forrest et al. 271.

455. Id. 272.

456. Center for Disease Control 1–2.

457. 432 U.S. 464 (1977).

458. See 35 Cong. Q. Wkly. Rep. 1199, 1200, 1640 (1977).

459. 85:3 U.S. News & World Report 63 (July 24, 1978).

460. Id.

461. 91:6 Newsweek 32 (Feb. 6, 1978).

462. Id.

463. See 10 Fam. Plan. Perspec. 362 (1978).

464. Newsweek 32.

465. Id.

466. U.S. News 63. See also Newsweek 32.

467. U.S. News 63.

468. R. Jackson, The Struggle for Judicial Supremacy 71 (1941).

469. J. Casper 84.

470. Id. 33.

471. Id. 48.

472. Id. 49.

473. Schenck v. United States, 249 U.S. 47 (1919); Abrams v. United States, 250 U.S. 616 (1919); Gitlow v. New York, 268 U.S. 652 (1925).

474. 274 U.S. 380 (1927).

475. Whitney v. California, 274 U.S. 357 (1927).

476. 283 U.S. 359 (1931).

477. 283 U.S. 697 (1931).

478. 299 U.S. 353 (1937).

479. 301 U.S. 242 (1937).

480. Dennis v. United States, 341 U.S. 494 (1951); Garner v. Board of Public Works, 341 U.S. 716 (1951); Adler v. Board of Educ., 342 U.S. 485 (1952).

481. 340 U.S. 332 (1951).

482. 342 U.S. 1 (1951).

483. 344 U.S. 183 (1952).

484. 343 U.S. 495 (1952).

485. Yates v. United States, 354 U.S. 298 (1957).

486. S. Wasby, Impact of Court 220.

487. See Frank 109, 123–28.

488. 351 U.S. 536 (1956).

489. 354 U.S. 363 (1957).

490. 359 U.S. 535 (1959).

491. 360 U.S. 474 (1959).

492. Miller, Subversion and the Cold War, in Third Branch of Government 204, 232 (C. H. Pritchett and A. Westin eds. 1963).

493. Barenblatt v. United States, 360 U.S. 109 (1959); Scales v. United States, 367 U.S. 203 (1961); Konigsberg v. State Bar, 366 U.S. 36 (1961).

494. 357 U.S. 513 (1958).

495. 367 U.S. 290 (1961).

496. 360 U.S. 684 (1959).

497. 357 U.S. 499 (1958).

498. 361 U.S. 516 (1960).

499. 364 U.S. 479 (1960).

500. See M. Harris & D. Spiller, After Decision: Implementation of Judicial Decrees in Correctional Settings (1977).

501. Frank 131.

502. R. Dahl, Democracy 202.

503. Dolbeare, The Public Views the Supreme Court, in Law, Politics and the Federal Courts 194, 211 (H. Jacob ed. 1967).

504. See, e.g., R. Johnson, The Dynamics of Compliance 124 (1967); K. Dolbeare & D. Hammond, The School Prayer Decisions 16 (1971).

505. For further discussion, see chap. 3, sec. III, B.

506. See Yudof 414–16; Casper, The Supreme Court and National Policy Making, 70 Am. Pol. Sci. Rev. 50, 63 (1976).

507. See Z. Chafee, Free Speech in the United States 53–55 (1948).

508. 413 U.S. 15 (1973).

509. 354 U.S. 476 (1957).

510. See, e.g., Jenkins v. Georgia, 418 U.S. 153 (1974). See generally Casper 62.

511. See Paulsen, The Persistence of Substantive Due Process in the States, 34 Minn. L. Rev. 91 (1950); Hetherington State Economic Regulation and Substantive Due Process of Law, 53 Nw. U. L. Rev. 226 (1958).

512. See, e.g., People v. Disbrow, 16 Cal.3d 101, 545 P.2d 272, 127 Cal. Rptr. 360 (1976); State v. Opperman, 247 N.W.2d 673 (S.D. 1976). See generally Howard, State Courts and Constitutional Rights in the Day of the Burger Court, 62 Va. L. Rev. 873 (1976); Note, Of Laboratories and Liberties: State Court Protection of Political and Civil Rights, 10 Ga. L. Rev. 533 (1976).

513. Cox, The Role of Congress in Constitutional Determinations, 40 U. Cinc. L. Rev. 199, 220–21 (1971).

514. J. Story, Miscellaneous Writings 428 (1835).

Three   The Fragile Character of Judicial Review

1. See chap. 1, sec. VI, E.

2. 49 Cong. Rec., pt. 5, p. 4292 (1913).

3. Gallup Poll, S.F. Chronicle, Apr. 13, 1978, p. 2, col. 5 (57% favor, 32% oppose).

4. Adams, American Public Opinion in the 1960s on Two Church-State Issues, 17 J. of Church & State 477, 479 (1975).

5. Gallup Poll, S.F. Chronicle, Jan. 23, 1978, p. 15, col. 1.

6. B. Cardozo, The Nature of the Judicial Process 106, 16 (1921).

7. Michigan Office of Criminal Justice Programs, The Michigan Public Speaks Out on Crime 56 (5th ed. 1977), cited in Israel, Criminal Procedure, the Burger Court, and the Legacy of the Warren Court, 75 Mich. L. Rev. 1319, 1425 n.440 (1977). See also Arizona State Legislature Criminal Code Comm'n, A Study of Opinions and Attitudes Relative to Crime and Criminal Justice, in Criminal Justice System Research 196, 252–53, 301–3, 499–500 (1974).

8. See W. Murphy, Congress and the Court 248 (1962).

9. Aug. 19, 1964, in 3 G. Gallup, The Gallup Poll: Public Opinion 1935–1971 at 1897 (1972) (47% favor, 30% oppose).

10. Kernell, Presidential Popularity and Negative Voting: An Alternative Explanation of the Midterm Congressional Decline of the President's Party, 71 Am. Pol. Sci. Rev. 44, 51–52 (1977), citing D. Kanouse & L. Hanson, Negativity in Evaluations (1972) and Jordan, The "Asymmetry" of "Liking" and "Disliking": A Phenomenon Meriting Further Reflection and Research, 29 Pub. Op. Q. 315 (1965).

11. Kernell 52 (footnote omitted).

12. Bloom & Price, Voter Response to Short-Run Economic Conditions: The Asymmetric Effect of Prosperity and Recession, 69 Am. Pol. Sci. Rev. 1240, 1244 (1975).

13. Steel, A Critic's View of the Warren Court—Nine Men in Black Who Think White, N.Y. Times Mag., Oct. 13, 1968, p. 56.

14. 1 C. Warren, The Supreme Court in United States History 388 (rev. ed. 1928) (hereafter cited as Supreme Court in History). See also 2 id. at 334.

15. L. Tribe, American Constitutional Law v (1978).

16. L. Levy, Against the Law 439 (1974).

17. Leflar, The Supreme Court in the American Constitutional System: The Task of the Appellate Court, 33 Notre Dame Law. 548, 551 (1958).

18. L. Hand, The Spirit of Liberty 163 (I. Dilliard ed. 3d ed. 1960).

19. Cox, The New Dimensions of Constitutional Adjudication, 51 Wash. L. Rev. 791, 816 (1976). See generally M. Harris & D. Spiller, After Decision: Implementation of Judicial Decrees in Correctional Settings (1977); Cox 813–21; L. Lusky, By What Right? 277–78 (1975).

20. See generally S. Wasby, The Impact of the United States Supreme Court 42–56 (1970) (hereafter cited as Impact of Court). For earlier discussion of the matter, see chap. 2, sec. VI.

21. See Stumpf, The Political Efficacy of Judicial Symbolism, 19 W. Pol. Q. 293 (1966) and studies discussed therein.

22. See Berkson, Supreme Court Justices: Effective Encoders of Supreme Court Decisions, 14 Am. Bus. L.J. 391, 393 (1977).

23. See secs. IV, B, and VIII, B of this chap.

24. The Federalist, No. 65 at 278 (C. Beard ed. 1959).

25. Schmidhauser, Berg & Melone, The Impact of Judicial Decisions: New Dimensions in Supreme Court–Congressional Relations, 1971 Wash. U. L.Q. 209, 238.

26. Warren, Legislative and Judicial Attacks on the Supreme Court of the United States—A History of the Twenty-fifth Section of the Judiciary Act, 47 Am. L. Rev. 1, 3–4 (1913).

27. 9 U.S. 115 (1809).

28. 14 U.S. 304 (1816).

29. 2 U.S. 419 (1793).

30. See 1 C. Warren, Supreme Court in History 100.

31. 30 U.S. 1 (1831).

32. 31 U.S. 515 (1832).

33. 62 U.S. 506 (1858).

34. 71 U.S. 333 (1866).

35. Russ, The Lawyer's Test Oath during Reconstruction, 10 Miss. L.J. 154, 160 (1938).

36. See, e.g., Murphy, Lower Court Checks on Supreme Court Power, 53 Am. Pol. Sci. Rev. 1017 (1959); Warren, Federal and State Court

Interference, 43 Harv. L. Rev. 345 (1930); Note, Evasion of Supreme Court Mandates in Cases Remanded to State Courts since 1941, 67 Harv. L. Rev. 1251 (1954); Note, State Court Evasion of United States Supreme Court Mandates, 56 Yale L.J. 574 (1947).

37. Canon, Organizational Contumacy in the Transmission of Judicial Policies: The Mapp, Escobedo, Miranda, and Gault Cases, 20 Vill. L. Rev. 50 (1974).

38. Beatty, State Court Evasion of United States Supreme Court Mandates During the Last Decade of the Warren Court, 6 Valp. U. L. Rev. 260, 283 (1972).

39. See generally Longaker, Andrew Jackson and the Judiciary, 71 Pol. Sci. Q. 341 (1956). But cf. Burke, The Cherokee Cases: A Study in Law, Politics, and Morality, 21 Stan. L. Rev. 500, 527–29 (1968).

40. 17 Fed. Cases 144 (1861).

41. See 1 C. Warren, Supreme Court in History 269–315.

42. See 3 F.D.R.—His Personal Letters, 1928–1945, at 459 (E. Roosevelt ed. 1950).

43. See Perry v. United States, 294 U.S. 330 (1935).

44. Dixon, Congress, Shared Administration, and Executive Privilege, in Congress against the President 125, 133 (H. Mansfield ed. 1975).

45. For detailed discussion, see, e.g., W. Murphy; C. Pritchett, Congress versus the Supreme Court (1961); C. Warren, Congress, the Constitution, and the Supreme Court (1925).

46. Currie, The Three-Judge District Court in Constitutional Litigation, 32 U. Chi. L. Rev. 1, 5 & n.27 (1964).

47. W. Murphy 58.

48. See generally id. 57–62.

49. 2 H. Ickes, The Secret Diary of Harold L. Ickes 172 (1954).

50. Dred Scott v. Sandford, 60 U.S. 393 (1857).

51. 157 U.S. 429 (1895).

52. 156 U.S. 1 (1895).

53. 298 U.S. 587 (1936).

54. See Murphy & Tanenhaus, Public Opinion and Supreme Court: The Goldwater Campaign, 32 Pub. Op. Q. 31 (1968).

55. See Gallup Poll, N.Y. Times, Feb. 16, 1969, p. 47, col. 1.

56. See Warren, 47 Am. L. Rev. at 3–4; 1 C. Warren, Supreme Court in History 308, 333. For a more current accounting, see Elliott, Court-Curbing Proposals in Congress, 33 Notre Dame Law. 597 (1958).

57. See S. Nagel, The Legal Process from a Behavioral Perspective 263–64 (1969).

58. Compare §215 with §203(b).

59. 18 U.S.C. §§3501, 3502.

60. 388 U.S. 218 (1967).

61. See the child labor law cases: Hammer v. Dagenhart, 247 U.S. 251

(1918) and Bailey v. Drexel Furniture Co. (Child Labor Tax Case), 259 U.S. 20 (1922).

62. 328 U.S. 303 (1946).

63. Miller, Toward a Concept of Constitutional Duty, 1968 Sup. Ct. Rev. 199, 224, n.105.

64. Dolbeare & Hammond, Inertia in Midway: Supreme Court Decisions and Local Responses, 23 J. Leg. Ed. 106, 108 (1970). And see the list of studies there cited.

65. Reich, Schoolhouse Religion and the Supreme Court: A Report on Attitudes of Teachers and Principals on School Practices in Wisconsin and Ohio, 23 J. Leg. Ed. 123, 125 (1970).

66. 333 U.S. 203 (1948).

67. Patric, The Impact of a Court Decision: Aftermath of the McCollum Case, 6 J. Pub. L. 455, 464 (1957).

68. Sorauf, Zorach v. Clauson: The Impact of a Supreme Court Decision, 53 Am. Pol. Sci. Rev. 777, 784 (1959).

69. 343 U.S. 306 (1952).

70. Sorauf 786.

71. Engel v. Vitale, 370 U.S. 421 (1962); School District v. Schempp, 374 U.S. 203 (1963).

72. Katz, Patterns of Compliance with the Schempp Decision, 14 J. Pub. L. 396, 407 (1965) (footnote omitted).

73. S. Wasby, Impact of Court 131.

74. Dolbeare & Hammond, 23 J. Leg. Ed. at 113.

75. Reich 142.

76. 387 U.S. 1 (1967).

77. See chap. 2, n.150.

78. W. Stapleton & L. Teitelbaum, In Defense of Youth: A Study of the Role of Counsel in American Juvenile Courts 36 (1972). For details, see Lefstein, Stapleton & Teitelbaum, In Search of Juvenile Justice, 3 L. & Soc. Rev. 491, 506–10 (1969).

79. Washington Post, Oct. 24, 1968, at G2, col. 3.

80. See, e.g., F. Graham, The Self-Inflicted Wound (1970), and the review by Silverglate, 84 Harv. L. Rev. 1748 (1971).

81. 384 U.S. 436 (1966).

82. Medalie, Zeitz & Alexander, Custodial Police Interrogation in Our Nation's Capital: The Attempt to Implement *Miranda*, 66 Mich. L. Rev. 1347, 1365–66 (1968).

83. Note, Interrogations in New Haven: The Impact of *Miranda*, 76 Yale L.J. 1519, 1614 (1967).

84. M. Harris & D. Spiller 259–61.

85. NAACP v. Alabama, 357 U.S. 449 (1958).

86. S. Wasby, Impact of Court 74; see generally id. 200–01.

87. 397 U.S. 254 (1970).

88. Mashaw, The Management Side of Due Process: Some Theoretical and Litigation Notes on the Assurance of Accuracy, Fairness, and Timeliness in the Adjudication of Social Welfare Claims, 59 Corn. L. Rev. 772, 813–14 (1974) (footnotes omitted).

89. I. Carmen, unpublished dissertation, quoted in Barth, Perception and Acceptance of Supreme Court Decisions at the State and Local Level, 17 J. Pub. L. 308, 311–12 (1968).

90. See sec. VIII, A of this chap.

91. These methodological difficulties were suggested to me by Martin Shapiro.

92. See Wasby, The Communication of the Supreme Court's Criminal Procedure Decisions: A Preliminary Mapping, 18 Vill. L. Rev. 1086 (1973) and studies cited therein.

93. Canon & Kolson, Rural Compliance with Gault: Kentucky, A Case Study, 10 J. Fam. L. 300, 318 (1971).

94. See Murphy & Tanenhaus, 32 Pub. Op. Q. at 34–35. See also Dolbeare & Hammond, The Political Party Basis of Attitudes toward the Supreme Court, 32 Pub. Op. Q. 16 (1968); Dolbeare, The Public Views the Supreme Court, in Law, Politics and the Federal Courts 194 (H. Jacob ed. 1967); Kessel, Public Perceptions of the Supreme Court, 10 Midw. J. Pol. Sci. 167 (1966).

95. Murphy & Tanenhaus, Public Opinion and the United States Supreme Court: A Preliminary Mapping of Some Prerequisites for Court Legitimation of Regime Change, in Frontiers of Judicial Research 273, 276–79 (J. Grossman & J. Tanenhaus eds. 1969).

96. See R. Dahl, Who Governs? 321, 324 (1961); Key, Public Opinion and the Decay of Democracy, 37 Va. Q. Rev. 481 (1961).

97. Johnson, Compliance and Supreme Court Decision-Making, 1967 Wis. L. Rev. 170, 183.

98. R. Johnson, The Dynamics of Compliance 144 (1967). See generally id., ch. 7.

99. S. Wasby, Impact of Court 230–31.

100. Id. 134.

101. Statistical Abstract of the United States 124 (1974).

102. N.Y. Times, Jan. 16, 1974, p. 75, col. 1.

103. See M. Tumin, Desegregation: Resistance and Readiness 153 (1958); Krislov, Constituency versus Constitutionalism: The Desegregation Issue and Tensions and Aspirations of Southern Attorney Generals, 3 Midw. J. Pol. Sci. 75, 77–78, 89–92 (1959); Beth, The Supreme Court Reconsidered I: Opposition and Judicial Review in the United States, 16 Pol. Studies 243, 246–47 (1968); Thompson, Transmission or Resistance: Opinions of State Attorneys General and the Impact of the Supreme Court, 9 Valp. U. L. Rev. 55, 69–71 (1974).

104. Shapiro, The Impact of the Supreme Court, 23 J. Leg. Ed. 77, 84 (1970).

105. See R. Dahl 324.

106. Hyman & Sheatsley, Attitudes toward Desegregation, 211:1 Scientific American 16, 20 (July 1964).

107. R. Jackson, The Struggle for Judicial Supremacy 27 (1941).

108. See Spong, The War Powers Resolution Revisited: Historic Accomplishment or Surrender? 16 Wm. & M. L. Rev. 823, 830–31, 836 (1975).

109. See R. McCloskey, The American Supreme Court 100 (1960).

110. S. Kutler, Judicial Power and Reconstruction Politics vii (1968).

111. Corwin, The Dred Scott Decision, in the Light of Contemporary Legal Doctrine, 17 Am. Hist. Rev. 52, 68–69 (1911).

112. See 2 C. Warren, Supreme Court in History 330.

113. McCloskey, Reflections on the Warren Court, 51 Va. L. Rev. 1229, 1258 (1965).

114. 2 C. Warren, Supreme Court in History 703.

115. See, e.g., Murphy & Tanenhaus, in Frontiers of Judicial Research 273; W. Muir, Prayer in the Public Schools 73–110 (1967); Dolbeare, The Supreme Court and the States: From Abstract Doctrine to Local Behavioral Conformity, in The Impact of Supreme Court Decisions 202, 206 (T. Becker & M. Feeley eds. 2d ed. 1973).

116. Dolbeare & Hammond, 23 J. Leg. Ed. at 120.

117. R. Johnson 148. See generally J. Brehm & A. Cohen, Explorations in Cognitive Dissonance 247–48 (1962).

118. Katz 408.

119. Id. 404, 408.

120. S. Wasby, Impact of Court 43.

121. Id.

122. See Way, Survey Research on Judicial Decisions: The Prayer and Bible Reading Cases, 21 W. Pol. Q. 189 (1968); Katz 406; Beaney & Beiser, Prayer and Politics: The Impact of Engel and Schempp on the Political Process, 13 J. Pub. L. 475 (1964).

123. S. Wasby, Impact of Court 127.

124. Beatty 284.

125. See generally W. Murphy 86–109.

126. See generally Stumpf, Congressional Response to Supreme Court Rulings: The Interaction of Law and Politics, 14 J. Pub. L. 377 (1965).

127. See Harris, Annals of Legislation: The Turning Point, 44:43 The New Yorker 68, 84 (Dec. 14, 1968).

128. United States v. Richardson, 418 U.S. 166, 188, 191 (1974) (concurring opinion).

129. W. Murphy 247 (footnotes omitted).

130. Westin, The Case for America, in United States v. Nixon xi, xii–xiii (L. Friedman ed. 1974).

131. See W. Murphy 245–46.

132. See F. Graham 22–25, 65; Allen, The Judicial Quest for Penal Justice: The Warren Court and the Criminal Cases, 1975 U. Ill. L.F. 518, 537–39. But see Israel 1347–48.

133. Maher v. Roe, 432 U.S. 464 (1977).

134. Westin, Also on the Bench: "Dominant Opinion," in The Supreme Court under Earl Warren 63, 71 (L. Levy ed. 1972).

135. S. Krislov, The Supreme Court and Political Freedom 42–46 (1968). See generally id. at 39–53.

136. CBS News, 60 Minutes, vol. II, no. 16, at 13, 16 (Apr. 14, 1970).

137. J. Casper, The Politics of Civil Liberties 1–2, 223–24 (1972) (footnotes omitted).

138. See, e.g., Leiken, Police Interrogation in Colorado: The Implementation of Miranda, 47 Den L.J. 1 (1970); O. Stephens, The Supreme Court and Confessions of Guilt, ch. 7 (1973).

139. Seeburger & Wettick, Miranda in Pittsburgh—A Statistical Study, 29 U. Pitt. L. Rev. 1, 8 (1967).

140. Note, 76 Yale L.J. at 1550–51.

141. S. Wasby, Small Town Police and the Supreme Court 117 (1976).

142. S. Wasby, Impact of Court 225.

143. See Reich, The Impact of Judicial Decision Making: The School Prayer Cases, in The Supreme Court as Policy Maker 44, 46–52 (D. Everson ed. 1968).

144. S. Wasby, Impact of Court 131–32.

145. Way 191.

146. Canon, The Exclusionary Rule: Have Critics Proven That It Doesn't Deter Police? 62 Judicature 398, 402 n.33 (1979).

147. Westin, in The Supreme Court under Earl Warren 63–64.

148. Daniels, The Supreme Court and Its Publics, 37 Albany L. Rev. 632, 658–59, 657 (1973).

149. Id. 640, 643.

150. Gunther, The Subtle Vices of the "Passive Virtues"—A Comment on Principle and Expediency in Judicial Review, 64 Colum. L. Rev. 1, 8 (1964).

151. Rosenblum, Justiciability and Justice: Elements of Restraint and Indifference, 15 Cath. U. L. Rev. 141, 147 (1966).

152. Linde, Judges, Critics, and the Realist Tradition, 82 Yale L.J. 227, 232 (1972).

153. 395 U.S. 486 (1969).

154. See C. Swisher, Dred Scott One Hundred Years After, 19 J. Pol. 167, 183 (1957); L. Hand.

155. See discussion in chap. 2, sec. V, B.

156. A. Bickel, The Supreme Court and the Idea of Progress 94–95 (1970).

157. See 2 C. Warren, Supreme Court in History 604 et seq.

158. See chap. 5, sec. III, D, 5, c, (6) (d).

159. 343 U.S. 579 (1952).

160. See A. Westin, The Anatomy of a Constitutional Law Case 73–74 (1958).

Four   The Scope of National Power vis-à-vis the States

1. See L. Tribe, American Constitutional Law 226 n.6 (1978); J. Nowak, R. Rotunda & J. Young, Handbook on Constitutional Law 414 (1978).

2. The Federalist, No. 58 at 249 (C. Beard ed. 1948) (hereafter cited to this edition unless otherwise indicated).

3. McCulloch v. Maryland, 17 U.S. 316, 435 (1819).

4. See John Marshall, Essays from the Alexandria Gazette, 21 Stan. L. Rev. 456, 495 (1969).

5. The words are those of Justice Johnson in 1830, quoted in D. Morgan, Congress and the Constitution at 91 (1966).

6. The Federalist, No. 58 at 249.

7. Id., No. 62 at 263.

8. See Gaffney v. Cummings, 412 U.S. 735, 752–54 (1973).

9. See Deckard, State Party Delegations in the United States House of Representatives—An Analysis of Group Action, 5 Polity 311, 333 (1973).

10. See R. Fenno, The Power of the Purse 54–61 (1966).

11. See Deckard 322–27.

12. The Federalist, No. 45 at 201.

13. See A. Holcombe, Our More Perfect Union 205–06 (1950).

14. Official Congressional Directory 4–194 (1975). See generally R. Dahl, Democracy in the United States: Promise and Performance 225–26 (2d ed. 1972) (hereafter cited as Democracy in the United States).

15. See Davidson, Congress in the American Political System, in Legislatures in Developmental Perspective 129, 151–53 (A. Kornberg & L. Musolf eds. 1970). See also R. Dahl, Pluralist Democracy in the United States: Conflict and Consent 187 (1967) (hereafter cited as Pluralist Democracy).

16. Davidson 151–52.

17. Truman, Federalism and the Party System, in Federalism: Mature and Emergent 115, 117–25 (A. Macmahon ed. 1955).

18. See E. Schattschneider, Party Government 158–63 (1942); V. Key, Politics, Parties and Pressure Groups 315 (5th ed. 1964).

19. See W. Keech & D. Matthews, The Party's Choice 179–80 (1977); L. O'Connor, Clout: Mayor Daley and His City 150–62 (1975).

20. L. Fisher, President and Congress 126 (1972).

21. Ranney, The Political Parties: Reform and Decline, in The New American Political System 213 (A. King ed. 1978).

22. L. Henkin, Foreign Affairs and the Constitution 247–48 (1972).

23. Beer, Federalism, Nationalism, and Democracy in America, 72 Am. Pol. Sci. Rev. 9, 17–18 (1978).

24. 426 U.S. 833 (1976).

25. Id. at 834–35.

26. 10 Wkly. Comp. of Pres. Docs.: Richard Nixon 264 (1974).

27. 30 Cong. Q. Almanac 10–S (1974). The details of the Senate vote described in the text that follows appear here.

28. 30 Cong. Q. Almanac 244, 28–H, 29–H (1974). The details of the House vote described in the text that follows appear at 28–H and 29–H.

29. B. Eckhardt & C. Black, The Tides of Power 21 (1976).

30. Huntington, The Founding Fathers and the Division of Powers, in Area and Power 150, 188 (A. Maass ed. 1959).

31. See Lofgren, The Origins of the Tenth Amendment: History, Sovereignty, and the Problem of Constitutional Intention, in Constitutional Government in America 331 (R. Collins ed. 1979).

32. The Federalist, No. 45 at 201 (J. Madison).

33. Id., No. 46 at 205 (J. Madison).

34. Id., No. 17 at 70 (J. Madison, ed. 1831) (A. Hamilton).

35. Id., No. 46 at 206 (J. Madison).

36. Id., No. 44 at 198 (J. Madison).

37. See Weidner, Decision-Making in a Federal System, in Federalism: Mature and Emergent 363, 370 (A. Macmahon ed. 1955).

38. Id. 371. See also id. 366.

39. See Stewart, Pyramids of Sacrifice? Problems of Federalism in Mandating State Implementation of National Environmental Policy, 86 Yale L.J. 1196, 1211–12 (1977).

40. The Federalist, No. 46 at 205.

41. Id., No. 46 at 204.

42. See D. Morgan 144–50.

43. C. Beard, The Enduring Federalist 6 (1948).

44. See L. Caldwell, The Administrative Theories of Hamilton & Jefferson 213 (1944).

45. See Fenno, The House of Representatives and Federal Aid to Education, in New Perspectives on the House of Representatives 283 (R. Peabody & N. Polsby eds. 2d ed. 1969).

46. See 9 Wkly. Comp. of Pres. Docs. 368–72 (1972).

47. See Stewart, The Development of Administrative and Quasi-Constitutional Law in Judicial Review of Environmental Decisionmaking: Lessons from the Clean Air Act, 62 Iowa L. Rev. 713, 726–27 n.66 (1977).

48. See 1 C. Warren, The Supreme Court in United States History 595 (rev. ed. 1928); J. Maxwell, The Fiscal Impact of Federalism in the United States 20 (1946).

49. See Myers, A Legislative History of Revenue Sharing, 419 Annals

1, 2–3 (1975).

50. See Tugwell, The Experimental Roosevelt, 21 Pol. Q. 239, 241 (1950).

51. Wechsler, The Political Safeguards of Federalism: The Role of the States in the Composition and Selection of the National Government, 54 Colum. L. Rev. 543, 558 (1954).

52. Quoted in Biddle, Louis Dembitz Brandeis, 29 A.B.A.J. 71, 73 (1943).

53. R. Dahl, Democracy in the United States 214.

54. See Cattanach, Have the States Become an Anachronism in the Federal System? The Case for a Negative Answer, 21 De Paul L. Rev. 649 (1972).

55. See Dam, The American Fiscal Constitution, 44 U. Chi. L. Rev. 271, 299 (1977).

56. See 1 Advisory Comm'n on Intergovernmental Relations, Significant Features of Fiscal Federalism, Trends 7 (1976).

57. See id. 59.

58. See id. 4.

59. Douglas, J., dissenting in New York v. United States, 326 U.S. 572, 594 (1946).

60. See Alabama v. Texas, 347 U.S. 272 (1954).

61. See Kohl v. United States, 91 U.S. 367 (1876); Kleppe v. New Mexico, 426 U.S. 529 (1976).

62. S.F. Chronicle, Sept. 7, 1972, p. 8, col. 1.

63. R. Dahl, Pluralist Democracy 344.

64. See, e.g., Heart of Atlanta Motel, Inc. v. United States, 379 U.S. 241 (1964); Katzenbach v. McClung, 379 U.S. 294 (1964); South Carolina v. Katzenbach, 383 U.S. 301 (1966). See also Jones v. Alfred H. Mayer Co., 392 U.S. 409 (1968).

65. In Oregon v. Mitchell, 400 U.S. 112 (1970), the Court, before the twenty-sixth amendment, held that this subject was beyond the national legislative power.

66. See, e.g., Employees of Dep't of Public Health & Welfare v. Dep't of Public Health & Welfare, 411 U.S. 279 (1973); Edelman v. Jordan, 415 U.S. 651 (1974); Fitzpatrick v. Bitzer, 427 U.S. 445 (1976). See generally Nathanson, Constitutional Problems Involved in Adherence by the United States to a Convention for the Protection of Human Rights and Fundamental Freedoms, 50 Corn. L.Q. 235, 240–42 (1965).

67. See, e.g., Dep't of Revenue v. James B. Beam Distilling Co., 377 U.S. 341 (1964) (claim that state tax violates export-import clause); Hostetter v. Idlewild Bon Voyage Liquor Corp., 377 U.S. 324 (1964) (claim that state regulation violates commerce clause).

68. See, e.g., Collector v. Day, 78 U.S. 113 (1871); Burnet v. Coronado Oil & Gas Co., 285 U.S. 393 (1932); Helvering v. Gerhardt, 304 U.S. 405 (1938); New York v. United States, 326 U.S. 572 (1946).

69. See, e.g., Fry v. United States, 421 U.S. 542 (1975); National League of Cities v. Usery, 426 U.S. 833 (1976).

70. 301 U.S. 324 (1937).

71. 315 U.S. 203 (1942).

72. 5 U.S. 137, 163 (1803).

73. 312 U.S. 100 (1941).

74. See Heart of Atlanta Motel, Inc. v. United States, 379 U.S. 241 (1964).

75. 384 U.S. 641 (1966).

76. See id. at 651 n.10.

77. Council of State Governments, Federal-State Relations, Report of the Commission on Organization of the Executive Branch of the Government, S. Doc. No. 81, 81st Cong., 1st Sess. 275 (1949).

78. See generally R. Harris, The Quest for Equality (1960); J. James, The Framing of the Fourteenth Amendment (1956); J. tenBroek, The Anti-slavery Origins of the Fourteenth Amendment (1951); Hurst, The Role of History, in Supreme Court and Supreme Law 55, 60 (E. Cahn ed. 1954); Frantz, Congressional Power to Enforce the Fourteenth Amendment against Private Acts, 73 Yale L.J. 1353 (1964).

79. See cases cited in n.125 infra. But see Oregon v. Mitchell, 400 U.S. 112 (1970).

80. 332 U.S. 19 (1947).

81. This is contrary to the dictum in Pollard's Lessee v. Hagan, 44 U.S. 212 (1845), repeated by the Court most recently in Oregon ex rel. State Land Board v. Corvallis Sand & Gravel Co., 429 U.S. 363, 374–75 (1977).

82. See Storing, The Constitution and the Bill of Rights, in Essays on the Constitution of the United States 32 (M. Harmon ed. 1978).

83. See Stern, That Commerce Which Concerns More States Than One, 47 Harv. L. Rev. 1335, 1337–41 (1934). Cf. W. Riker, Federalism: Origin, Operation, Significance 17–20 (1964). But see Strong, Bicentennial Benchmark: Two Centuries of Evolution of Constitutional Processes, 55 N.C.L. Rev. 1, 93–94 (1976).

84. 5 The Writings of James Madison 26 (G. Hunt ed. 1905).

85. W. Wilson, Constitutional Government in the United States 173 (1911).

86. Huntington 193.

87. 247 U.S. 251 (1918).

88. Bailey v. Drexel Furniture Co. (Child Labor Tax Cases), 259 U.S. 20 (1922). See generally R. Dahl, A Preface to Democratic Theory 106 (1956).

89. Carter v. Carter Coal Co., 298 U.S. 238 (1936).

90. Massachusetts v. Mellon, 262 U.S. 447, 483 (1923).

91. See, e.g., Willcuts v. Bunn, 282 U.S. 216 (1930).

92. R. Jackson, The Struggle for Judicial Supremacy 22 (1941) (emphasis added).

93. See United States v. Realty Co., 163 U.S. 427 (1896).

94. 50 Stat. 751 (1937), now codified in 28 U.S.C. §2403 (1970).

95. See, e.g., Schmidhauser, "States' Rights" and the Origin of the Supreme Court's Power as Arbiter in Federal-State Relations, 4 Wayne L. Rev. 101 (1958).

96. Wechsler 559 (footnote omitted).

97. O. Holmes, Law and the Court, in Collected Legal Papers 295–96 (1920).

98. McCulloch v. Maryland, 17 U.S. 316, 435 (1819) (Marshall, C. J.).

99. Helvering v. Gerhardt, 304 U.S. 405, 412 (1938) (Stone, J.). See also South Carolina State Highway Dept. v. Barnwell Bros., Inc. 303 U.S. 177 (1938) (Stone, J.).

100. See V. Key, Politics, Parties, and Pressure Groups 102 (3d ed. 1952); Willbern, The States as Components in an Areal Division of Powers, in Area and Power 70, 77–78 (A. Maass ed. 1959).

101. Graves v. New York ex rel. O'Keefe, 306 U.S. 466, 479 n.1 (1939).

102. See generally Dowling, Interstate Commerce and State Power, 27 Va. L. Rev. 1 (1940).

103. See Scharpf, Judicial Review and the Political Question: A Functional Analysis, 75 Yale L.J. 517, 524 (1966).

104. Freund, Review and Federalism, in Supreme Court and Supreme Law 86, 101–05 (E. Cahn ed. 1954).

105. The Federalist, No. 78 at 334.

106. 4 Letters and Other Writings of James Madison 349 (Congress ed. 1884).

107. 9 The Writings of Thomas Jefferson 518 (Ford ed. 1897).

108. 8 id. 311. See generally Krislov, Jefferson and Judicial Review: Refereeing Cahn, Commager and Mendelson, 9 J. Pub. L. 374 (1960).

109. 2 Messages and Papers of the Presidents 582 (J. Richardson ed. 1896).

110. 6 id. 9–10.

111. See W. Murphy, Congress and the Court 25 (1962).

112. See 1 C. Warren 761–64.

113. See M. Van Buren, Inquiry into the Origin and Course of Political Parties in the United States 342–43 (1867).

114. Cf. Beezer v. City of Seattle, 62 Wash.2d 569, 383 P.2d 895 (1963).

115. See, e.g., District of Columbia v. Train, 521 F.2d 971, 991 (D.C. Cir. 1975), vacated and remanded sub nom. EPA v. Brown, 431 U.S. 99 (1977). See also Note, Is Federalism Dead? A Constitutional Analysis of the Federal No-Fault Insurance Bill: S. 354, 12 Harv. J. Leg. 668 (1975).

116. The Federalist, No. 33 at 131.

117. See text at notes 275–76 infra.

118. See National League of Cities v. Usery, 426 U.S. 833 (1976), to be discussed in this section.

119. See, e.g., Gibbons v. Ogden, 22 U.S. 1 (1824); Champion v. Ames, 188 U.S. 321 (1903); Wickard v. Filburn, 317 U.S. 111 (1942); Heart of Atlanta Motel, Inc. v. United States, 379 U.S. 241 (1964); Katzenbach v. McClung, 379 U.S. 294 (1964); Perez v. United States, 402 U.S. 146 (1971). For judicial language authorizing virtually unlimited national control of navigation, see United States v. Twin City Power Co., 350 U.S. 222, 224–25 (1956).

120. McCulloch v. Maryland, 17 U.S. 316 (1819).

121. See, e.g., United States v. Doremus, 249 U.S. 86 (1919) (drug control); Sonzinsky v. United States, 300 U.S. 506 (1937) (gun control); United States v. Kahriger, 345 U.S. 22 (1953) (gambling control).

122. See, e.g., Steward Machine Co. v. Davis, 301 U.S. 548 (1937) (unemployment compensation); Helvering v. Davis, 301 U.S. 619 (1937) (control of social insurance). See particularly the judicial language in United States v. Gerlach Live Stock Co., 339 U.S. 725 (1950).

123. See Missouri v. Holland, 252 U.S. 416 (1920) (control of migratory birds).

124. See Oregon v. Mitchell, 400 U.S. 112 (1970).

125. See, e.g., Jones v. Alfred H. Mayer Co., 392 U.S. 409 (1968), Sullivan v. Little Hunting Park, Inc., 396 U.S. 229 (1969), Griffin v. Breckenridge, 403 U.S. 88 (1971), and Runyon v. McCrary, 427 U.S. 160 (1976) (thirteenth amendment); United States v. Guest, 383 U.S. 745 (1966) and Katzenbach v. Morgan, 384 U.S. 641 (1966) (fourteenth amendment); South Carolina v. Katzenbach, 383 U.S. 301 (1966) (fifteenth amendment).

126. See Griffin v. School Board of Prince Edward County, 377 U.S. 218 (1964).

127. See Swann v. Charlotte-Mecklenburg Board of Educ., 402 U.S. 1 (1971).

128. See authorities collected in W. Lockhart, Y. Kamisar & J. Choper, Constitutional Law: Cases—Comments—Questions 1439–40 n.a. (4th ed. 1975).

129. See Katzenbach v. Morgan, 384 U.S. 641 (1966).

130. See In re Rahrer, 140 U.S. 545 (1891); Clark Distilling Co. v. Western Maryland Ry., 242 U.S. 311 (1917); Prudential Insurance Co. v. Benjamin, 328 U.S. 408 (1946).

131. See Maryland v. Wirtz, 392 U.S. 183, 196 (1968); Fry v. United States, 421 U.S. 542, 547 n.7 (1975).

132. 426 U.S. 833 (1976).

133. Id. at 852.

134. Id. at 845, quoting Lane County v. Oregon, 74 U.S. 71 (1869).

135. Fry v. United States, 421 U.S. 542, 558 (1975).

136. 426 U.S. at 856 (Blackmun, J., concurring).

137. Id. at 847.

138. See cases cited in note 68 supra.

139. 426 U.S. at 840, quoting Fry v. United States, 421 U.S. 542, 547 (1975).

140. Id. at 852 n.17.

141. Id. at 855 n.18.

142. Fitzpatrick v. Bitzer, 427 U.S. 445, 451–56 & n.11 (1976).

143. Maryland v. Wirtz, 392 U.S. 183, 205 (1968) (Douglas, J., dissenting).

144. Fry v. United States, 421 U.S. 542, 554 n.1 (1975) (Rehnquist, J., dissenting).

145. See, e.g., Steward Machine Co. v. Davis, 301 U.S. 548 (1937); Helvering v. Davis, 301 U.S. 619 (1937).

146. See Brown, Beyond the New Federalism—Revenue Sharing in Perspective, 15 Harv. J. Leg. 1 (1977).

147. Office of Management and Budget, Special Analyses, Budget of U.S. Gov't: Fiscal Year 1979, at 175 (1978).

148. Percy, National League of Cities v. Usery: The Tenth Amendment Is Alive and Doing Well, 51 Tul. L. Rev. 95, 106 n.53 (1976).

149. See, e.g., The Federalist, No. 39.

150. Oklahoma v. United States Civil Service Commission, 330 U.S. 127, 129 n.1, 143 (1947).

151. Cf. Elrod v. Burns, 427 U.S. 347 (1976).

152. See, e.g., Screws v. United States, 325 U.S. 91 (1945).

153. See, e.g., Georgia v. Stanton, 73 U.S. 50 (1867).

154. 426 U.S. 833, 841.

155. See United Public Workers v. Mitchell, 330 U.S. 75 (1947); Broadrick v. Oklahoma, 413 U.S. 601 (1973).

156. 426 U.S. 833, 858.

157. Id. at 876–78.

158. Hand, The Contribution of an Independent Judiciary to Civilization, in The Spirit of Liberty 155, 164 (I. Dilliard ed. 1953).

159. Thayer, The Origin and Scope of the American Doctrine of Constitutional Law, 7 Harv. L. Rev. 129, 156 (1893).

160. Eakin v. Raub, 12 S. & R. 330, 355 (Pa. 1825) (Gibson, J., dissenting).

161. The Federalist, No. 60 at 261.

162. See text at notes 114–16 supra.

163. For earlier evaluation of this type of argument, see chap. 2, sec. III, A.

164. See, e.g., Evans v. Gore, 253 U.S. 245, 248 (1920).

165. 79 Cong. Rec. 13449 (1935) (quoting Wash. Daily News, Aug. 10, 1935).

166. 2 C. Warren 208–09.

167. 21 Cong. Rec. 2608 (1890).

168. D. Morgan 180 (footnotes omitted).

169. 104 Cong. Rec. 12458–59, 12468 (1958).

170. 110 Cong. Rec. 13434 (1964).

171. Civil Rights—The President's Program, 1963: Hearings on S.1731 before the Senate Comm. on the Judiciary, 88th Cong., 1st Sess. 204 (1963).

172. Mikva & Lundy, The 91st Congress and the Constitution, 38 U. Chi. L. Rev. 449, 483 (1971) (footnote omitted).

173. D. Morgan 336.

174. An analogous development in respect to judicial validations of government actions allegedly violative of personal liberties was observed in chap. 2, sec. V, B.

175. J. Thayer, Legal Essays 10 (1908).

176. See Note, The Case for an Advisory Function in the Federal Judiciary, 50 Geo. L.J. 785, 800–02 (1962).

177. 420 U.S. 35 (1975).

178. L. Fisher, Presidential Spending Power 192 (1975).

179. See D. Morgan 180.

180. See id. 254–65; Mikva & Lundy 472.

181. See C. Black, The People and the Court 34–86 (1960).

182. See Adamany, Legitimacy, Realigning Elections, and the Supreme Court, 1973 Wis. L. Rev. 790, 845–46.

183. P. Kurland, Politics, the Constitution, and the Warren Court 36 (1970).

184. 1 C. Warren 5 (emphasis in original).

185. See, e.g., 11 The Writings of Thomas Jefferson 50–51 (Lipscomb ed. 1905); 1 C. Warren 652.

186. Id. 514.

187. Id. 546.

188. Id. 519–20.

189. Id. 519.

190. Legal Tender Cases, 110 U.S. 421 (1884).

191. 2 C. Warren 656.

192. Id. See generally id. 654–59.

193. See Kilpatrick, Justice Black Has "Edited" Constitution, Miami Herald, Jan. 2, 1971, at A7, col. 5.

194. P. Kurland, Watergate and the Constitution 156–57 (1978).

195. The Report and Resolution of the National Conference of Chief Justices, Conclusions of the Report of the Committee on Federal-State Relationships as Affected by Judicial Decisions, 43 Mass. L.Q. 86, 87 (1958) (hereafter cited as National Conference of Chief Justices).

196. See sec. IX, B, 3, a of this chapter, and chap. 2, sec. III, C.

197. See, e.g., 1 C. Warren 642–53; National Conference of Chief Justices.

198. See Heller, A Turning Point for Religious Liberty, 29 Va. L. Rev. 440, 449 (1943).

199. See Note, The Court, the Bar, and Certiorari at October Term, 1958, 108 U. Pa. L. Rev. 1160, 1177 (1960).

200. See, e.g., United States v. Kras, 409 U.S. 434, 443 (1973).

201. Scharpf 536 n.59.

202. 48 U.S. 1 (1849).

203. 2 C. Warren, 193, 195.

204. 328 U.S. 549 (1946).

205. See Lewis, Legislative Apportionment and the Federal Courts, 71 Harv. L. Rev. 1057, 1088 (1958).

206. The Federalist, No. 81 at 347.

207. H. Hart & H. Wechsler, The Federal Courts and the Federal System 93 (1953).

208. M. Shapiro, Freedom of Speech: The Supreme Court and Judicial Review 30 (1966).

209. See D. Morgan 68, 259; Mikva & Lundy 494.

210. See D. Morgan, 143–59, 297–327; Frank, Review and Basic Liberties, in Supreme Court and Supreme Law 109, 122–23 (E. Cahn ed. 1954); Burt, Miranda and Title II: A Morganatic Marriage, 1969 Sup. Ct. Rev. 81; Mikva & Lundy 497.

211. See, e.g., S. Rep. No. 757, 93d Cong., 2d Sess. 6–20, 36–47 (1974).

212. See P. Brest, Processes of Constitutional Decisionmaking: Cases and Materials 15–31 (1975).

213. See D. Morgan, 16–21, 30, 184–203.

214. Mikva & Lundy 497–98.

215. See E. Corwin, The President 279 (4th ed. 1957).

216. See, e.g., D. Morgan 350; Mikva & Lundy 471, 497.

217. D. Morgan 9.

218. See id. 156–57; Mikva & Lundy 462–63.

219. See D. Morgan 202–03, 348–60.

220. Id. 335.

221. See, e.g., United States v. Five Gambling Devices, 346 U.S. 441 (1953); United States v. Bass, 404 U.S. 336 (1971).

222. 3 Letters and Other Writings of James Madison 349 (Congress ed. 1884). See also The Federalist, No. 39.

223. See text at note 105 supra. See also R. Berger, Congress v. the Supreme Court 203–05 (1969).

224. 3 J. Elliot, Debates in the Several State Conventions on the Adoption of the Federal Constitution 553 (2d ed. 1881).

225. 2 id. 196.

226. Id. 489.

227. Id. 131.

228. 1 Annals of Congress 840.

229. West Virginia State Board of Educ. v. Barnette, 319 U.S. 624, 667 (1943) (dissenting opinion).

230. New York v. United States, 326 U.S. 572, 594 (1946) (dissenting opinion).

231. 2 W. Crosskey, Politics and the Constitution in the History of the United States 1011 (1953). See also Ketcham, James Madison and Judicial Review, 8 Syr. L. Rev. 158 (1957).

232. Wechsler 558.

233. Levy, Judicial Review, History and Democracy: An Introduction, in Judicial Review and the Supreme Court 1, 6 (L. Levy ed. 1967). See also Hamilton's suggestion of no judicial review over questions of this type in The Federalist, No. 31.

234. See R. Berger 91–93.

235. Greene, Congressional Power over the Elective Franchise: The Unconstitutional Phases of Oregon v. Mitchell, 52 B.U. L. Rev. 505, 525–26 (1972) (footnotes omitted).

236. Huntington 193–94.

237. J. Acton, The History of Freedom in Antiquity, in Essays on Freedom and Power 49 (1949).

238. Bartkus v. Illinois, 359 U.S. 121, 137 (1959).

239. 1 W. Crosskey 702.

240. Id. 678.

241. Id. 705–06 (emphasis in original; footnotes omitted).

242. Feller, The Tenth Amendment Retires, 27 A.B.A.J. 223 n.2 (1941).

243. 307 U.S. 38 (1938).

244. Brief for the United States at 123, 127, id.

245. 1 Annals of Congress 458–59 (Gales & Seaton eds. 1789).

246. Kansas v. Colorado, 206 U.S. 46, 90 (1907).

247. See Martin v. Hunter's Lessee, 14 U.S. 304, 325 (1816) (Story, J.); McCulloch v. Maryland, 17 U.S. 316, 372–74 (1819) (Marshall, C. J.); Gordon v. United States, 117 U.S. 697, 705 (1864) (Taney, C. J.); Missouri v. Holland, 252 U.S. 416, 432 (1920) (Holmes, J.); United States v. Darby, 312 U.S. 100, 124 (1941) (Stone, J.).

248. J. Kilpatrick, The Sovereign States 15 (1957).

249. See generally R. Berger 260–63.

250. See generally Graham, Crosskey's Constitution: An Archeological Blueprint, 7 Vand. L. Rev. 340, 359–63 (1954).

251. 1 W. Crosskey 47.

252. 1 M. Farrand, The Records of the Federal Convention 357 (rev. ed. 1937).

253. A. de Tocqueville, Democracy in America 87 (Bradley ed. 1946).

254. J. Buchanan & G. Tullock, The Calculus of Consent 113–15 (1969).

255. Frankfurter, Mr. Justice Brandeis and the Constitution, in Mr. Justice Brandeis 84–85 (F. Frankfurter ed. 1932).

256. A. Vanderbilt, The Doctrine of the Separation of Powers and its Present-Day Significance 60–61 (1953).

257. National Conference of Chief Justices.

258. F. Frankfurter and H. Shulman, Cases on Federal Jurisdiction and Procedure ix (rev. ed. 1937); F. Frankfurter and W. Katz, id. vii (1931).

259. See generally Murphy, State Sovereignty Prior to the Constitution, 29 Miss. L.J. 115 (1958).

260. 3 J. Elliot 156.

261. 1 Messages and Papers of the Presidents 323 (J. Richardson ed. 1900).

262. Corwin, The Progress of the Constitutional Theory between the Declaration of Independence and the Meeting of the Philadelphia Convention, 30 Am. Hist. Rev. 511, 535 (1925).

263. See generally R. Berger, ch. 2.

264. Huntington 191–92.

265. See G. Wood, The Creation of the American Republic 608–09 (1969).

266. See M. Vile, Constitutionalism and the Separation of Powers 143–44 (1967).

267. The Federalist, No. 10 at 74. See also id., No. 51. See generally Huntington 179–96.

268. The Federalist, No. 27 at 109.

269. See generally Beth, The Supreme Court and American Federalism, 10 St. L.U.L.J. 376 (1966); E. Schattschneider, The Semi-Sovereign People 6–9 (1960); Carrington, Financing the American Dream: Equality and School Taxes, 73 Colum. L. Rev. 1227, 1250–51 (1973); Willbern 77–78; Potter, Changing Patterns of Social Cohesion and the Crisis of Law under a System of Government by Consent, in Is Law Dead? 260, 271–77 (E. Rostow ed. 1971).

270. See W. Riker 13–15.

271. Macmahon, The Problems of Federalism: A Survey, in Federalism: Mature and Emergent 1, 10 (A. Macmahon ed. 1955).

272. W. Wilson, Congressional Government 25–26 (9th ed. 1892).

273. See generally Cattanach.

274. See A. Cox, The Role of the Supreme Court in American Government 23–30 (1976).

275. C. Hughes, The Supreme Court of the United States: Its Foundations, Methods and Achievements 50 (1928).

276. See, e.g., H. Commager, Majority Rule and Minority Rights 49–54 (1950).

Five   Constitutional Conflicts between Congress and the President

1. A. Upshur, A Brief Enquiry into the True Nature and Character of our Federal Government 116–17 (1840).

2. See Frohnmayer, The Separation of Powers: An Essay on the Vitality of a Constitutional Idea, 52 Ore. L. Rev. 211, 219 (1973).

3. L. Henkin, Foreign Affairs and the Constitution 16 (1972).

4. Id. 28.

5. See M. Vile, Constitutionalism and the Separation of Powers 61 (1967).

6. C. Montesquieu, L'Esprit des lois (1748), quoted in L. Jaffe, Judicial Control of Administrative Action at 29 (1965).

7. 1 W. Blackstone, Commentaries on the Laws of England 146 (T. Cooley ed. 2d ed. 1872).

8. See W. Gwyn, The Meaning of the Separation of Powers 34 et seq. (1965); Miller, An Inquiry into the Relevance of the Intentions of the Founding Fathers, With Special Emphasis upon the Doctrine of the Separation of Powers, 27 Ark. L. Rev. 583, 588 (1973); A. Miller, Presidential Power in a Nutshell 16–18 (1977).

9. The Federalist, No. 47 at 211 (J. Beard ed. 1959) (hereafter cited to this edition without reference to the editor). See also id., No. 48.

10. 1 J. Richardson, Messages and Papers of the Presidents 219 (1896).

11. 4 The Works of John Adams 186 (C. Adams ed. 1865).

12. 3 The Writings of Thomas Jefferson 223–24 (P. Ford ed. 1894).

13. See, e.g., S. Huntington, Political Order in Changing Societies (1968); C. McIlwain, Constitutionalism and the Changing World (1936).

14. Youngstown Sheet & Tube Co. v. Sawyer, 343 U.S. 579, 613–14, 629 (1952) (concurring opinions).

15. Myers v. United States, 272 U.S. 52, 293 (1927) (Brandeis, J., dissenting).

16. M. Vile 30, 44.

17. See generally W. Gwyn ch. 5.

18. Quoted in Sharp, The Classical American Doctrine of "The Separation of Powers," 2 U. Chi. L. Rev. 385, 390 (1935). See also W. Gwyn 111; M. Vile 93.

19. Sharp 390.

20. The Federalist, No. 77 at 328.

21. Id., No. 49 at 221.

22. See chap. 2, sec. III, B.

23. 1 Annals of Congress 520 (1834).

24. Huntington, The Founding Fathers and the Division of Powers, in Area and Power 150, 159 (A. Maass ed. 1959).

25. M. Vile, 167, 171.

26. But cf. P. Kurland, Watergate and the Constitution 160 (1978) (hereafter cited as Watergate).

27. See G. Wood, The Creation of the American Republic, 1776–1787 at 608 (1969).

28. The Federalist, No. 49 at 223.

29. Id., No. 51 at 226. See also id., No. 48. See generally Carey, Separation of Powers and the Madisonian Model: A Reply to the Critics, 72 Am. Pol. Sci. Rev. 151, 157–64 (1978).

30. The Federalist, No. 48 at 218.

31. Id., No. 51 at 226.

32. Dietze, Hamilton's Federalist—Treatise for Free Government, 42 Corn. L. Q. 307, 326 (1957), quoting The Federalist, Nos. 70–73.

33. See T. Paine, Rights of Man, pt. 2, ch. 4 (1792).

34. The Federalist, No. 51 at 226.

35. Id., No. 70 at 299.

36. Id., No. 62 at 263–64.

37. J. Acton, Acton-Creighton Correspondence, in Essays on Freedom and Power 357, 364 (1949).

38. Myers v. United States, 272 U.S. 52, 294–95 (1927) (dissenting opinion).

39. Youngstown Sheet & Tube Co. v. Sawyer, 343 U.S. 579, 629 (1952) (concurring opinion).

40. The Federalist, No. 51 at 225.

41. L. Koenig, The Chief Executive 3 (1964).

42. S. Warren, The President as World Leader 431 (1964).

43. Quoted in R. Neustadt, Presidential Power: The Politics of Leadership 39 (1960).

44. G. Allison, Essence of Decision: Explaining the Cuban Missile Crisis 141–42 (1971) (footnotes omitted).

45. A. Schlesinger, The Imperial Presidency 260, 274 (1973).

46. R. Neustadt 23.

47. Id. 39. See generally C. Rossiter, The American Presidency 59–62 (2d ed. 1960); A. Schlesinger & A. de Grazia, Congress and the Presidency: Their Role in Modern Times 94–97 (1967); Cronin, "Everybody Believes in Democracy until He Gets to the White House ...": An Examination of White House–Departmental Relations, 35 Law & Contemp. Probs. 573 (1970).

48. G. Allison 67, 80–81, 145, 148.

49. M. Eccles, Beckoning Frontiers: Public and Personal Recollections 336 (1951).

50. 2 H. Truman, Memoirs: Years of Trial and Hope 165 (1956).

51. A. Schlesinger 343.

52. G. Allison 139.

53. Id. 129–30.

54. A. Schlesinger 274–75.

55. See P. Kurland, Watergate 176–79.

56. See generally R. Hilsman, To Move a Nation 541–62 (1967); R. Neustadt 37–38; C. Mills, The Power Elite (1956); N. Chomsky, American Power and the New Mandarins (1969).

57. D. Cater, Power in Washington 17 (1964).

58. C. Hardin, Presidential Power and Accountability: Toward a New Constitution 69 (1974).

59. The Federalist, No. 73 at 313.

60. Kolodziej, Congress and Foreign Policy: The Nixon Years, in Congress against the President 167, 171–72 (H. Mansfield ed. 1975).

61. 68 Dep't of State, Bull. No. 1769 at 652–55 (1973).

62. 9 Wkly. Comp. Pres. Docs. 861 (June 27, 1973).

63. See Eagleton, The August 15 Compromise and the War Powers of Congress, 18 St. L.U.L.J. 1 (1973).

64. See Hopkins, The Ninety-fourth Congress: Congressional Reform Progresses, 63 A.B.A.J. 211, 212–13 (1977).

65. 36 Cong. Q. Wkly. Rep. 1410–11 (1978).

66. D. Cater 90.

67. See Stassen, Separation of Powers and the Uncommon Defense: The Case against Impounding of Weapons System Appropriations, 57 Geo. L.J. 1159, 1168–76 (1969).

68. A. Schlesinger 246.

69. 31 Cong. Q. Wkly. Rep. 2156, 2414, 2868 (1973).

70. 33 Cong. Q. Wkly. Rep. 481 (1975).

71. 31 Cong. Q. Wkly. Rep. 2155, 2866 (1973).

72. Pub. L. No. 92–226, §658(a), 86 Stat. 20 (1972).

73. D. Cater 90. See generally L. Wilmerding, The Spending Power: A History of the Efforts of Congress to Control Expenditures (1943).

74. See E. Corwin, The President: Office and Powers 1787–1957 at 250–52, 462–63 n.72 (4th rev. ed. 1957).

75. See Kramer & Marcuse, Executive Privilege—A Study of the Period 1953–1960, 29 Geo. Wash. L. Rev. 623, 712 (1961).

76. See generally M. Benedict, The Impeachment and Trial of Andrew Johnson (1973).

77. See 119 Cong. Rec. 22521 (1973).

78. See Casper, Constitutional Constraints on the Conduct of Foreign and Defense Policy: A Nonjudicial Model, 43 U. Chi. L. Rev. 463 (1976).

79. Pub. L. No. 93–148, 87 Stat. 555 (1973).

80. Pub. L. No. 93–344, 88 Stat. 297 (1974).

81. See Fisher, Congressional Budget Reform: The First Two Years, 14 Harv. J. Leg. 413, 444–54 (1977).

82. Pub. L. No. 94–412, 90 Stat. 1255 (1976).

83. See Church, Ending Emergency Government, 63 A.B.A.J. 197 (1977).

84. See 33 Cong. Q. Wkly. Rep. 1712 (1975); Sparkman, Checks and Balances in American Foreign Policy, 52 Ind. L.J. 433, 438–39 (1977).

85. See 33 Cong. Q. Wkly. Rep. 2098 (1975); 30 Cong. Q. Alm. 662 (1974).

86. See Black, The Working Balance of the American Political Departments, 1 Hast. Con. L.Q. 13, 19 (1974).

87. A. Schlesinger ix.

88. See, e.g., J. Clark, Congress: The Sapless Branch (rev. ed. 1965).

89. L. White, The Federalists: A Study in Administrative History 89 (1948).

90. A. Schlesinger ix.

91. Schlesinger, The Future of Congress, Wall St. J., May 1, 1974, at 16, col. 6. See also B. Eckhardt & C. Black, The Tides of Power: Conversations on the American Constitution 13–14 (1976).

92. See, e.g., Morgan, The General Accounting Office: One Hope for Congress to Regain Parity of Power with the President, 51 N.C. L. Rev. 1279 (1973).

93. Sofaer, Executive Power and the Control of Information: Practice under the Framers, 1977 Duke L.J. 1, 47 & n.301.

94. See Kramer & Marcuse 856–60; Wallace, The President's Exclusive Foreign Affairs Power over Foreign Aid, Part II, 1970 Duke L.J. 453, 475–76.

95. See Hopkins, Congressional Reform: Toward a Modern Congress, 47 Notre Dame Law. 442, 460–62 (1972).

96. See D. Cater 8–9.

97. L. Henkin 114.

98. U.S. Commitments to Foreign Powers: Hearings on S. Res. 151 before the Senate Comm. on Foreign Relations, 90th Cong., 1st Sess. 108 (1967) (statement of Nicholas Katzenbach).

99. 22 U.S.C. §2422 (1974).

100. Zeidenstein, The Reassertion of Congressional Power: New Curbs on the President, 93 Pol. Sci. Q. 393, 399–400 (1978) (emphasis added).

101. Id. 405.

102. N.Y. Times, July 29, 1977, at A3, col. 6.

103. Zeidenstein 405.

104. L. Henkin 81.

105. A. Schlesinger 80.

106. L. Henkin 114.

107. D. Cater 142. See also Saloma, The Responsible Use of Power, in Congress and the Federal Budget 103, 177 (1965).

108. A. Vanderbilt, The Doctrine of the Separation of Powers and Its Present-Day Significance 71 (1953).

109. A. Schlesinger 118–19.

110. R. Dahl, Democracy in the United States: Promise and Performance 181 (2d ed. 1972) (footnote omitted).

111. 1 U.S.C. §112b (1976).

112. See Comment, The War Powers Resolution: Statutory Limitation on the Commander-in-Chief, 11 Harv. J. Leg. 181 (1974).

113. Rogers, Congress, the President, and the War Powers, 59 Calif. L. Rev. 1194, 1212–13 (1971).

114. A. Miller 191.

115. 400 U.S. 886 (1970).

116. Brief for The Constitutional Lawyers Committee on Undeclared War as Amicus Curiae at 76, Massachusetts v. Laird, 400 U.S. 886 (1970).

117. See generally Symposium, Legality of United States Participation in the Viet Nam Conflict, 75 Yale L.J. 1084 (1966); Note, Congress, the President, and the Power to Commit Forces to Combat, 81 Harv. L. Rev. 1771 (1968); Monaghan, Presidential War-Making, 50 B.U. L. Rev. 19 (Special Issue, Spring 1970); Velvel, The War in Viet Nam: Unconstitutional, Justiciable, and Jurisdictionally Attackable, 16 U. Kan. L. Rev. 449 (1968); Rostow, Great Cases Make Bad Law: The War Powers Act, 50 Tex. L. Rev. 833 (1972); L. Henkin 101–08; Van Alstyne, Congress, the President, and the Power to Declare War: A Requiem for Vietnam, 121 U. Pa. L. Rev. 1 (1972); Berger, War-Making by the President, 121 U. Pa. L. Rev. 29 (1972).

118. 67 U.S. 635 (1863).

119. See, e.g., Brief for Defendant at 22–24, 36–41, in Massachusetts v. Laird, 400 U.S. 886 (1970).

120. Compare Luftig v. McNamara, 252 F. Supp. 819 (D.D.C. 1966), aff'd, 373 F.2d 664 (D.C. Cir.), cert. denied, 387 U.S. 945 (1967); Holmes v. United States, 387 F.2d 781 (7th Cir. 1967), cert. denied, 391 U.S. 936 (1968); Velvel v. Nixon, 287 F. Supp. 846 (D. Kan. 1968), aff'd, 415 F.2d 236 (10th Cir. 1969), cert. denied, 396 U.S. 1042 (1970); Davi v. Laird, 318 F. Supp. 478 (W.D. Va. 1970); Gravel v. Laird, 347 F. Supp. 7 (D.D.C. 1972); Atlee v. Laird, 347 F. Supp. 689 (E.D. Pa. 1972); Da Costa v. Laird, 471 F.2d 1146 (2d Cir. 1973); Holtzman v. Schlesinger, 484 F.2d 1307 (2d Cir. 1973), cert. denied, 416 U.S. 936 (1974); with Orlando v. Laird, 317 F. Supp. 1013 (E.D.N.Y. 1970), aff'd, 443 F.2d 1039 (2d Cir.), cert. denied, 404 U.S. 869 (1971); Mottola v. Nixon, 318 F. Supp. 538 (N.D. Cal. 1970), rev'd, 464 F.2d 178 (9th Cir. 1972); Da Costa v. Laird, 448 F.2d 1368 (2d Cir. 1971), cert. denied, 405 U.S. 979 (1972).

121. L. Henkin 53.

122. Henkin, "A More Effective System" for Foreign Relations: The Constitutional Framework, 61 Va. L. Rev. 751, 766 (1975).

123. See L. Henkin 52; Henkin 766.

124. L. Henkin 53.

125. See A. Schlesinger 178.

126. See G. Reedy, The Twilight of the Presidency 38 (1970).

127. A. Schlesinger 287. See generally A. Miller 169–85.

128. 369 U.S. 186, 215 (1962).

129. See, e.g., Ratner, The Coordinated Warmaking Power—Legislative, Executive and Judicial Roles, 44 So. Cal. L. Rev. 461 (1971).

130. A. Schlesinger 77.

131. L. Henkin 106–07, 350 n.43.

132. Stassen 1165–66.

133. 81:17 Newsweek 22 (Apr. 23, 1973).

134. See Stanton, The Presidency and the Purse: Impoundment 1803–1973, 45 U. Colo. L. Rev. 25, 34–37 (1973).

135. L. Fisher, Presidential Spending Power 182–83 (1975).

136. Cox, Executive Privilege, 122 U. Pa. L. Rev. 1383, 1427–28 (1974).

137. Note, Executive Privilege and the Congressional Right of Inquiry, 10 Harv. J. Leg. 621, 649 (1973).

138. Id. 652–53.

139. N.Y. Times, Oct. 2, 1974, at 1, col. 2.

140. 33 Cong. Q. Wkly. Rep. 2097 (1975).

141. Id. 2572, 2711.

142. See Congressional Oversight of Executive Agreements—1975: Hearings before the Subcomm. on Separation of Powers of the Senate Comm. on the Judiciary, 94th Cong., 1st Sess. 43 (1975); Congressional Oversight of Executive Agreements: Hearings before the Subcomm. on Separation of Powers of the Senate Comm. on the Judiciary, 92d Cong., 2d Sess. 261 (1972).

143. A. Schlesinger & A. de Grazia 171.

144. A Schlesinger 105–09.

145. See Martin, When Lincoln Suspended Habeas Corpus, 60 A.B.A.J. 99, 102 (1974).

146. See A. Schlesinger 28, 91–92.

147. See AFL-CIO v. Kahn, – F.2d – (D.C. Cir.), cert. denied, 99 S.Ct. 3107 (1979).

148. But cf. A. Schlesinger, ch. 7.

149. See, e.g., Orlando v. Laird, 443 F.2d 1039 (2d Cir.), cert. denied, 404 U.S. 869 (1971); Da Costa v. Laird, 448 F.2d 1368 (2d Cir. 1971), cert. denied, 405 U.S. 979 (1972). See also Rehnquist, The Constitutional Issues—Administration Position, 45 N.Y.U. L. Rev. 628 (1970); cf. Church.

150. See B. Eckhardt & C. Black 7.

151. Mikva & Lundy, The 91st Congress and the Constitution, 38 U. Chi. L. Rev. 449, 497 (1971).

152. See 1 C. Warren, The Supreme Court in United States History 325–38 (rev. ed. 1928).

153. Hughes, Civil Disobedience and the Political Question Doctrine, 43 N.Y.U. L. Rev. 1, 16 (1968).

154. See Mishkin, Great Cases and Soft Law: A Comment on United States v. Nixon, 22 U.C.L.A. L. Rev. 76, 87 (1974).

155. See 84:8 Newsweek 16 (Aug. 19, 1974).

156. See, e.g., N.Y. Times, Apr. 13, 1974, p. 10, col. 4; id., May 12, 1974, p. 40, col. 7; id., May 27, 1974, p. 22, col. 1; id., June 14, 1974, p. 11, col. 8.

157. See Mishkin 77.

158. Westin, The Case for America, in United States v. Nixon: The

President before the Supreme Court xi, xiii (L. Friedman ed. 1974). See also G. Reedy 6; A. Schlesinger 148; M. Marcus, Truman and the Steel Seizure Case: The Limits of Presidential Power 34–36, 124–25 (1977).

159. Westin xii–xiii.

160. See chap. 3, sec. VIII, C.

161. See B. Eckhardt & C. Black 128–29.

162. R. Neustadt 26. See id. at 19–26.

163. Greenstein, Change and Continuity in the Modern Presidency, in The New American Political System 45, 69 (A. King ed. 1978).

164. R. Jackson, The Supreme Court in the American System of Government 62 (1955).

165. Frankfurter, J., dissenting in Baker v. Carr, 369 U.S. 186, 289–90 n.23 (1962) and citing cases.

166. See W. Gwyn 126–27.

167. See, e.g., Tufte, Determinants of the Outcomes of Midterm Congressional Elections, 69 Am. Pol. Sci. Rev. 812 (1975); Nelson, The Effect of Incumbency on Voting in Congressional Elections, 1964–1974, 93 Pol. Sci. Q. 665, 674–76 (1978).

168. R. Dahl 145.

169. G. Reedy 139.

170. A. Schlesinger 410.

171. D. Mayhew, Congress: The Electoral Connection 107 (1974).

172. A. Schlesinger 187.

173. International Herald Tribune, Jan. 8, 1973, p. 6, col. 6.

174. See N.Y. Times, May. 13, 1973, p. 5, col. 1.

175. S.F. Chronicle, Nov. 19, 1973, at 6, col. 1.

176. See N.Y. Times, Aug. 5, 1974, at 15, col. 2; id., Aug. 6, 1974, at 17, col. 7.

177. See L. Henkin 87.

178. A. Schlesinger & A. de Grazia 106.

179. 81:17 Newsweek 19 (Apr. 23, 1973).

180. R. Dahl 145.

181. P. Kurland, Watergate 172. See also C. Hardin 9; A. Schlesinger, chs. 3–5.

182. See United States v. Curtiss-Wright Export Corp., 299 U.S. 304 (1936).

183. See Steward Machine Co. v. Davis, 301 U.S. 548 (1937); Wickard v. Filburn, 317 U.S. 111 (1942); Katzenbach v. McClung, 379 U.S. 294 (1964).

184. See United States v. Grimaud, 220 U.S. 506 (1911); Currin v. Wallace, 306 U.S. 1 (1939); Lichter v. United States, 334 U.S. 742 (1948).

185. See Martin v. Mott, 25 U.S. 19 (1827); Prize Cases, 67 U.S. 635 (1863); Sterling v. Constantin, 287 U.S. 378 (1932).

186. See United States v. Belmont, 301 U.S. 324 (1937); United States

v. Pink, 315 U.S. 203 (1942).

187. See L. P. Steuart & Bro., Inc. v. Bowles, 322 U.S. 398 (1944).

188. See In re Debs, 158 U.S. 564 (1895). See also In re Neagle, 135 U.S. 1 (1890).

189. A. Miller 163.

190. 343 U.S. 579 (1952).

191. See, e.g., United States v. Schurz, 102 U.S. 378 (1880); Butterworth v. United States ex rel. Hoe, 112 U.S. 50 (1884); Noble v. Union River Logging R.R., 147 U.S. 165 (1893).

192. Quoted in A. Westin, The Anatomy of a Constitutional Law Case at 65 (1958).

193. 360 U.S. 474 (1959) (Secretary of Defense has no statutory or presidential authority to revoke employee's security clearance without affording confrontation and cross-examination).

194. 355 U.S. 579 (1958) (Secretary of Army has no statutory authority to use soldier's pre-military record as basis for less than honorable discharge).

195. Id. 581–82.

196. See, e.g., United States v. Smith, 39 F.2d 851 (1st Cir. 1930).

197. Wyoming v. Franke, 58 F. Supp. 890, 896 (D. Wyo. 1945).

198. Reprinted in A. Westin at 62–64.

199. See N.Y. Times, Apr. 28, 1952, at 1, col. 1.

200. See Brief for Solicitor General at 150–72, Youngstown Sheet & Tube Co. v. Sawyer, 343 U.S. 579 (1952).

201. Id. 102.

202. W. Taft, Our Chief Magistrate and His Powers 139–40 (1916).

203. T. Roosevelt, Autobiography 357 (1920).

204. 407 U.S. 297, 339 n.3 (1972).

205. 381 U.S. 1 (1965).

206. 10 Complete Works of Abraham Lincoln 66 (J. Nicolay & J. Hay eds. 1905).

207. 2 H. Truman 478.

208. 158 U.S. 564 (1895).

209. 318 F. Supp. 1293 (S.D.N.Y. 1970). But cf. United States v. Solomon, 419 F. Supp. 358 (D. Md. 1976).

210. 135 U.S. 1 (1890).

211. Proclamation No. 2039, in 2 The Public Papers and Addresses of Franklin D. Roosevelt: The Year of Crisis, 1933, at 24 (1938).

212. Exec. Order No. 9835, 12 Fed. Reg. 1935 (1947).

213. Exec. Order No. 8802, 6 Fed. Reg. 3109 (1941); Exec. Order No. 10308, 16 Fed. Reg. 12303 (1951); Exec. Order No. 10479, 18 Fed. Reg. 4899 (1953); Exec. Order No. 10925, 26 Fed. Reg. 1977 (1961); Exec. Order No. 11246, 30 Fed. Reg. 12319 (1965).

214. Exec. Order No. 11063, 27 Fed. Reg. 11527 (1962).

215. 55 L.R.R.M. 89 (1964).

216. Exec. Order No. 11387, 33 Fed. Reg. 47 (1968).

217. 45 C.F.R. §180 (1967).

218. Exec. Order No. 11905, 12 Wkly. Comp. of Pres. Docs. 234 (Feb. 18, 1976).

219. A. Miller 93.

220. See United States v. Yoshida Int'l, Inc., 526 F.2d 560 (C.C.P.A. 1975).

221. See FEA v. Algonquin SNG, Inc., 426 U.S. 548 (1976).

222. 1 Stat. 425 (1795), as amended, 10 U.S.C. §§332–34 (1970 ed.). See generally Pollitt, Presidential Use of Troops to Execute the Laws: A Brief History, 36 N.C. L. Rev. 117 (1958).

223. 343 U.S. 579, 586.

224. See generally Note, Congressional Reversal of Supreme Court Decisions: 1945–1957, 71 Harv. L. Rev. 1324 (1958).

225. See A. Westin 44–52.

226. See M. Marcus 98–99, 147–48.

227. Brief for Solicitor General at 102, 343 U.S. 579.

228. Id. 103 n.3.

229. 343 U.S. at 585, 630–32.

230. 28 U.S.C. §1491 (1970).

231. United States v. Causby, 328 U.S. 256, 267 (1946).

232. See P. Bator, P. Mishkin, D. Shapiro & H. Wechsler, Hart & Wechsler's The Federal Courts and the Federal System 1402–04 (2d ed. 1973).

233. See R. Berger, Congress v. The Supreme Court 330–31 (1969).

234. Seaboard Air Line Ry. v. United States, 261 U.S. 299, 304 (1923). See also Jacobs v. United States, 290 U.S. 13 (1933); Larson v. Domestic and Foreign Commerce Corp., 337 U.S. 682 (1949). See generally Dellinger, Of Rights and Remedies: The Constitution as a Sword, 85 Harv. L. Rev. 1532 (1972).

235. 106 U.S. 196 (1882).

236. 403 U.S. 713 (1971).

237. Brief for the United States at 13–14, id.

238. Cf. Mitchell v. United States, 369 F.2d 323 (2d Cir. 1966), cert. denied, 386 U.S. 972 (1967), discussed in A. D'Amato & R. O'Neil, The Judiciary and Vietnam 26 (1972).

239. 272 U.S. 52 (1926).

240. 295 U.S. 602 (1935).

241. See E. Corwin 86–87.

242. 5 U.S. 137, 158–61 (1803).

243. See also Morgan v. TVA, 115 F.2d 990 (6th Cir. 1940), cert. denied, 312 U.S. 701 (1941).

244. See Cole v. Young, 351 U.S. 536 (1956); Weiner v. United States,

357 U.S. 349 (1958).

245. 5 U.S. 137, 162–63 (1803).

246. See United States ex rel. Goodrich v. Guthrie, 58 U.S. 284 (1854). Cf. Bishop v. Wood, 426 U.S. 341 (1976).

247. See, e.g., Bailey v. Richardson, 182 F.2d 46 (D.C. Cir. 1950), aff'd per curiam, 341 U.S. 918 (1951); Peters v. Hobby, 349 U.S. 331 (1955); Vitarelli v. Seaton, 359 U.S. 535 (1959); Greene v. McElroy, 360 U.S. 474 (1959).

248. See, e.g., Service v. Dulles, 354 U.S. 363 (1957); Arnett v. Kennedy, 416 U.S. 134 (1974).

249. 272 U.S. 52, 67 (1926).

250. Id.

251. 279 U.S. 655 (1929).

252. P. Kurland, Politics, The Constitution and the Warren Court 41 (1970), citing a statement by Robert H. Jackson.

253. See 100 Cong. Rec. 6621 (1954); Executive Privilege, Secrecy in Government, & Freedom of Information: Hearings on S.858, S. Con. Res. 30, S.J. Res. 72, S.1106, S.1142, S.1520, S.1923 and S.2073 before a Subcomm. of the Senate Comm. on Government Operations and Subcomms. of the Senate Comm. on the Judiciary, 93 Cong., 1st Sess., vol. 1, at 24–26 (1973) (statement of Richard G. Kleindienst). See generally Rogers, The Papers of the Executive Branch, 44 A.B.A.J. 941 (1958).

254. See, e.g., R. Berger, Executive Privilege: A Constitutional Myth (1974); Schwartz, Executive Privilege and Congressional Investigatory Power, 47 Calif. L. Rev. 3 (1959).

255. See generally Dorsen & Shattuck, Executive Privilege, the Congress and the Courts, 35 Ohio St. L.J. 1 (1974); Kramer & Marcuse 827; Younger, Congressional Investigations and Executive Secrecy: A Study in the Separation of Powers, 20 U. Pitt. L. Rev. 755 (1959).

256. See Opinions of the Justices, 328 Mass. 655, 102 N.E.2d 79 (1951).

257. Senate Select Committee on Pres. Cam. Act. v. Nixon, 498 F.2d 725 (D.C. Cir. 1974). The question was specifically left open in United States v. Nixon, 418 U.S. 683, 712 n.19 (1974).

258. See, e.g., Cox; Sofaer, Book Review, 88 Harv. L. Rev. 281 (1974).

259. Cf. United States v. American Tel. & Tel. Co., 551 F.2d 384 (D.C. Cir. 1976); id., 567 F.2d 121 (D.C. Cir. 1977).

260. 418 U.S. 683 (1974).

261. 1 C. Wright, Federal Practice and Procedure (Criminal) §101 (1969). See also F.R. Crim. P. 6(a). Thus, the situation in Nixon v. Sirica, 487 F.2d 700 (D.C. Cir. 1973), which involved a subpoena from the grand jury itself, would appear to be yet a stronger factual setting for the Court's rationale.

262. See Fed. R. Crim. P. 48.

263. See McCormick's Handbook of the Law of Evidence §8 (2d ed. E. Cleary ed. 1972).

264. Van Alstyne, A Political and Constitutional Review of United States v. Nixon, 22 U.C.L.A. L. Rev. 116, 133 (1974).

265. Id.

266. 28 U.S.C. §§509, 510, 515, 516, 533 (1976).

267. Albert & Simon, Enforcing Subpoenas against the President: The Question of Mr. Jaworski's Authority, 74 Colum. L. Rev. 545, 558 (1974). But see Mishkin 82–83.

268. See Brief for United States at 36–38, 418 U.S. 683.

269. Id. at 43. See also Reply Brief for United States at 38–39 n.21, id.

270. Brief for Respondent at 28, id.

271. See sec. IV, E of this chap.

272. Van Alstyne, 22 U.C.L.A. L. Rev. at 139.

273. 347 U.S. 260 (1954).

274. 354 U.S. 363 (1957).

275. 359 U.S. 535 (1959).

276. Id. at 547 (Frankfurter, J., joined by Clark, Whittaker and Stewart, JJ., concurring and dissenting). See also United States v. Caceres, 99 S.Ct. 1465, 1473 n.18 (1979).

277. Cf. Nader v. Bork, 366 F. Supp. 104 (D.D.C. 1973).

278. See Ratner, Executive Privilege, Self-Incrimination, and the Separation-of-Powers Illusion, 22 U.C.L.A. L. Rev. 92, 101–02 (1974).

279. Compare Van Alstyne, 22 U.C.L.A. L. Rev. 116.

280. See text at notes 261–65 supra.

281. 433 U.S. 425 (1977).

282. Id. at 545 (Rehnquist, J., dissenting).

283. But see id. at 518 (Burger, C. J., dissenting).

284. Id. at 557 (Rehnquist, J. dissenting).

285. Id. at 502 n.5 (Powell, J., concurring).

286. See generally Kaye, Congressional Papers and Judicial Subpoenas, 23 U.C.L.A. L. Rev. 57 (1975); Kaye, Congressional Papers, Judicial Subpoenas, and the Constitution, 24 U.C.L.A. L. Rev. 523 (1977).

287. See, e.g., Long v. Ansell, 293 U.S. 76 (1934).

288. Cf. Calley v. Callaway, 519 F.2d 184 (5th Cir. 1975), cert. denied sub. nom. Calley v. Hoffman, 425 U.S. 911 (1976) (no due process violation).

289. See generally McCormick's Handbook of the Law of Evidence, ch. 12.

290. See Roviaro v. United States, 353 U.S. 53 (1957); Jencks v. United States, 353 U.S. 657 (1957).

291. 418 U.S. 683, 713.

292. Nixon v. Sirica, 487 F.2d 700, 716 (D.C. Cir. 1973). See also Committee for Nuclear Responsibility, Inc. v. Seaborg, 463 F.2d 788,

791 (D.C. Cir. 1971).

293. See Ratner 95–98. Compare 88 Harv. L. Rev. 61 (1974).

294. See United States v. Ragen, 340 U.S. 462 (1951).

295. Freund, Foreword: On Presidential Privilege, 88 Harv. L. Rev. 13, 33 (1974).

296. 345 U.S. 1 (1953).

297. Fed. R. Civ. P. 37(b)(2); Fed. R. Ev. 509(d) (R.D. 1971).

298. Compare Totten v. United States, 92 U.S. 105 (1875).

299. Cf. Sun Oil Co. y. United States, 514 F.2d 1020 (Ct. Cl. 1975); Dellums v. Powell, 561 F.2d 242 (D.C. Cir.), cert. denied sub. nom. Nixon v. Dellums, 434 U.S. 880 (1977).

300. See generally Bishop, The Executive's Right of Privacy: An Unresolved Constitutional Question, 66 Yale L.J. 477 (1957).

301. For description of these cases, see G. Schubert, The Presidency in the Courts 40–45 (1957).

302. See, e.g., Gelston v. Hoyt, 16 U.S. 246 (1818).

303. 71 U.S. 333 (1866).

304. Cf. United States v. Klein, 80 U.S. 128, 147 (1871), where the Court gratuitously discussed the scope of the President's pardon power vis-a-vis Congress.

305. Cf. Carlesi v. New York, 233 U.S. 51 (1914).

306. 419 U.S. 256 (1974).

307. 378 F. Supp. 1221 (D.D.C. 1974).

308. See Boudin, The Presidential Pardons of James R. Hoffa and Richard M. Nixon: Have the Limitations on the Pardon Power Been Exceeded? 48 U. Colo. L. Rev. 1, 28–29 (1976).

309. 419 U.S. 256, 264, 266.

310. See generally Note, The Conditional Presidential Pardon, 28 Stan. L. Rev. 149 (1975).

311. See 419 U.S. 256, 267.

312. Compare Burdick v. United States, 236 U.S. 79 (1915) with Biddle v. Perovich, 274 U.S. 480 (1927).

313. See Senate Select Committee on Pres. Cam. Act. v. Nixon, 498 F.2d 725 (D.C. Cir. 1974).

314. 2 U.S.C. §194 (1970).

315. This point was suggested to me by Meir Cohen.

316. See L. Tribe, American Constitutional Law 297 n.3 (1978).

317. See, e.g., Jurney v. McCracken, 294 U.S. 125 (1935); McGrain v. Daugherty, 273 U.S. 135 (1927).

318. Bishop 484–85.

319. A. Schlesinger 84.

320. P. Kurland, Watergate 30–31.

321. See, e.g., Prize Cases, 67 U.S. 635 (1863); United States v. Curtiss-Wright Export Corp., 299 U.S. 304 (1936).

322. See United States v. Pink, 315 U.S. 203, 249 (1942) (Stone, C. J.,

dissenting).

323. See United States v. Guy W. Capps, Inc., 204 F.2d 655 (4th Cir. 1953), aff'd on other grounds, 348 U.S. 296 (1955).

324. See T. Bailey, Diplomatic History of the American People 558–59 (1940).

325. See generally Murphy, Treaties and International Agreements Other Than Treaties: Constitutional Allocation of Power and Responsibility among the President, the House of Representatives, and the Senate, 23 U. Kan. L. Rev. 221 (1975).

326. See 2 N. Schachner, Thomas Jefferson, a Biography, ch. 53 (1951).

327. But see Edwards v. Carter, 580 F.2d 1055 (D.C. Cir.), cert. denied, 436 U.S. 907 (1978).

328. Cf. Ex parte Bollman, 8 U.S. 75 (1807); Cross v. Harrison, 57 U.S. 164 (1853); Santiago v. Nogueras, 214 U.S. 260 (1909).

329. Cf. Brown v. United States, 12 U.S. 110 (1814).

330. See Nobleman, Financial Aspects of Congressional Participation in Foreign Relations, 289 Annals Am. Acad. Pol. & Social Sci. 145, 160 (1953).

331. See generally C. Norton, Congressional Review, Deferral and Disapproval of Executive Actions (Library of Congress Congressional Research Service 1975) cited in Dixon, The Congressional Veto and Separation of Powers: The Executive on a Leash? 56 N.C. L. Rev. 423 at 425 n.11 (1978); Wallace, The President's Exclusive Foreign Affairs Power over Foreign Aid, Part I, 1970 Duke L.J. 293.

332. See Schwartz, The Legislative Veto and the Constitution—A Reexamination, 46 Geo. Wash. L. Rev. 351–52, 357–59 (1978).

333. See Dixon 489.

334. H.R. 8231, 94th Cong., 1st Sess. §1 (1975). See generally McGowan, Congress, Court, and Control of Delegated Power, 77 Colum. L. Rev. 1119, 1135–39 (1977).

335. See Watson, Congress Steps Out: A Look at Congressional Control of the Executive, 63 Calif. L. Rev. 983, 1004–06 (1975).

336. See Jackson, A Presidential Legal Opinion, 66 Harv. L. Rev. 1353 (1953).

337. See 9 Wkly. Comp. Pres. Docs. 1285 (Oct. 24, 1973); 10 id. 1279 (Oct. 12, 1974).

338. 97 Cong. Rec. 5374–75 (1951); 100 Cong. Rec. 7135 (1954); 111 Cong. Rec. 12639 (1965).

339. See Public Papers of the Presidents: John F. Kennedy: 1963 at 6 (1964); id.: Lyndon B. Johnson: 1963–64, vol. 2 at 1250 (1965).

340. See 8 Wkly. Comp. Pres. Docs. 1076 (June 16, 1972).

341. 12 Wkly. Comp. Pres. Docs. 1519 (Oct. 15, 1976).

342. See Dixon 432–33 n.29.

343. 36 Cong. Q. Wkly. Rep. 1623 (1978).

344. See Watson 1022.

345. See Wallace, 1970 Duke L.J. 453, 473–74.

346. 36 Cong. Q. Wkly. Rep. 1623 (1978).

347. See Miller & Knapp, The Congressional Veto: Preserving the Constitutional Framework, 52 Ind. L.J. 367, 374 (1977).

348. Buckley v. Valeo, 424 U.S. 1, 284–85 (1976) (concurring and dissenting opinion).

349. Atkins v. United States, 556 F.2d 1028 (Ct. Cl. 1977), cert denied, 434 U.S. 1009 (1978).

350. Clark v. Valeo, 559 F.2d 642, 685–90 (MacKinnon, J., dissenting), aff'd mem. sub nom. Clark v. Kimmit, 431 U.S. 950 (1977).

351. See Dixon 440–51.

352. 354 U.S. 1 (1957).

353. 354 U.S. 524 (1957).

354. See sec. IV, B of this chap.

355. Nathanson, The Supreme Court as a Unit of the National Government: Herein of Separation of Powers and Political Questions, 6 J. Pub. L. 331, 362 (1957).

356. See, e.g., The Chinese Exclusion Case, 130 U.S. 581 (1889).

357. See, e.g., Wong Yang Sung v. McGrath, 339 U.S. 33 (1950).

358. United States ex rel. Knauff v. Shaughnessy, 338 U.S. 537, 544 (1950).

359. Scharpf, Judicial Review and the Political Question: A Functional Analysis, 75 Yale L.J. 517, 579 n.218 (1966).

360. E.g., United States ex rel. Knauff v. Shaughnessy, 338 U.S. 537 (1950); Shaughnessy v. United States ex rel. Mezei, 345 U.S. 206 (1953).

361. Scharpf 579–80 n.218.

362. Harisiades v. Shaughnessy, 342 U.S. 580 (1952); Galvan v. Press, 347 U.S. 522 (1954).

363. Scharpf 580 n.218.

364. 335 U.S. 160 (1948).

365. 333 U.S. 103 (1948).

366. Id. at 111.

367. 194 U.S. 315 (1904).

368. See Banco Nacional de Cuba v. Sabbatino, 376 U.S. 398 (1964).

369. Guaranty Trust Co. v. United States, 304 U.S. 126, 137 (1938).

370. See generally Scharpf 543–45.

371. Ex parte Peru, 318 U.S. 578, 588 (1943). See generally Note, The Relationship between Executive and Judiciary: The State Department as the Supreme Court of International Law, 53 Minn. L. Rev. 389 (1968). See L. Henkin 56–64 for the view that the Court is reexamining this doctrine.

372. 279 U.S. 655 (1929).

373. See sec. IV, C, 4 of this chap.

374. See, e.g., S.1642, 92d Cong., 1st Sess. (1971).

375. See Bellamy, The Growing Potential of the Pocket Veto: Another Area of Increasing Presidential Power, 61 Ill. B.J. 85, 89 (1972).

376. See Eber Bros. Wine & Liquor Corp. v. United States, 337 F.2d 624 (Ct. Cl. 1964).

377. Kennedy v. Sampson, 511 F.2d 430 (D.C. Cir. 1974). The Justice Department did not seek review in the Supreme Court. 32 Cong. Q. Wkly. Rep. 3152 (1974).

378. Kennedy v. Jones, 412 F. Supp. 353 (D.D.C. 1976). The Justice Department agreed to the entry of summary judgment.

379. 302 U.S. 583 (1938).

380. 286 U.S. 482 (1932).

381. 5 U.S. 137, 166 (1803).

382. See Letter from Jefferson to William Johnson, June 1823, in S. Padover, The Genius of America 130 (1960).

383. 37 U.S. 524 (1838).

384. 59 Cong. Rec. 7026 (1920) (President Wilson's Message to Congress).

385. Senate Comm. on the Judiciary, Separation of Powers, S. Rep. No. 549, 91st Cong., 1st Sess. 13 (1969).

386. Note, Impoundment of Funds, 86 Harv. L. Rev. 1505, 1511 (1973).

387. Comment, Presidential Impounding of Funds: The Judicial Response, 40 U. Chi. L. Rev. 328 (1973).

388. Train v. City of New York, 420 U.S. 35 (1975); Train v. Campaign Clean Water, Inc., 420 U.S. 136 (1975).

389. See e.g., Guadamuz v. Ash, 368 F. Supp. 1233 (D.D.C. 1973); National Council of Community Health Centers v. Weinberger, 361 F. Supp. 897 (D.D.C. 1973); Pennsylvania v. Lynn, 362 F. Supp. 1363 (D.D.C. 1973).

390. See, e.g., W. Lockhart, Y. Kamisar & J. Choper, Constitutional Law: Cases—Comments—Questions 277–284 (4th ed. 1975) and articles cited therein. For earlier commentary, see Fisher, The Politics of Impounded Funds, 15 Admin. Sci. Q. 361 (1970) and articles cited therein.

391. See text at note 80, supra.

392. E. Griffith & F. Valeo, Congress: Its Contemporary Role 54 (5th ed. 1975).

393. Cf. Passaic County Bar Ass'n v. Hughes, 108 N.J. Super. 161, 260 A.2d 261 (1969).

394. Schechter Poultry Corp. v. United States, 295 U.S. 495 (1935); Panama Refining Co. v. Ryan, 293 U.S. 388 (1935). See also Carter v. Carter Coal Co., 298 U.S. 238 (1936); Washington v. W. C. Dawson & Co., 264 U.S. 219 (1924).

395. Arizona v. California, 373 U.S. 546, 626 (1963) (Harlan, J., joined by Douglas and Stewart, JJ., dissenting); Zemel v. Rusk, 381 U.S. 1,

21–23 (1965) (Black, J., dissenting); United States v. Robel, 389 U.S. 258, 272–73 (1967) (Brennan, J., concurring); California Bankers' Ass'n v. Schultz, 416 U.S. 21 (1974), 90–91 (Douglas, J., dissenting); 91–93 (Brennan, J., dissenting); 93 (Marshall, J., dissenting). Cf. National Cable Television Ass'n v. United States, 415 U.S. 336 (1974).

396. See S. Barber, The Constitution and the Delegation of Congressional Power (1975); T. Lowi, The End of Liberalism: Ideology, Policy, and the Crisis of Public Authority 297–98 (1969); Freedman, Delegation of Power and Institutional Competence, 43 U. Chi. L. Rev. 307 (1976); Wright, Beyond Discretionary Justice, 81 Yale L.J. 575 (1972); Ehmke, "Delegata Potestas Non Potest Delegari," A Maxim of American Constitutional Law, 47 Corn. L.Q. 50 (1961).

397. See Hampton v. Mow Sun Wong, 426 U.S. 88 (1976).

398. See generally 1 K. Davis, Administrative Law Treatise, ch. 2 (1958); Davis, A New Approach to Delegation, 36 U. Chi. L. Rev. 713 (1969); A. Miller 260–62.

399. See United States v. Paul, 31 U.S. 141 (1832); Franklin v. United States, 216 U.S. 559 (1910).

400. United States v. Curtiss-Wright Export Corp., 299 U.S. 304 (1936).

401. See, e.g., Kentucky Whip & Collar Co. v. Illinois Central R.R., 299 U.S. 334 (1937); Prudential Insurance Co. v. Benjamin, 328 U.S. 408 (1946).

402. See, e.g., Knickerbocker Ice Co. v. Stewart, 253 U.S. 149, 164 (1920).

403. See United States v. Dettra Flag Co., 86 F. Supp. 84 (E.D. Pa. 1949); cf. R. H. Johnson & Co. v. SEC, 198 F.2d 690, 695 (2d Cir.), cert. denied, 344 U.S. 855 (1952) ("quasi-criminal" sanctions).

404. Fahey v. Mallonee, 332 U.S. 245 (1947), reversing 68 F. Supp. 418 (S.D. Cal. 1946).

405. See generally Freedman.

406. Wright 586. See also McGowan 1127–30.

407. See B. Eckhardt & C. Black 48–53.

408. See Koslow, Standardless Administrative Adjudication, 22 Admin. L. Rev. 407 (1970); Miller, Statutory Language and the Purposive Use of Ambiguity, 42 Va. L. Rev. 23 (1956).

409. See, e.g., Greene v. McElroy, 360 U.S. 474 (1959); Kent v. Dulles, 357 U.S. 116 (1958).

410. See generally Stewart, The Reformation of American Administrative Law, 88 Harv. L. Rev. 1667 (1975).

411. See D. Morgan, Congress and the Constitution, ch. 10 (1966).

412. K. Davis, Administrative Law Treatise §2.04 (Supp. 1970).

413. See Stewart 1695 n.128.

414. See B. Eckhardt & C. Black 51.

415. 147 U.S. 282 (1893).

416. 161 U.S. 591 (1896).

417. 175 U.S. 423, 459–61 (1899).

418. 424 U.S. 1 (1976).

419. Williams v. Phillips, 360 F. Supp. 1363 (D.D.C.), stay denied, 482 F.2d 669 (D.C. Cir. 1973).

420. 357 U.S. 116 (1958).

421. 381 U.S. 1 (1965).

Six   Political Regulation of Judicial Authority

1. Ex parte United States, 242 U.S. 27 (1916).

2. See Gressman, The Constitution v. The Freund Report, 41 Geo. Wash. L. Rev. 951 (1973).

3. See Chandler v. Judicial Council, 398 U.S. 74 (1970).

4. See Merrill, "An Absolute Grant of Judicial Power," 26 Okla. L. Rev. 528 (1973).

5. See R. Scigliano, The Supreme Court and the Presidency 26 (1971).

6. See generally Note, All Legislative Rules for Judiciary Procedure Are Void Constitutionally, 23 Ill. L. Rev. 276 (1928); Kaplan & Greene, The Legislature's Relation to Judicial Rule-Making: An Appraisal of Winberry v. Salisbury, 65 Harv. L. Rev. 234 (1951); Pound, Procedure under Rules of Court in New Jersey, 66 Harv. L. Rev. 28 (1952).

7. See chap. 2, sec. IV, C; chap. 4, sec. I, C.

8. See the discussion of United States v. Nixon, chap. 5, sec. IV, D, 2.

9. 1 Stat. 73 (1789).

10. See, e.g., 2 W. Crosskey, Politics and the Constitution in the History of the United States, ch. 28 (1953); Corwin, The Supreme Court and Unconstitutional Acts of Congress, 4 Mich. L. Rev. 616 (1906); L. Boudin, Government by Judiciary (1932).

11. 2 Records of the Federal Convention of 1787, at 430 (M. Farrand ed. 1911). That Madison's views were far from consistent, however, has already been noted at chap. 4, sec. IX, E.

12. Hayburn's Case, 2 U.S. 409 (1792).

13. See Hart, Professor Crosskey and Judicial Review, 67 Harv. L. Rev. 1456 (1954); R. Berger, Congress v. The Supreme Court, ch. 6 (1969).

14. See also Banco Nacional de Cuba v. Sabbatino, 376 U.S. 398 (1964), discussed in L. Henkin, Foreign Affairs and the Constitution 60 (1972).

15. See also Ex parte Bakelite Corp., 279 U.S. 438 (1929); Williams v. United States, 289 U.S. 553 (1933).

16. See also Reid v. Covert, 351 U.S. 470, aff'd on rehearing, 354 U.S. 1 (1957); Kinsella v. Krueger, 351 U.S. 470 (1956).

17. For similar decisions, see 4 K. Davis, Administrative Law Treatise

§29.10 (1958). See also B. Eckhardt & C. Black, The Tides of Power: Conversations on the American Constitution 106 (1976).

18. See also Ex parte Siebold, 100 U.S. 371 (1879).

19. Textile Workers Union v. Lincoln Mills, 353 U.S. 448, 464–65 (1957) (dissenting opinion) (emphasis added).

20. Cf. United States v. Lee, 106 U.S. 196 (1882).

21. See United States ex rel. Milwaukee Social Democratic Publishing Co. v. Burleson, 255 U.S. 407 (1921).

22. See McDougal and Arens, The Genocide Convention and the Constitution, 3 Vand. L. Rev. 683 (1950); Parker, An International Criminal Court: The Case for Its Adoption, 38 A.B.A.J. 641 (1952).

23. Murray's Lessee v. Hoboken Land & Improvement Co., 59 U.S. 272, 284 (1855).

24. Crowell v. Benson, 285 U.S. 22, 51 (1932).

25. See, e.g., Rassmussen v. United States, 197 U.S. 516 (1905) (right to jury trial applicable in territorial courts).

26. 321 U.S. 414 (1944).

27. Crowell v. Benson, 285 U.S. 22, 87 (1932) (dissenting opinion).

28. See Martin v. Hunter's Lessee, 14 U.S. 304, 328–30 (1816) (Story, J.). See also 1 W. Crosskey, ch. 20; J. Goebel, 1 History of the Supreme Court of the United States: Antecedents and Beginnings 240–46 (1971); cf. Eisenberg, Congressional Authority to Restrict Lower Federal Court Jurisdiction, 83 Yale L.J. 498 (1974).

29. Cary v. Curtis, 44 U.S. 236, 245 (1845).

30. Battaglia v. General Motors Corp., 169 F.2d 254, 257 (2d Cir.), cert. denied, 335 U.S. 887 (1948).

31. Ohio Valley Water Co. v. Ben Avon Borough, 253 U.S. 287 (1920); St. Joseph Stock Yards Co. v. United States, 298 U.S. 38 (1936).

32. 106 U.S. 196 (1882).

33. 259 U.S. 276 (1922).

34. Cf. United States ex rel. Toth v. Quarles, 350 U.S. 11 (1955).

35. Cf. Jacobellis v. Ohio, 378 U.S. 184, 190 (1964) (opinion of Brennan, J.).

36. See St. Joseph Stock Yards Co. v. United States, 298 U.S. 38, 77 (1936) (concurring opinion).

37. This point was suggested to me by Paul J. Mishkin.

38. 285 U.S. 22 (1932).

39. See, e.g., The Steamboat Thomas Jefferson, 23 U.S. 428 (1825); Pennsylvania v. The Wheeling & Belmont Bridge Co., 54 U.S. 518 (1851); Marine Transit Corp. v. Dreyfus, 284 U.S. 263 (1932); Detroit Trust Co. v. The Thomas Barlum, 293 U.S. 21 (1934).

40. See, e.g., Missouri v. Fiske, 290 U.S. 18 (1933).

41. See Nowak, The Scope of Congressional Power to Create Causes of Action against State Governments and the History of the Eleventh and Fourteenth Amendments, 75 Colum. L. Rev. 1413 (1975).

42. See Fitzpatrick v. Bitzer, 427 U.S. 445 (1976).

43. See Nowak 1445–53; L. Tribe, American Constitutional Law 136–41 (1978); Hutto v. Finney, 437 U.S. 678, 704–10 (1978) (opinion of Powell, J.).

44. 2 U.S. 419 (1793).

45. See, e.g., Jagnandan v. Giles, 538 F.2d 1166 (5th Cir. 1976); Mauclet v. Nyquist, 406 F. Supp. 1233 (W.D.N.Y. 1976), appeal dismissed sub nom. Rabinovich v. Nyquist, 433 U.S. 901, reh. denied 434 U.S. 881 (1977).

46. See Jecker v. Montgomery, 54 U.S. 498 (1851).

47. United States v. Grossman, 1 F.2d 941, 952 (7th Cir. 1924) (Carpenter, J.).

48. Compare Nixon v. Sirica, 487 F.2d 700 (D.C. Cir. 1973) with Mississippi v. Johnson, 71 U.S. 475 (1867).

49. See Ex parte Grossman, 267 U.S. 87 (1925).

50. See Palmore v. United States, 411 U.S. 389 (1973); Swain v. Pressley, 430 U.S. 372 (1977).

51. Cf. Glidden Co. v. Zdanok, 370 U.S. 530 (1962).

52. See United States v. Allocco, 305 F.2d 704 (2d Cir. 1962).

53. The Federalist, No. 78 at 336 (J. Beard ed. 1959).

54. Glidden Co. v. Zdanok, 370 U.S. 530, 536 (1962). See also Evans v. Gore, 253 U.S. 245, 252 (1920).

55. See Tushnet, Invitation to a Wedding: Some Thoughts on Article III and a Problem of Statutory Interpretation, 60 Iowa L. Rev. 937, 944 (1975).

56. See Palmore v. Superior Court, 515 F.2d 1294, 1304–06 (D.C. Cir. 1975); United States v. Starling, 171 F. Supp. 47 (D. Alaska 1959).

57. Glidden Co. v. Zdanok, 370 U.S. 530, 536 (1962) (opinion of Harlan, J.).

58. See generally 4 K. Davis, Administrative Law Treatise, chs. 28–30 (1958); L. Jaffe, Judicial Control of Administrative Action, ch. 9 (1965); Strong, Judicial Review: A Tri-Dimensional Concept of Administrative-Constitutional Law, 69 W. Va. L. Rev. 249 (1967).

59. Crowell v. Benson, 285 U.S. 22, 87–88 (1932) (dissenting opinion). See also Hart, The Power of Congress to Limit the Jurisdiction of Federal Courts: An Exercise in Dialectic, 66 Harv. L. Rev. 1362, 1372–73 (1953).

60. See L. Tribe 40–43.

61. See generally L. Jaffe 381–89.

62. See Van Alstyne, A Critical Guide to Marbury v. Madison, 1969 Duke L.J. 1, 30–33.

63. See, e.g., Correpondence of the Justices, P. Bator, P. Mishkin, D. Shapiro & H. Wechsler, Hart and Wechsler's The Federal Courts and the Federal System 64–66 (2d ed. 1973).

64. 369 U.S. 186, 211, 217 (1962). See also Wechsler, Toward Neutral Principles of Constitutional Law, 73 Harv. L. Rev. 1, 7–10 (1959).

65. Luther v. Borden, 48 U.S. 1 (1849); Coleman v. Miller, 307 U.S. 433 (1939).

66. Baker v. Carr, 369 U.S. 186, 211 (1962).

67. 19 U.S. 264, 404 (1821). See also, e.g., Hyde v. Stone, 61 U.S. 170, 175 (1858); McClellan v. Carland, 217 U.S. 268, 282 (1910).

68. For one illustration of its use, see Illinois v. City of Milwaukee, 406 U.S.·91, 93 (1972).

69. Gunther, The Subtle Vices of the "Passive Virtues"—A Comment on Principle and Expediency in Judicial Review, 64 Colum. L. Rev. 1, 16 (1964).

70. 367 U.S. 497 (1961).

71. Id. at 508.

72. See Senate Select Committee on Pres. Cam. Act v. Nixon, 498 F.2d 725 (D.C. Cir. 1974).

73. See Banco Nacional de Cuba v. Farr, 383 F.2d 166 (2d Cir. 1967), cert. denied, 390 U.S. 956 (1968).

74. 418 U.S. 683, 705–06 n.16 (1974).

75. 48 U.S. 1 (1849).

76. Id. at 37.

77. Id. at 42.

78. Id. at 43 (emphasis added).

79. Id. at 47 (emphasis added).

80. 2 U.S. 408 (1792).

81. Id. at 411 (emphasis added).

82. Id. at 410.

83. See, e.g., Muskrat v. United States, 219 U.S. 346 (1911).

84. 2 U.S. at 411 (emphasis added).

85. Id. at 412–13 (emphasis in original).

86. 401 U.S. 493 (1971), relying on Massachusetts v. Missouri, 308 U.S. 1 (1939).

87. 401 U.S. at 495–96.

88. Id. at 497.

89. Id. at 499.

90. Id. at 497.

91. Id.

92. Id. See also Massachusetts v. Missouri, 308 U.S. 1 (1939); Illinois v. City of Milwaukee, 406 U.S. 91 (1972); Washington v. General Motors Corp., 406 U.S. 109 (1972); United States v. Nevada, 412 U.S. 534 (1973).

93. 401 U.S. at 497–98.

94. Id. at 499.

95. Gunther 16, quoting A. Bickel, The Least Dangerous Branch: The Supreme Court at the Bar of Politics 127 (1962) (emphasis added).

96. Scharpf, Judicial Review and the Political Question: A Functional Analysis, 75 Yale L.J. 517, 549 & n.110 (1966).

97. A. Bickel 55.

98. Gunther 10.

99. Scharpf 549.

100. Finkelstein, Judicial Self-Limitation, 37 Harv. L. Rev. 338, 363 (1924). For earlier discussion of this approach, see chap. 5, sec. III, D, 5, c, (6) (d).

101. National Mutual Ins. Co. v. Tidewater Transfer Co., 337 U.S. 582, 647 (1949) (dissenting opinion).

Cases Cited in Text

Index